JEAN PARVULESCO

VLADIMIR PUTIN & EURASIA

OMNIA VERITAS

JEAN PARVULESCO
(1929-2010)

VLADIMIR PUTIN & EURASIA

Vladimir Poutine & l'Eurasie - 2005

Translated from French by Omnia Veritas Limited

Published by
Omnia Veritas Ltd

www.omnia-veritas.com

© Omnia Veritas Limited - 2021

All rights reserved. No part of this publication may be reproduced by any means without the prior permission of the publisher. The Intellectual Property Code prohibits copying or reproduction for collective use. Any representation or reproduction in whole or in part by any means whatsoever without the consent of the publisher is illegal and constitutes an infringement punishable by the articles of the Intellectual Property Code.

JEAN PARVULESCO 15

PREFACE 19

THE GEOPOLITICAL DOCTRINE OF THE USSR AND ADMIRAL G.S. GORSHIKOV'S FUNDAMENTAL OCEANIC PROJECT 27

Belgrade, Dalmatinska Uliça 27
Admiral G.S. Gorchkov's "Fundamental Ocean Project 30
The fatal turn of a fatal historical development 32
The final confrontation of two antagonistic conspiracies 33
The fundamental theses of the Red Army's "geopolitical groups 34
"Taking the lead" 40
The essential vehicle 42
Knowing in advance, it's all there 42

THE SIN-KIANG RED LINE 44

The Falcon's Strategy 44
Europe defends China 45
Superpowers trade China for the Middle East 46
A well-developed scenario 47
Escalating countermeasures 48
The August 69 precedent 49
Moscow will have to strike 50
Beijing turns to NATO 51
Senator Jackson and the Shadow Falconers 52
Sin-Kiang is no longer in Sin-Kiang 54
Safety pays 54

TOWARDS A NATIONAL-COMMUNIST NATIONAL-COMMUNIST EUROPE? 56

Preventive war, "stupefaction and paralysis 57
Geopolitics trumps ideologies 58
From the "Polarka Plan" to the "Volcano Plan 59
Moscow plays the Portuguese example 61
Time for captains everywhere 62
The destiny of Soviet national-communism 63
The game is far from over 64
Preventing relaxation at all costs 64

YURI ANDROPOV AND THE NIGHT SIDE OF THE SOVIET UNION 66

YURI ANDROPOV, AND THE NIGHT SIDE OF THE SOVIET UNION, (SUMMARY) 70

In the shadow of the Kremlin, the liberated breath of the old mystagogically marries the inner emptiness of the new 71
A vote secured by the elite Kantemirov division 71

The lost testament of L.I. Brezhnev, and his vision of the next 'cosmic spring' 72
About John Paul II's extraordinary envoys to L.I. Brezhnev, and their top secret mission 72
Yuri Andropov is no longer Yuri Andropov 73
At present, two-faced powers are secretly fighting for supreme power in the USSR. What are Y.V. Andropov's choices? 73
A Secret Government in the Soviet Union"? Is Y.V. Andropov the great commander, or just a necessary tool? 75
Polar fraternities in the Red Army, and Russia's thousand-year reign 75
Another view of the political-historical career, mission and mystery of V.I. Lenin and his apparently unelected successor, I.V. Stalin 76
The Hitler-Stalin pact, irreversible foundation of the Soviet continental line 76
Vanguard Soviet geopolitics seen in the light of the coming millennium 76
Geostrategic developments by General Valeri Varennikoy, Deputy Chief of Staff of the Red Army 78
The Red Line of Sin-Kiang 78
Afghanistan, the home front of Asia Mysteriosa's approach 84
The USSR and Islamic fundamentalism 87

THE GRU GALAXY 89

"The highest ambition" 89
I.V. Stalin, the final vision of a Eurasian Empire 91
The same nocturnal movement 92
The agony of the Berzine era 94
Non-being has just overtaken being" 96
Askania Publishing 98
Hans Werner Neulen : 99
The great secret mission of the Gral. Col. SM. Chtemenko 101
From Berlin to Sin-Kiang 106
Sowing and Harvesting 109
The Amtorg, in the heart of Wall Street 116
The ice is broken 118

THE SUPRAHISTORICAL SIGNIFICANCE OF THE OF THE MASSACRE OF THE LAST ROMANOVS 126

History, and the concept of dogmatic irrationality 126
The inner workings of the 'special turmoil'. 128
The extinction of the Romanov race had a 'precise objective'. 129
The time had come". 134
The visionaries of the great disaster announced, of the immense turmoil prepared underground 136
Russia's recovery 139
A testimony from the current Russian political power 142

Samuel Huntington, and the Eurasian grand-continental vision............145
The great imperial secret of Nicholas II..147
A testimony by Karl Haushofer 149
The last word, the 'appearance of the final saviour 150

ORTHODOXY AND CATHOLICISM, THE GREAT RESTART? 151

The end, and the beginning of a great cycle 151
The anti-continental strategy of the Orthodox-Catholic divide 152
The paraclete spirit of John Paul II's pilgrimage to Romania 153
Working in the shadows of the 'fiery spiritual heights'. 155
The birth, and the shedding of blood, of the 'Burning Bush' group 156
Fulgens Corona...158

WE ARE THE CHURCH OF THE END 162

History as a fighting Mariology 162
The dogma of the Cosmic Coronation of Mary 165
The end of communism and the reunification of the Great Continent 167
There is no New Empire without a renewed religion 168
The failure of Rome in Western Europe 169
The Two Standards: Tradition versus Anti-Tradition................................172
Same Faith identifications 174
The oath of John Paul II 175
We are the Church of the End 176

RUSSIA'S EUROPEAN MAINLAND MISSIONS 178

The Franco-German axis is a World Revolution.......................................178
Blessed are the Pacifics 179
Immense negative powers, hidden..181
The movements of Middle-earth 182
The Marian horizon of the New Russia 184
The order of emergencies 186

THE COUNTER-GLOBALIST STRATEGY OF THE PARIS-BERLIN-MOSCOW AXIS 192

THE MYSTERIOUS RISE OF VLADIMIR PUTIN 202

(1) Vladimir Putin, the end of a cycle..202
(2) The secret services in power 204
(3) Vladimir Putin, the predestined 205
(4) Geopolitical views..205

WHAT EUROPE EXPECTS OF VLADIMIR PUTIN THE ESCHATOLOGICAL DESTINIES OF THE NEW RUSSIA 209

(1) The Seventh Seal 209
(2) Vladimir Putin's eschatological imperial 'grand design....................211
(3) What recovery tasks? 213

- (4) The Paris-Berlin-Moscow axis 216
- (5) Serbia, and South East Europe 217
- (6) The four Christological invitations 218
- (7) "The Spirit is born and grows". 221

VLADIMIR PUTIN AND THE "EURASIAN EMPIRE OF THE END 223

- A foundational document, "The Eurasian Imperial Pact 226
- The 'sign of departure': the appearance of a new 'absolute concept', a new 'providential man 227

WHAT IS THE "BIG SECRET" LINKING VLADIMIR PUTIN TO JOHN PAUL II? 233

- Vladimir Putin's Roman inclination 233
- How can this final reunification of Catholicism and Orthodoxy be achieved? 235
- The current disasters of the Catholic Church 237
- The duty of a predestined generation 239
- The Return of the Great Times 240

FOR A FIRST EURASIAN CONTINENTAL CONFERENCE ON THE "GREATER SIBERIA PROJECT 242

- The current reversal of Europe's political axis 244
- Towards the complete liberation of Western Europe 246
- The current moment in continental geopolitics 247

ON THE ULTIMATE PREDESTINATION OF ROMAN AMERICA 251

- Like China, Fundamentalist Islam, an anti-continental weapon of the United States 253
- Roman America, bridgehead and advanced metastrategic base of the Great Eurasian Continent 254
- Six operative geopolitical theses 255
- Roman America in a state of self-defeat 257
- A decisive generation 258
- You are in a state of total war, in the visible and in the invisible 260

JUNICHIRO KOIZUMI AND JAPAN'S 'GREAT AWAKENING 263

- It would be a disaster for the United States'. 264
- Junichiro Koizumi, bearer of a new destiny for Japan 265
- The life-saving use of the Armed Forces 267
- The mystical outline of our future struggles 268
- "New missions". 271

TO BLOCK THE PARIS-BERLIN-MOSCOW-NEW DELHI-TOKYO EURASIAN AXIS: THE US WILL OCCUPY AFGHANISTAN AND PAKISTAN 273

    The East of the "Eurasian Island" is already liberated. But not yet the West 275
    On the vast globalist operation of strategic diversion underway 276
    Europe's current dual positioning..278
    Current states of dialectical warfare 280

GEOPOLITICS OF A FINAL GLOBAL SITUATION 283

INDIA, THE FUTURE 'POLAR CENTRE OF THE GLOBAL ARCHIPELAGO 292

    What is transcendental geopolitics?...292
    India, the future 'polar centre' of the Planetary Archipelago....................294
    India's National Revolution, and its external supporters 297
    The conditions for a total revolutionary upliftment of present-day India...298
    The intervention of the Negative Powers..300
    By supporting the Indian Revolution we celebrate our return to the roots of our own identity...301

CHINA DOES NOT BELONG TO THE EURASIAN GRAND-CONTINENTAL COMMUNITY OF DESTINY 303

    What supra-historical justifications? 305
    Guido Giannettini's geopolitical theses on China......................................305
    Europe must reclaim China's northern half...308
    History is prophecy..311

WE URGENTLY NEED TO TAKE AN IDEOLOGICAL AND STRATEGIC STAND 312

    The current general US counter-offensive against Eurasian continental reunification 312
    The five current directions of the US strategic counter-offensive against Greater Europe...314
    In the interregnum of the planetary dialectical war 320
    The internal dialectical struggle of the European camp in crisis 321
    Immediate battles...323

THE SUMMER OF 'FINAL REVERSAL'. 326

    The current underground of a European Trotskyist surface organisation .327
    Overall plans for social-communist provocations......................................329
    Unitary structure, superstructure, and infrastructure 331
    Do not betray the operational secrets of our final counter-strategy 333
    The "Planetary Superpower of the United States" as the suprahistorical enemy of the Greater Europe...333
    Washington and Moscow...334
    Fighting on two fronts 335

THE TRANSCENDENTAL MEANING OF THE UPCOMING GERMAN ELECTIONS (SEPTEMBER 2002) 337

The new Franco-German 'Refounding Pact *338*
Nothing will happen without Vladimir Putin's 'New Russia *341*
Faced with the US 'Planetary Empire', a new deflagration dialectic *343*
Taking the side of Iraq is taking the side of Europe *345*
The ''parallel hierarchies'' of Greater Europe *346*

GERMANY, AND THE ULTIMATE FATE OF EUROPE 348

Facing a certain historical disaster of Germany; its causes, and ways of recovery *350*
The Putin Directive *353*

TURKEY, THE VANGUARD OF THE SECRET ACTION OF AL QAEDA IN EUROPE 355

VLADIMIR PUTIN, IN THE ESCHATOLOGICAL PERSPECTIVE OF THE "THIRD ROME" : THE "MAN OF THE KREMLIN", THE MAN OF THE FINAL BATTLES 361

The time of conspiracies *361*
The fundamental internal antagonism of the former Soviet power is now being covertly perpetuated on a European scale. *363*
Why Vladimir Putin? *365*
Bringing down the socialist-Trotskyist fortress of Berlin at all costs *367*
Faced with the ''Planetary Superpower of the United States'', the great-continental, ''Eurasian'' Europe is rising up today *369*
The Three Suns of the End *370*

THE ASSUMPTION OF VLADIMIR PUTIN 372

The American Democratic Party, and its double *372*
A socialist-Trotskyist conspiracy against Russia? Why is that? *373*
The basic steps of Russia's final recovery *374*
The nuptial dialectic of the Imperium Ultimum and the Religio Novissima *377*
Is there a "Vladimir Putin mystery"? *379*

OTHER TITLES 383

JEAN PARVULESCO

Jean Parvulesco (born 1929 in Romania, † in Paris in 2010) is a French writer and journalist. He calls himself a Catholic and heir to the thought of the Tradition in the line of René Guénon and Julius Evola.

Born in Wallachia and having attended cadet school, Jean Parvulesco decided to flee the communist regime after the Second World War and swam across the Danube to Yugoslavia in July 1948. He was arrested and sent to a political camp for forced labour near Tuzla, but escaped to Austria in August 1949. The former Romanian dissident arrived in Paris in 1950, and took courses in philosophy and literature at the Sorbonne, but did not devote himself seriously to them, preferring to frequent the literary, artistic and cinematographic avant-garde circles.

Frequenting nationalist-revolutionary circles alongside Jean Dides (among others) from the end of the 1950s, this strange activist was close to the OAS – which did not prevent him from theorising a 'geopolitics of great Gaullism'. He later wrote geopolitical articles in various publications, including the daily Combat, advocating, following the work published in early 2002 by Henri de Grossouvre, the establishment of a 'Paris-Berlin-Moscow axis' to counter Anglo-Saxon hegemony, a concept previously put forward by Gabriel Hanotaux and evoked by Raymond Abellio (to whom Jean Parvulesco was close) in his novel Les Militants.

The author of an abundant and varied body of work (novels, essays and poetry), Jean Parvulesco began publishing in the 1980s, claiming numerous literary influences in his novels. (Source babelio.com)

He who politically unifies Eurasia prevents the formation of a unipolar world, he who prevents the formation of a unipolar world breaks the ambitions of the United States, he who breaks the ambitions of the United States saves the world.

Michel d'Urance

Guy Debord once said that what characterises the present times is the fact that revolutionaries have become secret agents and secret agents have become revolutionaries. It is this double reversal that constitutes the basis of what is currently happening in the depths.

For Udo Gaudenzi, this book is a revolutionary limit fight committed on the line of passage towards the 'history at its end'.

PREFACE

In these tumultuous beginnings of 2005, absolutely decisive events are manifesting themselves, with force, sheltered from their own concealments at work, which would seem to be responsible for obturating, for attenuating their true importance, the certain character of a tragic convergence, engaged in the direction of a final reversal of times and of the current meaning of world history at its end. For it is now a given that we are ineluctably heading towards 'the end of a world', an expression borrowed from René Guénon.

Of course, the current paranoid gesticulations of what Bill Clinton called the 'Planetary Superpower of the United States', engaged as it is in its incredible enterprise of interference – in the terms of an armed conflict of planetary dimensions and implications – in the Middle East, under the pretext of the definitive control of Iraq, and the liquidation of the national-revolutionary regime of Saddam Hussein, which was still in power in Baghdad yesterday, captivate for the moment the entire horizon of current events, mobilising exclusively our attention (very wrongly, as we will see in the course of the present brief text, which is also something other than a simple preface).

This attempt at interference by the United States in the Middle East is, in any case, nothing more than a repetition, at a much higher level, of its previous undertaking of direct interference in the former Yugoslavia – in Bosnia, Kosovo, Macedonia, and Serbia itself – which ultimately led to the total political and strategic control of the United States over the whole of the South-East of the European continent, with Albania as a base of control and rear manoeuvre.

However, contrary to certain misleading appearances, the real centre of gravity of the current planetary political situation is not in the Middle East, and is only relatively concerned with the aftermath of the US offensive against Iraq, even as regards the hidden and even more than hidden reasons for this assault with its avowed aims of total devastation. The real centre of gravity of the current planetary politics as a whole is, in reality, in Europe, and concerns the current efforts of European imperial integration around the Franco-German Carolingian Pole and the subsequent relations that this one intends to urgently initiate, and deepen in terms of destiny-in the very terms of the "greater destiny", both historical and supra-historical-with Vladimir Putin's "New Russia": In reality, it is the still relatively confidential project, currently underway, of the Paris-Berlin-Moscow transcontinental axis that marks the truly decisive advance of the current revolutionary changes on the grand-continental European scale of Eurasian imperial dimension and predestination.

However, the current European grand policy is – and absolutely cannot be – a fundamentally conspiratorial policy. We must not be afraid of words. A fundamentally conspiratorial policy because all of its major operational options take place in the shadows, essentially in the shadows, protected by special devices of strategic diversion and controlled disinformation, aimed not so much at diverting the attention of the United States from what is happening in Europe at the moment – nothing can really remain hidden in the face of the permanent surveillance of Washington's politico-strategic intelligence services – but so that, but so that, as far as possible, the *immediate appearances of* the current course of events are kept on the sidelines, de-substantiated, deported from the true reality, from the decisive scope of the ongoing process of European imperial integration. A false alternative reality permanently replaces the real reality in action, the political future in its immediately revolutionary dimensions, a false reality which we must know is emasculated on purpose, subversively pushed forward so that it distracts, de-dramatises, disarms the alerts that are too close to the underbelly of things. So that the European imperial revolutionary reality does not risk being seen as an abrupt provocation to the *'general line' of the* vital interests of the United States; and also so that the latter does not manage to grasp everything about the process of grandcontinental European imperial integration which, subterraneanly, continues in an ineluctable way. It is going ahead, despite the obstacles of the American negative strategy committed to countering, in the shadows, the succession of great political operations planned jointly by Paris, Berlin, Moscow and also by New Delhi and Tokyo, with a view to one and the same final politico-strategic objective, which is that of the imperial affirmation of the greatest continental Europe of 'Eurasian' dimensions, of the revolutionary affirmation of the great 'Eurasian Empire of the End'.

Even if Jacques Chirac thought he had to talk about a 'Pacte Refondateur' of the 1963 Franco-German de Gaulle-Adenauer treaty, the official celebrations of this treaty, which took place in Versailles at the end of January 2003, did not give away what was behind it: The official celebrations of this event, which took place in Versailles at the end of January 2003, did not, however, give any hint of what was behind it: the setting in motion of the subterranean process of the political integration of France and Germany, so that, in the long run, we would arrive at what Aleksandr Dugin called, in a resounding editorial from Moscow, the 'Franco-German Empire'. Long live the Franco-German Empire", he entitled his truly revolutionary editorial, as decisive as it was visionary, and which will remain as such in the history of the greater Europe to come.

For it is a question of a 'Franco-German Empire' which must constitute the historically founding pole of the great continental Eurasian *'Imperium Ultimum'*, its 'West Pole', the other pole, the 'East Pole', having to be constituted by Russia and, behind Russia, by India and Japan: A fortnight after the formal recognition, in Versailles, of the Franco-German "Refounding Pact", President Vladimir Putin made an official state visit to Paris, while

Jacques Chirac's Prime Minister, Jean Pierre Raffarin, went, at the same time, to New Delhi, where he was pursuing confidential politico-strategic talks with the Indian Prime Minister, Atal Bihari Vajpayee. And one could perhaps consider that Jean-Pierre Raffarin's talks in New Delhi with Atal Bihari Vajpayee had been prepared during the recent official visit of several days to Paris of the Indian Deputy Prime Minister, L. K. Advani, representative, within the Indian Union government, of the hard-line, revolutionary wing of the ruling Bharatiya Janata Party (BJP). For those in the know, history, the 'big story', while pretending to happen in the open, only ever develops the tragic spiral of its march behind the scenes, in the deep shadows of what is allowed to be seen by those who are 'not'.

In any case, one thing is absolutely certain: what has now been set in motion will never stop. In secret, or not.

The time has come, however, for us to no longer conceal the still veiled reality of a de facto situation with no way out other than that of a total planetary conflagration: if the greatest continental, 'Eurasian' Europe is created, which today, conspiratorially, is precisely in the process of being created, the United States would find itself relegated, by this very fact, to the situation of a second – or even third-rate power. It is therefore quite obvious that the supreme planetary political and strategic goal of the United States can only be to oppose by all means the advent of the great-continental 'European Empire' of the end. And indeed by all means, including that of a preventive war – a nuclear war – of the United States against the European Empire. This is what European politicians, those who hold the future destiny of the Greater Europe in their hands, must always bear in mind. For this is the final word, the stumbling block and the ultimate test. *The test of fire.*

This is a situation of permanent rupture. And this is precisely what, in the context of this unstable, essentially equivocal and tragic 'ultimate limit', will explain the conspiratorial conditions in which the grand-continental European imperial process is currently initiated and pursued behind the façade of disinformative appearances and engaged in the active dialectics of a permanent diversion strategy, This is the facade of the *visible situation of* things that is purposely kept in a singularly disappointing light, as if it were trampling indefinitely on the spot, lost in indecision and weakness, deprived of any chance of 'reaching its goal'. Disinformation, therefore.

While the *invisible situation is the* exact opposite of what its strategically doctored, concealing appearances show, the project – for example – of the Paris-Berlin-Moscow axis being, at the moment, practically in a state of success. But the Paris-Berlin-Moscow axis is our decisive battle.

For, for some time to come, the great European continental policy will have to be conducted as a policy with two identities, with two antagonistic levels of visibility, an essentially conspiratorial policy, a policy that is both visible and invisible. A false visible politics, and an invisible revolutionary reality in action.

And it is here that the extraordinary direct revolutionary importance of the activist – and for some time now, over-activated – grand-continental European chains constituted by the 'geopolitical groups' is going to be surprised – as I have been saying for a long time now – , whose mission had been – and still is – that of watching over the uninterrupted development of a certain imperial geopolitical national-revolutionary consciousness within the countries of the Greater Europe, a movement acting, already, beyond the national cleavages, in an increasingly imperial perspective, a decisive movement, a movement carrying the 'great history' in its underground march.

Thus, in the present work, which is a singularly dangerous book, not to be placed in all hands, I myself have done nothing more than to bear witness, in continuity with the march forward, to the consequent developments of a certain revolutionary imperial consciousness in Europe. Step by step. Thus accompanying its own course, and more often than not anticipating it, and by a long way: it was not a follow-up analytical work that I undertook to do there, but a fundamentally visionary work, whose own horizon was situated in the history of the beyond the end of history.

The first article in this book, entitled *The Geopolitical Doctrine of the USSR and* Admiral G. S. Gorshkov's *"Fundamental Oceanic Project"*, was published in February 1977, and the last, entitled *"The Assumption of Vladimir Putin"*, in December 2004. From one to the other, the process of the birth and revolutionary developments of the current European grand-continental political consciousness is traced over a quarter of a century and more: each chapter of this book marks an ascending stage of the new supranational revolutionary consciousness with imperial, secretly eschatological aims, of which this book is the vanguard.

And this is precisely as the evolution of visible and invisible events in ongoing world history was itself increasingly engaged in a dialectic of imperial convergence, following the gradual emergence of the concept of a new final revolutionary 'grand destiny' to integrate the geopolitical ensemble of what we call the 'Eurasian Empire of the End'.

In fact, this concept of a new European imperial 'great destiny' was itself a response to the anticipated emergence of the 'New Russia' in the course of current European world history: a *'New Russia'* seen, therefore, as the predestined revolutionary agent of the abysmal changes that were eventually to take place. The call of history, resounding from the depths, won out over the dogmatic sleep of Russia prevented from being. And the 'New Russia' itself appeared – or rather, did it not *reappear in* the course of current history through the providential advent of the 'predestined man', the 'absolute concept' Vladimir Putin, embodying the 'New Russia' and all that it means in relation to the immense changes already underway or to come in the history of the world caught up in the vertigo of its own final destination.

Thus, the set of texts constituting the present book represents the inner journey of the spiral of a grand-continental imperial geopolitical awareness that was bound – in advance, and very necessarily – to lead to the final conclusions that are now, here, its own. And, as such, the present work must be recognised as a book of total combat, showing what are the current paths of any grand-continental imperial geopolitical awareness. At the same time, beyond the paths of the intimate evolution of a certain final geopolitical consciousness, one can find in it the acting secret, the living secret of the peak spiritual experience, which is that of the *dialectical illumination* attached to the appearance of this very consciousness, a peak spiritual experience that can be held to be a liberation, a deliverance, a secret takeover.

The great geopolitics, the "transcendental geopolitics" is, in fact, a revolutionary mysticism in action, which must lead to the absolute power of consciousness over politics and, beyond politics, over "great history" itself, because the final geopolitical consciousness is now identified with the march of "great history" towards its ultimate, eschatological, imperial conclusion, a conclusion which is situated in the history beyond the end of history.

Now other times are coming'. In the perspective already opened before us of this history beyond the end of history, the scale of importance of the political-historical problems changes completely. There, the twofold ultimate limiting objective of the 'New Russia' appears to be that of the liberation of Constantinople and the deliverance of the Hagia Sophia, as well as that of the establishment of a new and at the same time extraordinarily ancient foundational relationship with India and, behind India, with Tibet, Korea and Japan. Russia," says Alexander Dugin, "is the bridge from Europe to India.

Didn't William II write to his cousin Nicholas II, whom he called the 'Emperor of the Pacific', that the fact that Korea belonged to Russia's direct sphere of influence was an obvious and indisputable fact? Wasn't Nicholas II ardently obsessed with in-depth intervention, with Russia's effective presence in Tibet and India? Had he not undertaken, following Badmaieff's advice, major secret operations in the direction of Tibet and India? For his part, did Vladimir Putin, by mystically espousing the abysmal cause of total Russia, by personally overseeing the regime of the Pravoslavian canonisation of the Imperial Family bestially massacred by Soviet communism, not make all the eschatological missions of 'Holy Russia' his own? Didn't he involve the Orthodox Church directly in the management of Russia's current great politics, thus reintroducing the sacred into Russia's march towards its renewed destiny, towards its great suprahistoric missions to come? Does he not openly confess his own Christian faith, the fire of faith that has never ceased to inhabit him since his childhood, rekindled by his visit to Jerusalem? Doesn't he have occult, but ongoing, links with Rome?

Thus, the current nuptial reunion of Russia and Europe will have to impose the return of the living sacred within the Great Continental imperial community. This, in turn, will shift once again, and definitively, the spiritual centre of gravity of the 'Great Continent', from the materialistic positions of the Trotskyite conspiracy supporting the social democracies – finally driven out of power, all over Europe – to the horizon of a history once again open to the intervention – to interventions – of the supernatural. Thus the sunny times of a new great revolutionary return to being and the saving abandonment of the subversive dominations of non-being are announced. Vladimir Putin and the 'Eurasian Empire' is being and the return of being. The sunshine beyond the end. That day will come.

But perhaps we should reconsider a certain point. Indeed, I have been strongly criticised for having produced, in this book, a long series of articles following each other over time, rather than presenting something like the final synthesis of the material proposed by all of them; their integration, therefore, in a book that would have given a unitary, concentrated, global image. A book of synthesis rather than this long succession of articles. But that would have been to proceed in a way that was completely opposite to what I really wanted to bring out in my approach to the subject, namely the advent on the agenda of the concept, both politico-historical and suprahistorical, of the 'Eurasian Empire of the End' and its predestined relations with President Vladimir Putin. The rise of a geopolitical thought captured in its own becoming.

For, if, in the final analysis, geopolitics is a gnosis, as some of us are already deeply convinced, what would be important then would be to be able to reveal also the very process of the gnostic birth, of the advent to the day of the final, accomplished geopolitical consciousness. To surprise, therefore, the initiatory process of the geopolitical consciousness in the process of rising from itself to the supreme West of its own final, *definitive* identity. In fact, if the birth to itself of the ultimate geopolitical consciousness reproduces the heroic ascent of the initiatory spiral towards what attracts it to the heights, it is certain that this ascent itself must be shown, here, at least as much as the ultimate awareness to which it finally intends to lead. Not only its outcome, but also its path.

Now, to surprise the process of the initiatory ascent on the way to its ultimate accomplishment-the ultimate geopolitical path, in this case, of this one towards the concept of the 'Eurasian Empire of the End'-is in reality no other than to follow its path through the series of articles whose succession will have constituted, in time, this very ascent: there is there the whole explanation of the choice of the structure of exposition that I thought I had to impose on the present work. A simple series of articles? Perhaps. But, beyond that, there is also *something else*. A series of articles, ablaze with the fire of an 'ultimate consciousness'.

Will we have understood it? It is the lived testimony concerning the experience in progress of a geopolitical consciousness in the process of being accomplished that constitutes itself this consciousness, whose accomplishment goes however beyond the experience that will have conveyed it, because it is itself the conceptual assumption of it and, beyond this, what must end up bringing it to the immediate revolutionary action, to the 'direct action'.

And the conclusion of all this will thus appear, I believe, as if by itself: as it is, the present work has no other ambition than that of making it the decisive counter-strategic tool of a total combat, of the final imperial combat of our own.

The secret revolutionary experience of geopolitics founds by anticipating the becoming of the greatest history in progress, its occult ministry is not at all, as one might think, that of accompanying by trying to explain the forward march of history: on the contrary, it is geopolitics as an abysmal gnostic experience of history that poses its ultimate goals, and tends to the ultimate eschatological reasons in action.

The successive grid of cutting-edge politico-revolutionary combat articles, a mobilised grating at work day after day, which constitutes the very substance of the present work, is there to testify, over a quarter of a century, to the fact that avant-garde geopolitical consciousness has not finished preceding the revolutionary becoming of history in progress; that, in fact, history in progress does not cease to follow the visionary emergence of a certain geopolitical consciousness, whose occult foundations are thus revealed as being of a providential nature. This is precisely what, in the highly confidential internal correspondence of the Society of Jesus, was called, in the 18th century, the 'secret design of the Emperor'. Not the Emperor of Vienna, but the 'Emperor of Heaven'. And there, everything is said.

Geopolitical action thus has a double nature of its own: it conveys the direct providential inspiration of history, of the greatest history, and thus leads, at the same time, secretly, the politico-historical developments of history in its immediate forward march.

So, in a certain sense, it is the sum in motion of the circumstantial articles gathered in this book that will have made the history of the world currently in motion and already so close to its end; and this whether we know it or not.

So many steps forward towards the revolutionary awareness that should lead to the constitution of the 'Fortress Greater Europe' called to face the politico-military encirclement being installed by the United States engaged in its policy of final planetary takeover, the planned 'Fortress Greater Europe', also, to destabilise, to neutralise the new politico-historical directions of a world which is approaching, subversively, and in an increasingly accelerated way, the 'final planetary crisis' envisaged by the secret designs of the 'Anti-Empire' already in place in Washington. The 'Great European Fortress' whose planetary counter-strategic centre of gravity is subterraneanly mobilised by Vladimir Putin's 'New Russia', whose final imperial and eschatological predestination will soon change the face of the world and of history. Indeed, one can predict that *everything will change,* and definitively.

Jean Parvulesco

THE GEOPOLITICAL DOCTRINE OF THE USSR AND ADMIRAL G.S. GORSHIKOV'S FUNDAMENTAL OCEANIC PROJECT

> *Which of the two camps will prevail over the other? The one that will be able to let the will of destiny of the providential man appear within it, who will also be the man of the last battle.*
>
> *When will it come? Inevitably, at the appointed time.*

Belgrade, Dalmatinska Uliça

The forced stay that I had to make in Belgrade, in the summer of 1948, in the armoured cell number 15 of the special UDBA prison, in the Dalmatinska Uliça of gloomy and bloody memory, gave me, among other things, the opportunity to talk for days and nights with one of the most important leaders of the clandestine political group that, in the years 1946–1948, had tried to act, even within the Titist power in place, along a doctrinaire line, nights, with one of the most important leaders of the underground political group which, in the years 1946–1948, had tried to act, from within the Titist power in place, along a kominformist doctrinal line, in other words, Stalinist and anti-tatist, Prof. MT. MT. The latter, astonishingly under-educated, or suicidally reckless, had been escaped by Rankoviteh's political services and placed in total isolation in the Dalmatinska Uliça on the very day he returned from Moscow to Belgrade. Since 1947, Prof. MT had been the head of the Permanent Economic Commission of the Cominform in Moscow, behind which the South-East European Directorate of the operational political-strategic services was hidden, doubling the open political apparatus maintained by the Cominform in Romania, Bulgaria, Yugoslavia and Albania, and, in a more covert way, in Greece as well.

But the real reason for the anti-Kominformist stance of the National Titist Government in Belgrade, which was forced to respond both defensively and preventively to the attacks – the encirclement – to which Yugoslavia had just been subjected by the Stalinist-Kominformist front in Eastern Europe, the real reason, therefore, for the major, irreversible break between Yugoslavia and the

Soviet Union in July 1948, concerned precisely the underground plans of Marshal Tito and his front man, Vukmanovic, between Yugoslavia and the Soviet Union in July 1948 concerned, very precisely, the underground projects of Marshal Tito and his front man, Vukmanovic-Tempo, who were preparing to set in motion a vast movement for the federal *regroupment of* South-East Europe, a regroupment predetermined by Belgrade and which was to be aligned, in the long term, with positions defined by Belgrade.

It was Vukmanovic-Tempo, a close companion of Marshal Tito and for a long time the Federal Minister of Labour – at least he was during my forced internships in 1948–1949 in the labour camps of the Litva-Banovic mining zone near Sarajevo – who seems to me to be at the origin of the anti-Kominformist line on which Yugoslavia had embarked from 1948. The vast clandestine counter-strategic operation that Vukmanovic – Tempo at the time, the master builder of the 'great South-East European geopolitical design' secretly nurtured by Marshal Tito and his close associates – had set up was none other than that of the accelerated constitution of a South-East European Federation comprising, under an implicitly Yugoslav political leadership, Greece, Albania, Yugoslavia, Bulgaria and Romania.

Through the Cominforn, LV. Stalin was to react so harshly that the break between Belgrade and Moscow was, so to speak, immediate and final. Moscow having mobilised the entire pro-Soviet Eastern bloc on its side, Yugoslavia was immediately banished from the 'socialist camp', cast into the outer darkness, pushed back to the political fields of the 'third way' (which, later, would lead to the Titist strategies of 'non-alignment').

One would not think of attacking the zones, the spheres of imperialist influence without expecting the worst. Indeed, Marshal Tito had only been able to avoid the Soviet-Kominformist 'normalization' of Yugoslavia, and only just, by abruptly suspending the underground operations in progress on the South-East European federal line of Yugoslavian influence, whose top leader, Vukmanovic-Tempo, had thus been brought to the level of a sort of Che Guevara of Eastern Europe. A Che Guevara before his time, and who owed his personal salut to the dialectical intelligence and manoeuvring boldness with which Belgrade had managed, on the one hand, to disengage from South-East Europe and, on the other, to negotiate the counter-turn of its national retreat into the 'Yugoslav fortress'. And all this while managing to maintain the necessary distance from the Western camp through what was to become 'non-alignment', a Yugoslav doctrine of replacement, support and blockade that had to offer the subsequent career that we know.

But let us return, after this brief introduction to the subject, to my own personal relations with Prof. MT. When I met him at the UDBA prison in Dalmatinska Uliça, his strict isolation had already been lifted a month earlier. Relaxed, trying to get his act together in May, he thought that his transfer to a common cell had a singularly positive meaning. But he too was wrong, like so many others. In fact, Prof. MT disappeared for good in the whirlwind of the great anti-Kominformist repression of those years, executed, I was assured, in the winter of 1949, in a secret anti-Kominformist camp near Mitroviça. But I have kept intact the memory of his cell confidences, the main part of which concerned his talks in Moscow with I. V. Stalin and his private secretary, General Alexander Poskrebychev. Prof. MT was one of the few who at that time, with an iron fist, spasmodically squeezed his right arm:

—You, comrade MT, are talking tonight in my house like that Trotskyite Kardelij, your dear comrade from the Political Bureau in Belgrade. I find this extremely regrettable. Do you really believe that we do not know what Kardelij's clandestine activities are, his relations with world Zionism and the effeminate Trotskyites of *the* British *Intelligence Service*? Besides, in Belgrade, Kardelij is not the only one who has scabrous connections, if you can see who I am talking about and at the same time not talking, if you can see who I am referring to. All this we know only too well, and much more. But to you, comrade MT, to you personally, I want to trust you. I know that you are with us, that you are one of us, and that you are the only intelligent Yugoslav, much more intelligent than that pheasant Djilas. Besides, you are Serbian, and you speak Russian like the rest of us. You see, this very morning, when I woke up, I was thinking of you. For I know that your time will come, and perhaps sooner than you think. For we have our eye on everything. So, as General Poskrebyshev says so well, be *careful*, Comrade MT. We have defeated Hitler's Germany and wiped out Nazism, but there are still, at home-even at home, I mean-things that are wrong. There is, you see, there is, again and again, the Trotskyite conspiracy from within, which, coiled under the floor, in our own house, and supported from without by the anti-Soviet line of world Trotskyism, is slyly watching for the right opportunity to raise its head again. And yet, we thought we had crushed the head of that snake. But we have to start again every day. This is our secret revolutionary task, that every day we take up the same ice pick, that every day we prevail over death and the forces of death by appealing to death, by manipulating death itself. As long as it lets us, I mean it...

So General Poskrebychev is right to be so keen to watch over the words of our ceaseless struggle. For it all fits together. The only concept that completely covers our strategic vision or, as General Chtemenko would say here, our geostrategic vision of proletarian internationalism, is that which concerns the 'planetary mission' of Soviet Russia. We Soviets have always sought to support, complement and exalt our continental power-our great continental power-with a Fleet different from those of the other great maritime powers, a Fleet that can stand on its own, that does not need external bases: an Oceanic Fleet, our *Okeanska*. We have always looked for a way out to sea, a way out to the Atlantic as well as to the Pacific. But for us, the Pacific has always been and remains the most important. I say: the Pacific above all. The planetary mission of Soviet Russia can therefore be considered to be on the way to being accomplished the day our Ocean Fleet cruises freely, and I would even say – Sovereignly, in the Pacific, the day the Red Flag flies in the wind of the South

Islands. Comrade MT, have you ever heard of Easter Island? No, does Easter Island mean nothing to you? Nothing at all? And yet, remember, because I am telling you a great thing, *everything happens on Easter Island.*

But we have nothing to fear, the United States has no destiny of its own, its planetary imperialism is an imperialism of merchants and zombies manipulated by others, in the shadows. An imperialism without a destiny. For this is what I would like you to remember again tonight: the United States does not exist. Before the end of this millennium, the United States will be out of the history of the world. In fact, history itself is very close to its end.

—Thank Comrade Stalin very much, he has just entrusted you with very great things. Go on, Comrade MT, kiss his hand,' whispered General Poskrebyshev, urging him towards I. V. Stalin, who, smiling enigmatically, distantly and vaguely, stood motionless before the red-covered table, 'petrified, and as if shrouded in night.

—And I kissed his hand as if he were a Metropolitan,' Prof. MT had to admit to me, troubled, as he was in turn a victim, like so many others, of the secret spell of the former Tbilisi seminarian, a fellow student of Gurdjieff and an initiate of the *Rasputy*.

Admiral G. S. Gorchkov's Fundamental Ocean Project

But how can we fail to recognise that, as I.V. Stalin said, *everything fits together.* For, using as a relay the agitation-propaganda and counter-information structures of Taiwan, solidly implanted, as we know, in Hong Kong, Singapore and in the whole of South-East Asia, the Maoist Then Wu – the Taiwan vector is, without doubt, unknowingly, or almost, very often used by the Then Wu – insisted on disseminating, in August 1976, a document of high anti-Soviet use, which, in order to be quite probably a prefabrication, does not contain any less an indisputable part of truth. It is the English translation of a so-called *"Fundamental Oceanic Project"* by Admiral G. S. Gorshkov, a sort of general plan for the world politico-strategic expansion of the USSR from the oceanic and maritime geostrategic positions already assumed, or increasingly to be assumed, by the Soviet Fleet.

The major importance of this document stems, however, from the fact that it could obviously only have been produced (if it is really a production at all) on the basis of a certain amount of concrete data, proven elements which cannot fail to be authentic, including, in particular, and according to the latest state of analysis, the *embbiding* of a secret manual of operational naval geostrategy currently in use at the Leningrad Higher Naval Academy.

And *everything fits together* because the conclusions of Admiral G.S. Gorshkov's 'Fundamental Oceanic Project' give 1977 as the decisive date for the setting up of a great Soviet naval geostrategy whose avowed aim would be the total domination of the inter-oceanic planetary spaces, a goal for which a strong development time of seven years, 1982–1989, is set. However, it is also the case that the limit-objective of the 'Fundamental Oceanic Project' in question, which is to be achieved and stabilised in the years 1982–1989, and which is to polarise the entire inter-oceanic power of the Soviet Fleet, concerns, as it should, the South Pacific expanses defined by the neuralgic zone, by the 'suprasensitive zone' of Polynesia and, paradoxically, by the metapolitical *Trefpunkt of* Easter Island. Which obviously brings everything back, and in what a mysterious way, to the words that I.V. Stalin had let himself say, but perhaps on purpose, and who knows for what distant, elusive purpose, one night in 1948 in the Kremlin.

On the other hand, it may not be entirely without interest to note that, from the point of view of what is now called 'great astrology', Soviet Russia, with its essentially Neptunian sign, was to reach the peak of its own Neptunian-oceanic destiny in the years 1982–1989.

Also, in his last metapolitical novel, *The Pit of Babel*, Raymond Abellio wrote: " ... the three 'occult' planets, Uranus, Neptune and Pluto, which currently seem to be related to the respective destinies of the United States, Russia and China, thus mark three great crises, in 1962–1968, 1982–1989 and 1999–2015" (Raymond Abellio, *The Pit of Babel*, Paris, 1962) 1982–1989, the time period concerned, precisely, by Admiral O.S. Gorchkov's "Fundamental Oceanic Project".

It is the profound Neptunian inevitability of the present times that governs the oceanic obsession of Soviet Russia. Following the geostrategic impetus of Admiral O. S. Gorchkov's "Fundamental Oceanic Project", Russia has thus put itself in a position to ensure total control – in principle – of intercontinental maritime and oceanic spaces, a control that will decide the very direction of world history in the years 1982–1989.

That a continental superpower should thus become, in the space of a quarter of a century, an oceanic superpower, what more Neptunian sign of the final reversal of planetary geopolitical polarities, where the clear sign of the great imperial periods to come also appears?

Moscow's most secret dream remains that of achieving control of the Pacific. The day the Soviet Union gains a foothold in Polynesia, the face of the world will change for a thousand years", Andréa de Winter, the central character in *Atlantis*, said openly in Paris shortly before she met her dramatic and dark end.

Finally, during the visit to Peking in September 1976 of the Head of State of Western Samoa, Mailetoa Tanumafili, the Prime Minister and supreme head of all the intelligence and security services of the P.R. of China, Hua Kuo-feng, whose new political-administrative position is quite elevated, and who will have to rise even higher, took the opportunity to denounce the fact that he had been a member of a group of people who had been working in Western Samoa for many years. Hua Kuo-feng, whose new and very high political and administrative position is known and who will have to rise even higher, took the opportunity to denounce the 'new front of strategic infiltration' opened 'in the Pacific' by a "superpower which claims to be the natural ally of the Third World and which, in reality, constitutes the most dangerous war zone for the future of the Third World", a superpower for which "strategic investment in the Pacific, and more particularly in the South Pacific, is today a very important objective".

No one is unaware of this today in the Pacific: from Beijing, it is Hua Kuo-feng who is personally leading the political battle to stop Soviet investment in the Pacific and who, firmly determined to win, is building the barrier that will prevent the Soviet Union from accessing the oceanic paths of its planetary projects that are already under way. The large-scale action undertaken by Hua Kuo-feng, as we know, also mobilises, on its back, anti-Soviet options of the first importance, and which know how to give themselves occult support even within the political power currently in place in Moscow.

The fatal turn of a fatal historical development

The process has thus begun, which must decide the future politico-historical destiny of the USSR and make, therefore, either that it commits itself totally to the paths required by the offensive geostrategic conception of its Armed Forces and Fleet, or that it undergoes and assumes, fully, the slide which, in fact, would represent a subversive return to the anti-national and anti-continental positions of what I. V. Stalin called, in his talks with Prof. MT, the 'Trotskyite conspiracy from within'.

Thus, marking the inexorable end of a crisis that could become exponential at any moment, of an internal rupture of the Soviet regime itself, announcing the fatal turning point of a fatal historical evolution, the *line of passage of* the year 1977 appears to be absolutely decisive, because, if it is a crisis that is perhaps still invisible, or at least not easily discernible on the surface, it is already reaching a paroxysm in its depths, the only possible outcome of which implies that the regime itself, without procrastination and irrevocably, must commit itself in one direction or the other.

Of course, the essentially negative powers currently acting in the Soviet Union, more or less clandestinely, on positions of self-dislocation, internationalist subjugation and preventive historical resignation, represent, in reality, only the groups of cosmopolitan and degenerate intellectuals who, agitating around gatherings of the kind of the Soviet Committee for Human Rights set up by the misguided Andrei Sakharov, gatherings which are nothing more than staples, even provocative apparatuses manipulated by the KGB rather than organisations for political action, only involve a minority which is singularly insignificant in relation to the deep political and social reality, in relation to the living social reality of the Soviet Union today.

The danger of a resurgence of what I. V. Stalin called the 'Trotskyite conspiracy from within' remains, in fact, quite different: namely, the danger that this one manages to manoeuvre thoroughly, and all the more so if the politico-social evolution of the moment lends itself to it, to mobilise on itself, and to divert to essentially subversive, anti-national and anti-Soviet ends, the formidable revolutionary capital of the discontent, of the social despair of the Soviet masses, to make of it the counter-revolutionary whirlwind in a position to prevent, and at its most crucial hour, the internal evolution of the present Soviet regime towards continental national-communist positions, towards the setting up of an overall geostrategic device capable of assuring to Soviet Russia the politico-historical weapon of its final 'planetary mission'.

However, is it conceivable that the Red Army could allow things to happen like this? In order to break the straitjacket of the Party, of the Marxist-Leninist administration of the Party in the State, the Red Army may itself dialectically find itself in the imperative obligation to call upon the emergence, the mobilisation of social – or anti-social – forces of chaotic dissolution, whose subsequent handling will certainly not be without risks, and risks which may suddenly become what General de Gaulle called, in May 1968, *immense risks*. 0 are, it must be clearly understood, the very conditions, the active conditions, on the ground, of the final confrontation of two conspiracies: antagonistic within the same State power. Until further notice.

The Soviet Armed Forces are on a war footing, ready to carry out their national and international duty alongside the combatants of the countries of the socialist community", declared the Soviet Minister of Defence, Marshal Ustinov, on 7 November 1976 in Red Square, Moscow.

Faithful to the sacred principles of proletarian internationalism and protecting the interests of socialism, the work of freedom and independence of the peoples, the Soviet Armed Forces", added Marshal Ustinov, "follow with extreme vigilance the activities of the internal and external enemies of Peace".

The final confrontation of two antagonistic conspiracies

Inside the soviet power, two tendencies, or rather two conspiracies, are confronting each other, at the present time, in depth, and it is precisely this confrontation in action that defines and arms the total political crisis to which the year 1977 can absolutely not fail to provide, in one way or another, the *decisive* outcome: on the one hand, and still using the expression of I.V. Stalin, the 'Trotskyist conspiracy from within', and, on the other hand, what should be called, from now on, the actual conspiracy of the proponents and groups serving the geopolitical line of the Red Army, the 'geopolitical groups' in action from the Red Army's positions of strength within the Soviet State.

For European revolutionary nationalists, the most urgent and, in the present circumstances, the only fundamental doctrinal task appears, therefore, to be that of an immediate and as thorough as possible approach to the new revolutionary ideology which today brings forward the still hidden leaders of the new Soviet continental geopolitical line.

If we look at things in the right way, if we take only the essential point, it was I.V. Stalin himself who, by taking the lead in the anti-Trotskyist struggle and by liquidating, thereafter, the leaders and the sources of the anti-national infection within the regime, was to initiate the national-revolutionary turn of Soviet socialism, of Soviet 'national-communism', to lay the foundations of the German-Soviet Pact of August 1939 which, whatever was said about it and whatever happened afterwards, was to constitute the first politico-historical act of the future continental geopolitical mobilisation, the magnetic lines of march and the most profound petition of destiny of which we are trying to identify today. For, secretly centred on the great Eurasian *heartland* included in the triangle formed by the Gobi desert, Sin-Kiang and Tibet, it is indeed this continental geopolitical mobilisation presaged by the German-Soviet Pact of August 1939 that is preparing, today, to bring together and reactivate, once again, the Great Continent, from the Atlantic to the Pacific, from the Pacific to the Atlantic. And let us not forget either that it is in the heart of the triangle constituted by the Gobi desert, Sin-Kiang and Tibet that, according to the earliest traditions, the Dejung, or Shamballa, 'the occult centre of the visible and invisible world' and, according to Alexandre Saint-Yves d'Alveydre and René Guénon, the dwelling place of the 'King of the World', would be found.

Also, on the other side of the barricade and on a completely different level, the Slansky episode, or that of the liquidation of Laszlo Rajk, shady arrangements if ever there were, and with them, but on a much larger scale, the equivocal and prevaricated rectification, The Soviet 'normalisation' of the 'Prague Spring' in 1968 represent, among a number of similar obscure affairs, more or less visible layers of an iceberg submerged under the icy waves of the occult war for planetary domination in progress, an iceberg named, in this case, the fight to the death between the two antagonistic tendencies of the Soviet power currently in place, namely the 'Trotskyite conspiracy from within' and, in opposition to it, the political-military power groups which, in the USSR, have supported and still support a national-revolutionary line, what is called, today, the 'geopolitical line'.

A submerged iceberg whose next moves will secretly decide the final meaning of the current world history.

The fundamental theses of the Red Army's geopolitical groups

As we know, several Western intelligence agencies are already following closely, with varying degrees of success, the current evolution of the conceptions, commitments, occult tests of strength and more or less muted manifestations of the Soviet national-revolutionary home front, whose convergence is asserting itself and intervening both in the higher ranks of the

Red Army and in the offensive social and political intellectual, and even confessional, fringe: The convergence of the two groups is taking place both in the higher ranks of the Red Army and in the offensive social and political intellectual and even religious marginalities which, feeling themselves to be at least implicitly supported by the Red Army and its structures of influence, are progressively intensifying their pressures and activities, without, however, trying too hard to move on to the stage of concerted action aimed at bringing about a significant change in the situation, and certainly in the regime itself, before the time has really come for this.

Having recently had access to active integration files dealing with problems concerning, on the one hand, 'the grand-continental geopolitical line within the Armed Forces and Fleet of the Soviet Union' and, on the other hand, 'the current regime of the national-revolutionary nebula admitted to exist and manifest itself in the USSR, and particularly in the organisations of the Soviet youth', on behalf of an American para-governmental intelligence agency, we had to go immediately to the evidence of the current reality of the USSR, and more particularly in the organisations of the Soviet youth", files of integration constantly fed by sources in direct contact with the current reality of the USSR, we had to immediately realise the very extreme national thrust at work, today, in the undergrounds of Soviet history. A history that has already been solicited by the vast turning point that marks the 'decision threshold' of 1977 and, consequently, the space of subsequent repercussions ordered by this threshold, the space of the 'Neptunian years' of the USSR, the years 1982–1989, when everything will have to be done or undone. What a spectral analysis of the depths of a great history in the making that the direct instruction of these files and the documents they contain, documents ranging from special reports from the interior or the external action groups of the emigration to tracts, manifestos, memoirs, newspapers and other clandestine publications from youth organisations, universities, Soviet military and naval academies, etc., and this enumeration is not intended to be exhaustive. This list is by no means exhaustive.

It was thus by putting to use some thirty documents belonging to these files, of which I had been more or less allowed to take copies, that I was able to constitute the concept from which the fundamental theses of action of the Soviet national-revolutionary front and of the 'new turn' that the latter now claims to propose, if not yet to impose on the regime currently in place in the USSR, emerged.

Thus, according to the latest state of the information and documentation material in our power, and taking it upon ourselves to organise, dialectically situate in relation to an overall operational concept, to simplify and reduce, to compact, the fundamental theses of the 'geopolitical groups' acting from within the Soviet Yearly Forces as well as within the politico-social and cultural marginalities controlled by them or under their direct influence, would be, at present, the following:

(1) The Great Eurasian Continent is 'one and indivisible', 'from the Atlantic to the Pacific'; India, China and South-East Asia implicitly represent the 'areas of geopolitical predestination and direct continental expansion of the central Eurasian power'. The fundamental task of our generation", says a document from Moscow, "is to set in motion the process of full political-historical integration of the entire Great Eurasian Continent". The political war, the 'direct politico-strategic intervention' against the regime currently in place in Beijing appears, therefore, as an 'immediate continental task', to which must be subjected, or which must engage 'all the revolutionary national availabilities of the Eurasian continent'.

(2) The European policy of Soviet Russia could therefore only be a policy of continental unity, centred on the positions of strength of a Europe mobilised around its own sub-continental *heartland*, i.e. around the 'total integration', in the same 'community of destiny', of France and Germany.

It should be stressed, however, that in the continental vision of the 'geopolitical groups' acting within Soviet Russia, Europe had long been conceived in terms of Germany, and Germany alone.

In this regard, it is important to recall here that in October 1949, on the occasion of the foundation of the German Democratic Republic (GDR), I. V. Stalin sent the following telegram to the President of the new state, Wilhelm Pieck:

The experience of the last war has proved that the greatest sacrifices were made by the German and Soviet people, that these two peoples have, of all the peoples of Europe, the greatest possibilities of accomplishing acts of world-wide significance.

Through the German Democratic Republic (GDR), I.V. Stalin, and it is essential that we understand its meaning very clearly, was addressing, barely four years after the last war, the whole of Germany, and in the terms of a planetary project from which he purposely banished any ideological proposal concerning communism, any Marxist-Leninist commitment, to express himself exclusively in terms of geopolitics, in terms of destiny.

Now, if, at the present time, in the continental doctrine of the 'geopolitical groups' acting more or less clandestinely in the USSR, Western Europe is conceived and defined by the new Franco-German 'community of destiny' to the exclusion of any other European conception, This is due to the abrupt rectification of perspective introduced by the return of Gaullism to power in 1958, and more particularly by the personal action of General de Gaulle himself, in Europe (Germany, Eastern Europe, the Soviet Union), as well as at the planetary level (in the 'storm zones' of Africa, Asia and Latin America and, less fortunately, in Canada; When a dismal scoundrel like André François-Poncet thought he could afford to criticise General de Gaulle unfairly, and in the columns of Le *Figaro,* for the French action undertaken by the latter in favour of Quebec and French Canada, the *Krasnaya Zvezda* and the

Komsomolskaya Pravda did not hesitate to recognise in it an attempt at 'national liberation').

(3) On the other hand, it is often insisted that the political-historical unity of the Great Eurasian Continent must be pursued, also, and completed, supported, through the establishment of a common structure of economic and political relations, but especially economic, and increasingly active, with its 'zones of transcontinental geopolitical repercussion', which are defined, in an article of December 1975, as the 'bloc of three external supports', 'Japan, the Arab world, Indonesia'. On the other hand, other documents present Japan, quite often, and even more often, as an 'integral part' of the Great Eurasian Continent.

(4) However, the "fundamental enemy" of "Eurasian geopolitical unity" remains, in any case, the "enemy across the Atlantic", the United States.

But not as a people, which, against all odds, appears to be a 'white people, by blood, history and destiny', but as a politico-historical tool of a world conspiracy which, sheltered from the present states of the American superpower, sheltered, therefore, from a so-called "world democratic superpower", represents, on the planetary level, the external projection of what I.V. Stalin called the 'Trotskyite conspiracy from within'; hence, also, it is argued, the 'permanent anti-Soviet mobilisation' drained, on the planetary level, of what I. V. Stalin called the 'Trotskyite conspiracy from within'; hence, too, it is argued, the 'permanent anti-Soviet mobilisation' drained, on a planetary level, by the 'occult proponents' of the successive governments in place in Washington, a mobilisation that has awakened, maintained and strengthened the present anti-Soviet commitments of the P. R. of China and, above all, of the United States.This mobilisation has awakened, nurtured and strengthened the present anti-Soviet commitments of the PR of China and, above all, has set up and led, in the shadows or quite openly, the 'planetary conjunction' of 'capitalist-plutocratic imperialism' and the 'world imperialism of Zionism'.

Today", write the authors of the "Appeal to the Great Soviet Nation", "we are faced with the threat of a biological degeneration in the short term and without appeal, a threat that concerns not only ourselves, but already the white race as a whole. And the deep root of this threat is called democracy". And in another document: "We have now recognised and unmasked the enemy of our race: it is democracy".

(5) Until now, it is mainly at the level of doctrinal proposal that some underground or semi-subterranean groups of national and continental geopolitical action claim to be, in the Soviet Union, vanguard national-revolutionary action groups, reinforcing, thus, from below, the positions of the politicomilitary infrastructure of the government and the regime, which, if one really had to subscribe to the recent allegations of a Leonid Plyushch, would be, already, themselves, a 'government' and a 'regime' of 'openly national-socialist' orientation, and the use that Leonid Plyushch makes of the term 'national-socialism' must be understood, here, according to its most direct 'Hitlerian' connotation. A 'government' and a 'regime', says Leonid Plyushch, which would no longer be a government or a regime in the usual sense of the terms, but new forms of a new 'National Socialist conspiracy'.

How can we doubt it? A high-level academic, and recognised as such in the West, where he has found the welcome and unconditional support of his own people, a dissident of the importance of Leonid Pliouchtch must indeed know very well what he is talking about, what he intends to denounce and what he tells us to fear: it is the very ambivalence of his allegations which, for us, constitutes the very value of his testimony.

To the 'class antagonism' of Marxism-Leninism, the 'geopolitical groups' oppose the 'race antagonism' and the 'great intercontinental race wars' to come, affirming at the same time the 'historical responsibility of the white Aryan race in its totality' and the 'historical mission of vanguard', or the 'planetary mission of vanguard' of Russia in this 'end of the XXth century', which will be a 'period of racial conflagration on a planetary scale'.

Russia's historical mission is not over, it has only just begun", states the "Pan-European Manifesto of the RSFSR". The Manifesto concludes with a provocative reference to Hitler's slogan 'One People, One Empire, One Leader' (*'Ein Volk, ein Reich, ein Führer'),* in a double sense, since it concerns both the 'Greater Russia' and the entire Eurasian 'Great Continent'. The inferno of a new messianism is smouldering under the increasingly equivocal ashes of the Marxist-Leninist interlude and the immense catastrophe that it will have imposed on the Russian people, on Europe and on the whole world. Maü, 'Shouldn't salvation set the House of Darkness ablaze first and foremost?' asks a young poet from the Leningrad *samizdat* in the 'Christmas 1976 issue' of *'Russian Iconostasis".*

In the same series of semi-clandestine documents, it is insisted that Russia's "historical mission of vanguard", far from implying a "will to imperialist power", announces, on the contrary, "a will to sacrifice, a will to destiny and to sharing", which cannot be realised otherwise than by the "profound communion" of all the "white Indo-European" nations in the same "historical direction of destiny".

We shall see to it that the fatal error of Hitler is never again repeated, who, by placing the destiny of the German people, the 'destiny of the German nation', above the interests of the entire white Indo-European race, has led us all into the historical impasse of our present decline, A dead end in which our race, our civilisation, which is in danger of dying, can no longer pull itself out of the decree of annihilation that has been issued for it, nor can it avoid the fateful slope of an ethnic, moral and biological degeneration that may now have no return. This is how civilisations undermined from within always perish. Hence the counter-current movement on which we are now playing our last chance of being and surviving".

It is, I believe, of extreme interest to note that the document from which I have just quoted this more than revealing fragment was also the object of a fairly wide circulation in German translation – using, for this purpose, the channels of an already continental clandestinity – in certain political circles of the Federal Republic of Germany, where it intended to give itself the status of an "appeal from the national revolutionary Soviet youth to the German and European youth of today".

Yet another document, this one dated May 1976, "demands", verbatim, the "politico-military integration", "in Asia", of the United States, Soviet Russia and India, with the aim of "containing", and "repressing, neutralising once and for all, the rising tide of the Yellow Peril of imperialism of the People's Republic of China". The latter document is signed by "a group of astronaut cadets" belonging to a semi-clandestine organisation called *Vetche*.

(6) At the same time, and rather paradoxically, it would seem that the problems of the new Soviet and continental economic organisation are – for the time being, at least – of very little interest to the leaders of the "geopolitical action groups".

If their projects of change foresee, nevertheless, and as a simple question of principle, the continental planning of large-scale industry and its maintenance in the ownership and under the control of the State, their attention is solicited, on the other hand, and even rather intensely, by the problem of the *Ruskoye Polie, of* the "Russian Land", of which the "Russian peasant" must become the "sole master". In this sense, the work of the economists of the line of V. Jouline, of I. Kopyssov, are followed with the most interested attention, and constitute, in the interpretations of the national-revolutionary *samizdat*, the basic ideological weapon for the mobilisation on the spot and the subterranean supervision of the Russian peasantry, a task involving, also, the acting instances of the neo-orthodox underground currents. For it must be acknowledged that the fiery rivers of the oldest Russian Orthodoxy continue to flow under the *Ruskoye Polie*.

(7) It remains to approach a last aspect of the problem, which is certainly not the least difficult to identify. This is the religious, or rather the orthodox, aspect, even though the Catholic clandestinity, which is even more profound and perhaps even more active in the shadows than the present orthodox clandestinity, will one day have to do something extraordinarily new and, above all, unforeseen, extraordinarily unforeseen, when it appears.

But what kind of orthodoxy is this? For, behind the supposedly clandestine activities of the Constantine Leontiev Seminary – a "private seminary", it goes without saying – as well as behind the stirrings of an increasingly offensive obscurantist mysticism in the peasantry and the most underprivileged social strata of the big cities, mining concentrations, etc., unsuspected avenues are now opening up, all of which are leading to the rising tide of an Orthodox revival. In this context, unsuspected paths are now opening up, all of which will eventually lead to the rising tide of an orthodox revival akin to what I would like to call the orthodox "Great Vehicle", just as we say the Buddhist "Great Vehicle".

In this regard, it is sufficient to take note of the thin "elementary patent" – printed, and perhaps printed within the USSR itself – describing the spiritual career of the "three holy starets" of Kiev, "John, Elijah and Alexander".

Setting out on foot from Kiev, "the day Stalin died", the "three holy starets", "John, Elijah and Alexander", shared the task of the "great spiritual renewal of the End", each assuming apostolic responsibility for a religious area "to be set on fire": John takes Europe, Elijah Russia and Alexander the "Great Siberia" (let us specify that the "Great Siberia" covers Soviet Siberia, Sin-Kiang and the religious archipelago of Chinese Orthodoxy, Mongolia, India and Tibet, or the "Great Tibet").

The doctrine manifested by the "three holy starets" of Kiev announces the "final renewal" of Orthodoxy, and predicts the imminent advent of the "Holy Spirit Paraclete", who is presented as having to become "incarnate" in the person of the Holy Wisdom, in the person of "Saint Sophia the Great", preaches cosmic salvation through the "very high fire of the holy cosmic liturgy" of "illuminations". The "illuminations", a most mysterious activist concept, foresee thousands and thousands of small candles being lit, at night, during the day, on top of the hills, "from hill to hill", along the paths, or in the windows of isolated farms, houses, collective dwellings, boats on the rivers in the interior of the country, "from Siberia to the Crimea". Waiting, too, for the day when thousands and thousands of other small candles will cover the streets, the pavements, the large squares suddenly invested and fervent in all the Soviet capitals, thus submerged by the "Holy Fire", when the hour will ring, the hour of the "new sanctification", which will also be the hour of the "Final Transfiguration" of the Soviet Union and the historic advent of the "New Holy Russia".

Let us recall that, in his novel *Incognito*, Petru Durnitriu, a guaranteed unconscious bearer, relates, outside of any conspiratorial scheme, the prodromes of the "internal change" of the pro-Soviet communist regime in Romania, an "internal change" obtained by the mere presence, presence on the spot, a presence that is both deeply clandestine and deeply active, of one of the three "holy starets of Kiev", Brother John, vainly pursued for years by the "political security" of Bucharest.

"Taking the lead"

The fragmentary and circumspect presentation of the intelligence, research and ideological-political documentation material used to identify and define the 'fundamental theses' of the new 'geopolitical current' now at work in the USSR, stems from the very nature of the investigation thus pursued, our contractual obligations to ensure that, on the one hand, the presentation and developments we have undertaken cannot in any way be used for the manoeuvres of a possible repressive approach *in the field* – Vladimir Ossipov, the head of the *Vetche* think tanks and publishing house, was eventually arrested, and was sentenced to eight years in prison-nor, on the other hand, does it appear to be, in any way, a *denunciation of* what it is about, when our positions regarding the renewal and national-revolutionary advancement of geopolitical consciousness, of the new grand-continental and European consciousness of certain ideological and action groupings at work in the USSR are intended to be and are above all positions of support, of exacerbating participation, of common struggle and of a common will for the grand-continental re-appropriation of Europe and its greater imperial destinies to come.

All trends merged into a single bundle of wills polarised by the "new great-continental destiny" of the Soviet Union, the names of V. Ossipov, G. Chimanov, V. Chalmaev, A. Sofronov, V. Vandakourov remain, for us, as many heroic landmarks, as many heralding and fighting landmarks, as many vanguard landmarks of the terrible, the terrible, the terrible, the terrible, the terrible. Sofronov, V. Vandakourov remain, for us, as many heroic landmarks, as many heralding and fighting landmarks, as many vanguard landmarks of the terrible, immense groundswell that is currently rising in the East, the "third groundswell" that Ungern von Sternberg, the visionary of "Anterior Asia", had glimpsed in other times.

In any case, we are not unaware that the American para-governmental intelligence agency, whose special documentation on the new geopolitical consciousness at work underground in the USSR I have had to use here, and which can only do what it is ordered to do, intends, for its part, to have recourse, in the short term, to the complicit and stipendiated diligences of a Soviet dissident – with the profile of a young academic, historian or sociologist, recently emigrated from the USSR – for the production of a book on all the problems concerning the national-communist revival in the USSR, a "national-socialist revival", as they say, and which the university presses of Princeton or Berkeley will make it their duty to publish and *endorse* according to a well-honed procedure. A book, I mean, necessarily conceived and written according to a requirement of violent denunciation, warning and provocation aiming at intervening directly in the process of geopolitical overvaluation in progress as well inside as outside the Soviet Union. This intervention was planned to act on the level of anti-European agitation-propaganda in certain circles in Washington, and unknowingly gave a glimpse of what our great political battles of tomorrow will be like if, to the offensive of the irreducible anti-European enemy acting from within European lines, we will have to oppose the counter-offensive of the great continental fortress whose greatest name to come will be that of the Eurasian Empire of the End, the *Regnum Ultimum* of the "Enlightened Brothers of Asia".

A great offensive of anti-European and anti-continental ideological denunciation is thus in the process of mobilising its negationist means, whose operational epicentre and direction of march we have identified, as well as the invisible enemy who secretly commands its subcontracting.

That is why we have just *taken the lead*.

The essential vehicle

That a new national-revolutionary thought should break through openly or clandestinely in Soviet Russia, and that the impact of its domestic front of action should grow ever stronger, is not inconceivable, on the contrary.

But what appears to be very extraordinary in this case, and indeed is so, is the support, even if only to the second or third degree, given to this current by the groupings, the national faction of the government and the regime, as well as – in the front line – the Soviet Armed Forces and the Fleet, whose infrastructures of supervision, agitation and politico-military control have become its essential vehicle. For it is, among others, the services of General A.A. Epichev, head of the central political direction of the Soviet Armed Forces, as well as those of Admiral V. Grichanov, head of the central political direction of the Fleet, which, at the present time, are working to activate, in a barely confidential manner, the national-revolutionary networks manipulated by the "geopolitical groups". The latter, implanted even in the innermost circles of the *Stavka*, of the General Staff of Moscow, represent therefore, in the present circumstances, the occult detonator of the great political explosions whose time is becoming, we believe, more and more imminent, and include in their ranks names as prestigious as those of Marshals Vassilievki and Koniev.

Now, this hour, as we are beginning to realise more and more indisputably, the hour of the deflagrating deadlines that will change everything, is announced, with total certainty, without fail, for the year 1977, and its most critical instance, its intimate line of rupture being situated, according to the very march of the tensions currently in play, on the line of passage of next summer, from June to August 1977. Soon, very soon, we shall see whether we know or do not know how things are.

Knowing in advance, it's all there

History, the great history, is never what those who are subjected to it think, blinded on purpose as they are by its occult leaders. The active secret of history must be sought in the living reasons of those who make and unmake it, in the silence and darkness of the *underworld*, far from the gaze and attention of the masses, and they know that history moves forward or backward, that it lights up or darkens, each time, according to the inner workings of a will that maintains itself beyond the course of history, a transhistorical will.

It is in the light of this internalizing conception of history that it will be necessary to know-know *in* advance-who, in the Soviet Union, will eventually prevail, at the desired time, over the other side, relentlessly, to immediately commit itself to changing-in one direction or the other-the direction and even the very face of world history. Today, as in the past, this is the *single goal: to* change the face of the world. However, in the perspective of the single goal, which of the two camps will win over the other? The one that will be able to let the will of the destiny of the providential man appear within it, who will also be the man of the last battle. When will he come? Inevitably, at the appointed time.

February 1977, in *Correspondance Européenne*

THE SIN-KIANG RED LINE

Every large-scale Soviet counter-offensive is currently attempting to neutralise, or at least to undermine, the recent Chinese offensive in favour of strengthening Europe's political-strategic unity.

France must find the means of integrating the North Atlantic Treaty Organisation as quickly as possible, because no European country is now capable of taking care of its own defence or of facing up to the intentions of Soviet social imperialism in Europe on its own", Chou En-lai confided to a French politician who was irredeemably in decline, but whose notorious anti-Soviet interests were sufficient for Peking to pretend to concede him an out-of-class reception.

This is because, for Chou En-Lai and the strategic command of China's 'grand policy', the fundamental problem of China's external security remains, in principle, the Soviet Union and, in practice, what Beijing considers to be the current Soviet attempt to encircle the 'Chinese Island' of Chungwa Kuo.

China's overall response essentially involves the establishment of a strategic nuclear insurance posture along the north and north-western Sino-Soviet border, the "Sin-Kiang red line", as well as the political counter-assurance of a multi-directional warhead offensive bar, particularly with regard to the following thrust beams

1) South East Asia, Indonesia, the South Pacific,

2) Ceylon, India and its "cam crown",

3) the "intercontinental operational area" of the Indian Ocean,

4) Western Europe and the Mediterranean fixation axis, which, through the Maghreb Island (Algeria, Morocco, Tunisia, Libya) directly targets the Middle East and the "black gates" of the Soviet Union (Baku, Tiflis, Maïkop area).

A special-status operational area includes Albania, Yugoslavia and Romania, pro-Soviet Eastern Europe (GDR, Czechoslovakia, Hungary and, above all, Poland), and the territory of the Soviet Union itself, including Siberia.

The Falcon's Strategy

In its overall dimensions, therefore, the great Chinese defensive thrust runs from North to South and then from East to West, in the same direction as the original rotation of the Mongol swastika. All Mongolian thrusts throughout the previous history of the race have been in the same imperial direction, from East to West. In this regard, and for a more recent deciphering of the deep waves of history, it is only time to reread Ferdinand Ossendowski's memoirs haunted by the bloody shadow of Colonel Baron Ungem von Sternberg.

In any case, it could be said that the East-West direction taken by the Mongolian imperial attempts throughout their succession holds its secret, its secret both immanent and active, in the doctrine known as the 'three cavalcades': for the sacred strategy of the: For the sacred strategy of the Mongols, for the Strategy of the Falcon, the heart of the objective is only attacked after having gone around it three times.

Now, just as it had been before for the Mongols, the core of the objective appears to be the total political hold, the 'imperial hold' on the 'Middle Lands' of the Eurasian continent. The geopolitical location of this "Middle Land" coincides with the large continental areas beyond the Urals that today belong to the Soviet Union, from the Black Sea to the Sea of Okhotsk.

However, the idea of locating the "Middle Lands", an earlier version of Sir Halford Mackinder's *heartland*, in the very heart of the Eurasian continent, is an obsessive Mongolian idea, which in fact has nothing to do with the Chinese conception of the world and of history. For the profound Chinese worldview, the "Middle Lands" are exclusively constituted by the lands of the interior of China, which has always called itself Chungwa Kuo, "Middle Land". For China, the "Middle Lands" are never to be conquered but always to be defended. Hence the Great Wall, and the legendary Chinese vision of Chungwa Kuo, surrounded on all sides by Barbarians. Every time China found itself in a situation where it was engaged in an offensive enterprise towards the Eurasian *heartland*, it was because it was forced to do so by a class, by a ruling group of Mongolian origin.

This is far from being irrelevant today, given the Mongolian origins of Chou En-lai and most of the elements he surrounded himself with in the strategic command of China's grand politics.

Europe defends China

But here, what also appears to be very obvious, is that the crucial point, the *Trefpunkt of* the external strategic counter-assurance system set up by China is not, as one would no doubt be tempted to believe, on its South Asian route, the train of which continues, without a solution of continuity, from Hong Kong to Aden, but in Western Europe, where this system finds its current culmination, and its most advanced point of impact.

It is thus Western Europe that constitutes the ganglionic epicentre of the current political counter-insurance mechanism set up by the Chinese People's

Republic against the Soviet Union. For the strategic command of the Chinese "grand policy", defined by Chou En-lai and put into action from Beijing by Teng Hsiao-Ping, Western Europe is currently an integral part of China's external defensive line.

At the same time, the non-geopolitical character of Sino-American relations, which is foreign to the active reality of the force of things, is also apparent, as relations between Beijing and Washington have always been circumstantial and of an exclusively political order.

For, for US imperialism, there has never been a decisive Chinese threat in the Pacific, where the only danger Washington has ever recognised is that of the *Dai Nippon*, the "Greater Japan". Here too Haushofer was right.

Superpowers trade China for the Middle East

With the precedent of August 1969 helping in a somewhat dramatic way, Beijing's current alarms are mainly a response to the dialectical implications, the hidden but certainly active reasons for the change in the attitude of the Soviet Union and the United States in the Middle East, a double change that occurred too perfectly simultaneously not to be suspect.

For one thing appears to be quite certain in the eyes of the political leaders in Beijing: the Soviet Union has given in to the United States in the Middle East, and given in a way which, given its apparently irreversible political and strategic positions in this part of the world, constitutes the equivalent of a surrender in open country. In the present state of affairs, the only counter-value that can justify, on the part of the Soviet Union, the current disengagement from its best established positions in the Middle East, is the American commitment not to intervene in the event of a preventive strategic expedition of the Soviet Union in China, even and especially if it is a nuclear operation.

A preventive expedition that took the gloves off and pretended to be, or at least claimed to be, not an aggression with clear and precise war aims, but an operation similar to the *normalizations* already carried out by the Soviet Union in Budapest in 1956 and in Prague in 1968.

It would therefore be in exchange for the more or less implied right to proceed with the nuclear normalisation of the Chinese People's Republic that Moscow would have agreed to stall in the Middle East, and one would understand much less the alarms and emergencies that this eventuality would not have failed to trigger in Beijing.

The proof is the haste, perhaps a little ill-considered, with which Chinese political leaders have come to incite, from Beijing, the reinforcement of the economic and politico-strategic unity of Western Europe, and even to support the positions of the North Atlantic Treaty Organisation with regard to the Soviet bloc. And even more so, to openly encourage anti-Soviet subversion in

Eastern European countries, as seen most recently in Beijing's denunciation of the Soviet Union's control and prohibition of nuclear production and technology in the GDR, Czechoslovakia and Hungary, etc. The work of provocation in depth is masterfully undertaken.

A well-developed scenario

Indeed, as we later learned, the Soviet plans for the democratic decentralisation of the Chinese People's Republic advocated at that time bringing the regions with Turko-Mongolian nationalities, such as Sin-Kiang, Cinghai, Inner Mongolia and Manchuria, into the sphere of direct Soviet influence, while Tibet would have regained its total independence, under the dual guarantee of India and the Soviet Union.

Following the stages of a perfectly worked-out scenario, on 13 August 1969 the Soviet-Chinese border incident at Yumin, on the north-western border of Sin-Kiang, broke out, undoubtedly the most important in the series that had begun on 2 March with the Chinese provocation on Damanski Island, on the Ussuri, since at Yumin the Soviet side was already participating with specialised units supported by helicopter gunships and heavy tanks: Yumin opened the series of incidents that would later justify Soviet intervention in China and the setting in motion of the ideological-administrative, military and economic mechanisms of normalisation.

But it was also at this time that Washington decided to intervene to prevent the Soviet action against the People's Republic of China.

In the US presidential elections of November 1969, Richard Nixon's candidacy won thanks to the support of domestic forces that demanded precisely the change in US policy towards China, unconditional support for the state of Israel and a visible and real anti-Soviet hardening, a pact that the new president kept until the end of 1972.

It is also clear that rapprochement with China required the liquidation of the state of war in the Indochinese peninsula and the eventual withdrawal of US forces from Southeast Asia.

And it is indeed the rupture of this inner pact of American politics, a rupture for which President Richard Nixon is primarily responsible, which today commands the whole of the anti-presidential campaigns centred on the so-called Watergate affair.

The rupture of the pact from which came the new American-Soviet rapprochement and its major political and diplomatic consequences, namely the exchange between the two superpowers of the polar zones of geopolitical influence, China and the Middle East, leading to the resumption of Soviet plans for the normalisation of China and the abrupt change of the American line in the Middle East. Fearsome forces have thus been set in motion that will not stop.

Escalating countermeasures

Already in March 1969, a certain "Conference for Relations between the West and China", or "Conference for Relations with China", brought together in New York the two eminences grises of the Republican and Democratic parties, Arthur Golberg and Jacob Javits, as well as, among others, Edwin Reischauer, Henry Kissinger and Arthur Schlesinger, the latter two having since taken over, one of them, the Department of State and the other the Pentagon. In its conclusions, the New York Conference on Relations with China called on Washington to urgently initiate a process of diplomatic recognition of China by the United States, and to support China's application to the UN, all with a view to defining a grand policy of joint Sino-American alliance and global action. It is perhaps important to note that among the conclusions of the New York conference on relations with China was the "return" to Beijing of the investigative films obtained by American satellites over the territory of the People's Republic.

Following the New York conference on relations with China, the escalation of American countermeasures in favour of Peking was not long in coming, leading to direct, albeit subterranean, American intervention in the preliminaries of the Soviet attack on China.

In any case, it was only on 11 August that it became known in Washington that Moscow was aware of the US counter-manoeuvre, through an unsigned commentary by the Novosti Agency, which denounced in a rather languid manner the collusion between the Chinese People's Republic and "American imperialism".

Not hesitating to take advantage of its total political control over Eastern Europe, writes the New China Agency, "the Soviet Union appropriates more than 90% of the uranium ore production extracted in Czechoslovakia, which represents about one fifth of Soviet uranium resources". A similar situation, continues the New China Agency, is being made by Moscow to the GDR and Hungary, whose uranium production is held entirely at the disposal of the Soviet Union.

And not only do the Soviet revisionists control the exploration, mining and transportation of Czechoslovakia's uranium ore, says the New China Agency, but Soviet specialists are forbidden to pass on any technical information to Czechoslovakian comrades working with them in this sector". Any attempt to use nuclear energy domestically in Eastern Europe was strictly forbidden by the Soviet Union, and this ban also extended to any discussion of nuclear technology within Comecon.

The Soviet secret services ensured that specialised technicians from the uranium-producing countries of Eastern Europe could not under any circumstances make direct contact with each other, and that any exchange of technical information had to take place exclusively through the Soviet Union.

The direct exploitation of this double operation of denunciation/provocation mounted with particular care by the Chinese agitation and propaganda services in Eastern Europe is now reaching its climax. At the same time, the Chinese services have managed to make it known that it is thanks to Beijing, through Beijing, that Bucharest has been able to obtain contracts in Canada for the installation in Romania of several nuclear power stations for civilian use, but similar to those that have just enabled India to produce the plutonium needed to make its own atomic bomb.

The August 69 precedent

But what, in Beijing, will have contributed above all to defining the new global political-strategic line of the Chinese People's Republic according to the eventuality of a Soviet nuclear attack on its northern and north-western borders, is, as we have already said, the "precedent of August 1969".

It was at the plenary meeting of the Central Committee of the Communist Party of the Soviet Union on 26 June 1969 that the decision was taken to launch a Soviet nuclear attack against the People's Republic of China. The group of the General Secretariat-headed by Leonid Brezhnev, and followed, at that time, by Piotr Chelest, who, on the strength of the quite positive results of the Soviet intervention in Czechoslovakia, the initiative of which belonged to him to a very large extent, represented the General Staff of the Armed Forces-was not to encounter any serious difficulty in winning, at that meeting, the decision concerning the nuclear normalisation of China. The date of the clash was to be left to the discretion of the Joint Chiefs of Staff, but on no account was it to be later than the end of August.

The plans of attack, chosen by the Stavka within the emergency timeframe agreed on 26 June, provided for the following operational developments:

—Combined nuclear spot operation and specialised commandos on China's nuclear infrastructure nerve centres, concentrated in Sin-Kiang;

—Arrow on Peking of a fast armoured strategic group, from Outer Mongolia and with the support of some elite units under the command of General Batin Dozj: head of the Ulaanbaatar Armed Forces; operation conceived with the political aim of neutralising on the spot the power of unity and politico-military action of the Party and the Government, as well as to release the elements of a new central power, of pro-Soviet orientation, and to support its installation;

—Combined fast armoured/airborne operation on Manchuria's industrial nodes and internal communication lines, with the minimal aim of neutralising the logistical effort of production, and the major aim of occupying and securing control of the decisive area where China's new industrial power is being forged;

—Unconditional and immediate local support for all national protests against the central government in Beijing, creation of pro-Soviet national governments against Chinese cultural and political pressure.

Finally, around 23 August, a note verbale from the government in Washington, acting as a confidential message from the President of the United States to Leonid Brezhnev, warned the Soviet Union against any initiative of decisive dimensions that the latter might undertake towards the Chinese People's Republic

At the same time, the CIA was sending sufficient documentation about Soviet plans for intervention in China to more or less selected sectors of the American press, with the task of using this material in a vast operation of preventive mobilisation of American and international public opinion, "but without pushing too hard either".

Moscow will have to strike

Faced with this ambiguous situation, Moscow could not but back down and suspend operations already underway.

Today, five years later, the situation is the same again, this time without the political-military blockade of the United States and with an infinitely more thorough resolution on the part of the Soviet Union.

If Beijing's political leaders do not succeed in inventing, in due course, a replacement dam that will compensate for the withdrawal of the United States from the game and that will count against the Soviet Union in terms of decisive deterrence, the fate of the regime currently in power in China is cast.

Sooner or later, Moscow will have to strike, and this time there will be no holding back its thrust.

Some people are even thinking about the next August: August 1969-August 1974 is a good time. The time it took Hulgu's Pan-Mongol armies to invade and destroy Baghdad, when the "last Caliph" was executed in 1258.

More than ever, therefore, the Mongolian staff that Chou En-lai managed to mobilise around himself in the small group that, under the leadership of Teng Hsiao-Peng, watches over the destinies of China's great politics, should meditate on the words of Temutchin, who became Genghis-Khan by power, the Oceanic Khan: "…on a clear day, be vigilant like a hardened wolf; on a dark night, be cautious like the black raven''.

Beijing turns to NATO

What must be kept in mind in these analyses is that the possible investment of China by Soviet intervention forces is not at all aimed at what, in terms of conventional strategy, would be called the "occupation of Chinese territory". The purpose of any Soviet operation in China would be to normalise a political situation considered abnormal to the interests of the People's Republic itself, a situation abnormal to the interests of the Chinese people and the Chinese Communist Party. The Soviet operation would be the equivalent of a political war of liberation, the setting in motion of an enterprise of thorough de-alienation of the Chinese Communist Party and the central power, both "hijacked" in their goals and in their political-administrative structures, by "groups deviating from the power currently in place in Beijing". It is not a question of expropriating, forbidding or liquidating the politico-strategic line of a Chinese communism, of a "Chinese way of communism", but of rectifying it, of bringing it back to its "popular and socialist" direction, to its "most just democratic line".

But China is not Czechoslovakia, and there is no doubt that the unpredictable elements of the Chinese domestic situation following a possible Soviet action of politico-strategic rectification risk at any moment to engage the whole operation in ways that are at the very least equivocal, if not excessively dangerous for the Soviet Union itself.

On the other hand, it remains quite obvious that the political and other counter-assurances that Beijing is trying to provide itself along the southern borders of the Eurasian continent remain rather uncertain, at least for the time being. In this regard, Pakistan's gradual slide out of China's orbit remains fraught with both lessons and uncertainties.

On the other hand, the work of strengthening and over-activating some of its already acquired positions appears to be more immediately rewarding for Beijing in its Eastern European areas of operation, as well as in the establishment of a range of new special political and diplomatic relations with Western Europe.

In fact, for a long time now, Chou En-lai and the strategic command group of the Chinese "grand policy" have been taking positions in favour of the economic and politico-strategic unity of Europe, and also in favour of the North Atlantic Treaty Organisation. It is certain that NATO seems to be the most appropriate western structure for Beijing to set up a common western and Chinese security mechanism to deal with the permanent threat posed to each other by the weight of the Red Army's presence along the Lübeck-Trieste continental separation line.

China has become one of NATO's hottest supporters, its passion to serve far outstripping the commitments of some other countries that are members of the military bloc'', writes the *Krasnaya Zvezda, the* official organ of the Soviet

Armed Forces, and the *New York Times* has just written that China is becoming "a far more sincere supporter of NATO than some of the organisation's full members". This is also the firm belief, repeatedly expressed in recent times, by the acting Secretary General of the North Atlantic Treaty Organisation, Robert Luns.

On the other hand, in its most recent external propaganda offensive, the Tass Agency has been aggressively attacking the relations that Chou En-lai and his group have been trying to establish with political circles, pressure groups and political leaders who openly profess their irreducibly anti-Soviet and anti-socialist positions, citing, in this connection, the way in which Edward Heath, the leader of the British National Opposition, and Franz-Joseph Strauss, the Bavarian leader of the anti-socialist opposition in West Germany, were received in Peking by Chou Enlai. This is how Peking is developing its relations with all those in reactionary circles who are ready to collaborate in China's international action in the field of anti-socialism, and more particularly against the Soviet Union," the Tass agency said.

Senator Jackson and the Shadow Falconers

But the big shake-up of Soviet counter-propaganda was triggered, in fact, by the visit to Peking of the Democratic Senator from Washington State, Henry "Scoop" Jackson.

The latter, leader in the Senate of the hardest Democratic fraction and whose anti-Soviet intransigence is reputed to be unfailing, was received in Peking by Chou En-lai personally, and the Soviet press underlines, in order to emphasize the exceptional character, and even, in a way, the subversive implications, that this meeting took place in the Peking hospital, where the Chinese Premier was "undergoing treatment for a serious illness". It is also known that the democratic hawk Henry "Scoop" Jackson was received, during his visit to Peking, by Chou En-lai's deputy for strategic problems of the "grand policy", Teng Hsiao-Peng, as well as by the vice-minister of Foreign Affairs, Houah-Houa.

Finally, the guidelines reported in the Chinese press were intended to highlight the global nature of Senator Henry Jackson's meetings with Beijing politicians, both in terms of the issues discussed and the decisions taken together on this occasion, which should be put into action as quickly as possible.

It was therefore to be expected that Moscow would react, and it did not take long. At the dinner in the Kremlin in honour of President Richard Nixon on 27 June, Leonid Brezhnev said: "The détente in Soviet-American relations, as in international relations in general, is meeting with rather strong resistance. I do not need to speak in detail on this subject because our American visitors know better than we do and in greater depth those who speak out against international détente in order to revive the arms race and who want to return to the methods and customs of the Cold War. I only wish to express my firm conviction that the policy of these people, whether they are aware of it or not, has nothing to do with the interests of our peoples. This is undoubtedly a direct attack on Senator Henry Jackson and the pressure groups behind him who are doing everything possible to neutralise the US-Soviet détente policy, to sabotage the work that has already been done between Washington and Moscow. Work which, according to President Richard Nixon, was only made possible, in the end, "because of the personal relations established between the General Secretary of the Communist Party and the President of the United States".

An exchange of declarations hiding, under their lying transparency, under their apparent simplicity, but, in fact, terribly trapped, a vertiginous historical importance, and that nobody understood, or almost nobody, those who understood all the importance had better pretend to have understood even less than the others.

A new American operation to rescue the so-called Maoist regime was therefore underway, more or less identical to the one that had been mounted in 1969 through the New York conference on "relations with China". The difference, which is fundamental, is that this time the US government, and President Richard Nixon in particular, are committed to positions that are essentially opposed to those of the pro-Maoist supporters represented, on the ground, by Senator Henry Jackson and others like Abe Ribicoff, whose activities and hype are increasingly seen by specialists as the "tip of the iceberg".

Faced with the most diverse abortive manoeuvres of the die-hards of the anti-Soviet line, the political administration in Washington has to reckon, at the same time, with the machinations of the pro-Chinese nebula, an outgrowth and subterranean continuation of the Institute for Pacific Affairs, of dismal memory.

However, for Beijing, the thrice fatal illusion would be to let itself be persuaded that the action of the intervention and influence groups which, in Washington, manoeuvre to put in the way of the American-Soviet rapprochement in progress, would go straight in the direction of the interests of China, as the professionals of the diversion of the class of Henry ''Scoop'' Jackson never tire of making believe. For it is not for the safeguarding of the politico-historical interests of the Chinese People's Republic that the hooded Democratic hawks and the great faceless falconers hiding in the favourable shadow of anti-Soviet intransigence act in Washington, but to slow down the process, to hinder and neutralise the exchange of zones of influence operated by Washington and Moscow on the Middle East, to sabotage while there is still time, the implications of the new pro-Arab line adopted by the current Republican administration of Richard Nixon.

For the shadowy hawks in Washington, support for China serves to sabotage the ongoing rapprochement with the Soviet Union, and sabotage of the rapprochement with the Soviet Union serves to sabotage Washington's rapprochement with the Arab world in the Middle East.

Sin-Kiang is no longer in Sin-Kiang

Today, the "Sin-Kiang red line" no longer runs only in the north and northwest of China, along the Soviet-Chinese nuclear confrontation zone, but everywhere in the world where China can politically and strategically counter the Soviet Union's positions. Whenever the problem of the Soviet Union's political presence and security is posed in terms of crisis or challenge, in the Indian Ocean, in the Middle East, in Eastern or Western Europe, China is involved, dialectically called upon to engage all its oppositional and politico-strategic forces.

The Sin-Kiang red line is thus no longer only a line of direct nuclear confrontation between the Chinese People's Republic and the Soviet Union, but also and above all a line of permanent confrontation between those who, in the current march of world history, are likely to take sides with one or the other of the two great geopolitical camps in presence, the camp of Beijing and the camp of Moscow.

If Beijing wins its political battle in Europe, and succeeds in making Europe take on the status of a factor of politico-strategic uncertainty on the western rear of the front opened by the Soviet Union against China, Beijing will thus have turned, politically, and reversed the front of any possible direct offensive of the Soviet Union towards the heart of Chinese interior spaces.

If, in the near future, the overall analyses put forward by the strategic command of the Chinese "grand policy" were to be proven by the very march of history, it would be on the line which, today, and since 1945, separates Europe into two still antagonistic parts, that the "red line of Sin-Kiang" should mark, above all, the passage of destiny. For it will undoubtedly be in the hollow of this internal splitting of Europe, separated within itself between a Western Europe and an Eastern Europe, that the final outcome of the Soviet-Chinese confrontation will be played out in due course.

Safety pays

In these conditions, will China be able to achieve its 'conceptual breakthrough', will it be able to envisage achieving it in time?

In this game, Beijing's trump card remains, more than ever, the North Atlantic Treaty Organisation and, within it, the West European implantation of a certain idea of an Atlantic community of destiny between the United States and Europe. Relations between the United States and Western Europe had become somewhat strained in the aftermath of the October War in the Middle East," writes the New China Agency. However, faced with the ambitions and military threat of Soviet social-imperialism and its efforts to politically disintegrate Western Europe, the leaders of the United States and the Western European states found it necessary to draw closer together again''.

It is to this overall situation that the Soviet Union is trying to respond, at the present time, with the acceleration of its project of a "Conference for the Continental Security of Europe", of which it remains, however, rather doubtful that it will ever become something politically effective, a structure of European historical presence and intervention in a position to respond to the planetary challenges that concern it directly. Unless, of course, there are profound changes in the Soviet Union's next historical choices towards Western Europe, historical choices that would give Europe's continental security its greatest dimensions, weight and geopolitical destiny. If the Soviet Union wants absolute security on its western rear, it should pay the price.

29 July 1974, in *Combat*

TOWARDS A NATIONAL-COMMUNIST EUROPE?

In an Eastern European embassy in Paris, a high-ranking diplomat recently made the following reflections, which one would hope were remote-controlled: "The little importance that seems to have been attached in Paris to the talks that Georges Marchais had last July in Moscow, and in particular with Leonid Brezhnev, seems to me to be quite appalling. The political leaders of Western Europe seem incapable of understanding that the current evolution of the situation in the camp controlled by the USSR is mobilised by a single political and strategic objective: to be in a position to respond to the certainty that, from now on, the Soviet-Chinese confrontation is absolutely inevitable, and that it risks taking on, at any moment, the immediate dimensions of a world conflagration". It was precisely the day after the Brezhnev-Marchais talks of 27 July last that *Pravda*, raising the problem of the imperative need for a new conference of the European Communist parties, a conference which would enable them to "strengthen their action with a view to achieving détente in Europe", declared the following: The international communist movement is currently characterised by the need to strengthen unity on the basis of Marxism-Leninism and to take joint action. The Peking government is developing anti-Sovietism and allying itself with the imperialists against socialism and peace. For this reason it is wrong to think that the dangers of war are non-existent. The fundamental problem of Soviet diplomacy in Europe thus becomes a problem of "European security", in the particular sense that this concept means the politico-military security of the Soviet Union's western rear in case the latter should find itself in direct engagement with China. The current aims of Soviet diplomacy in Europe are therefore twofold: on the one hand, to get the European Communist Parties to form a block behind the anti-China line of the CPSU ("to strengthen unity", "to carry out joint actions"), and, on the other hand, to secure the implicit support of the European countries in the event of an open politico-military conflict with the People's Republic of China ("it is wrong to think that the dangers of war are non-existent", etc.).

In the present circumstances of its great continental policy, the Soviet Union has no choice for the pursuit of its diplomatic urgencies of the moment, Moscow must rely primarily on France, and on the PCF. France, in other words the new regime of Valéry Giscard d'Estaing, to act diplomatically and politically in Europe, Georges Marchais and the PCF to act on the increasingly tense dialectical level where the problem of Soviet influence on the European Left is posed at the moment. Hence the joint declaration by the two General Secretaries of the Soviet and French Communist Parties on relations between the Soviet Union and France: "The two Communist Parties attach immense importance to the development of cooperation between the USSR and France, a cooperation which responds to the interests of both peoples and which is destined to become an important factor in guaranteeing peace in Europe".

In the same joint communiqué, the General Secretaries of the Soviet and French Communist Parties, Leonid Brezhnev and Georges Marchais, also referred to the ongoing work of the European Conference on Co-operation and Security and recalled that "the rapid completion of the work of this 'summit' conference responds to the interests of general peace and that of the broad masses of the people", while taking care to point out the need to "complete international political détente with military détente". It might remain to be pointed out that the man in Moscow who bears the current responsibility for the alignment of the European Communist Parties with the leading anti-China positions demanded by the new Soviet strategy is the Secretary of the Central Committee, Boris Ponornarev, and his task is far from easy. In any case, Boris Ponomarev's visit to Paris closely preceded the CPF General Secretary's trip to Moscow.

It would be difficult to expect more clarity from others.

But who, at the present time, in Europe would be able to grasp the full importance of this confession, and the very precise scope for immediate action? Who could understand, one wonders, the extraordinary power of political-diplomatic manoeuvre that this could provide, if only they still wanted to, the game of a certain French continental line of action?

Preventive war, stupefaction and paralysis

At the same time, international public opinion is wondering, not without some trepidation, about the meaning of the formidable psychological conditioning campaign launched by the Tel Aviv government, which aims at the accelerated creation of a war psychosis within the Israeli nation as well as outside.

Indeed, according to the Israeli Minister of Defence, Shimon Pères, "the plausible risks" of a resumption of the Arab-Israeli war have just reached, in recent days, a threshold of no return, "turning on all the warning signals". There is therefore no longer any doubt that if the Tel Aviv government is thus setting in motion an internal and external psychological conditioning device intended to forge the lure of the imminence of a new Arab offensive against Israel, it is precisely to mask and to divert the decision of a forthcoming Israeli preventive action against the Arab front, and above all, most certainly against Syria. Israel, General Gur has just declared, could be the first to choose the utilitarian option, if the political options prove ineffective.

The psycho-technical manipulation of the masses that always precedes the launching of a preventive action has the aim of dialectically reversing the terms of the situation, so that the attacker ends up posing as the attacked, and the attacked as the attacker. This is a fundamental requirement of the current conditions of political warfare, which none of the confronting parties can afford the fatal oversight of ignoring.

The same emergency procedure, coupled with a first-class intention to stun, is currently being used by the Soviet Union against China. For Moscow it is not only a matter of warning international public opinion and mobilising the Soviet masses in the face of the real, supposed or fabricated Chinese danger, but also of psychologically paralysing the ideological-racial adversary beyond Sin-Kiang, of inflicting on him the certainty of the forthcoming attack under the guise of a stupefyingly fascinating terror, with all the weight of an "overwhelming fatality", etc.

However, the truly decisive stage in the setting in motion of an agitation and psychological framework in terms of 'war psychosis' is the one where, in the process, the potential protagonists come to rid themselves of all hindrances, all ideological impediments, and where only the direct planning of the planned confrontation matters, where the problems of the operational concentration of the forces involved abruptly override any other consideration.

Geopolitics trumps ideologies

This is where the most unexpected ideological information appears, such as, for example, the mobilisation of a certain European extreme right, which has its roots in fascism and collaboration, in the service of the particular politico-historical interests of the State of Israel.

But it is the Soviet-Chinese confrontation which is currently provoking, assuming and supporting in force a series of ideological reversals which are probably already irrevocable and which, in any case, cancel out the ideological justifications of the current world war, which is a total and permanent world war, in favour of its geopolitical justifications alone.

So we are obliged to witness the tango of fascination which, apart from any ideological consideration, leads the People's Republic of China today to make a qualified solicitation towards the still functioning leaders of the Third Reich, and of all the previous great battles against the Soviet Union and "world Bolshevism". Everything is there. In Canada, Ukrainian emigration, which is strongly anti-Soviet and anti-Russian, is the object of a manoeuvre of nucleation and intoxication carried out by the services of Peking, a manoeuvre which, under the cover of an external front for the liberation of the "captive nations of the USSR", is currently trying to set up a vast machine of subversion destined to mobilise the whole of the anti-Soviet emigration of Canada and, from Canada, in the whole world on site. And why, precisely, from Canada? That is the question, a question that is not without an answer.

At the same time, the Soviet special services were well aware of the real Chinese "rush" on the Third Reich's senior executives, who, like former minister Albert Speer, appeared to be essentially recoverable, economic, cultural and technical executives. Thus, the former head of the Hitlerjugend and hero of the Battle of Berlin, Arthur Axmann, went to Peking several times at the personal invitation of Chou En-lai, bringing with him a whole group of industrialists and technicians from the economy and political youth organisations who had belonged to the Third Reich.

Only recently, at a large reception held by the People's Republic of China in Bad-Godesberg, the sculptor and architect Arno Breker, a close friend of the Chancellor of the Third Reich and referred to by Charles Despiau as a new Michelangelo, was received with marks of deference bordering on outright provocation towards the Social Democratic government of the Federal Republic, whose representatives on the spot were beaten cold, and very ostentatiously, by the Peking ambassador who was receiving him, and by his entire entourage. It is therefore not at all excluded, it is suggested, that in the near future Arno Breker will visit Peking, officially invited by the People's Republic of China.

Finally, it is well known in the specialised services that Beijing agents are currently combing the circles of German survivors in Latin America, and in particular Brazil and Argentina, for contacts with the assembly groups of former SS and other special political formations, who are being offered quite exceptional contracts provided that they agree to go to the People's Republic of China for a period of at least three years.

On the other hand, if Israeli state radio is to be believed, Chou Enlai felt obliged to convey to the Tel Aviv government last July, using the eager services of Democratic Senator Henry Jackson, the assurance that the People's Republic of China wished to help guarantee the existence of an Israeli state strong enough to oppose and effectively resist the "activities of Soviet imperialism", the assurance that the People's Republic of China wishes to help secure the existence of an Israeli state strong enough to effectively oppose and resist the "Soviet imperialist drive" in the Middle East, and strategically able to counteract the Soviet presence in the Indian Ocean.

From the Polarka Plan to the Volcano Plan

On the other hand, and still following the internal dialectic of total world war, which requires the replacement of ideological justifications by the direct operational commands of geopolitics, one can catch the USSR taking upon itself, at the present time, the destinies of a new ''risorgimento'' of Greater Croatia, and thus ensuring the succession, thirty years later, of an idea that had been supported by the Third Reich, and which had already led to the creation of a new world war, the destiny of a new "risorgimento" of Greater Croatia, and thus ensure the succession, thirty years later, of an idea that had been supported by the Third Reich, and which had already led to the creation of a Croatian National State, headed by the Poglavnik Ante Pavelitch.

It was from 1969 onwards that certain political leaders of the Croatian national emigration sought contact with the USSR, with the Soviet embassy in Bonn serving as the first intermediary in this operation, which later, but always in the shadows, was to take on decisive dimensions and which today is still bearing fruit. Paradoxically perhaps, the share of the Croatian national emigration and its forces acting, secretly, inside, appears much more important, in the current state of the Soviet plans concerning the project of a Croatian Socialist Republic, than that of the communist government in Zagreb and the cadres of the Croatian Communist Party set up by Belgrade.

This is because the USSR deliberately played the card of the Ustasha and the Ustasha-controlled Croatian National Front both externally and internally, which is extremely significant.

After the revelations of a Czechoslovak defector, General Sejna, the Soviet project of politico-military normalisation of Yugoslavia, known as the "Polarka Plan", was improved and simplified, improved and simplified by the exclusion, in particular, of the part that foresaw the passage of Soviet forces through Carinthia, an Austrian territory, to take Yugoslavia in a pincer movement with the thrust of a second offensive front advancing from the south.

The new Soviet plan, which again included, as in the "Polarka Plan", two directions of thrust separating at the moment of departure, proposed to secure Croatia and Slovenia by starting from Hungary and heading towards the Adriatic, with the port of Pula as the fundamental objective, while a mixed Soviet-Hungarian offensive corps would be satisfied with investing the north of Serbia, along the Hungarian border, as well as the Yugoslav Banat. This would allow the installation of a Croatian Socialist Republic on the Adriatic, controlled by the USSR, and the complete isolation of Romania, while preserving the appearance and even the reality of a reputedly independent Federal Yugoslav Republic (but amputated of Croatia and Slovenia).

It is by analysing the satellite survey of the layout and the directions of march of the two Soviet offensive corps based in the south-western part of Hungary in the strategic region of Lake Balaton, that we were able to reconstitute more or less in its essential lines the new Soviet plan of military intervention in Yugoslavia, This plan is referred to in specialized circles as the "Volcano Plan" and is said to have been personally conceived by the Warsaw Pact Deputy Commander-in-Chief, General Chtmenko.

Let us add that, in the terms of the "Volcano Plan", the major problem of any military intervention in Yugoslavia, i.e. Belgrade's arrangements for the launching of a war of total defence of the territory, is evacuated, in principle, by the fact that the Soviet forces are supposed to stop on the borders of "Greater Serbia", their direct action concerning only zones where nationalism is turned either towards the outside (Banat) or towards itself (Croatia). This is why

Belgrade has been quick to set in motion an urgent updating of the anti-Russian doctrine of "Greater Serbia", which, in the recently published anti-circulation book by Prof. Miko Milenkovic, tries to demonstrate that Croatia, Macedonia, etc. are "properties of Greater Serbia and of the historical and racial expansionist power of the Granderbian stock".

Moscow plays the Portuguese example

This situation itself, the new destiny that seems to be given by the Soviet Union to the Great Croatia project, far from being a circumstantial situation, the by-product of a conjuncture that it is a question of using tactically as long as it lasts, represents on the contrary, the direct beginning of one of the new structures of politico-strategic action, set up by the USSR, in Europe, from 1969 onwards.

Indeed, having understood that the Communist Parties in Western Europe, and above all, within the framework of a maintained alliance with social democracy and the so-called revolutionary lefts, have no chance of appropriating political power in due course, Moscow is currently playing the card of the ritual suicide of the Communist Parties of Western Europe within a common front with the national armed forces. What happened in Portugal, where the Communist Party now serves only as an operational relay between the Armed Forces Movement and the popular masses, will eventually happen in Spain, Greece and most certainly in Italy, too, it is thought in Moscow.

In this respect, it is extremely interesting to recall that all the organisations of direct politico-strategic action, brought together by Guido Giannettini in the CNDR (National Committee for the Defence of the Republic), an extreme right-wing formation that has been acting illegally in Italy for two years by means of terrorist action and clandestine political agitation, have declared themselves, and on several occasions, in favour of a rapprochement with the Italian Communist Party, on condition that the current team of the ICP General Secretariat, led by Berlinguer, decides to eliminate from the Party the Trotskyist and internationalist elements that have made it the bridgehead of international leftism, and which continue to sabotage and rot the European national left from the ICP.

Now that things have reached this point, it should also be remembered that Guido Giarmettini's CNDR makes no secret of its claim to be considered the first element of a clandestine provisional government of the future Italian Socialist Republic, and that its action is increasingly oriented towards contacts with the Armed Forces and the accelerated infiltration of the political and administrative structures in place. A part of the State is already behind them", wrote *L'Espresso* in its editorial of 11 August.

Time for captains everywhere

The hour of the captains has come in Europe, and in Europe the hour of the captains will be the hour of national-communism.

Captains are in power in Lisbon, tomorrow they will probably be in Madrid, Rome and Athens, as they are already in Tripoli and Algiers. With Colonel Vasco Gonçalves as President of the Council and General Otello Carvalho as head of the Continental Operational Command (Copcon), Lisbon has become the political-strategic epicentre of the new European revolutionary struggle, which is the continental struggle of national-communism. Today, therefore, General Otello Carvalho has at his disposal, through the Operational Command of the Continent (Copcon), the only European armed force with an exclusively political mission, and he directs, from the military region of Lisbon, which he is also in charge of, the only political battle corps currently available in Europe. A national-communist battle corps.

It is also known that on the eve of Caramanlis' return to Athens, a group of Greek officers belonging to the elite arms, including military security, were in Lisbon on a confidential mission for the Northern Army Group, and it is also known that the political orientation of these officers was not at all what one might think. The line of immediate ideological confrontation on which your politico-military groups will have to meet in the coming days in Athens, due to the liquidation of a regime that has been rotten on its feet for a long time, is already engaged in the direction of an evolution foreseen by your analyses that show national-communism as the winner in the long run on the two shores of the Mediterranean, from Lisbon to Athens and from Algiers to Cairo.

And it is this new situation, which is currently taking place in Europe, in terms of Immediate history, which will also risk giving a chance to a total reconsideration of the problem of German reunification. For, in the perspective of what is happening or is being prepared, in Lisbon as well as in Rome, Athens or Madrid, East Germany is destined to win dialectically over the adulterated and socially ultra-subversive political conceptions of West Germany, ruthlessly devoured by the occult canker of stateless super-capitalism. And to the extent that the armed forces and the Party in East Germany have long since found the way back to the only active reality of a national destiny and a national consciousness.

If, in 1969, no one had tried so hard to kill de Gaulle to prevent him from doing what they knew he was going to do at all costs, Europe today would be, in its direction of travel, in its very being and in its very breath, a Gaullist Europe. Now, after the Petit Clamart, so brilliantly successful in 1969, Europe will be something else. The same continuation will have to take very different paths, paths that are undoubtedly infinitely more dangerous than those that Gaullism and Gaullist Europe would have chosen if de Gaulle had been able to stay.

The destiny of Soviet national-communism

In a forgotten book, *De Gaulle Dictator*, a forgotten politician, de Keritlis, concluded his lived analysis of Gaullism with the following definition, which is still quite extraordinary, and which dates back to 1945: Gaullism is a National Socialism that played the winning party card.

Soviet national-communism is a national-socialism that has succeeded in turning itself into a socialism, and whose nationalism thus becomes a continental nationalism. Soviet national-communism is a continental national-socialism insofar as any authentically and totally national European policy must appropriate, in order to act, the space of continental geopolitical development that goes from the Atlantic to the Pacific.

This same deep historical current, which today we must call, perhaps for lack of a better term, national-communism, will end up, on the other hand, and there, in a way, as if by a return of the wave, by announcing itself also in the Soviet Union, a groundswell coming from Lisbon, from Madrid and Athens, from everywhere. Soviet national-communism, whose most current meaning is that of an overall continental geopolitics, will then become a national-communism turned towards Europe, a movement of essentially European destiny and consciousness, insofar as European national-communism will succeed in bringing back to Europe, in terms of consciousness, the backlash of the original seismic impulse, which was part of it in terms of destiny.

It is since 1969, as has already been said, that the Soviet Union has been preparing the installation of national-communism in Europe, which means that a dividing line crosses the political history of Russia, a dividing line that announces, in fact, that the Soviet state ideology is no longer Marxism-Leninism, but geopolitics. Final evacuation of Marxism-Leninism, return to the living and active values of a national geopolitical vision turned towards the immediate historical assumption of a national destiny of continental and world dimensions: this is where the movement of internal neutralisation of Marxism-Leninism, a movement initiated by Stalin by the massive liquidation of the Party's cadres that his project of the German-Soviet pact demanded, was to find, and finds, today, its final outcome. On top of Stalinisation, Leonid Brezhnev was thus continuing, and fulfilling, the hidden aims of the national geopolitical line of Soviet communism embodied by I. V. Stalin.

The part of Heraclitus that acts underneath a Hegel, says endlessly and without respite: nothing is made in history except by the negation of negation. It is by geopolitically negating the Chinese dialectical negation that the Soviet Union today manages to dialectically find itself in terms of total geopolitics, and to lay the foundations for another historical restart of its own continental destiny in Europe and in the world.

Of course, the game is far from over: there are powers at work which, in Moscow as elsewhere, can still call everything into question, and change everything.

The game is far from over

Commenting on the summer meetings between Leonid Brezhnev and the Secretaries of the Communist Parties of Eastern Europe, meetings which have now become a tradition, the Belgrade daily *Politika*, whose sources of information are always considered exceptional, stated that, in the present circumstances, these meetings would take on the value of a summit conference intended to prepare, still kept secret, the great "red council" of world Communism which Moscow would like to be able to convene for next year. Why this haste and secrecy, why this implied tension? It is because Leonid Brezhnev has also let himself be caught in the quicksand of a phase where, if he wants to win, he has to play tight, fast, and without the slightest tactical setback. Beyond Vienna, things are being decided now.

Indeed, there is no doubt that the silent but still very powerful group which, in the Central Committee of the CPSU and elsewhere, opposes the general line taken by Leonid Brezhnev, will try to use the political liquidation of Richard Nixon to counter-attack, and it is also well known that the anti-Brezhnev group in Moscow has effective and fierce support in almost all the Communist Parties of Eastern Europe and elsewhere, especially in Prague and Rome.

The key phrase of the last American-Soviet summit meetings, uttered by Richard Nixon in Moscow, which some people immediately rushed to interpret in the sense of an attempt at personal publicity, but which will remain in the history books as the tragic tear through which the depths of invisible history bear witness, It was a tragic tear in history, in which the depths of invisible history bore witness to the march of visible history, and it was the beginning of a fatal chain of events for Leonid Brezhnev, who would in due course be reproached for having linked Soviet global policy to the options of a US President who was deemed incapable of fulfilling his commitments, "for the sake of the gallery". Richard Nixon, it will be recalled, stated that the current state of rapprochement between the Soviet Union and the United States had been made possible, above all, "because of the personal relationship established between the General Secretary of the Communist Party and the President of the United States".

Preventing relaxation at all costs

One thing, in any case, is certain: J. F. Kennedy was liquidated because he was about to play the Soviet card, and that, once J. F. Kennedy was out of the way, nothing was done between Washington and Moscow. Robert Kennedy, in his turn, was liquidated at the very moment when he was in danger of taking over the Presidency of the United States, because once in the White House he too would have played the Moscow card. Richard Nixon, finally, was liquidated because he managed to do what the Kennedys had been prevented from accomplishing, and above all because his political elimination could not fail to call into question once again the current achievements of the American-Soviet rapprochement.

But here too there are still a few things to be said. The first is that the Kremlin is fortunately not the White House. The second is that, despite the demented hype that the international left has been making for years about the actions of the so-called "war criminal" Richard Nixon, never since 1945 has the world been so close to the apocalyptic risk of a pre-emptive nuclear conflagration as it was when Richard Nixon was shot down in flames, Moscow is now wondering whether it would not be better to play its decisive strategic cards in one fell swoop before the whole world finds itself united in a democratic crusade, or rather in a new democratic crusade designed to impose on it the law of a world imperialism whose equivocal sign no longer manages to conceal its still unavowable aims. The third thing to be said is that, taking the part of the fire, it is also possible that the scenography set on the cleaning by the vacuum of the White House goes dry, on a historical unforeseen event before its point of departure in the very trap that Richard Nixon's politico-administrative "killers" had set up so well, too well: because, behind Gerald Ford, the sharp shadow of Ted Kennedy is already looming, who will not miss his shot. It's always the third time that's the charm. The fourth and last thing to say is that a strange analogy seems to have played, and is still playing, in the shadows, in Washington as well as in Moscow, at the ultimate point of the overall plan to bring down Richard Nixon and, later, if possible, Leonid Brezhnev. Indeed, it would now appear that, on balance, it is CIA Director William E. Colhy, who bears operational responsibility for Richard Nixon's downfall. And some also believe that it is the head of the Committee for State Security, Yuri Andropov, who, through a vast system of relays, is covering, from Moscow, the setting up of the current campaign against Leonid Brezhnev.

Now, in any case, the pale bitches of the Apocalypse are unleashed. By the time anyone really noticed, it would already be the "time of the inferno" again. The present calm is no more than the torrid, dreary lull before the storm breaks, before the fire breaks out. At the deepest level, the parties involved are hastily setting up their new secret relays, their intervention forces and their manoeuvring masses. For having let itself slip so pitifully out of the great game, does France imagine that it will be spared, at the time of the next European tragedy, at the time of the next deal of iron dice?

The losers are always marked by fate.

16 August 1974, in *Combat*

YURI ANDROPOV AND THE NIGHT SIDE OF THE SOVIET UNION

In January 1981, a KGB colonel stationed in London under diplomatic cover, V. R. Nikolsky, had, as was so well known at the time, 'chosen freedom' (because, it was claimed in Russian émigré circles in London, of a young Jamaican singer, who was no doubt multi-talented, rather than for imperative ideological reasons, as he himself claimed).

As he had been in charge of Anglo-Soviet "active cultural relations" for the last two years – close monitoring of the politically and culturally active circles of Soviet refugees in Britain, their ongoing contacts with the underworld of the Soviet *Samizdat in the* interior, etc. – he was able to make a significant contribution to the development of the Soviet Union. -V. R. Nikolsky, once freed – in principle at least – from the terrifying shackles of the Soviet secret services, hastened to create – by setting up, as they say, on his own account – a sort of commercial office for the permanent distribution of more or less unpublished manuscripts coming directly from the Soviet *samizdat* inside, which he offered to the various European publishing houses interested in this kind of peculiar, and even somewhat dangerous literature.

A summary of V. R. Nikolsky's unpublished manuscript, *"Yuri Andropov and the Night Side of the Soviet Union"*.

In August of the same year, V. R. Nikolsky went to Paris and offered to take it upon himself to negotiate with a major publishing house of my choice for the publication of an important manuscript – more than four hundred pages long – of which he himself was the author, in which he proposed to give a direct, exhaustive, revealing and entirely accurate picture of the internal political realities of the Soviet regime in power at that time, as well as of certain of its external activities.

From the first reading, V. R. Nikolski's manuscript – in English – appeared to me to be a political document of extreme topicality, importance and usefulness: it was exactly what it claimed to be, a revealing probe into the most secret heart of the Soviet power apparatus in action. A major blow, with immediate and most unpredictable repercussions.

The Parisian publishing house to which I had proposed V. R. Nikolski's manuscript had then asked me to write a summary of about twenty pages, which I did not hesitate to provide urgently. I did not hesitate to provide it as a matter of urgency, because we had to save time and not drag our feet.

But finally, for very obscure reasons, the envisaged editorial transaction having failed, nor any of the long series of attempts that followed it, V. R. Nikolski, exasperated by all this procrastination, by the increasingly dubious bogging down of our efforts to reach an arrangement and publish her manuscript, in which she was wrongly accused of being the author of a book. Nikolski, exasperated by all this procrastination, by the increasingly dubious bogging down of our efforts to reach an arrangement and the publication of his manuscript, in which, rightly or wrongly, he had pinned all his hopes, abruptly decided to leave Europe, and flew to Brazil, where I soon lost track of him for good.

All that remains of this distressing adventure is the summary I made of V. R. Nikolski's manuscript, *Yuri Andropov and the Night Face of the Soviet Union.* It is a document which, especially in the perspective of what was to happen later in Russia, seems to me to be of such importance that I cannot help but include it in this book. Once again, I recognise in it an exceptional political testimony on the hidden and at the same time posed – paradoxically enough – without any concealment, very openly, of the great imperial geopolitics of the USSR's Forces Years, of their inner tendencies, their mentalities and their *ultimate goals.* Which have remained unchanged to this day. And which, now, are in danger of succeeding. In the more or less long term, and in a totally changed politico-historical context, because its raison d'être will no longer be Marxist-Leninist, but imperial and Eurasian orthodox, "transcendental".

In fact, Yuri Andropov's political biography is part of a long anti-Soviet conspiracy pursued from within the regime itself. Since his secret plans for the internal transformation of the regime could not succeed during his lifetime, Yuri Andropov, by betting on Mikhail Gorbachev, had ensured its impersonal continuation in the march of history already underway. The contents of the letter in which Yuri Andropov appointed Mikhail Gorbachev to the Political Bureau as his successor as General Secretary of the Party are now known.

Under the nefarious influence of the more than suspicious Alexander Yakovlev, the 'man of the powers in the shadows', Mikhail Gorbachev had quickly initiated – through the two devastating concepts of 'glasnost' and 'perestroika' – the process of the self-transformation of the Soviet regime from within, This process was soon to lose control of, leading immediately – or almost immediately – to the liquidation of the Soviet regime and of the Soviet Union itself.

What, over and above the hallucinatory, bloody, infernal eclipse of communism in power, finally made possible Russia's present reunion with its own former identity, was the shaking, the original jolt engineered by Yuri Andropov from the start, and with what subversive visionary power.

Do I need to explain? The summary I had to make, for the Parisian publishing house that was interested in it, of R.V. Nikolski's manuscript in English, *The darkface of the Soviet Union, did* not in any way mention my possible personal ideological-political positions concerning all the problems dealt with by this book: I only gave an objective account of its content, from which I drew the essential lines of force.

Nevertheless, I think that what should be noted is, above all, the very particular level at which R. V. Nikolski placed his revelations, his analyses and his own comments, a level that reveals the true nature of the clandestine activist concerns of certain occultist, 'polar' circles. Nikolsky placed his revelations, analyses and his own comments at a level that reveals the true nature of the clandestine activist preoccupations of certain occultist, "polar", "transcendental" and "archaic" circles, acting from within the higher operative structures of the KGB on the eve of the collapse – which remains, all in all, extraordinarily mysterious – of the Soviet Union, of which we can repeat what Plato had already said, 360 years before Christ, about Atlantis: In the space of a single fatal day and night, the island of Atlantis sank beneath the waves of the sea and disappeared''.

And to remember that a direct and deeply hidden relationship appears between, on the one hand, the special "subversive", "anti-Soviet" politico-strategic action of Yuri Andropov and his personal staff and, on the other hand, the current imperial and eschatological Eurasian revolutionary positions of Vladimir Putin: So, in the final analysis, it is as if what Yuri Andropov started, Vladimir Putin is now completing.

So it was not for nothing that one of the first initiatives Vladimir Putin took when he entered the Kremlin was to have a golden plaque sealed in memory of Yuri Andropov. For this is an equally fundamental and revealing symbol and admission.

Finally, I may have to acknowledge the very bitter regrets I feel because, while I had at my disposal the original manuscript by R. V. Nikolski, I had not been able to give – even at the time – all the attention I should have given to the last part of it, which concerned the ultra-secret background of the Soviet intervention in Afghanistan, the aims of which would indeed seem to have been very different from what was claimed. Because, I know, Afghanistan – and the area of high geopolitical storms of which it is the seismic epicentre – will be in the news again. Soon.

A few words about V. R. Nikolski himself. A character who seemed to have escaped from one of Raymond Abellio's terminal novels, *The Pit of Babel, Unmoving Faces*, he seemed to me to represent, in a way, the "great Jewish race" of the secretly enlightened, turned in on themselves, indistinguishable from the outside, but nevertheless acting from the invisible to the visible, in the terms of who knows what unavowable special mission. Totally transformed – I don't know if I can say transfigured – by Communism, in which he had thought he had found a dream greater than the dream of Judaism itself, and which had burnt his life to the ground, once he had detached himself from it, he had thereby ceased to be himself, having lost the part of the absolute which had possessed him for so long. He had lost the part of the absolute that had possessed him for so long, becoming not an undead, but a living-dead, the counter-zombie of himself, the shadow of his shadow.

I don't know what V. R. Nikolski ended up doing or not doing in Brazil, but something tells me that after a while he had to leave Brazil for Canada and that from Canada he would have gone to the United States. Because that's the way it's usually done. And in the United States, of course, emerging as someone else, because he would have become someone else.

As for the final assessment of the background information and analysis put forward in his manuscript, I have supported and still support what I believe to be its fullest veracity. Unquestionably. And I know exactly what I am talking about.

What might seem to be inconsistent with the particular language of communist offensive intelligence agents would, in the case of V. R. Nikolsky, be due to the fact that, having belonged to ultra-secret, counter-strategic ideological nuclei operating at very high levels, hidden within the communist apparatuses in action and even acting, at times, against them, he had had to undergo a series of specific mutations in his way of thinking, speaking and behaving. But these are undoubtedly too technical, unconventional and confusing in their approach and use.

In any case, I know that V. R. Nikolski had never been able to secure the confidence of the British security services, to whom the obviously too special character of his assertions and *revelations* seemed to be the very proof of their immediate unreliability, and of the essentially suspicious situation of his own personality. An insurmountable misunderstanding, a *sign of the times.*

Having said this, it is no less certain that, subsequently, the political and strategic information provided by V. R. Nikolsky was verified by the evolution of the internal situation in Russia and, finally, by the appearance of Vladimir Putin, as well as, above all, by what this appearance signifies *as irrevocable.* For it is the advent of the "New Russia" that V. R. Nikolsky was in fact announcing.

A successful conspiracy that continues.

YURI ANDROPOV, AND THE NIGHT SIDE OF THE SOVIET UNION, (SUMMARY)

> *Which of the two camps will win over the other? Does the transmission of supreme power in the USSR still reveal the survival, buried in the depths, of the shamanic warrior rite known as the "severed head"?*

November 1979 – November 1982: rigorously controlled, through the KGB and with the support of the Red Army, by Y. V. Andropov and his power group, the subterranean process of de-Brezhnevisation dialectically precedes, foresees and succeeds in demanding, when the time comes, the ritual killing of L. I. Brezhnev. In the shadows, once again, we return to the procedures of the most ancient Russia, to the abysmal mystagogies of the Scytho-Chamanic Paleolithic. The sacrifice of the supreme leader, and the figuration of his cosmological support by the Mystery of the Severed Head thus appears as an essentially warlike mystery. Napoleon, at the moment of his death: "The Head of the Armies". From I. V. Stalin to Y. V. Andropov, only the military ranks, only the terrible warrior qualifications of the Kshatriyas sanction and legitimise the ultimate political hierarchies of the Communist Party in relation to the Soviet State, in other words, in relation to the occult transhistorical reality of the "Red Empire of the End of the Cycle". The transmission of the supreme power can only be done, in the Red Kremlin, by the mystagogic assassination of the political-military leader in place, by the murderous elimination of the declining Great Leader, the twilight *generalissimo*. Thus V. I. Lenin was assassinated by I. V. Stalin, I. V. Stalin by L. Beria, L. Beria by N. S. Khrushchev, N. S. Khrushchev by L. I. Brezhnev, and L. I. Brezhnev by Y. V. Andropov. The long politico-strategic agony of L.I. Brezhnev, undead rather than alive-dead, and the KGB's new anti-personnel neutralisation technologies. On 23 November 1981, during his visit to Bonn, L. I. Brezhnev took a very personal and leading position in favour of nuclear arms reduction in Europe. Seizing this opportunity, the KGB set out to clear the air around him: the highly confidential file on social malpractice, even corruption of L. I. Brezhnev's relatives and his own family, was officially handed over by the KGB to the MVD, to the "Special Office for Combating the Dismantling of Socialist Property", the dreaded O.B.Kh.S.S.; L. I. Brezhnev's brother-in-law, General

S. Tsvigun, Vice-President of the KGB, is the victim of a technical suicide; the Department (A) of the First KGB Directorate (Disinformation, Activnyyé Meropriatya), acting in close liaison with L. Zamiatin, head of the information services of the International Department of the Central Committee, launched an intensive internal and external disinformation campaign aimed at spreading the rumour of L. I. Brezhnev's progressive mental debilitation and his imminent physical incapacitation; finally, the Leningrad review *Aurora* took the liberty of publishing, under the direct control of the Party Secretary, G. Romanov, an unbelievable article, in fact, an open attack, about "a certain personality, which is dying all the time".

In the shadow of the Kremlin, the liberated breath of the old mystagogically marries the inner emptiness of the new

Under the black walls of the Kremlin, super-charged medium, and in front of the open grave of L.I. Brezhnev, in front of the half-unveiled Kaaba of the world conspiracy of communism, Y.V. Andropov pronounces, three times, the ritual words of the initiatory passage of powers: "Farewell, then, dear Leonid Ilyich Brezhnev". The next moment, the drums and the shamanic brass will carry the *old* into the nothingness of nothingness while bringing back its imperishable breath into the emptied chest of the *new:* thus, each time, the new is only made of the breath of the oldest which returns occultly to the light of life.

Now, how can we fail to recognise, in this sombre science of the ritual passage of powers, the extraordinarily deep persistence of a consciousness prior to any science of the present day, the persistence of a shamanic and preglacial conception of the manipulation of breaths, of which perhaps only the hypnagogic visions of P.H. Lovecraft would be in a position to give an account today? It was in the confessions that the future Marshal and Chief of Staff of the Red Army, Michail Toukhatchevsky, was to make to Rémy Roure, during their common captivity at the fort of Ingolstadt, during the First World War, where the future President of the Republic was also present – for *everything is connected*, General Charles de Gaulle, that the first testimony to the secret return of the greatest Bolshevik hierarchies to a racial and transhistorical identity subject to the Being of the Abyss appears.

A vote secured by the elite Kantemirov division

However, three days later, surrounded by the armoured units of the Kantemirov shock division, the Central Committee, where Constantin Chernenko's current had a majority, and a large majority, carried Y. V. Andropov to the General Secretariat of the Party by a suggestive blocking vote: it was the Kantemirovka which, in fact, voted for Y. V. Andropov. Why didn't Y. V. Andropov call on the I Armoured Division

Dzerzhinsky, belonging to the KGB itself, under the command of General S. Chomikov? Through the Kantemirovka, the power of strategic support in the interior would henceforth be, for Y. V. Andropov, an exclusively military power.

The lost testament of L. I. Brezhnev, and his vision of the next 'cosmic spring'

The Party's corpse suddenly pulls itself together and babbles in the wings. On the lost testament – misplaced, they say – of L. I. Brezhnev, which we know had a rather enigmatic title: ''The Soviet Union, fundamental and perpetual guarantor of World Peace. The near advent of the great Cosmic Spring''. Some light on L. L. Brezhnev's letters to Indira Gandhi, and on his apocalyptic terrors. To avert, at any cost, the unbearable horror of a nuclear confrontation, whatever it may be. To preserve the Soviet Union and Europe from it, by whatever means necessary: that is my true aim, that is, I am convinced, my true mission. The Brezhnevian conspiracy to block and neutralise the state of nuclear armaments took on worldwide dimensions, which worried the Atlantic camp as much as the socialist camp itself. Informed by leaks from Indira Gandhi's immediate entourage, the head of the large KGB plant in New Delhi personally went to Moscow to warn Y. V. Andropov. The latter informed the Chief of the Army Staff, Marshal Ogarkov, of the situation in the greatest secrecy. Emergency constitution, at the top of the operational staffs of the KGB and the Armed Forces, of a permanent and special crisis cell, directed against the underground activities and the pacifist deviationism of the General Secretary of the Party and his personal action group. Constantin Chernenko, who, it has just become clear, "travels a lot, even too much", and who seems to control quite closely, "too closely", the Party's cadres and internal organisation, becomes the special cell's number two target.

About John Paul II's extraordinary envoys to L. I. Brezhnev, and their top secret mission

The secret mission of Professors Jérôme Lejeune, of the Faculty of Medicine in Paris, and Marini Bettolo, of the Pontifical Academy in Rome, extraordinary envoys of John Paul II to Moscow, to L. I. Brejnev. The highly confidential meetings of the Pontifical Academy at the Casa Pio Quarto in Rome and the apocalyptic conclusions of its work. Two reports were drawn up for the exclusive use of John Paul II: *the absolutely secret report* and *the absolutely incommunicable report*. John Paul II took it upon himself to make the contents known to L. I. Brezhnev. Brezhnev replied to Rome, but the content of this reply remained a deep mystery, and John Paul II hastened to cover it with papal secrecy.

In January 1983, Y. V. Andropov proposed to the Vatican the establishment of a special, direct and permanent occult channel of communication between John Paul II and himself. On the current consequences of this proposal. The active bases of a new underground diplomacy of the Church.

The *reserved authorisations of* John Paul II's Secretary of State, Mgr. Casaroli, a convinced supporter, even activist, of the most extreme openness to the East, and the broad outlines of the metastrategic operation underway under the cloaked name of *"Project Dark Side of the Moon"*.

The persistent shadow of L. I. Brezhnev's late mother, whose death had profoundly changed him, reappears. Under the total influence of a mystical group in Kazan, L.I. Brezhnev's mother had spent the last years of her life under the black veils of the underground, nocturnal congregations of the Old Believers, and in the convulsive memory of the "great burnings" of 1682. On the advice of his mother, L. I. Brezhnev had brought the thaumaturgist Duna Davitashvili to Moscow in the greatest secrecy and had her installed in the private clinic of the Gosplan leaders. Duna Davitashvili herself had then called and mobilised the most essential elements of the mystagogic and thaumaturgical action group by her side, gathering them in one of the large residential suburbs of Moscow, of which she had been, in Alma Ata, Kazakhstan, the "living and bloody heart" and the "true mother of life". Particular correspondence from Moscow states that the groups under the influence of Duna Davitashvili are still in place, operating under somewhat slower conditions but essentially unchanged, in this month of March 1983 when "so many decisive things are being prepared, things known in advance".

Yuri Andropov is no longer Yuri Andropov

Yuri Vladimirovich Andropov, or the latest KGB super-montage, its *transcendental montage:* Yuri Vladimirovich Andropov is not, or is no longer Vladimirovich Andropov. Does the mystery of the philosophical transmutation of metals contain the active principle of the manipulations that can lead to the change of the abysmal identity of a determined subject? Beyond the primary techniques known as brainwashing, can we already obtain, in the specialised high-tech services, the *whitening of the being*? An allegorical return to Richard Condon's novel, *The Mandchurian Candidate*, and the subliminal action film made by John Frankenheimer.

At present, two-faced powers are secretly fighting for supreme power in the USSR. What are Y. V. Andropov's choices?

Visible or invisible, forces both metapolitical and immediately political are occultly fighting for supreme power inside the entrenched camp of the USSR and in the Central Cell of the world conspiracy of Soviet-influenced communism. The new and abysmal emergence, in the USSR, of a counter-power, a Trotskyist parallel power, back on track and active again since the death of I.V. Stalin, with paroxysmal peaks under the influence of L. Béria (including, in particular, the rehabilitation of the Jewish doctors of the criminal conspiracy at the top known as the "white coats"), and, also, but somewhat differently, under that of N.S. Krouchtchev. In this regard, the extraordinary visionary testament of Rasputin, discovered in Odessa in 1927 and made public in the West, thanks to a leak organised in London, in 1973, a leak that Professor Renzo Baschera was able to seize, for purposes that are, all in all, rather obscure. Rasputin's terrible, fascinating and all too clear visionary testament foresees the decisive confrontation between the Trotskyist "snakes" and the Stalinist "eagle" and, although it was written in 1912, it not only announces the annihilation of the Soviet Union, but also of the Soviet Union, announces not only the final annihilation of the Trotskyist "snakes" as a harbinger of the bloody liberation of the "Holy of Holies", the "Most Holy Russia", but also and above all the "conversion of Red Russia" and the eventual advent of "a Great King who will at last be able to render True Justice".

It was in Rasputin's own hand that this prophetic testament was written in 1912 for the Tsarina Alexandra, who became Saint Alexandra Romanoff: the fullest measure of the fundamental prophetic importance of this text lies in the sickly, even paranoid, attention with which it was regarded by I.V. Stalin (but how can one resist the temptation to recognise, in the "conspiracy of companions with the subtle weapon of venom", the plot of the "white coats" thwarted, no doubt far too late for some, by the inspired vigilance of the doctor Lydia Timachouk, a radiologist at the Botkine Hospital). At present, it is already known that it was Y.V. Andropov himself, as well as some of his closest supporters, are feverishly scrutinising the brief but terrible prophecy of the Pokorvskoye mystic: the conclusions of this prophecy concern the very time of their own coming to power, and if everything else has already come true, and come true to the letter, there is no reason why the rather peculiar end announced therein should not come true as well. Lastly, an absolutely significant sign of the state of mind which is today that of the Soviet people in its most nocturnal, most intact layers, a state of mind overheated by the seismic movements, by the shifts which it senses in the depths, at least two circuits of *Sviatye Pisma*, of "holy letters", with their epicentres respectively in Odessa and Leningrad, have taken up with fervour and clarity, since the end of last year, the essential impulses of the bloody prophecy of Rasputin, the Siberian Enlightened One, and in particular those which concern its apocalyptic conclusion.

A Secret Government in the Soviet Union? Is Y. V. Andropov the great commander, or just a necessary tool?

Is the Soviet central power, at present and for a long time already, a politico-military occult power? Is Soviet central power, at the same time, occultly predetermined by an internal theocratic-imperialist counter-power?

A secret government in the Soviet Union, *Nostra* claimed in February 1982. *Nostra:* "An Order, organised according to a neo-medieval system similar to that of our knights. Its aim: to dominate the earth at the end of our century. And also: "The society that the "Order" dreams of would be a sort of neo-medieval Russia, ruling by military province chiefs over the whole of Eurasia: a hierarchical society, powerfully mobilised". The "inner secret" of this Order would be, still according to Nostra, the following: "Not to believe in Marxism, but to use it for the "greatness of the Empire", i.e. of the USSR, called to dominate the world".

The pre-ontological figure of the Soviet Union's Millennial Reign, a figure deeply active in the political-military circles that are currently deciding the future destinies of the Soviet Union and the worldwide conspiracy of Soviet-influenced communism from behind the scenes.

Polar fraternities in the Red Army, and Russia's thousand-year reign

The top-secret penetration of the Polar Brotherhood into the Red Army, before, during and after Marshal M. Tukhachevsky's tenure on the Army Staff. Why did I. V. Stalin have to proceed to the physical neutralisation of Marshal M. Tukhachevsky? First of all, and whatever the other reasons might have been, imperatively, of a politico-military nature, so that he could take over himself, within the Red Army, the occult leadership of the Polar Brotherhood; which he would later hand over to General S. Chtemenko, Chief of the Army Staff, in whom, very exceptionally and not without mystery, he had put all his trust.

With the arrival of Y. V. Andropov at the General Secretariat of the Communist Party of the USSR, the flamboyant star of Marshal Ogarkov, Chief of the Armed Forces Staff, rose on the horizon of the Supreme Command of the Red Army. Alongside Marshal Ogarkov, General Valeri Varennikov, Deputy Chief of Staff of the Armed Forces, is currently working to define the new overall geostrategy of the Red Army, the external version of what has just been called the pre-ontological figure of the "Millennium Reign of the Soviet Union". On this subject, see the extremely significant article by Jacques Guillemé Brulon in *Le Figaro* dated 30 January 1983: *Cinquante ans après l'ascension de Hitler au pouvoir. A "thousand-year-old" USSR.* The rapprochement of the Soviet Union and the Third Reich is indeed not without bringing back to light the common continental project and the occult transhistorical foundations of the two great Eurasian imperial attempts of the end of the 20th century.

Another view of the political-historical career, mission and mystery of V. I. Lenin and his apparently unelected successor, I. V. Stalin

In fact, V. I. Lenin, and I.V. Stalin even less, were not at all what we are used to think of them. A different light, a light of rupture and dialectical reversal of the doctrinal and activist work of V. I. Lenin and I. V. Stalin – a work which, in the light of the history of the Soviet Union, is not only the work of V. I. Lenin, but also of I.V. Stalin's doctrinal and activist work – a work of which, in the end, only the secret geopolitical splitting will count – would it not deliver the keys to the most unsuspected, mysterious and forbidden identity of the Soviet Union and of the so-called world revolution of communism of which it wants to be, since 1917, the politico-strategic epicentre and the historical vanguard on the march? Emmanuel Le Roy Ladurie, in 1980: "The Soviet Union has become, today, the absolute centre of world totalitarianism".

The Hitler-Stalin pact, irreversible foundation of the Soviet continental line

The memory, not yet obscured, for some, of 23 August 1939: to know how to recognise, today, in the Hitler-Stalin Pact, the supreme pole of the great Eurasian continental policy of the Soviet Union and its planetary projects still and always hidden behind the diversionist doctrinal semantics of Marxism-Leninism. Communism is not, and has never been, in the Soviet Union, an end in itself, but the means of totalitarian development of an occult imperial project.

On the double language of the general policy report presented by I. V. Stalin on 10 March 1939 in the St. Andrew's Hall of the Kremlin at the opening of the 18th Congress of the Communist Party of the USSR.

1977–1982, decisive years of what 'great return'? The precedent of the German review of Buenos Aires, *Der Weg*. Towards a clandestine re-actualisation of G. V. Astakhov's "operational line"?

Vanguard Soviet geopolitics seen in the light of the coming millennium

In-depth clarifications, positions of activist intelligence concerning the geopolitical line of the USSR, from V. I. Lenin to Y. V. Andropov, and the fundamental principles of a certain transcendental geopolitics in a position to expose, precisely, the pre-ontological concept of the Soviet Union's "Millennial Reign".

Already, in February 1977, the monthly *Correspondance Européenne*, published in Paris, wrote: "Inside the Soviet power, two tendencies, or rather two conspiracies, are confronting each other, at the present time, in depth, and it is precisely this confrontation which defines and arms the total political crisis to which the year 1977 can absolutely not fail to provide, in one way or the other, *the decisive outcome:* on the one hand, to use, once again, I. V. Stalin's expression, the ''Trotskyist conspiracy from within'', and, on the other hand, what should be called, from now on, the current conspiracy of the ''geopolitical groupsV. Stalin, the ''Trotskyist conspiracy from within'', and, on the other hand, what should be called, from now on, the current conspiracy of ''geopolitical groups'' in action from the Red Army's positions of strength''. And also: "For the European revolutionary nationalists, the most urgent and, in the present circumstances, the only fundamental doctrinal task appears, therefore, and is imposed as an immediate approach and as thorough as possible of the new revolutionary ideology which carries forward, today, the still hidden leaders of the new soviet continental geopolitical line".

On the counter-strategic concept of ''ideological bridgehead'' applied to the Trotskyist destabilisation attempt put into action in Prague in 1968. The secret opposition of two polar conceptions, the Arctic Conception and the Antarctic Conception, and its significance as a dialectical break with Horbiger's doctrines of the foundational cosmogonic struggle "of Ice and Fire". The opposition of the Arctic Conception and the Antarctic Conception has been exploited covertly since 1977 by the advanced research services working under the direct control of the USSR Ocean Fleet Staff. For his part, Y. V. Andropov personally supports, from strategic rear bases in Karelia, the establishment of a top-secret advanced Soviet presence in the Far North, and of a permanent special mission in the immediate vicinity of the North Pole. Under the supervision of Fleet Admiral G. S. Gorshkov's personal staff, the USSR Ocean Fleet, the *Okeanska,* penetrates deep into the "inner spaces" of Antarctica.

In *The Assumption of Europe,* Raymond Abellio dialectically reverses the data of the problem and, considering the opposition of the Arctic and Antarctic polar conceptions from the point of view of the Central Fire of the Earth, The most secret part of this genetic cosmology is in line with the essence of Horbiger's doctrines, while at the same time opening up to the final intelligence of an overall Polar Conception, and whose most immediately operational vision would seem to lend itself to the approach and manipulation of what has been called, with a hedged expression, the Great Galactics. Abellian-influenced covert action groups are making theurgic approaches between Peru and Japan; extremely dangerous operations are being pursued, covertly, in certain lands of the South Atlantic (which does not fail to interest, most keenly and decisively, elements in place *of* Admiral G. S. Gorchkov's *Okeanska*).

Geostrategic developments by General Valeri Varennikoy, Deputy Chief of Staff of the Red Army

Following very closely the current doctrinal commitments of the Chief of the Armed Forces Staff, Marshal Ogarkov, his closest collaborator, Deputy Chief of the Armed Forces Staff, General Valeri Varennikov, is working to define the new geostrategic lines of march of the central politico-military group of which Y.V. Andropov is himself, at the present time, the *supreme concept of active polarisation:* return to the policentrist dialectic of the world revolution of communism and the planetary anti-imperialist struggle; ontological super-strengthening of the Central Lands, and their intercontinental confrontations with the proponents of the Oceanic Establishment; a new general Soviet line towards China, the USA and Latin America, towards India, South-East Asia and Japan, towards the Arab world and the Middle East, and in Europe towards Western and Eastern Europe and the operational complex of South-East Europe; Greece, perhaps, as a platform for new and highly unpredictable departures.

The Deputy Chief of the Armed Forces General Staff, General Valeri Varennikov, wrote in the *Izvestia:* It is therefore urgent, and of the utmost importance, that new means be set in motion to constantly perfect the preparation of the Armed Forces of the Soviet Union, so that they may be brought ever closer to the maximum point of all their operational possibilities, and, also, so that this permanent preparation may henceforth be carried out in very close liaison with the front of all the Armed Forces of the countries belonging, in Europe, to the same battle camp as us''.

These declarations of General Valeri Varennikov are very important indeed. For they lay down, for the first time, the decision, implicitly advanced, of a forthcoming reinforced integration and, later, of a total integration of the Armed Forces of the Warsaw Pact, the first stage of the political-administrative integration of all the socialist countries of Eastern Europe into a federal unit of the Soviet type, and whose decisive and ultimate political infrastructure would be constituted by Moscow.

Y.V. Andropov, on 16 November 1982, in Moscow: ''The policy of Eastern Europe, and even more so the policy of the Balkans, is not made in Bucharest or Belgrade. It is made, exclusively, in Moscow''.

The Red Line of Sin-Kiang

For Guido Giannettini, who remains unquestionably the founder of the new European continental geostrategy and therefore of a new planetary geostrategy, the founder of *total geostrategy*, it is Eurasia which, geopolitically, constitutes the "Middle Earth", whereas the continental geopolitical frontier of the USSR and China, the frontier of race and destiny, corresponds to what was called, elsewhere, the "Middle Earth", The continental geopolitical frontier of the USSR and China, a frontier of race and destiny, corresponds to what has been called, elsewhere, the "Sin-Kiang red line".

In *The Conquest of Middle-earth* Guido Giannettini wrote in August 1971: "On the basis of the elements of geopolitics we have discussed, the interests of Eurasia are common, because Eurasia is a natural unit; and this unitary character should become more evident precisely today, in the era of the great blocks and great concentrations of States. Against Eurasia, the heart of the main mass of land masses, stands the great primordial ocean, the Pacific, which today has found its axis not only geographically, but also politically, in the 40th parallel of Washington and Beijing. Disputed by two worlds, the border walk, the 'middle land'. And just like four thousand years ago, the possession of the "middle land" is still of interest to the European descendants of the ancient *Reitervolkers of* the steppes. In fact, if Hitler's Drang *nach Osten* had succeeded, Europe (but, above all, Eurasia) would today be on the front line on the Altai Mountains and the borders of Sin-Kiang. This did not happen because the same forces now allied with China succeeded in preventing the peaceful unification of the Eurasian continent-which both Hitler and Stalin seemed to be striving for-and then the attempt at unification led by arms. But the substance of things is not changed. Europe will be reborn and will not be able to escape the fatal *Erulkampf* for the conquest of the "Middle Land", a final struggle that will thus decide its fate.

Now it is quite obvious that, at the present time, the Chief of Staff of the Red Army, Marshal Ogarkov, could very well risk signing these analyses by Guido Giannettini, in which he would in any case not fail to find the essence of the new Soviet continental geostrategic thinking of which it would seem that he was the leading ideological figure.

However, it seems no less certain that Y. V. Andropov would start, in an early phase, a process of diversionary and delaying approach towards Beijing, using for this purpose the exceptional skills of the high-class sinologists he has been able to attract confidentially in the new Soviet diplomacy and in the university, led by Mikhail Kapitsa. Appointed Deputy Foreign Minister on 16 December 1982, it is now taken for granted that, as part of the general plan for the investment of power devised by Y.V. Andropov's personal action group, Mikhail Kapitsa should very soon succeed the current incumbent of the Soviet Foreign Ministry, A.A. Gromyko, in Smolensk Square. Former ambassador to Islamabad and then responsible, successively, for South-East Asia and the Far East at the Moscow Foreign Ministry, Mikhail Kapitsa has in fact just succeeded in the rather abrupt task of establishing a line of relations that is not yet official, but effective, and completely consistent, with the number one man in Peking, Den Xiaoping, a fierce contemptor, only a few months ago, of

"Soviet social-imperialism, heir to mystic-tsarist imperialism and its most occult designs for continental domination in Asia". However, in his approach to Deng Xiaoping, Mikhail Kapitsa had acted, and from the beginning, under a special mandate from Y. V. Andropov and under the latter's personal supervision, to whom he constantly reported on the progress of his mission. On the other hand, it is now known that it was indeed under the direct influence of Mikhail Kapitsa that, on his return from an inspection tour in South-East Asia, the Chief of the Armed Forces Staff, Marshal Ogarkov, had advised and obtained that the permanent delivery of Soviet war materiel to Hanoi, heavy equipment, missiles and advanced electronic equipment, should be reduced very significantly. However, these Soviet deliveries of counter-strategic military support were constantly denounced by Beijing as "absolutely intolerable". Deng Xiaoping himself, in July 1982: ''The Soviet boil in Hanoi must be punctured at any price'' (so it was, but we still don't know the real price).

It should be added that the Soviet military retreat from China, which was completed in Hanoi, was at the same time coupled with a very hard retreat on *the ground:* Since December 1982, all the parallel politico-military organisations, irreducibly anti-Chinese, which had been preventively implanted in the disputed border regions and whose rear bases were in Inner Mongolia, were abruptly put to sleep, and most often without the slightest care, forcibly suppressed by the special operational services of Victor Chebrikov's new KGB.

Finally, and infinitely more significantly, it was through the intermediary of Mikhail Kapitsa that the new Minister of Defence of the P.R. of China, General Zhang Aiping, was able to learn of Marshal Ogarkov's latest political and strategic treatise. of China, General Zhang Aiping, was able to take note in due course of Marshal Ogarkov's latest politico-strategic treatise, a top secret work if ever there was one, which, in a feature article recently published in *The Red Flag, the* central doctrinal organ of the CCP, General Zhang Aiping has just taken on board, such as it is, and, we believe, very deliberately as it is – because this strange compilation at first degree is intended to be, in fact, the open challenge of a politico-strategic provocation of very great size, of a politico-strategic provocation given as quite decisive – all the fundamental theses, namely

(1) The exclusively scientific and technological nature of the major political-historical confrontations of the near future being more than widely proven, an *absolutely unconditional priority must be imposed on the Armed Forces' nuclear armament effort, an armament which must be essentially national, unencumbered by external servitudes,* and comprising a strategic nuclear arsenal as well as a tactical nuclear arsenal, both of which imply the accelerated diversification of the delivery systems and specialised bearers

(2) the mobilisation of the entire active nation for a *super strengthened acceleration of the development of all the economic and industrial sectors*

engaged, directly or indirectly, in the service of the technological-military effort in the process of starting the final process of its "great leap forward",

(3) the immediate establishment of the *Higher Scientific and Technological Committee of the Armed Forces and Defence*, which already has extremely extensive powers of its own, powers of "vertical high command", i.e. free from any control, delay or political-administrative impediment.

Undeniably, the most secret politico-strategic, or rather strategic-administrative theses of the Chief of the Soviet General Staff, Marshal Ogarkov, have been seized upon by the new Chinese Minister of Defence, General Zhang Aiping, with a very worrying power of dialectical integration in depth, a power of integration that is quite immediate and as if over-activated by the very urgencies of what constitutes the essential problems that the Armed Forces of the P. R. China are abruptly called upon to face in their current turn. But there is an iron law of the universe, and it is the law of the people. But there is an iron law: it is the enemy who will always be the best student. What Commander Charles de Gaulle could only have had a premonitory, doctrinal vision, it was General Reinz Guderian who found himself in a position to realise it in terms of action.

In the final analysis, Marshal Ogarkov, as well as his too-gifted disciple, General Zhang Aiping, announce more than they propose the irresistible rise of a new great military society: the historical safeguarding of the new societies to come and of the new great States currently in the process of regrouping requires, from now on, their total militarisation.

But, on the other hand, must not every new advent of a total military society appear, and every time, as a harbinger of the imminent return to the heroic and fiery season of the Great Empires?

The advent of Y.V. Andropov to the supreme levers of the politico-military command in the USSR means, first of all, the probably definitive destabilisation of the Party and of the *apparatchik* corps of its overall politico-administrative apparatus, as well as, on the other hand, and quite tragically, the abrupt displacement-the displacement of revolutionary rupture, one could, eventually, dare to say-of the greatest soviet power towards the inner centre of gravity of the Red Army, towards the polar cell of decision, towards the most forbidden and occult polar heart of the ideological-operational high command of the Soviet Armed Forces.

Zbigniew Brzezinski, who was asked in January 1983 whether Y. V. Andropov "inspired confidence" in him, had to answer bluntly: "Not in the least. His appointment underlines a dangerous shift in the centre of gravity of power in the USSR away from the CPSU apparatchiks and towards the year and the secret services. These two institutions are the most repressive and also the most *nationalistic*. Andropov succeeded where Beria, in 1953, and Zhukov, in 1957, had failed.

Now, everything is subversively linked, and everything is connected by the very course of events. Through the WRONS, through the Military Committee for National Salvation set up by General Jaruzelski, Polish society as a whole is predetermined by an infrastructure of an exclusively military nature, which acts permanently and totally in the open. The current missions of the WRONS and the Polish Armed Forces are ideological-political, social, administrative, economic and trade union, educational, diplomatic and religious: all the authentically living, authentically revolutionary forces of Poland under General Jaruzelski's military-political regime have to pass, in order to be and to act, through the channels preconceived and purposely set up by the Polish Armed Forces. (And doesn't the WRONS itself, the Military Committee of National Salvation, remind us, in a strange and very significant way, of the Committees of Public Salvation of the generals, or rather of the national-revolutionary captains of Algiers, during the great politico-military battles of leadership carried out by the Secret Army Organisation, by the OAS? For those who are still in a position to judge what is behind the cards, this connection is far from being fortuitous. Its value would be, rather, of an extreme prophetic and activist actuality).

Thus, although it may not be quite there yet, Poland is on the way to becoming, under the leadership of General Jaruzelski, the first openly military socialism in Europe today. Now, it is certainly worth noting that General Jaruzelski himself is one of those who best approached and grasped the strategic-administrative thinking of Marshal Ogarkov, to whom he owes a good part of his career and, above all, the security of his present situation.

Today, as in the past, the inner strength of the armies that support, openly or more covertly, the tragic adventure of the nascent Empires, has always been the politico-military strength of its young captains. Thus, we must remember that when taking a brutal stand against the uncertain and negative situation of the strategic readiness of the Groups of the Soviet Armed Forces in Germany, Marshal Ogarkov did not fail to declare that the future and even the very destiny of the Red Army rested on its young captains, that the Red Army must be and will be "an army of young captains".

On the other hand, in his New Year's message for 1983, the recently dismissed Chief of Staff of the French Army, General Jean Delaunay, declared, prophetically perhaps, or otherwise, that *1983 would be the year of the captains in France*. It is on the shoulders of its young captains, General Delaunay also declared, that the immense effort represented by the "operational efficiency of the French Army, the traditional guardian of French soil, is held today.

Finally, and as if to take a step back, let us also recall that, in a major doctrinal text entitled, precisely, *Towards a National-Communist Europe,* the now defunct *Combat* wrote, on 16 August 1974: "The hour of the captains everywhere. The hour of the captains has just sounded in Europe and, in Europe, the hour of the captains will be the hour of national-communism. And then there are these lines, too, which, in this case, you have to be adventurously in a position to intercept, beyond the provisional denial that seems to have been inflicted on them by the very course of events, the secret premonitory dimensions and the very secret topicality that is to come, or rather to come back: 'The captains are in power in Lisbon, tomorrow they will probably be in power in Madrid, Rome and Athens, just as they are already in power in Tripoli and Algiers. With Colonel Vasco Gonçalves as President of the Council and General Otello Carvalho as head of the Continental Operational Command (Copcon), Lisbon has become the political-strategic epicentre of the new European revolutionary struggle, which is the continental struggle of national communism. Today, therefore, General Otello Carvalho has at his disposal, through the Operational Command of the Continent (Copcon), the only European armed force with an exclusively political mission, and he leads, from the military region of Lisbon, which he also commands, the only political battle corps currently available in Europe. A National Communist Battle Corps'.

With the plenary complicity and all the necessary support of Y. V. Andropov and his group, is Marshal Ogarkov trying, at the present time, to bring to fruition in China what he has not yet been able to set in motion in the Soviet Union itself? Could it be that the China of general Zhang Aiping, like the Poland of general Jaruzelski, is in the process of becoming, in a very subversive way, the test bed for the new politico-military vision of the internal and external imperialism of the greatest Russia, just as Hungary would be its trans-Marxist economic test bed, and Romania its mystagogical test bed, subterraneanly orientated towards the most terrible theurgico-cosmological approaches to the worlds and dominations of the External Powers?

This, then, would be the ultimate meaning, the unfailingly occult meaning of the Leninist-Stalinist concept of the *division of socialist labour* projected on a planetary and even supra-planetary, galactic and external scale by those in Moscow, in the membership of the central group, who would seem to be already ready for the most inconceivable of "great beginnings"?

What is actually happening along the Sin-Kiang 'red line'?

Knowing that, like the new Deputy Foreign Minister Mikhail Kapitsa, the Chief of Staff of the Armed Forces, Marshal Ogarkov, is himself part of the "central group", the rather small personal group of Y. V. Andropov's unconditional followers, one is obviously entitled to ask what the meaning of these manoeuvres of veiled super-opening towards Beijing can be, a multi-headed opening whose importance must be measured. Andropov, one is obviously entitled to wonder what the meaning of these manoeuvres of veiled super-opening in the direction of Peking can be, a multi-headed opening whose decisive politico-strategic importance, and undoubtedly much more than decisive, must be measured as accurately as possible, and whose ultimate responsibility can only belong, in any case, to Y. V. Andropov himself.

An immensely dangerous responsibility, a responsibility on the brink of the abyss: at least in the first degree, the current manoeuvres towards China, and more particularly for what is the underground Mikhail Kapitsa-Zhang Aiping relationship, are indisputably directly related to high treason.

However, it is no less certain that, in spite of all appearances, in spite of all the opening facts that may claim the contrary, an abysmal dialectical war is occultly engaged, and at the present time more than ever, between Moscow and Peking, a war of an absolutely new type in which only someone like Marshal Ogarkov, whose weapon of origin is genius, and who knows, it is said, how to handle the new mathematical logics in their most advanced states, can assume the task of maintaining the operational front line, of subterraneanly predetermining its realities, and who knows, it has been said, how to handle to perfection the new mathematical logics in their most advanced states, can assume the task of maintaining the operational front line, of subterraneanly predetermining the real objectives and all the pass codes of an approach so powerfully, so actively multiplied outside of itself, if not, also, and above all, against itself. For, in the final analysis, the new Soviet-Chinese rapprochement conceived by the immediate operational group of Y. V. Andropov is already putting into action a strategy of indirect investment and a dialectic of dialectical appropriation of the present, *post-Maoist China-Mao's* Widow China, which, against all odds, like Mao's Widow herself, will remain there forever, increasingly obscured, impotent and annulled – a subterranean offensive, imperialist, totalitarian strategy and dialectic, whose sole aim is the final annihilation of the antagonist's life forces and the complete subversive expropriation of its permanent geopolitical being and having.

Thus, to have the last word on this, should we not go back a little, to the analyses, already quoted, of Guido Giannettini? For, if the means of politico-strategic action change, the goals and the deep reality of the great geopolitics, its *objective fatality*, will always remain the same, unchanged.

To reach *the Imperium*, the Greater Russia must still appropriate the Middle Lands. To reach the Middle Lands, *the Imperium* must, above all, with an expression of I. V. Stalin, strike at the head, dialectically annihilate the politico-historical consciousness of present-day China, and then appropriate its gigantic remains, decapitated, but geopolitically still alive. *Drag nach Osten*, indeed.

Afghanistan, the home front of Asia Mysteriosa's approach

The real stakes of the politico-military control of Afghanistan, considered, to begin with, in the light of certain revelations by Saint-Yves d'Alveydre and Ferdinand Ossendowski, and, subsequently, by René Guénon.

What Unknown Superiors, to speak as René Guénon, and what Higher Secret Societies have been sheltering, since, perhaps, the 1950s, in the high, inviolable, out-of-reach valleys of the Hindukuch, at the Dust Gates of Samarkand?

From 1941 onwards, the *Ahnenerbe*'s remote research services (Heinrich Himmler, Wolfram von Sievers) compiled a top-secret file concerning certain special investigations by *the Ahnenerbe* in Afghanistan, registered under the covert name of *Sonderaktion Kandahar*, "SK". This file materially disappeared during the German debacle of 1945.

The nearly complete *Ahnenerbe/Sonderaktion Kandahar* file was found in the German Democratic Republic (GDR) in January 1976 and was immediately retrieved by local agents of the mysterious Section (Vil) of the KGB (the 'Esoteric Section', or KGBIKARIN) and immediately forwarded to Moscow.

Notes directly from the incommunicable/reserved papal report transmitted from Belgrade in November 1978 by Prof. Dr. Bruno Wellensteg of Zurich to the Vatican Secretariat of State, dealing with the current aftermath of the occult operational takeover and revitalisation of the *Ahnenerbe! Sonderaktion Kandahar* by the KGB/KARIN in Afghanistan (Prof. Dr. Bruno Wellensteg being, in fact, the former SS colonel at the disposal of Albrecht-Georg von Kantzow, who was formerly in charge of Reichsführer Heinrich Himmler in Berlin and was personally responsible for the entire *Ahnenerbe/Sonderaktion Kandahar*).

On the great and small mysteries of the KGB/KARIN operational headquarters in Baku, Azerbaijan. The updating of the old doctrine of the 'outer enclosures' and the 'core of quiet darkness'.

From the Baku headquarters, the KGB supports and strengthens the underground promotion of the great Shiite esotericism and Sufism throughout the Islamic world. Directly responsible for the operations concerning the 'revival of secret Islam' as well as the 'overactivation of the great anti-imperialist revolutionary and national liberation currents', is the local KGB chairman of Azerbaijan, Geidar Aliyev. Later, in order to openly engage in more political and religious, even spiritual, activities, Geidar Aliyev was promoted to the position of First Party Secretary in Baku, thus assuming full political and administrative control of Azerbaijan.

However, immediately after the disappearance of L. I. Brezhnev, Geidar Aliyev was urgently called to Moscow by Y. V. Andropov himself, who immediately invited him to join the Political Bureau. On the other hand, in Moscow, Geidar Aliyev was immediately invited to be part of the "central group" which acted in the shadow of Y. V. Andropov. It is undoubtedly Geidar Aliyev who will be in charge, at the scheduled time, of the implementation and of the overall triggering of the "world Islamic grand design" which seems to haunt, and as if to radiate, the most secret planetary visions of Y. V. Andropov. Geidar Aliyev's rising star is the mysterious green star of Anterior Asia, of the *Asia Mysteriosa* of the Polar Fraternities.

Statement by Geidar Aliyev, an activist element of Y. V. Andropov's "core group", to a group of revolutionary activists of the Kandahar PDPA Andropov, to a group of revolutionary activists of the Kandahar PDPA: For the USSR and for its new planetary anti-imperialist strategy, the promotion and support of Islam, and of Islam in its double external and internal face, is, today, in the proper space of the Third World marked by the struggles of its second liberation, of its post-colonial national liberation, of the same urgency, of the same immediate politico-historical importance as the deep understanding, the support advanced by the whole socialist camp, to the great underground currents for peace currently in action in Western Europe and even in the United States itself" (Moscow, February 1983).

In today's Afghanistan, behind certain hidden things, other things are hidden, even more hidden: the great mystagogic manipulations of Moscow, undertaken more or less in application of the teachings intercepted through its hold on the *Ahnenerbe/Sonderaktion Kandahar* material, are deeply, and very subversively, sheltered behind the politico-strategic covers provided by the very particular circumstances of the Soviet presence there.

Thus, on [1] January 1983, the Communist Party of Afghanistan, the People's Democratic Party (PDPA), announced at the official celebration of its 18th anniversary that it had put an end to the existence of two parallel dissident organisations – **(1)** the Fareham of President Babrak Karmal, and **(2)** the Khalq of former leaders Taraki and Amin – and had thus succeeded in re-establishing, once and for all, its inner unity.

On the other hand, in Moscow, Andrei Alexandrov, an essential element of Y. V. Andropov's "central group", published on 31 December 1982, through the official channel of the Tass Agency, a declaration intended, in principle, to put an end to the "insinuations" on the policy of the USSR towards Afghanistan, "insinuations propagated recently" by "certain politicians and press organs, essentially from countries that are waging an undeclared war against Afghanistan". Finally, to cut short the preventive disinformation manoeuvres suggesting that Y. V. Andropov was planning to change the Soviet line towards Afghanistan by starting a *disengagement* process in the more or less short term, Andrei Alexandrov also wrote: "Attempts to condition relations between the USSR and the United States, between the East and the West, by events around Afghanistan cannot fail to arouse surprise and disapproval. Who would be impressed by these attempts? Do we really think that, under their influence, the USSR will change its position towards democratic Afghanistan and its legitimate government? Let us say it unequivocally: these calculations are illusory. The USSR will fulfil its internationalist duty to protect Afghanistan against foreign military intervention to the end. Andrei Alexandrov concludes by saying that the USSR has no intention of "keeping its troops in Afghanistan forever".

(Nevertheless, if, as everything would seem to indicate, Y. V. Andropov's "central group" was able to retain, and even adopt, the preventive conclusions that are necessary from any attempt to update and deepen the direct operational aspects of the *Ahnenerbe/Soruleraktion Kandahar* dossier, it is obvious that the USSR would hardly be willing to engage in the slightest process of disengagement in Afghanistan. On the contrary, the nameless and faceless leaders of the "Secret Order" who are said to have seized the levers of command in Moscow must have perfectly understood, themselves and their political-military proxies, to what point of extreme non-return the continuation of its super strategy in motion already requires that after Afghanistan, and within a timeframe that can no longer tolerate any delay, the new imperial power of the USSR the new historical emergence of the Greatest Russia accelerated and superintensified its push towards the Indian Ocean by imposing its real presence, its immediate politico-strategic weight on Pakistan at the same time as on the separatist South-East of Iran, and on Iran itself, more and more subversively invested and turned inside out by the double Soviet device of direct political penetration, Marxist and Islamo-progressive:While it was the internal and external intelligence and security services of the Soviet Armed Forces, the GRU, which, in 1976, had intercepted the constitutional files of *the Ahnenerbel Sonderaktion Kandahar* in the GDR, and that, consequently, it was the GRU which should have ensured any possible updating of them. The KGB president at the time, Y. V. Andropov, requested and obtained, but not without difficulty, that the GRU be discharged and that the KGB actually take control of it. It was therefore the KGB's takeover in 1976 that opened up the new operational career of the *Ahnenerbe/Sonderaktion Kandahar* dossier and suddenly offered unexpected opportunities to some of its former German agents who had survived the furnace of 1945, including, precisely, SS Colonel Albrecht-Georg von Kantzow, who, since then, has shown that he has been able to step up his game again, most certainly on special instructions.)

The USSR and Islamic fundamentalism

However, in Moscow, at the level of the Central Committee's "internal operational cells", it is not unknown that through its current politico-military confrontations in Afghanistan, the Soviet Union is engaged in the front line of a vast emerging planetary conspiracy, prepared underground by the British special services – structures under cover of the Foreign Office, and MI6 – with a view to organising a general uprising of Fundamentalist, Shiite and Wahabi Islam.

An uprising whose offensive opening of the future politico-strategic front is aimed, at the beginning of the horizon of the third millennium, and even well before, on the one hand, at the revolutionary conflagration, first of all, of the soviet republics of Central Asia, with a fundamental focus of irradiation in Tehran and, later, in Kabul, and, on the other hand, at the blocking of the politico-strategic "Euro-Arabic" line put in place by General de Gaulle. The aim is to dismantle it, to render it inoperative as quickly as possible, and by other means as well.

Fundamentalist Islam should win, in the long run, because of its mystic-revolutionary excesses and secretly supported in this operation by the United States and Great Britain bloc, both on the international level and in the Arab countries of the "Gaullist line", Iraq, Syria, Egypt, Algeria, etc., as many national socialist regimes with a political-military structure to be dislodged and replaced by "new type" regimes with a fundamentalist Islamic identity, essentially religious, fanatically religious, etc. These are all national socialist regimes with a politico-military structure to be dislodged and replaced by regimes with a fundamentalist Islamic structure and identity of a "new type", "essentially religious, fanatically religious".

The planetary uprising of Fundamentalist Islam, which is in the process of underground preparation, will have to act transversally, through the two American and Soviet blocks, trying to clear a "third way" which will not be at all the current "third way" of the "non-aligned", but a "third way" of abysmal, definitive, total revolutionary rupture, in a way post-historical, because it will be based on religious positions that overturn the conventional order of the current ideological-doctrinal commitments, whatever they may be, and will put into practice planetary offensive strategies of a "new type", where, in response to the presence of a discontinuous, non-continuous and, for the most part, non-visible front, new offensive strategies will be put into action, based on mass terrorism and the use of special means of combat (chemical, biological and even nuclear warfare on a reduced scale).

Thus, the fighting strategy of the future Fundamentalist Islamic Front will be, essentially, a strategy based on terrorism, and on the all-out fight against any other form of political reality other than that of the Islamic religion. The total war of an entity of a totally new type).

THE GRU GALAXY

An extended operational analysis of Pierre de Villemarest's book, *GRU, le plus secret des services soviétiques*, 1918–1988, Stock, Paris, 1988.

The editions Stock, Paris 1988, have just published a new book by Pierre de Villemarest, *GRU, le plus secret des services soviétiques, 1918-1988*. It is well known that, in addition to publishing specialised works on the USSR, contemporary espionage, terrorism, and Soviet-German relations, Pierre de Villemarest, founder of the *European Information Centre* (CEI) in 1970, pursues multiple activities, (active address, *European Information Centre* (CEI) and its official publications, at La Vendomière, 27 930 Le Cierrey, France, tel. (16) 3 237 0024, telex 17 2640 Infocei).

The highest ambition

Following a somewhat dispersed order of march, and situating itself, at the outset, in an overall politico-historical and revolutionary perspective which, all things considered, is only relatively ours as well, the research undertaken by Pierre de Villemarest on the intimate history of the GRU, "the most secret of the Soviet services", research going from 1918 to 1988, nevertheless leads, as if in the final analysis, to a grid of geopolitical conclusions that are activated and over-activated, to theses of immediate operational affirmation, explicit or *implicit*, which interest us, which must interest us to the highest degree and in a way that we find directly relevant to what we consider to be the most urgent current events on our own combat front.

In his *GRU, the most secret of the Soviet services, 1918–1988*, Pierre de Villemarest pursues a particular task, a task of *spetsloujba* as they say in the "military department 44388", in Khodinka: to establish an ontological differentiation between the KGB and the GRU, a differentiation which, moreover, would follow – follows – very closely that which, in other times and in other circumstances, opposed, underground, the SD and the Abwehr within the political-military security apparatus of the Third Reich.

Indeed, the basic thesis of Pierre de Villemarest's analytical work on the GRU is as follows, and to be as direct as possible I quote from the back cover: ''The KGB is an emanation of the Party: the GRU comes from the Army. The difference is enormous: by vocation, the army protects the State while the KGB protects the Party which has invested the State. Behind the USSR, that of

Gorbachev, we see the shadow of the army reappear. You have to know what the GRU is to understand what will happen now in Moscow.

And, still speaking of the GRU, Pierre de Villemarest also argues that "it cannot be repeated enough that it is an intelligence service, and was not, and is not, a service of repression". And then: "We must remember this on every page of its history: in relation to the Soviet power and its secret police, it is what the Wehrmacht's general staff and its intelligence service, the Abwehr, were in relation to the Nazi party and the Sicherheitdienst, this parallel espionage service of the single party".

Finally, to conclude his book on the GRU, Pierre de Villemarest wrote: ''It would be wrong to imagine that everything is said in an alliance between the political-military apparatus and the Gorbachev group against the old Party cadres and the support they find in the KGB apparatus. It may be that Gorbachev tolerates the military's influence only as a temporary expedient, while he asserts himself and recovers the economy. But he also knows that the time when marshals and generals bowed their heads to Stalin and his henchmen, or out of opportunism and careerism, to Khrushchev, Brezhnev or Andropov, is over. The extreme technicalisation of armaments, the high qualifications of the officers of the commands, such as those of the GRU, led to a state of mind which instinctively placed itself at the service of the state much more than at that of the Party. The slogan 'patriotism in the service of internationalism' no longer captivates the cadres of this army, for which the GRU continues to be the eyes and ears beyond the borders. Today's army serves the Soviet state to protect and maintain it. Proud of its mission, it is less and less willing, despite the KGB, to safeguard the dominant role of the Party at the risk of the state being crushed in a global conflict. It is becoming – whether the KGB state likes it or not – the irresistible component of a new era, if only because of East-West relations, on which its advice is indispensable. To portray the USSR's senior officers as a kind of "go to war", to cast suspicion on them because their nationalism outweighs communism, would be to cast them into a dangerous national-Sovietism. National-Sovietism is an SS army at the orders of the single party. Nationalism, except for imperialist drift, is an army at the service of a state within its borders. The last lines of Pierre de Villemarest's book on the GRU are these: ''But it is not because an empire is, like a river, forced to return to its bed, except to spread out and get lost in the sands, that it loses its dynamism. On the contrary, the current, narrowed in its banks, gains in cohesion and strength. *History teaches us vigilance,* such was the title of Marshal Ogarkov's last book. It teaches it to the Soviet Union. It teaches us too.

Pierre de Villemarest, *GRU, the most secret of Soviet services, 1918–1988:* it is therefore, and in the first place, a book of advanced ideological-political combat, of which the workers responsible for a certain European and continental intelligence cannot disregard or omit to use it, in one direction or another, or even to recover it as such, to the ends that we can well suppose, possibly and if we think, with Guy Debord, that the "highest ambition" of some would be, today, to succeed in making sure that "secret agents become revolutionaries, and that revolutionaries become secret agents".

I. V. Stalin, the final vision of a Eurasian Empire

Thus it seems to us that, following a thorough reading of his very important work on the GRU, Pierre de Villemarest would seem to hold the occult political history of the USSR to be the fact of a permanently mobilised military conspiracy facing a political-administrative counter-conspiracy. Conspiracy and counter-conspiracy merging, at a certain level, with the history of the dramatic, self-intensifying, shadowy and ultimately bloody opposition between, on the one hand, the Red Army and the GRU and, on the other hand, the Party and the General Secretariat of the Party and its own overall politico-strategic control and security services (NKVD, KGB).

This is reduced, also, and more particularly for the paroxysmal period of I. V. Stalin's unfailing control over the General Secretariat of the Party, to the underground and total fight between the Red Army and I. V. Stalin, the Red Army considering that the fundamental enemy of the USSR is Germany and the Third Reich, while I. V. Stalin, on his side, had understood, in a visionary way, that it was on the alliance – and even, in the long run, on the great-continental integration of the USSR and the Third Reich that the destiny, the greatest destiny was going to be played out.

Therefore, the decisive years that were to be, for I. V. Stalin, the years 1936–1939, can be understood – really understood – only in the perspective of a ruthless *internal fight*. Years of reprieve, of underground preparation and counter-conspiracy that allowed him to stop, neutralize and, later on, annihilate the internal resistance, of exclusively trotskistocosmopolitan order, that had managed to subversively seize the General Staff of the Red Army and the GRU with the aim of opposing the confidential "grand design" of I.V. Stalin, obsessed with the final vision of a Eurasian Empire, a Great Continental Empire integrating the USSR and the Third Reich and, from the central Soviet-German *heartland*, the whole of continental Europe.

All the Soviet internal policy, from the arrival of I. V. Stalin to the General Secretariat of the Party until June 1941, had thus pursued only one secret fundamental goal: the setting up of the internal counter-structures of the Soviet power able to allow this one to lead, at the desired time, to the great-continental integration of the USSR and the Third Reich, an integration whose summit prefiguration had appeared at the time of the diplomatic instrumentalization of the Germano-Soviet pact of August 1939.

In this regard, Pierre de Villemarest will quote the 'complete and secret' report of Himmler and Heydrich, dated 22 March 1937, which assured that *Germany was no longer the target of the Comintern or of other Soviet activities.* In continuation, Pierre de Villemarest states that, according to the confidences made to him by Commodore H. Wichmann, former director of the Abwehr for Great Britain, Colonel Walter Nikolaï, former chief of military intelligence to the Kronprinz and, subsequently, under the Third Reich, responsible for the Office of Jewish Affairs, "was one of those who, as early as 1919, believed that a well-conducted German-Soviet entente would determine the fate of Europe and Eurasia. So much so that both Captain Patzig, the first head of the Abwehr in the 1920s (the German equivalent of the GRU) and his successor in December 1935, Admiral Canaris, forbade Nikolai access to their offices". And Pierre de Villemarest adds: "For a while Nikolai put his personal knowledge at the service of von Ribbentrop, whose entourage was full of intellectuals and civil servants who despised the unconditional and narrow-minded policemen with whom Hitler had surrounded himself since 1934. Then Nikolai managed to get into the good graces of Heydrich, the man who ran the Nazi spy ring around the world, the SD, rival of the Abwehr. And Nikolai got on well with Martin Bormann who, after the flight of Rudolf Hess in 1941, became the eminence grise of power. Nikolai, who in 1937 created the Office of Jewish Affairs to serve as his cover, was one of the secret pivots of the GRU. We do not know whether he was a volunteer or paid agent, but we do know that when the vanguard of the Red Army entered Berlin in 1945 – that is, the special units of the NKVD – this man, still green at seventy-two, rushed to the Soviet side, rather than fall to the Allies.

The same nocturnal movement

On the subject of Colonel Walter Nikolai's supposed connections with the GRU, a fable as evanescent as it is ambiguous, although one must know how to distinguish between relations ordered from one service to another, even if they are ultra-clandestine for the needs of the cause, and the subjection of what is commonly referred to as a double agent, on the subject of Colonel Walter Nikolai's supposed connections with the GRU, Pierre de Villemarest does not even refrain from quoting his sources. Personal files", he asserts, made up "on the basis of enquiries with the survivors of the Canaris team, including Commodore Wichmann, Colonel Wagner (head of the Abwehr for the Balkans), and General Gehlen's deputies", and also on the basis of "cross-checking with the industrialist Arnold von Rechberg, who warned the French services in vain before 1940".

The operational theses of the anti-National Socialist disinformation line practised in the early 1960s by the agents of the Gehlen Organisation, who, working from Pullach in Bavaria for obscure, as yet unresolved, purposes, are to be found again in a most outrageous form, had tried to launch the singularly laughable montage of Martin Bormann's (Pakbo's, supposedly) alleged membership of the GRU's combatant networks and of the latter's presence, after the war, in the USSR (whereas, as some people know, it was in Spain that Martin Bormann had hidden for a long time).

For his part, and in the same vein, Pierre de Villemarest adds, innovating: "Thanks to Nikolaï's advice, the GRU will actively recruit, from 1937 to 1941, in the Gestapo and the SD, and even one of Himmler's assistants. In his own time, Martin Bormann will enter the scene".

Thus, when we do *too much,* it will always be too much: because, in the end, by trying to prove too much, we prove nothing at all.

Himmler, Heydrich, Bormann, "Soviet agents", the SD and the Gestapo deeply infiltrated by the GRU, the national socialist apparatus of Greater Germany manipulated, in the shadows, by the nocturnal creatures of the dismal Kiusis Peteris, alias Ian Karlovitch Berzine, "Starik" (the "Old Man"), and by his successors?

It is a little too quickly to forget, however, that it was the despicable, abject "Admiral" Canaris, convicted of high treason against his own country and the armies of his country engaged in a total war, a traitor to his fallen comrades, who was hanged from a butcher's hook, the symbol of a justice that was no doubt belated but at last clear-sighted. The lame reprieve that "Admiral" Canaris had obtained by having Heydrich assassinated in Prague in 1942, a criminal manoeuvre designed to loosen the stranglehold that Heydrich was closing more and more around himself and his followers, the SD having finally begun to understand, The supreme opprobrium of the butcher's hook was written into his destiny in advance, just as it is written into the uncertain shadow of every great treason.

The metahistorical and sacrificial adventure of National Socialism depraved by the uses made of it, through who knows what pro-Soviet subjugations of its leaders, by the faceless bosses of Moscow's great occult game? It would also mean forgetting the millions of young Germans and Europeans of all nationalities who, 'inhabited by the Hölderlinian light of death', as Martin Heidegger said, heroically gave their lives to save civilisation, who, inhabited by the Hölderlinian light of death'', as Martin Heidegger put it, heroically gave their lives for the sake of civilisation, of being and of the European and Western destiny of the world and of the present history – the final history – of the world, who made their shed blood the incorruptible concrete of the ontological and sacrificial foundations of the future great Western history of the world, opening up again to the mystery of its own future metahistory in the renewal of the cycles.

If, in the depths, a double movement of great-continental mixing had approached, in those *decisive years,* and before the irreparable happened – decisive years that are now coming back – the double revolutionary and metahistorical adventure of the USSR and the Third Reich, this double movement had found its own centre of gravity elsewhere than in the murky waters of the low police force of the two sides, outside the terrible advances of the high national and continental treason perpetrated, in the USSR, by the supporters of the Trotskyite-cosmopolitan conspiratorial bloc and, in

Germany, by the otherwise disguised agents of the same nocturnal tendency. The same movement at work, too, in London, Washington and elsewhere. And, also, who said that history does not repeat itself?

Cari Düssel, in 1944: 'Why do you Germans keep quiet? Why don't you say clearly and intelligibly how you see the future, our future, the future of Europe? ''.

The agony of the Berzine era

However, in the light of what we have since learned, it is now perfectly certain that the person directly operationally responsible for the subversive build-up undertaken by the Trotskyite-cosmopolitan conspiratorial apparatus opposed to the grand continental and European vision of LV. Stalin, was none other than the very head of the GRU, Ian Karlovitch Berzine, the "Starik", the "Trotsky from within". The harder the fall, the better.

For, on the day LV. Stalin had decided that he had to put an end, abruptly, to the barrier erected, from within the central Soviet power, against his plans of great-continental rapprochement between the USSR and the Third Reich, a barrier tirelessly erected and straightened by the conspiracy of the Trotskyisto-cosmopolitan bloc having found asylum, behind Ian Karlovich Berzin, in the GRU, this barrier was dismantled, by I. V. Stalin, inside and outside the USSR, in the shortest possible time – dazzling, I would say – and without paying too much attention to the considerable risks involved. The Trotskyite-cosmopolitan apparatus covered by the GRU of Ian Karlovich Berzin and his agents inside and outside the USSR was then annihilated – annihilated man by man, or almost, and the politico-administrative agony of Berzin's ardent wake lasted until 1941 and beyond, not to say that it would still last today, as we will see below, because *it is not over*.

Had these "anti-fascist fighters" of the hardest line, the "Berzine line", had time to understand that they were purely and simply sacrificed by L. V. Stalin to the demands – *objective demands,* it was said – of his policy of continental rapprochement with Adolf Hitler's Greater Germany?

Pierre de Villemarest: ''Strange blindness or morality that these men did not perceive that from 1937 onwards, from Switzerland to the suburbs of Albacete, the agony of the Berzine era had begun, and led straight to the German-Soviet pact of August 1939! Were they unaware of the order given by Stalin as early as December 1936 ''Cease all activity against Germany! ''. Didn't they wonder why Iagoda and then Iejov had launched killing squads all over the world, 70 per cent of whose victims were Jews, and 100 per cent were opponents of Nazism? ''.

And Pierre de Villemarest again, from whom we must quote here these analytical pages seizing, at the same time admirable and terrible, indisputable, the very march of the greatest history in the process of taking one of its irrevocable turns, "without return". It is enough to reread Stalin's speech pronounced in January 1934 before the XVIIth Congress of the CP of the USSR, to review the agreements made with Berlin in 1935, to know the steps taken that same year by several emissaries of Stalin's personal secretariat and of the 00 to the leaders of the *Sicherheitdienst* and the secret conversations of the diplomat David Kandelaki, to understand that the shadow of death extends over those who belonged to the first phalanx of the Revolution, if they are suspected of not being unconditional towards the Party, i.e. Stalin.

At the beginning of 1936, things were sufficiently advanced on the Berlin side for Stalin to summon Semione Ouritzki, acting director of the GRU since the previous summer, to the Kremlin. He gave him the order that Walter Krivitzky had also received at the head of the networks covering Europe: "Stop all work against Germany! ". How could the fate of Berzine, Unschlicht and Ouritzki not be sealed when, in April 1937, David Kandelaki brought to Berlin the first draft of the German-Soviet pact, which, with a few nuances, was to be the pact signed in August 1939?

Spain, where Berzin acts for the best with his specialists: Vladimir Antonov-Ovseenko, A. Wronski, Gorev, Stern, the future Marshal Malinovski, Generals Rodintzev and Smoukhevitch Spain is the tomb of an era. Even the NKVD killers, who murdered suspected Trotskyites or anarchists behind their backs, would fall in their turn once they returned to the USSR. Except for a few insiders.

Recalls from abroad began in May 1937. Defections began. Krivizky already. Ignace Reins, head of the GRU in Switzerland, is executed before he can escape. Marshal Tukhachevsky presides over his last parade that month. When he arrived at the Kremlin rostrum, Marshal Iegorov pretended not to see him. This was a bad sign. But what to do? It is too late. Tukhachevsky is going to die, and hundreds of men with him. Nicolas Iejov, eight weeks after the Marshal's death, sends a directive: "Exterminate all the members of a highly ramified spy network... ".

Unschlicht replaced Ouritzki as head of the GRU. For five months, he would multiply his efforts, based on the Spanish war and what survived of the network leaders, to maintain and reconstitute this organisation. Iejov took the job from him in May 1938. Until the following December, there was a massacre in the ranks of the GRU: Unschlicht was shot in June for treason; Vassili Blücher, who had just routed the Japanese units on Lake Khasan, was recalled to Moscow and executed on 9 November. Even in the NKVD, people are afraid. There is good reason for this: 3,000 Chekists are murdered. General Lyushkov, head of the NKVD border guards in the Far East, fled to Manchuria, on the Japanese side, offering his adversaries all the information on the Soviet Union's military apparatus. The execution of Vassili Blücher irrevocably closed an entire era.

In Moscow, Stalin placed Lavrenti Beria behind Iejov in July 1938. Now that he no longer has to fear the popularity and efficiency of the army high command, the space is free to place docile pawns in the direction of the agreement with Berlin''.

Even today, who can really understand it? The only objective, the profound objective of the entire Stalinist policy, both internally and externally, from 1934 to 1940, was that of agreement with Berlin, agreement with Hitler.

Non-being has just overtaken being''.

Two continental superpowers, the USSR and the Third Reich, each engaged in its own revolutionary and totalitarian experience using the dialectic and the activist impositions of the One Party, will thus end up being invested, each one, Each of these two superpowers is thus divided and opposed, in themselves, against themselves, while at the same time opposing each other.

What, then, is the conflictual structure of the hold on internal power of each of the two superpowers in presence, a structure, therefore, fundamentally common to both? What is the internal conflictual structure common to both Soviet and National Socialist power in Moscow and Berlin respectively?

he gives the following definition: divergent, centrifugal, cosmopolitan and anti-national, fundamentally also anti-continental forces, establishing their internal offensive bases at the General Staffs and their intelligence and security services – General Staff of the Wehrmacht as well as General Staff of the Red Army, Abwehr and GRU – are opposing, in an increasingly consistent manner, increasingly vehement but also increasingly covert, subversive, to the forces of national and grand continental revolutionary convergence at the disposal of the One Party-PC of the USSR, NSDAP – whose ultimate goal would seem to be that of pursuing the final integration of the two opposing states – USSR, Third Reich – into a single meta-historical unity of destiny, namely the Grand Continental Confederation of Eurasia. While the opposition from within, at work in Moscow as well as in Berlin, an opposition from within that is paradoxically cosmopolitan and military, even militaristic, "reactionary" and irreducibly anti-continental, prepares-in Moscow as much as in Berlin-the armed confrontation of the USSR and the Third Reich, the "final war", the transcontinental and planetary Endkampfin wished for by Karl Haushofer and Rudolf Hess, while appealing – each side on its own side – to the "External Powers" of Anglo-Saxon liberal democracy, "oceanic" and anti-continental powers, which, at the same time, are doing their utmost to keep France under their degrading and over-eliminating influence, or even as a somnambulistic hostage of its own anti-destiny.

Now, if it was the intra-continental war and not the grand continental integration that finally won in terms of history – in terms, too, of anti-destiny – it is urgent and more than urgent that we recognise this, and that we recognise it in all clarity: it was not because of the USSR, but because of the inconceivable, disastrous and completely demented blindness of the Third Reich, which committed all its forces in June 1941 to an intra-continental war of rupture against the USSR, when the latter had fought, *right up to the very last moment,* to avoid the irreparable disaster, that the irreparable disaster negatively changed the course of the European history of the Great Continent

On the night of 21–22 June 1941, when the Wehrmacht was attacking from Finland to the Black Sea, LV Stalin's ambassador in Berlin, Vladimir Dekanozov, went in the middle of the night to the home of the Third Reich's foreign minister, Joachim von Ribbentrop, in Dahlem, Lenz Allee, to bring him an urgent personal message from LV. Stalin. The General Secretary of the CP of the USSR, LV Stalin, wanted to go personally, and as soon as possible – said the message – to Berlin, for a "supreme conference" with Chancellor Adolf Hitler. But the dice of nothingness had already rolled, the darkness of non-being had won.

And, according to Arno Breker's confidences, I can myself testify that, on the morning of 22 June 1941 – the sun had barely risen – Martin Bormann, leaving – or should I say deserting – his post in the Reich Chancellery, went to see Arno Breker in Jâkelsbrueh, in a state of somber disarray, in order to confide in him, at the risk of his own life, his despair in the face of the irretrievable, now done. Martin Bormann: ''Non-being, on this June day, has just won out over being. Everything is consumed. All is lost''.

Arno Breker: ''His visit was mysterious, and it will always remain so. It seemed to me that at the last moment he had not said what he had wanted to say to me. He stopped again, his hand on the handle, turned around once more, as if he wanted to say something, but he remained silent.

How far we were suddenly from the abysmal myth of *Total Weltrevolution*. Could things have happened differently? In history in progress, only what has been counts. But there is still the future, of which we are, still and always, the metapolitical soldiers, of which we constitute, in the face of darkness, the visionary protection force.

In its July 1980 issue, *Jeune Nation* wrote: 'So it was that Hitler's Germany missed its chance, and it is very fortunate that it missed it; for things had to happen as they did, and not otherwise. Why should the Europe of the End have been a German Europe? The Europe of the End must and will be European, the Europe of the End can only be European. For this is, at the present time, the only truly and totally revolutionary question, the only liberating question: deep within themselves, will the European nations rediscover, when the day comes, and which is already here, the burning reality of the "nation before the nations", the transcendental legacy of the "Indo-European nation" of our earlier origins? The iron dream of absolute irrationality, a dream that General de Gaulle called 'superhuman and inhuman', having ended, once and for all, in the blackened ruins of the Berlin Chancellery, it remains for us to face, without flinching, the black sun of what is still to come. But beyond this sun of darkness, and if the abyss calls for the abyss, will there ever be *anything else* for us? Is there nothing beyond the disaster? Nothing beyond blackness and emptiness?

Borrowed from *Jeune Nation,* the fragment I have just quoted was entitled, precisely, the *"Genius of Renewal".*

Askania Publishing

These analyses should not, however, be interpreted in the sense of any implicit hostility to the European armies in combat during the last two world wars, 1914–1918 and 1939–1945, and even less as a distrust that could undermine the military honour of our people and of all those who were led to make the heroic sacrifice of their young lives for a political or metahistorical cause, for a total revolutionary cause.

If there is hostility, and mistrust, deep mistrust, this active hostility and this mistrust only concern, in any case, the very occult nuclei of treason and degrading anti-national and anti-revolutionary duplicity that we have come to detect within the German OKW, nuclei of treason at work before, during and even after the 1939–1945 war, or their counterpart within the Soviet Stavka, deeply infected, for example under Tukhachevsky, by the cosmopolitan and Trotskyite-cosmopolitan remanences that we know and inevitably led, thus, towards the active and unceasingly activated dialectics of high treason, defeatism and anti-revolutionary obstructionism and subterraneanly opposed to the grand continental and European Stalinist line.

Thus, to put it in terms of a new foundational myth, the young dead of the Battle of Stalingrad are no longer, for us, German, Soviet or Romanian dead, but the young heroes of the same great European and continental cause, the young dead of our own life to come.

Herbert Taege, director of Askania Publishers and of the magazine *Askania Annuel* (active address, Postfach 17, 3067 Lindherst, Federal Germany), comments in the August-September issue of Robert Steuckers' magazine *Vouloir* (active address, BPB 41, 1970 Wezembeek-Oppem, Belgium) on Hans Werner Neulen's book, *Europa und das 3. Reich. Einigungsbestrebungen im deutechen Machtbereich 1939-45,* Universitas, München, 1987. Herbert Tage's commentary, which is much more than a mere commentary, is entitled, in an interrogative form, *"European Confederation"* or *"European Nation"*? and we will find in it revelations that are as decisive as they are clear for the definition of a unitary metahistorical concept of this "great continental and European cause" that we urgently need to update.

Herbert Tage's article and, obviously, even more so the book it deals with, take on a symbolic and immediately ideological-political value that is quite extraordinary in the present circumstances: It clearly shows the emergence, the action taken, the confidential history, the principles and the doctrine, the ideological-political theses that eventually prevailed in Berlin within the Supreme Command of the SS (SS Hauptamt), from the years 1942–1943, a revolutionary doctrine and action expressing a grand-continental and European line absolutely identical to that which we are trying to define ourselves today, and, by that very fact, in its time, a visionary, even prophetic line.

According to Herbert Taege, the head of the planning office and of Amtegruppe D (Europa Amt), Alexander Dolezalek, was responsible in Berlin for the Great Continental and European line within the SS Supreme Command (SS Hauptamt). Alexander Dolezalek's ideological and political work was immense.

Hans Werner Neulen:

The idea of a peaceful order in Europe had not yet fully emerged from National Socialism, but had nevertheless propagated the beginnings of solutions in domestic and foreign policy, solutions which provided for the abandonment of the totalitarian *Führerprinzip* and the German claim to absolute domination of the continent'.

A long way had been travelled from the idea of a coercive Germanic state under absolute German hegemony to the sublime ideal of a 'European confederation', where each people would be free to shape its own political order and could freely shape its own political destiny.

According to one of the official documents presented by Hans Werner Neulen in his book, entitled *Die europdische Friedensidee 1944145* ('The idea of peace for Europe 1944/45'), Germany's 'war objective', as it was then defined by the Supreme Command of the *SS* (SE Hauptamt), led to the following conclusion: Germany is waging this war to achieve a positive objective: to build the European Confederation, the socialist community of the peoples of Europe''.

Herbert Taege: ''The immanent opposition to the National Socialist system had already formed in 1942, i.e. before Stalingrad, and, within the SS leadership, had found its spokesman in the person of Richard Hildebrandt. As early as 1943, Himmler had made contact with the followers of this opposition within his senior officer corps, with the aim of working towards the establishment of a constitutional *Führerstaat*''. Richard Hildebrandt, ''in a sworn statement just before he was handed over to the USSR for execution, described the aims of his activities and revealed the names of the personalities who surrounded him. There were survivors of this circle, including Dolezalek, head of the SS Hauptamt planning office, who was able to verify the writings left by Hildenbrandt. What was the ultimate goal, the *fundamental goal* of this "immanent opposition" to the "National Socialist system" operating from within the SS Hauptamt in Berlin? Herber Taege also said: "What undoubtedly constituted the salient point of this 'opposition' was the goal of foreign policy, which was already outlined at the time and which would eventually find expression in the plan for the 'European Confederation'. According to the official documents of the SS Hauptamt quoted by Herbert Taege in his article, the SS Hauptamt's plan for the 'European Confederation' called for the following: ''Renunciation of any claim to German hegemony beyond the natural borders of German ethnicity and, therefore, a return to the party programme. Creation of the United States of Europe on the basis of the equal rights of all the peoples included in this entity. Subordination of all national points of view to this great common goal.

It was, on the other hand, with the offensive for the creation of the National Liberation Army of Russia of Soviet General Vlassov, hero of the battle of Moscow, that the "immanent opposition" within the SS Hauptamt had to fight one of its decisive battles. Unfortunately, the leaders of the "immanent opposition" in the SS Hauptamt lost this battle at the last level, coming up against Hitler's irreducibly negative positions towards Russia and the "peoples of the East", a disaster with fatal consequences.

Herbert Taege: "It is understandable why the German officials and officers who had supported Vlassov's movement felt betrayed. Many withdrew from the game, before Goebbels abandoned the idea of creating a post he had planned: that of a 'chargé d'affaires for Eastern problems', attached to the Ministry of Propaganda. For this post, Goebbels had considered Günter Kaufmann, editor-in-chief of the magazine *Wille und Macht,* intended for the leaders of the *Hitlerjugend.* Kaufmann, together with his colleague from *Das Schwarze Korps,* Günter d'Alquen, had been campaigning for years for a radical change of course in Russian policy. In the April-June 1943 issue of *Wille und Macht,* Kaufmann had published General Vlassov's open letter under the title *Russen gegen Sowjets* (''Russians against the Soviets''). And then: 'In the circle around Vlassov, to which the writer Edwin Erich Dwinger also belonged, all agreed that "openness must be the unconditional precondition for relations between the German government and the Russian liberation movement". It was welcomed that General Vlassov's name had finally been mentioned in the German press, especially in the magazine *Wille und Macht.* In a special issue, Vlassov's appeal was not only quoted in full but also commented on in no uncertain terms.

This documentary overview of the revolutionary European theses professed, in the middle of the war, in the shadows and then very openly, by the "immanent opposition" of the SS Hauptamt in Berlin, serves to prove that it is indeed the European and continental eschatology that constitutes, in Europe, the only fundamental idea of the 20th century. This documentary overview of the European revolutionary theses professed in the midst of the war, in the shadows and then very openly by the "immanent opposition" of the SS Hauptamt of Berlin, serves to prove that it is indeed the European and grand-continental eschatology which constitutes, in Europe, the only fundamental idea of the political twentieth century, an idea present in all the camps, conveying all the ideologies, and conveyed by all the ideologies present, and at the same time fought to the death, in all the camps, by the enemy who, in all the camps – and even in the antagonistic camps – appears to be, always and everywhere, the same. Unceasingly annihilated, unceasingly evacuated from history, repressed into non-history, Great European eschatology is nevertheless reborn indefinitely from its ashes.

The great secret mission of the Gral. Col. SM. Chtemenko

Always, impenetrable are the ways of the metahistory in action: long term work, the annihilation, by I.V. Stalin, of the subversive structures set up, inside the central politico-military power of the USSR, by the permanent conspiracy of the trotskisto-cosmopolitan line of which one of the last avatars was, in 1953, the "white coats conspiracy", will have dialectically invented, on the field, the "objective conditions" that were to open the doors of history to those responsible for the "geopolitical line" within the USSR Armed Forces, a "geopolitical line" whose polar figure remains, to this day, General Colonel Serguei Matveievitch Chtemenko (7.2.1907-23.4.1976).

With S. M. Chtemenko and his action groups of the "geopolitical line", LV. Stalin will have won, beyond his death, in the most distant future, the visionary bet of his grandcontinental politics. The political armies of the great stalinist continental revolution, the political armies of the revolutionary setting in motion of the future Eurasian Empire, which had been dreamed of by the leading elements of the "immanent opposition" within the SS Hauptamt of Berlin, became a political-military reality with the advent of the generation of S.M. Chtemenko in the soviet staffs.

The man whom Pierre de Villemarest calls ''one of the first geopoliticians of the USSR, perhaps even the first of all'', the Oral-Col. S. M. Chtemenko was, successively, and acting, as Pierre de Villemarest says, "sometimes in the shadows, sometimes on the front stage", the head of the GRU, the head of the General Staff of the USSR and the head of the Warsaw Pact's Military Staff: the weight of his avant-garde politico-military action was immense, and immense was also the turning point that he managed to impose, confidentially, on the current and future destinies of the Soviet Armed Forces and the USSR itself, the geopolitical turning point of the "Great European and continental imperial line", or even the "oceanic exit" of the Great Eurasian Continent and its dialectical penetration into the "final planetary game" with *the Okeanska*, the Oceanic Fleet of Admiral Serge Gorschkov, the latter identified as one of the leading elements of the "S. M. Chtemenko clan" and of the "S. M. Chtemenko".M. Chtemenko clan'' and its ''core geopolitical groups''.

On the Gral. Col. S. M. Chtemenko, Pierre de Villemarest wrote that "he belongs to a clan of senior officers, certainly 'Soviet', but above all Great Russian in spirit, and perfectly expansionist". And also: "For this caste, the

USSR is an empire called to dominate the Eurasian continent, not only from the Urals to Brest, but from the Urals to Mongolia, from Central Asia to the Mediterranean. And then: "On this last point, Chtemenko is indeed the man who invented, from 1948 to 1952, not the eventual invasion of Afghanistan, but its slow absorption by continuous economic interpenetration, with accompanying subversion. And, at the same time, the irruption of the USSR in the Arab capitals, in Beirut, Damascus, Cairo and Algiers. At the end of 1948, he already explained that at the intersection of the East and Asia, Afghanistan offered the strategic means to cover the fleets that Admiral Serge Gorshkov, one of his personal friends, was beginning to develop to exit from the Black Sea into the Mediterranean.

And Pierre de Villemarest adds: "When in the summer of 1948 the failure of the Jdanov plan in Western Europe took the latter to the grave (apart from the fact that it embarrassed Stalin and dangerously competed with Malenkov and Beria), Chtemenko was one of the inspirers of the anti-Semitic politico-military group, in the Soviet Union and in the satellite countries, of which the "White Coats plot", in January 1953, was the culminating manoeuvre. Everything is linked: Moscow then moves from supporting Israel (1947) and the international Jewish networks, to the strategy of the Arab, or more exactly Muslim, card.

On the passage of the Gral. Col. S. M. Chtemenko to the command of the General Staff of the Warsaw Pact Armies, Pierre de Villemarest underlines: "After a period of eclipse, following the disgrace of Marshal Zhukov, in October 1957, Chtemenko will reappear as Chief of the General Staff of the Warsaw Pact Armies. A position made for him, because he was also the man who, twice at the head of the GRU and constantly placed in the general staff, took the initiative to double the Soviet spy networks in the world thanks to personnel specifically chosen in the secret services of the states satelliteized by Moscow, or of the states associated by cooperation treaties with the USSR.

Finally, I must also remind you that it is the Gral. Col. S.M. Chtemenko and his "geopolitical groups" for study and action were behind the counter-strategic plans *Polarka*, modified *Volcano* – "normalisation" of Yugoslavia and the whole of South-East Europe – and *Genghis-Khan* – nuclear "normalisation" of Sin-Kiang and People's China – plans which, in the sixties, almost "changed the face of the world".

In the end, however, none of this happened. For what "objective reasons" – in other words, in the terms of what top-secret confrontation of internal and external forces competed *at that time* – the "changes of destiny" involved in the implementation of the great counter-strategic plans of Gral. Col. S. M. Chtemenko and his "geopolitical groups" could not have been made, could not have *passed into history*? Let's say that the answer to this question carries with it the spectral diagnosis of the situation created, at present, in the USSR and in the heart of the Eastern "socialist bloc", by the rise to power of Mikhail

Gorbachev and the unavoidable forces that are hiding behind him, while waiting for what comes next.

Thus, the very exceptional and praiseworthy merit of Pierre de Villemarest will have been – and how can we fail to recognise this, and to congratulate him warmly for it – that of having been able to detect and grasp, with certainty, the great hidden destiny, the true dimensions of the doctrinal and revolutionary identity, and the activating and all-encompassing value of the counter-strategic commitments defined and implemented by the Gral. Col. S. M. Chtemenko, and therefore the extreme importance, in the recent past, and in the future too, in the most distant metapolitical future, of those clandestine and unofficial politico-military influence nuclei that were, and still are, his "geopolitical groups". And this Pierre de Villemarest has done in a way that is all the more notable because he is the only one, in France at least, to have understood and dared to say it when it was necessary and, above all, as it was necessary.

I think it is also worth noting that, for his part, General Guido Giannettini, in his studies and research on the "advanced geopolitical approach" to the grand-continental history of Europe and its Eurasian hinterland, revealed the attempt by Chou Enlai, who, in the years of his supreme power, tried to take over – on behalf of the Greater China, the "Chinese Continental Island", the Chungwa Kuo – the grand-continental geopolitical doctrines, and tried – or almost tried – to impose the Greater China, the "Chinese Continental Island", the Chungwa Kuo, of the Greater China, of the "Chinese Continental Island", the *Chungwa Kuo* - the great-continental geopolitical doctrines, and pretended – or almost – to impose on China a Eurasian confederal mission assuming the imperial destiny – the same imperial destiny – which had already been dreamt of by the "immanent opposition" of the SS Hauptamt of Berlin and the "basic geopolitical groups" of the Gral. Col. S. M. Chtemenko. And I can – and must – also testify to the quite operational interest that General Guida Giannettini and his services did not fail to show, from 1958 to 1978, and *even afterwards* – if one can see what that means – in the doctrinal positions, the counter-strategic commitments of Gral. Col. S. M. Chtemenko and of the nuclei of influence he had set up in the USSR and in the armies of the Eastern "socialist bloc".

More than that: In the same vein, let us also reveal that, in order to stem the wave – successive waves – that preceded and succeeded, under the direction of the same occult extra-European epicentre, the Trotskyisto-cosmopolitan explosions of May 1968 throughout Europe and, above all, in France, where the Gaullist regime in place was directly targeted General Guido Giannettini and his underground influence structures had confidentially tried to install, everywhere, and especially in France, within the apparatus of the already dying Gaullist regime, "basic geopolitical groups", or "Geopolitical Groups". This operation culminated in the attempt to capture and turn around (Dominique de Roux) the politico-military uprising (the "Carnation Revolution") which, in Portugal, ended in the deviationist failure that we know.

Why, in France and throughout Europe, this repeated failure of the grand-continental geopolitical line? Rather than a doctrine of action, geopolitics is essentially the direct action of a doctrine, *a doctrine in action.* Direct geopolitical action is absolutely not usable for the march to power, for the "seizure of power". Direct geopolitical action can only be used from the absolute centre of a politico-military power already in place, can only act from within a politico-military power already totally in place.

In any case, it remains a certainty that, thanks to General Guido Giannettini's interventions, as confidential as they were followed, the Western study of the "geopolitical line" in action in Moscow and in the "socialist bloc" of the East, the monitoring of the "sometimes in the shadows, sometimes at the forefront" of the career, of the personal approach of Gral. Col. S.M. Chtemenko, did not cease for a moment to be at an immediately operational level.

Is all this already in the past? In geopolitics, for the great geopolitics, *everything is present.* Hence the extraordinary importance, hence the extraordinary topicality that we must acknowledge, again and again, to the action undertaken by the Gral. Col. S. M. Chtemenko in his time, and according to the means that were objectively granted to him by the situation. A polar personality for a polar ideology''. It should be remembered that, for the major supporters of the great-continental geopolitical line, the absolute centre of the ideological and politicomilitary power of the USSR is not in Moscow, but at the "North Pole", and that the "geopolitical groups" set up by Gral. Col. S. M. Chtemenko within the fighting units of the Red Army are also called "polar lodges".

Having said all this, I don't think I can fail to take the opportunity to recall, here, and as if for a polar purpose, the name of General Alexander Poskrebychev, head of the personal secretariat of I. V. Stalin and, as such, responsible for the *Spezialne Sektor.* Who was, within the Stalinist regime – and at its peak – what Martin Bormann, supposed by some – including Pierre de Villemarest – to have been in the service of the USSR, will not have been, within the National Socialist regime – and at its peak – while having been, with Adolf Hitler, what General Alexander Poskrebyshev had been with I.V. Stalin

For General Alexander Poskrebyshev was, and the time has finally come to reveal it, the man in Berlin who was precisely where he had to be, and where he managed to do everything he had to do.

However, if Marshal G. K. Zhukov came to be the intractable military protector of Gral. Col. S. M. Shtemenko, it was basically thanks to the support and tireless work of General Alexander Poskrebyshev that Gral. Col. S. M. Chtemenko was able to act and continue his geopolitical action on the great continent, his "polar task".

On the other hand, insofar as the rather long General Secretariat of Leonid Brezhnev was, in fact, only a later, and perhaps final, reverberation of

Stalinism, it can be taken as provable and proven that the great-continental geopolitical line doctrinally and operationally installed by I. V. Stalin himself, from 1936 onwards, and later magnified by Gral. Col. S.M. Chtemenko, was more or less maintained in power until the disappearance of Leonid Brezhnev and the dismantling of the "Dniepopetrovsk group". It is also known that Leonid Brezhnev was himself, in a more or less secret way, a renovator of the already acquired Soviet grand-continental positions, which he exacerbated insofar as, updating the USSR Defence Council to serve his own interests of power, he had made it – or strongly influenced it – into a new structure, He had turned it into – or strongly tried to turn it into – a politico-military tool of strength, intended to allow him to invest in a policy of continental rapprochement with Germany which, in the long run, implied not only the reunification of the two German states, but a total refocusing, a *total turning* of the USSR towards Germany and Western Europe.

The German reluctance, responding to hidden, deeply anti-German and anti-European interests, was nevertheless going to cause Germany and Europe to lose, by sabotaging – and knowingly, I mean *deliberately* – the great continental advance, the pro-German advance of Leonid Brejnev, years perhaps forever irredeemable, just as in the sixties they had also sabotaged – the same *reluctance*, the same hidden interests – the visionary effort undertaken by General de Gaulle in the same grand continental and pro-German convergence, in the corridor of magnetic attraction of the same great polar loyalty.

I. V. Stalin may already be far away in his corridor of darkness, but the attraction of Germany still mysteriously exerts itself on Soviet Russia. Over Siberia, in the airliner which, at the personal invitation of Chou En-lai, was taking him on a visit to Peking, Arthur Axmann – a confidence which he told me in Madrid, in the presence of Otto Skorzeny – was suddenly surrounded by a number of senior Soviet officers, well aware of the aims of his trip. The speech they had given him at the time, to persuade him that Germany's 'new continental mission' concerned the USSR and not People's China 'nor Chou Enlai's continental expansionist plans', Arthur Axmann told me, 'a veritable high-staff geopolitical session', was of such grand continental orthodoxy that he found himself, at the time, recalling in the depths of his memory some of the most tense words he had once had to intercept in the circles of the 'immanent opposition' within the SS Hauptamt in Berlin. Arthur Axmann: ''It was, it seemed to me, the *return of the times*''.

Arthur Axmann's meeting, above snowy Siberia, with the elements in action of a 'geopolitical group', a 'polar lodge' of the General Staff of the Red Army, which makes me irresistibly think of the film that John Frankenheimer had made in 1962 from a novel by Richard Condon, *The Manchurian Candidate*. By a very strange coincidence of fate, it was the same evening I met Arthur Axmann in Madrid that I was to see *The Manchurian Candidate*. It all fits together.

From Berlin to Sin-Kiang

The last battle that Gral. Col. S. M. Chtemenko had to fight within the Red Army, and which he won, was that of the full re-establishment of the strategies of the use of conventional forces in parallel with the new ballistic super-strategies of the "intercontinental war". Pierre de Villemarest will quote, on this subject, the article of "doctrinal rupture" that Gral. Col. S. M. Chtemenko had published in February 1965 in the central organ of the Soviet Armed Forces, *Krasnaya Zvezda*, in which he stated that "the USSR's defence policy cannot be based solely on intercontinental ballistic missiles".

However, it was precisely the General Secretary of the Party, Nikita Kruchtchev, who was at the head of the political-military group supporting, at the top of the ruling power, the thesis according to which "from now on, the defence policy of the USSR will have to be based exclusively on the use of intercontinental ballistic missiles".

Pierre de Villemarest is therefore right to suggest that the real reason for the dismissal of the General Secretary of the Party, Nikita Krouchtchev, which was perpetrated with a brutality all the more extreme because it had to be *masked*, was the fundamental strategic choice, infinitely prejudicial, and which could even have become fateful, imposed – in principle at least – by Nikita Krouchtchev and his followers on the Ministry of Defence and the General Staff, a choice that would have totally given precedence to the new intercontinental ballistic super-strategies over conventional strategies and, above all, over the very reality of the Red Army as a permanent and organic summation of the Soviet Armed Forces, having its own destiny, and considered, this reality, in its continental deployment as a whole, "from Berlin to Sin-Kiang".

Once things were done, the *Krasnaya Zvezda*, Pierre de Villemarest notes, would write, not without vehemence, that "the strategy to which we were finally turning our backs was the product of a stupid brain". And the bloody laundry continued in the shadows. Exactly eight days after Khrushchev was *deposed*," observed Pierre de Villemarest, "Marshal S. S. Biriouzov, the new chief of the General Staff, appointed by Nikita Khrushchev, architect of the Soviet missile installation in Cuba in 1962, and an unconditional supporter of Khrushchev's doctrines of intercontinental nuclear *blitzkrieg*, disappeared on October 19, 1964, in a plane accident of exceptional opportunity. In the same plane crash, General N. Mironov, responsible for the "Intercontinental Nuclear Blitzkrieg", also disappeared. Mironov, head of the "administrative organs", also died in the same plane crash. Pierre de Villemarest: "It has been established that the plane crash had been *prepared"*. One could hardly be more lapidary.

A phenomenon as singular as it is dizzyingly rapid, the 'dekruchtchevisation' was completed in less than a month: indeed, there was great danger in the house.

Urgent and direct, the Red Army's response had been perfectly adequate to the challenge whose stranglehold was about to serve it a devastating challenge.

It is that the endangerment, by the supra-strategic doctrines of Nikita Krouchtchev and his followers, or, if you like, the eventual perishing of the Red Army as – as we have just said – a permanent and organic summation of the Soviet Armed Forces, having *its own destiny,* and considered, this summation, in the whole of its continental deployment, "from Berlin to Sin-Kiang", was not – was absolutely not – a single affair, the simple affair of the choice – even if it was a capital one – of a strategic doctrine of defence. Behind the matter of the choice of a strategic defence doctrine, far, very far behind it, was another choice, a *completely different choice.* What other choice, what completely different choice? That of dialectically denying, and then proceeding to the de facto dismantling of what constituted the implicit national mission, the metapolitical and immediately charismatic mission of the Red Army as defined by Gral. Col. S. M. Chtemenko and his ''basic geopolitical groups'': the mission of high guarding the national integrity, the very being and national consciousness of the ''Soviet people'' and of the Greater Soviet Russia, and even-and, perhaps, above all-the ''polar predestination'' of the latter, the concept of ''polar predestination'' to be understood, of course, in the most Chtemenkian sense of the term.

For the "basic geopolitical groups" acting within the Red Army in the "polar" direction set by Gral. Col. S. M. Chtemenko and by those – or rather, those – who stood behind him, the Red Army was, and should be, above all, a state of perpetuated consciousness. The Red Army was to be the very thing of which the Communist Party could only be the poor and obscure counterfeit, the decoy preventively pushed to the front line. Thus the Red Army had to be, without any solution of continuity, living connective tissue, form of being and way of life. And, at a much greater subversive depth, it will also have been, whatever the "external", "collaborationist" avatars, the "underground mission" of the Russian Orthodox Church and, in the Ukraine and the Baltic States, that of the clandestine Catholic Church, always the fire burning under the dead ashes.

Dismantled as a national mass organisation, fallen into disuse and becoming, more and more, due to the very degradation of its own political and social reality in the face of the rise, in the short term, of a nuclear praetorian guard at the particular service of the external options, defensive or offensive, of the general secretariat of the Communist Party held by the "Khrushchevian line" – a nuclear praetorian guard conforming to a supra-specialised organisation, of reduced structure, separated from the national masses of the soviet people and constituted, exclusively, of superior technicians, of "mercenaries of the interior" – the Red Year saw itself thus forbidden of any living presence, of any action, of any soviet social and national breathing, of any deep counter-interpretation of the only impositional reality of the Communist Party. It was therefore necessary to react to this immediately, and the Red Year reacted to it. Just as, from now on, it will react, immediately, and at the necessary cost, to any attempt to encroach upon or alienate the secret "polar line" that it has given itself to follow internally, or even externally. *Outside?*

Outside, certainly. As well as the head of the GRU, Gral. Col. S. M. Chtemenko had fought to give the military intelligence services of the "socialist bloc" countries in the East a permanent status of shared responsibility and equal action in the pursuit of overall operational tasks, their interpretation and exploitation, by taking command of the General Staff of the Warsaw Pact Forces, he will establish, with the most exemplary rigour, the right of the national representations within the Warsaw Pact to a direct participatory use of the concept of their commitment in the whole of the Eastern European "socialist front". This included the emergence of a permanent state of conflict with the proponents of the doctrine of an exclusively Soviet command of the Warsaw Pact, or one that would have granted only formal participation status to other staff delegations.

This situation is paradoxically reminiscent of the fierce battles waged by *Obergruppenführer* Berger, who, as the man in charge of the non-German European fighters in the Waffen SS, refused – and he was not the only one to do so – to accept any German preponderance of command or status with regard to the soldiers, NCOs, officers and general officers of the Waffen SS, officers and general officers of the Waffen SS, and, also, as to German ideological-doctrinal exclusivity in the 'shaping of the new post-war grandcontinental European order' (on this subject, see Hans Werner Neulen, *An deutscher Seite Internationale Freiwillige von Wehrmach und Waffen* SS, Universitas, Munich 1985).

It is a fact, I believe, that the activist usefulness of these cross-references, of these political-historical transversals whose impact sheds light and teaches in depth, cannot be sufficiently tested. In this respect, let us remember the dramatic and more than singular conditions that were those of the setting up of the French strategic nuclear deterrent force by General de Gaulle, conditions that provoked – and required the emergence, perhaps irremediable, of an immense fracture within the French Army, thus mortally wounded, and for a very long time to come, by the dark and dubious after-effects of the "Algerian affair". Played out on the edge of the abyss, and at what paroxysms of entrapment, the elusive "Algerian affair" by which, the "objective reasons" requiring it at that time – "it's take it or leave it, right then and there", General de Gaulle said, as if hallucinated, to Pierre Joxe – it was imperative that the French strategic nuclear deterrent force be put in place, and that it be put in place *in good time*.

Strange and disturbing is the significant analogy between the "plane crash" that caused the disappearance of General Georges Ailleret, himself a tragic actor in the "Algerian affair" before becoming the super-patron of the French strategic nuclear deterrent force, and the "plane crash" that caused the disappearance – for the reasons we have just mentioned – of Marshal S. S. Biriousov, super-patron of Soviet intercontinental warfare ballistic missiles.S. Biriousov, superpresident of the ballistic missiles of the Soviet intercontinental war. The comparison is obligatory, and its meaning more than obvious.

Any army that is not, very fundamentally, a "secret armed organisation", or, if we want to go even further, a Secret Armed Organisation, is not a real army, nor can it in any way be the body of a destiny in arms, the embodiment of a metahistorical destiny, of a *predestination*. Every truly great army is an Order, and a Secret Order.

Sowing and Harvesting

Since the death of Leonid Brezhnev, the internal situation in the USSR has been evolving in an increasingly accelerated spiral, which some also consider to be increasingly unpredictable. With the rise of Mikhail Gorbachev to power, a rise that was singularly resilient and hardly ever took place without clashes or hidden breakage, things seem to have entered a phase that can now be considered final: what is being undone in the Soviet world will never be done again, while what seems to be being done with force and continuity risks being undone at any moment. Just as in October 1917, world history is changing, world history is being renewed, revolutionarily forged in Russia. But in a direction that now risks being totally opposed to the changes that occurred in 1917. A direction that only St. Maximilian Kolbe could have foreseen, and of which the Catholic Church had held the formidable, inconceivable secret since the year of the Marian apparitions of Fatima, in Portugal, apparitions that took place precisely in 1917. It is known that in one of his great mystical visions, St. Maximilian Kelbe had seen "the statue of the Virgin Mary, radiant, placed on the highest tower of the Kremlin", and that on July 13, 1917, the Virgin Mary had appeared to him in the form of a statue. On 13 July 1917, the Virgin Mary had told the young visionary of Fatima, Lucia dos Santos, that, subject to certain mystical demands, demands which it would be up to the Catholic Church alone to bring to full fruition when the day came, "Russia will be converted, and Peace will win out in the end".

And I also intend to quote Jacques Vergès' testimony here: "If the roots hold, no hope is lost. Look at Russia and see how, after sixty years of the Gulag, the slavophile and Christian themes retain their strength. Russia's mission will always be to defend Europe against the Asian cultural revolution''.

Now the USSR is changing, and will definitely change. A change, as we have just said, which, from now on, risks being accomplished more or less quickly, and in a more or less tumultuous way, but, in any case, in a different direction, if not totally opposed to the one taken, in October 1917, by the revolutionary movement from which the USSR then emerged, and which had to install the USSR in the ''new destiny'' that it so tragically imposed on itself and the world.

Can we already foresee the first course of the change that the USSR is currently preparing to take in its great political and, in the long run, metapolitical turn, the configurations of rupture and counter-establishment, or even what it will be appropriate to consider, one day, as its own identity?

The avowed aim of our present study is no different. In fact, it is the very data of the problem, thus defined, that predetermine, prospectively, the only answer. An answer whose name can only be that of a New Destiny.

In the more or less long term, but from now on, without waiting too much longer, the "new USSR", the USSR of the "final turn" of its destiny, will be – will have to become – exactly what the Secret Order – what we have just called, here, the Secret Order – will want it to be, to come to be. I mean the Secret Order instructed, within the Red Army, by the "polar line" of the "basic geopolitical groups" that Gral. Col. S. M. Chtemenko, and by what was hiding behind it after having followed – supported – the "grand continental line" of I. V. Stalin.

What this New Destiny of the USSR, and hence of the entire future "socialist bloc" of the East, will be made of, and how it will be made, of which it will have to be both the outcome and the abysmal metahistorical justification, is beginning to appear, at present, to let itself be surprised under the spectral illumination of the doctrine of the Secret Order acting, having acted, since the years 1934–1936, in the underground infrastructure of the Red Army and, from the Red Army, mobilising – and, today, in an increasingly *exposed* manner – the political, historical and economic totality of the USSR and of the "Soviet State" invested from within.

Thus, when Marshal N. V. Ogarkov, then chief of the General Staff of the USSR, called for – and tried to impose the doctrine of – the "integral militarisation" and the "general and permanent mobilisation" of the industrial production apparatus and of the Soviet economy as a whole, the very small number of those who are said to be "in the know" – a "very small group" present, and confidentially at work in the USSR as well as in Eastern and Western Europe – had not failed to understand that the "Secret Order" was about to go on the final offensive. Hence, almost immediately, the dismissal of Marshal N. V. Ogarkov, who temporarily – but should we not rather say subversively – returned to the shadows, waiting for the next step. Because the time, one would have to believe, had not yet come for this "final offensive" nor, above all, for what it would imply and make irreversible on the still untried plan of the great Soviet politico-military strategies renewed by the open resumption of the Eurasian continental line. As usual, those who are in the greatest hurry lose nothing to wait for the final ripening of the times, their *fatal ripening*.

However, the very burning question for us today, indeed the *only question*, is whether Marshal N. V. Ogarkov is the successor, at the head of the Secret Order of the Red Army, of Gral. Col. S. M. Chtemenko? I am strongly tempted to think so, and to proceed accordingly.

And this is the reason why I would like to point out that, in France, at the present time, only two specialists seem to have understood, or at least really glimpsed, the true dimensions, political or otherwise, of Marshal N. V. Ogarkov's transcendental career. These two specialists in the USSR are Alexandre Adler, the official sovietologist of *Libération*, and, much less widely known perhaps but no less wise, Pierre de Villemarest, whom we must follow as closely as possible.

Although he had nothing to report on information of a reserved nature, everything that Pierre de Villemarest wrote in his work on the GRU on the power approach attributable to Marshal N. S. Ogarkov must be of particular interest to us, in a way that I must consider to be of primary importance: the most urgent counter-strategic advance of our own action is, at this moment, directly challenged.

Pierre de Villemarest :

The man who most contributed new dimensions to Soviet strategy, from the mid-sixties, but especially in the last ten years, was Marshal Nikolai V. Ogarkov, whom Marshal Zakharov had taken under his protection shortly after Leonid Brezhnev came to power. Ogarkov, whom Marshal Zakharov had taken under his protection shortly after Leonid Brezhnev came to power. For about twenty years the KGB had had its own disinformation service, which was raised to the status of a department in 1969. Thanks to Ogarkov, the GRU staff had its own department from 1967. Under the name (at the time) of the thirteenth directorate of the high staff, it worked in permanent consultation with the relevant GRU office. Ogarkov was the man who, in the weeks leading up to the paratroopers' intervention at Prague airport and the onslaught of armour that surrounded Czechoslovakia, was able to blind the West to Soviet preparations. This was because he circulated false and contradictory information to Western governments from sources believed to be reliable, and because in the hours leading up to the invasion he managed to jam NATO's radar. Four years later, when the American and Soviet delegations signed the Salt I agreements, the man standing next to Brezhnev was neither the Prime Minister, nor the Chief of Staff, nor a member of the Politburo, but General N. V. Ogarkov, who thus seemed to endorse with his technicality these peaceful intentions. Brezhnev's irony towards the smiling and relaxed American delegation. Honour for Ogarkov who was so good at luring Washington during these negotiations that he was promoted to Marshal of the USSR and appointed Chief of the General Staff.

Additional remark by Pierre de Villemarest: "It is true that, according to our sources at the Pentagon, Henry Kissinger, although not very specialised in armaments, wanted to discuss alone, without American technicians, with those of the USSR, in the final phase of these negotiations. Ogarkov's work was greatly facilitated by this.

And Pierre de Villemarest adds: "Marshal Ogarkov has been, for twenty-two years, the grand master of *maskirovka*, i.e. the art of disinforming the West on the strategic intentions of the USSR, through a thousand channels of which the officers and agents of influence of the GRU are the vectors throughout the world. It should be noted that Marshal S. F. Akhromeiev, current Chief of the General Staff (since 1984), was his successor in 1974 at the Directorate of Military Disinformation.

On the other hand, Pierre de Villemarest notes that Marshal N. V. Ogarkov was personally behind the creation of the Soviet special operational forces, the black commandos of the *Spetsnaz*.

Pierre de Villemarest :

Nikolai Ogarkov is above all the inventor of a theory that revolutionised the art of Soviet warfare. It is essential to know the principle. It directly involved the GRU through the use of its special units, called *Spetsnaz*, which existed in each of the forty-one land divisions and in the form of naval brigades. On Ogarkov's initiative, operational manoeuvre groups appeared, which were sets of highly mobile units, including these new air assault brigades, joined to the airborne forces of the usual framework, which decoupled the Soviet armed forces' capacity for in-depth action. The *Spetsnaz* brigades are intended to dive, just before the H-hour of D-Day, far behind the adversary's borders, in the heart of its territory, on the vital points of its economy, its transmissions, its defence, its road, rail and air communications, its energy production or reserves. All the motorised infantry and armoured divisions were transformed into extremely flexible attack units, capable of autonomous operations. Helicopters have been integrated into these assault forces. Everything is planned, designed, prepared for surprise warfare, in close coordination with the *Spetsnaz* units which, projected behind the borders (up to 500 kilometres), are divided into intelligence groups, sabotage groups and intervention groups against human targets; possibly dangerous civilian and military authorities".

And further on: "The *Sptesnaz* undergo continuous training, and are sent on temporary stays in the countries that would be assigned to them in the event of a conflict... and under various covers: sports, cultural, trade union or tourism missions. They were hosted by 'sleeper' agents, recruited long ago, not to spy, but to serve as guides on D-Day. This is reflected in Soviet writings by texts such as that of General Yuri Ya. Kirchin:

Within the capitalist and developing countries, forces will fight against their governments, and to the extent of their means, assist the socialist coalition in the war.

And to conclude: "These texts date from 1987. Colonel Henri Paris, in *Stratégique*, insisted on this problem: "Based in a general way on the offensive, and more particularly on the offensive in depth, the Soviet air-land concept leads to the abolition of any notion of continuous front". It is the GRU, in particular its fifth directorate, which plans and plans the secret means of support for this offensive in the world, the directorate in question having under its permanent responsibility the *Spetsnaz* distributed in each of the sixteen military land districts and each of the main fleets. It also has similar brigades, directly under the orders of the head of the directorate, for punctual intervention at the request of the chief of the general staff".

Things being what they are – and even more so, things *being what they are – it* seems to me to be imperatively urgent and necessary that we ourselves should devote, in the shortest possible time, in-depth research, research of immediate counter-strategic operational use on all the problems polarised by the personal politico-military situation which is, which must be, at present, that of Marshal N. V. Ogarkov, the situation, also, of the evolution and the active states of his doctrines and the positions which emerge from them to act-act, for the moment, in a rather singular way. V. Ogarkov's personal politico-military situation, a situation, also, of the evolution and of the active states of his doctrines and of the positions which emerge from them to act-act, for the moment, in a rather singularly confidential way, and even too confidential for it not to be, by this very fact, significant of an *operational intention in progress* – both in the USSR, where Marshal N. S. Ogarkov seems to be taking over from Gral. Col. S. M. Chtemenko at the head of the "Secret Order" of the Red Army, as well as within the socialist bloc of the East and, by way of dialectical imposition, even within the lines of our own camp, reduced, from now on, to the sub-continental space of Western Europe alone.

Now, what is this *operative intention in progress*, which we have come to speak about here, by bringing to its ultimate and most actual conclusion our investigation into the real activities of Marshal N. S. Ogarkov? For it is powerfully to be remembered that, after his forced dismissal-or supremely *arranged*, so goes the maskirovka-from the General Staff of the Red Army, Marshal N.S. Ogarkov was entrusted-or he demanded to be entrusted-with the direction of the "theatre of operations" in the West, in other words, with the active responsibility for the plans and the command of any possible Soviet enterprise of penetration and politico-military investment of Western Europe.

Now, given the balance of forces thus challenged by any possible Soviet politico-military commitment in the direction of Western Europe, this commitment, projected in the next few years and considered from the sole Soviet point of view, could not objectively be posed in any other way than in the form and in the terms of the *resultant theatre* of a combined sub-continental manoeuvre with nuclear cover in principle.

Nuclear cover, in fact, imperiously non-active, or very partially active at the tactical level only, nuclear cover, therefore, exclusively *of principle*, and combined manoeuvre comprising, on the one hand, a sub-continental penetration operation of avant-garde, in charge of the *Spetsnaz* strategic intervention groups and, on the other hand, and at the same time, an investment operation, The latter was entrusted to the armoured forces who were called upon to define, by their very march, not so much the "front line" – there would be none, there could be no "front line" to speak of – but the political-administrative advance of the European sub-continental "normalisation" that was taking place.

I would add that the combined strategy – breaking through, penetrating the lines and overthrowing in depth at the charge of the special strategic forces, investing and securing the territory by the deployment of the shock tanks – conceived by Marshal N. V. Ogarkov for the coming appropriation, for the "normalisation" of the Soviet continental predestination space, has already been tried and tested on a smaller scale. Ogarkov for the future appropriation, for the "normalization" of the space of Soviet continental predestination, has already been tried and tested on a smaller scale, and in Czechoslovakia and Afghanistan – let us remember the dazzling capture of Prague by the *Spetsnaz*, their performance in Kabul – and each time – already under the direct command – albeit quite covert – of Marshal N.V. Ogarkov himself

It also seems to me that we must do great justice to the inspired insistence with which Pierre de Villemarest endeavours to define the eminent ministry, in the politico-military ideology of the great Soviet continental strategies, of the operational disinformation apparatuses in charge of the GRU, whose special tasks are echoed right up to the level of the General Staff of the Red Army. And also for not having failed to impose, in his book on the GRU, the violent illumination that was necessary to uncover the fundamental and, strictly speaking, decisive responsibilities of Marshal N. V. Ogarkov in the doctrinal, operational and command establishment of the great strategies of Soviet offensive disinformation: at the end of the day, isn't the "master of the *maskirovka*" of today the "master of the world" of the years to come?

Guy Debord: ''Secrecy dominates the world, and first of all as the secret of domination''. And also: ''Where disinformation is *named*, it does not exist. Where it exists, it is not named''.

However, in order to provide these scenarios with their overall framework of validity, certain political conditions of state would have to be predetermined on the Western European side, conditions which, first and foremost, would have to be such as to exclude any slide towards *a state of war* in the conventional sense of the term, a state of war arising from the fact of the Soviet politico-military advance and its investment of the European sub-continental space: These political conditions should be able to concede to the subcontinental advance of Soviet special forces the status of an enterprise of 'normalisation', very exclusively, and the major doctrinal difficulty lies in the need to define the situation in which the differentiation of the 'state of war' and that of 'normalisation' would be exhibited as obligatory, obvious and certain. In other words, as accepted by all parties involved, and accepted as such.

However, and especially *in anticipation of events,* the definition of the political conditions that could concede the Red Army's western advance a status of 'normalisation' is itself an integral part of the concept of Soviet continental investment of the West European subcontinent and, as such, constitutes an 'operational secret' defended by the offensive strategies of the great Ogarkovian *maskirovka*.

The establishment – I venture to say – of the conditions that could – and should – grant – I mean impose – the Soviet continental investment in Western Europe a status of "normalisation" excluding the "state of war", established in great secrecy, bears the operational code name of *Sowing and Harvesting* (or *Posev* i *Jatva)*.

Is the operational secret of *Sowing and Harvesting* penetrable? I think so. Let us say, briefly, that, practising ourselves the ways of approach, of reversal and of dialectical counter-investment of the problems solicited, dialectical ways usually followed by the soviet politico-military thought, we believe that we have been able to determine that the *Sowing and Harvesting* operation will have to watch over and provide for the underground implementation, of a vast situation of imposition – of self-imposition – and of revolutionary surge, of Trotskyite-cosmopolitan leftist orientation, a crisis situation destined to "spread" in order to totally – irrevocably – destabilise, to totally *disintegrate* the political and social space of the countries of Western Europe. Thus, calling for a kind of 'May 1968' of European sub-continental dimensions. But this time, of course, in a completely opposite sense to that of May 1968.

Reversal, therefore, and counter-investment of the structures of the Trotskyite-cosmopolitan leftist operation of May 1968 which, at that time, had attempted – on behalf of the occult centre that we know – to bring down the Gaullist regime in power in France and, From France, the movement tried to spread to other Western European countries, including, for reasons that we may suspect, the countries opening up to the Mediterranean.

Guy Debord again: "The most important thing is the most hidden. Nothing, for twenty years, has been covered with so many ordered lies as the history of May 1968. Useful lessons have nevertheless been drawn from a few demystified studies on these days and their origins; but this is the secret of the State.

The Amtorg, in the heart of Wall Street

The best chapters of Pierre de Villemarest's book on the GRU, such as *Les années Berzine (1924–1935), Et puis le désastre (The* Berzine *Years)*, are those that deal with Soviet infiltration of the world of economy and industry, trade unions, university and culture, political power, intelligence and diplomacy, in the United States and Great Britain, and above all between the two World Wars: It is a pitiless account of an unprecedented social catastrophe, the aftereffects of which are still being perpetuated today, and which continues to measure the putrefactive grip of the black cancer of treason that a society doomed to perdition has invented and maintained in its midst, a black cancer of treason produced and carried by the congenital cretinism of a decadent, irredeemably degenerate social class. Darkness infiltrates through those who call it.

Dennis Wheatley's extraordinary novel, *Toby Jugg the Possessed*, just published (Paris, 1988) by Nouvelles Éditions Oswald (Neo), should be read urgently, and to the second or even third degree: The revelations concerning this *black cancer* make this great and little-known book the ardent breviary of all those who find themselves called upon to venture along the forbidden and dangerous frontiers where politics confronts metapolitics, where the putrefactions of historical and social decadence, even if they are best disguised and best concealed from the untrained eye, meet the chasms inhabited by *other darknesses*.

The special documentation gathered and produced by Pierre de Villemarest on the subject of Marxist infiltrations – or so-called Marxist infiltrations, which amounts to the worst – at work in the folds and folds of shadow and permanent betrayal of a certain Anglo-Saxon society that has long been in agony, I must also point out the excellent quality of the reference works that Pierre de Villemarest constantly sends to support his denunciation and uninterrupted updating.

I will cite, for example, and among many others, *The Climate of Treason*, by Andrew Boyle, Hodder and Stoughton, London, 1979, *The Storm Petrels*, by Gordon Brook-Shepherd, Ballantine Books, New York, 1977, *Kennwort: Direktor*, by Heinz Uhne, Fischer Verlag, Frankfurt, 1970, *Der Angriff*, by Graf Ranz Huyn, Verlag Fritz Molden, Munich, 1987, *Wall Street and the Bolchevik Revolution*, by A.C. Sutton, Arlington House, New York, 1974, *Mole*, by William Hood, Ballantine Books, New York, 1982, *The Grand Design of Egon Bahr*, by Walter Hahn, in *Orbis*, 1973, and *Brandt and the destruction of Nato*, by Stefan Possony, Heinz Tirnrnermann, Walter Hahn, in Foreign Affaire Publishing Co Ltd, London, 1973.

This is a formidable sample, a front-line sample of a literature of testimony if not confession, engaged in the demystification of the criminal trials of an era singularly devoid of trials, and all the more edifying, this sample, because it might well contain something like a sub-message reserved for the attention of a few, and not the least.

But, on the other hand, can we ignore the fact that powerful obstacles often prevent us from accepting the political analyses produced by Pierre de Villemarest? Does he tell us that General Heinrich Müller – former head of the Gestapo and, according to reserved sources to which Pierre de Villemarest seems to fully subscribe, a covert agent of the GRU – who had taken refuge in Central America after the war and then in South America, had been kidnapped in 1955 "by a Czech team" and brought back to Prague, "where his life has since depended on the results of his work for Moscow"? Or, also, that, besides, of course, Gral. Col. S. M. Chtemenko, the group of general officers and admirals who had to follow a committed line of action against the intolerable permanent conspiracy of the Trotskyite-cosmopolitan concentration in place within the Soviet central power – and there, Pierre de Villemarest citing the names of Marshals Vasilyevsky, Koniev, Govorov ("chief of the military police"), and Admirals Kuznetzov and Levchenko – were thus only manifesting the "anti-Semitic background of a fraction of the high staff"?

All of these things are of the highest, most certain interest to us, *the interpretation of* which, however, calls for doctrinal choices which may or may not be the same for some and for others, for Pierre de Villemarest himself, for example, and for ourselves, who hunt in many other undergrowth and with other packs.

On the other hand, I would like to repeat, when Pierre Villemarest turns to the informational dismantling of Marxist penetrations in Great Britain, in the United States – see the chapter, quite excellent, "Businessmen disguised as Red Cross humanists", or the elucidation node titled "The Amtorg, at the heart of Wall Street" – we can only say how much we respect his work, his active lucidity and his unfailing vigilance over so many years; we can only say, too, how much we hope that our efforts will one day be directed in such a way that they act in concert and, perhaps, with all the means that are due to them.

A final word. In carrying out what I called the "spectral analysis" of his book on the GRU, I had begun by noting Pierre de Villemarest's half-confessed inclination – or something like it – for some of the national, traditionalist and military modalities *of* the *Abwehr,* which, moreover, are perpetuated, which, moreover, are perpetuated, as the "profession of the lord" obliges.

The fact is that the anti-Marxist work of the Abwehr was, and probably still is, an irreplaceable achievement, both internally and externally: if only mythologically, I see it as a guarded pass for some and for others, a guarded pass in the high mountains.

Pierre de Villemarest quotes, from a personal source, Litvinov's advice to Berzin and his deputies, namely: "If one knows how to infiltrate those who are themselves infiltrating British society from above, one will be able to penetrate it with them, while benefiting from their cover". Together, let's return this strong and brilliant advice from a top-class specialist to the sender. And, by the way, the very spiral of Dennis Wheatley's cult book, *Toby Jugg the Possessed*, *can be* found here. These things hold together.

The ice is broken

And all this once said, established and, how to say, *triggered*, not to forget, in no case not to forget that the so long research undertaken by us starting from the book of Pierre de Villemarest on the GRU, that the "spectral analysis" to which we have just subjected this book remain tended by an extremely precise goal, an extremely precise goal which, him, is located well beyond this book itself: Now, our goal being that of giving an immediately reliable definition of the ultimate meaning and the fundamental secret of the current changes of state in progress in Soviet Russia, a definition thus operationally ready to be used on the ground, a counter-strategic definition, we have tried to find, to invent, precisely from Pierre de Villemarest's book on the GRU, a line of departure for the implementation of a "work of ensemble" intended to lead us to this definition which, as such, should also carry a decision to be taken in terms of direct action. A definition whose urgency and necessity seem to me to be self-evident, and even tragically obvious. A decision whose time will also be that of our own destiny, in the vanguard of what we have just called the New Destiny and of its greatest future metapolitical battles. A New Destiny commanding the current future of the visible and invisible history of the USSR and, therefore, of the most profound history to come of the Great Eurasian Continent.

This definition, implicitly carrying a great counter-strategic decision, immediate and even as if already in action, of which all the current or dialectically still to come deployments constitute the most urgent task of our own direct commitment today, this definition conveying the terrible secret of the New Destiny and of a new beginning of the Great Eurasian Continent, can we affirm that we have established it, are we able to claim that we are already using it, that it is already informing the current states of our work? And, if so, what is this counter-strategic definition already in action, and whose action is already going to change the face of the world and the very meaning of the history of the Europe of the End, our history, our destiny and our secret mission, our dreamed tragedy and our tragedy in arms?

What is this definition, I will say it, exhaustively, during the next meeting of our own "basic geopolitical group", a meeting which will be very shortly convened for this purpose, and where our group, as "basic geopolitical group number 1" will be called to assume, to proclaim itself offensively as the counter-strategic revolutionary epicentre of the great movement of European and continental awakening that is coming, a seismic movement whose setting in motion will have to mark the metahistorical passage of our present times towards the times of the New Destiny.

I must therefore limit myself to suggesting today that this definition is called upon to dialectically bring together, oppose, integrate and surpass, in the direction of an as yet undetermined future and in an increasingly active, and perhaps soon even increasingly paroxysmal, manner, the two major polarities of the inner geopolitical field, of the unitary geopolitical concept governing the current identity and future of the Great Eurasian Continent.

So what are these two inner polarities today, these two over-activated polarities of the Eurasian continental field whose resolution is already calling for the abysmal secret of its New Destiny?

—On the one hand, the movement set in motion, in the USSR and within the Eastern "socialist bloc", by Mikhail Gorbachev and by what Mikhail Gorbachev is in the process of becoming the "absolute concept", and this movement of the Gorbachevian petition for change, of self-transmutation, having itself to face, in a confrontation of dramatically confidential conditions, on the summits of the *maskirovka*, the "Secret Order" of the Red Army and its "polar groups" at the disposal of Marshal N.V. Ogarkov who, since 1984, had been plunged into "action under cover" ("sent back into the shadow of the hierarchy", said Pierre de Villemarest).

—On the other hand, Western Europe in its most current states, where Federal Germany has been initiating, since October 1988, its "new grand-continental project" in the direction of the USSR, a project inspired by Hans Dietrich Genscher and by what shelters behind him, while, at the same time, Western Europe has to deal with the equivocal and decadent positions, essentially subversive and occultly anti-European positions of France, which is once again a prisoner of its own "internal enemy", and which is fought by "covert action", by the high clandestine work of a certain "Gaullism of the end", still without a face or controllable identity.

In any case, it is now a given that the visit of West German Chancellor Helmut Kohl to Moscow in October 1988, and the immediately grand-continental doctrinal, economic and geopolitical overtures made by this visit, take on the decisive value of an "initiatory threshold": Whether Moscow believes that it should accept the West German overtures or whether it thinks that it should not accept them, the fundamental question has thus been made available to all the great diplomatic and politico-strategic debates to come between the proponents of the inner destinies of the Great Continent, and there is *no turning back*.

It is known that the "new grand-continental project" of the Federal Republic of Germany, presented in Moscow in October 1988 by Chancellor Helmut Kohl, a project inspired by his Foreign Minister, Hans Dietrich Genscher, had already been presented by the latter personally in February 1987 at the International Economic Forum in Davos, Switzerland.

And let's say that, summarising in the extreme, the speech presenting the "new grand-continental project" of the Federal Republic of Germany made by Hans Dietrich Genscher in Davos in February 1987 could fit into the grid of the six doctrinal proposals that follow, doctrinal proposals that, one day from now on perhaps the closest, risk becoming so many theses of direct geopolitical action, immediately operational:

1) We are fully prepared, already ready, to enter into wide-ranging economic cooperation with the Soviet Union, which will help it to modernise its economy, develop this huge country with its great natural resources, while helping us too, by providing jobs and increasing our growth.

2) We are also ready to adopt, to make our own the concept of a "common European home" put forward by Mikhail Gorbachev, and to make this home, with the support of the Soviet Union, a truly common home, a home in which all the inhabitants would live as equals, free and at peace, a home in which the wall of separation between those who live in the East and those who live in the West would tend to disappear, and in which human rights would be respected

3) At present, the economic exchanges between East and West are-if one considers the potential in place on both sides-at a surprisingly low level.

For the Federal Republic of Germany, for example, which is CAEN's main trading partner, trade with the East accounts for only 4% of foreign trade.

Eastern Europe thus appears to be an essentially inward-looking trading bloc.

4) Mikhail Gorbachev seems to be well aware of all this. He is aware that in order to modernise his country he needs economic and technical co-operation with the West, business co-operation on a broad basis and, at least for the time being, large credits.

On the other hand, this would open up a huge economic space in the West, a huge opportunity whose mobilisation could be a driving force behind the mobilisation and growth of the entire world economy.

5) It is up to the Federal Republic of Germany to judge today, in a more realistic and less prejudiced way, the new developments in the Soviet Union and the future prospects, the new perspectives for the future that these open up before us and before the whole of the world economy.

It is also the task of the Federal Republic of Germany to ensure that the new developments now taking place in the Soviet Union are not in danger of being mistaken for an outwardly directed propaganda enterprise. It is a question of really taking them for what we already know they cannot not be, of exploring their content and of making immediate use of the beginnings that already exist, already in action, so that from this, and in the first place, we come to a de facto improvement in East-West relations.

6) It is a matter of trusting the sense of the changes being imposed in the Soviet Union by Mikhail Gorbachev. It is a question, therefore, of taking Mikhail Gorbachev at his word, of offering our capital of trust.

For the Federal Republic of Germany, it is now a question of daring to take the side of a great opening to the East and, consequently, and to begin with, to initiate without further delay a movement of economic cooperation on the largest scale with the Soviet Union.

(Hans Dietrich Genscher, [1] February 1987, to the International Economic Forum in Davos, Switzerland. For the text of the entire proceedings of the International Economic Forum in Davos, Swiss federal source. Summary of the speech by Bans Ditrich Genscher, also Swiss federal source).

However, it should not be forgotten that, three months before the Chancellor of the Federal Republic of Germany, Helmut Kohi, was led to present, in Moscow, the de facto overtures constituting the essence of the "new German grand-continental project", Mikhail Gorbachev, for his part, had already taken a position, in July 1988, in Warsaw, on the principle of a Greater Europe bringing together Eastern and Western Europe, a rapprochement in principle accompanied, in addition, by the proposal to bring together a "European Union", In Warsaw, Mikhail Gorbachev had already taken a position on the principle of a Greater Europe bringing together Eastern and Western Europe, a rapprochement in principle accompanied by the proposal to convene a "pan-European summit" in order to "make significant progress in the reduction of conventional armaments in Europe".

Mikhail Gorbachev, in July 1988, in Warsaw: We see in the future a Greater Europe in which East and West would no longer threaten each other with weapons pointed at each other, but which, on the contrary, would find a basis for unprecedented progress in the exchange of goods and work, of experience and knowledge, of people and ideas, a Greater Europe of people who would have learned to see each other as partners in a single vast project and not as antagonists engaged in endless confrontation''.

Thus the doctrinal apparatus is already in a state which, under the cover of what Hans Dietrich Genscher calls the "project of large-scale economic cooperation" between Federal Germany and the Soviet Union, is at least as diversionary as it is self-serving, This project is intended to define and ensure the political and diplomatic implementation of a new German continental grand design acting as a bridgehead for the whole of Western Europe, and to which, for his part, Mikhail Gorbachev, by taking the lead, has not failed to commit himself to welcoming a plenary acceptance, even if, for the time being at least, confined exclusively to the level of a petition of principle. But it is no less obvious and certain that much has already been done, and that a sort of tectonic shift of destiny would seem to have been irreversibly set in motion somewhere in favour of a metahistorical renewal of the grand-continental European idea.

Nevertheless, in order to give substance to the "operational definition" that it is important for us to make emerge from the meaning in action, from the ultimate meaning of the profound changes currently underway in the USSR and from the exposure of the "terrible secret" that governs them from below, we must also take into account, and take into full account, the formidable fields of forces intervening, inexorably, in each of the Western European camps, of Eastern Europe-whose antagonistic polarities-less and less antagonistic, it is already claimed-constitute, at the present time, or reconstitute, rather, the concept and the visionary reality, the project in progress-already in progress, and we have just seen how-of the Greater Europe, the renewed foundation or in the process of renewal of a metahistorical return to the ancient idea of the Great Eurasian Continent.

What, then, are the fields of force, the formidable fields of force that predetermine, from within, the current states of the antagonistic polarities whose double thrust, revealing itself from the new dialectical confrontation of Western and Eastern Europe, goes to reconstitute, to call to life, to renew, the politico-historical concept of the Greater Europe? To answer this overall analytical question, inciting and preconceived, raised by us, *here* and now, with the aim of putting it into action later on, this will be precisely the task of the next meeting of the "basic geopolitical group number 1", whose special mission we have just defined, its mission as the counter-strategic centre of the "great European and continental awakening movement" that is coming, the very movement of the New Destiny.

In the meantime, it seems to me that a certain number of problems need to be raised today, to be tackled preventively, if only to take a step forward in our own current work.

First of all, it is necessary to recognise that Gorbachevian *perestroika* has already liberated two formidable fields of antagonistic forces in the USSR, the paroxysmal rise of which seems to me to be very difficult, if not impossible, to curb. Above all, I would cite the rise of Trotskyism to the light of day.

To recognise, therefore, that the liberation, the sudden unleashing of all the leftist, anti-social and anti-national, "anti-imperial", anarco-nihilist and abjectly "Tolstoyist" relics perpetuating in the deepest sewers of the "dark unconscious of the Russian peoples", The rise of the sewers is currently maintained and subject to an artificial revival as a result of the rehabilitation of Leon Trotsky and hence of Trotskyism and, behind this rehabilitation, by the very process of putting back on the official track the Trotskyistocosmopolitan line against which the Soviet State, according to the Stalinist conception of the term, and supported, in the shadows, by the "Secret Order" of the Red Army, has not ceased to fight for more than half a century, without, however, succeeding – as far as it seems – in neutralising it in a decisive manner, "without return".

Everything happens. In *Pravda* of 9 September 1988, the moron in charge, General Volkogonov, wrote: "In his years of intense activity in the Party (1917–1924), Trotsky had not been an enemy of the revolution, nor of socialism. On the other hand, he was already an enemy of Stalin. We cannot fail to pay tribute to him: unlike many, he did not bow to Stalin's dictatorship.

The element, more than close to Mikhail Gorbachev, which, on his behalf, now controls and supports – or supports at all, and not only on behalf of Mikhail Gorbachev – the rise-political-administrative rise of the Trotskyite-cosmopolitan conspiracy already in place within the Soviet central power – which it must be believed has never quite had to leave its nocturnal summits – is the dreaded and increasingly feared AN. Yakovlev, former USSR ambassador to Canada, at the time of his disgrace and now back in the saddle by the grace of the latter, member of the Central Committee and the Political Bureau and, in the Central Committee, head of the Foreign Affairs Commission.

Now, in Moscow, A. N. Yakovlev is indisputably held to have been, at the time when he was still posted in Ottawa, the "inspired inventor" – and inspired by whom, as we shall see below – of the dialectic of internal change of Soviet power called upon to act through the concepts of *glasnost* and *perestroika,* an acting dialectic on which Mikhail Gorbachev saw himself having to base the "new line" of his own internal and external power. A "new line" of which he wants to be and claims to be the inspirer, and the direct and open inspirer, whereas he is, in fact, and whatever one may say, nothing more than the inspired one in the shadows, in the shadows, I mean, of a secret which, for the moment at least, exceeds him and holds him.

In Ottawa, A. N. Yakovlev had had the opportunity, no doubt prepared at length, to meet frequently and significantly with someone who, an old acquaintance perhaps, for some, actually represented – under the cover of confidential dealings with a Chicago nuclear industrial company – Israel's external interests. This "someone", whose "group skills" had already had to instruct, at other times, the Prague ambassador to Tel Aviv, Dr. David Goldstücker – we have not forgotten that Dr. David Goldstücker had to be the hidden inspirer and architect of the so-called Prague Spring, against which men like Generals S. M. Chtemenko and N.A. K. Kovac had to act on the spot. M. Chtemenko and N.V. Ogarkov – was also, in Ottawa, the covert instructor of ambassador A.N. Yakovlev. It was thus through a direct channel from the same occult centre that had already been involved, through Dr. David Goldstücker, in the manipulations that led, according to the plans, to the so-called Prague Spring, that the ideological-political arrangements for the implementation of the Soviet anti-nationalist and Trotskyite-internationalist "new line", precisely the "new line" that was to emerge through Gorbachevian *perestroika,* were conspiratorially inculcated into the then ambassador A.N. Yakovlev, then posted in Ottawa. As much on the doctrinal level, involving the revival under control of a neo-Trotskyism claimed to be exclusively dialectical, anti-

Stalinist, as on the level of the manoeuvres to be operationally engaged on the spot when the time came, the instruction, in Ottawa, of the present head of the Foreign Affairs Commission of the Central Committee of the Communist Party of the USSR, ambassador A.N. Yakovlev, had therefore been made *from outside, a* fact which I do not think is in any way liable to be withheld.

It seems to me that I can take it for granted that this fact had been, in its time, and especially afterwards, I mean since the return of A.N. Yakovlev to the ultimate spheres of the present Soviet power, powerfully retained, indeed, by the military special services of the Federal Republic of Germany, and one can imagine the way in which the military special services of the Federal Republic of Germany had to be used. Yakovlev in the ultimate spheres of the present Soviet power, was indeed strongly retained by the special military services of the Federal Republic of Germany, and one can imagine the use that will not fail to be made of it, by Bonn, at the most opportune moment for the developments, already in progress, of Hans Dietrich Genscher's "project of large-scale economic cooperation" presented, in Moscow, by Chancellor Helmut Kohl.

However, the emergence of a field of subversive Trotskyite and Trotskyisto-cosmopolitan forces in the current states of Gorbachevian *perestroika* and following the action at the top of the politico-strategic cell instructed, at the level of the Central Committee, by A. N. Yakovlev, must not be considered otherwise than within a front of overall change. Any interpretation that was not carried by the demand for a definition of the whole line of change assumed, today, in the open, by Mikhail Gorbachev, will end up appearing totally random.

For *perestroika*, the movement in progress of *perestroika* itself, has, on the other hand, also liberated, and in a no less significant way than the abscess of Trotskyism and its nebula, the impetuous, irrational and seemingly unstoppable torrents of the "Christ-like soul" of the Russias, and this along a line of emergence that is quite extraordinarily unforeseen. In fact, it is not Orthodoxy that is being carried forward today by the breaking of the dikes, by the tumultuous waters of the Christic rebirth of the Russias, but, in Ukraine and even more so, perhaps, in the Baltic States, Catholicism. Catholicism?

Irrepressible and totally exposed, setting in motion demonstrations of hundreds of thousands of faithful suddenly brought out of the shadows, the Catholic explosion in the Baltic States remains one of the most incomprehensible of all the seemingly incomprehensible things that are happening in the Soviet Union today in the wake of the first earthquakes of Gorbachevian *perestroika*. And what is yet to come will be even more irrationally unpredictable. Unpredictable for all except, at this time, for John Paul II and the Catholic, Apostolic and Roman leadership of the "reverse side of contemporary history", "contemporary history" which, as we know, is now becoming, at the cyclopean gates of the third millennium, a definitively planetary history.

Mikhail Gorbachev said, commenting on the very concrete results of Helmut Kohl's visit to Moscow in October 1988: "The ice is broken", and should we not also see it as a petition of principle concluding the first major stage of the ongoing Gorbachevian *perestroika*? In any case, it is hardly as long as it is still dialectically in the process of becoming that we can hope to understand it, to grasp its inner "terrible secret", but only at the time of its ultimate outcome, "when everything will be done, when everything will be finished" and when the "grand design" of the "Secret Order of the Red Army" will be fully accomplished, and *accomplished in history: It* is not while it is still going on, it is with the arrival of Gorbachevian *perestroika* that its "terrible secret" will be revealed, that the inconceivable will suddenly become history in renewal and the metahistorical threshold of another history, of a "different history". In the times of the history of the end, only the *outcome* counts.

For the moment, the revolutionary – or rather, already trans-revolutionary – process of Gorbachevian *perestroika* serves exclusively the personal struggle of Mikhail Gorbachev, but of Mikhail Gorbachev as the "absolute concept" of *perestroika*, by conveying, on the ground, its implacable dialectical march towards total power. Thus the operational goal of *perestroika* is twofold: to bring Mikhail Gorbachev to total power, and to open up an emergency corridor for the Soviet Union towards the "total cultural revolution" which still conceals its name, towards the great internal transmutation of its economic, technological-industrial and social structures, which alone can still enable it to catch up in the race for planetary domination on which the third millennium is already opening. While, in the shadows, the "Secret Order" of the Red Army watches, inspires and conspires, controls, decides and directs, slows down or accelerates, and makes things happen that must be done underground.

The process of ontological transmutation of the internal organisational structures of the Soviet Union once completed, the "Secret Order" of the Red Army will emerge into the full light of day, the meaning of Soviet power will change, history, the greatest European continental history will find there a new passage towards trans history, a new passage identifying, then, both with the "terrible secret" of Gorbachevian perestroika and with what we, ourselves, called the New Destiny. But nothing will stop this movement now. The ice is broken.

Text of the lecture delivered on 24 February 1989, in Lausanne, to the Board of Directors of the Atlantis Institute for Special Meta-strategic Research (IRMSA)

THE SUPRAHISTORICAL SIGNIFICANCE OF THE MASSACRE OF THE LAST ROMANOVS

> *Mysterious forces are leading you and your people to an inevitable doom.*
>
> Grand Duke Alexander Mikhailovich,
> in a 1917 letter to Emperor Nicholas II.

History, and the concept of dogmatic irrationality

History is impenetrable, and very paradoxically becomes transparent, luminous, only at the final moment when its dogmatic irrationality reaches the paroxysm of mystery, of incomprehensibility, when the suprahistorical powers reputed to be out of reach, "eternal", that lead it occultly let themselves be surprised naked, exhibit themselves temporarily inside its very becoming, a supplicated becoming that they then exalt and dazzle while devastating it in the short term, inflicting irremediable ravages on it. There is an immense inner sun of history, whose approach is both divine and fatal, calcinating, and always alien if not enemy to the tranquil beaches of reason held to be discursive and which, in fact, is never anything more than an acceptable diversion in the face of the abysmal conduct of dogmatic irrationality on the march according to its own plans, inconceivable on the human scale.

What can we still understand, at the present time, of the cyclone of ardent light that was the transcontinental adventure of Alexander the Great, and of the absolutely incomprehensible fact that his cyclopean tomb could have disappeared without a trace? How can we admit, too, that with the dazzling appearance of Frederick II Hohenstaufen there was, for the last time, at the dawn of present times, the declared imperial incarnation, and held to be so, visible and accepted by all, evident, of the divine principle of the *Imperium,* of the Sun God, of the *Sol Invictus* immediately present in history? And the disappearance, in the underground of a certain occult history, of the bloodline of the annihilated Merovingians, *made nothing?* And the miraculous fainting of Louis XVII from the Temple, who emerged from history like a wall that opens up to receive you? What about Adolf Hitler's accession to total, suprahistorical power out of nothing, and both equally dreamlike, the creation of the Third Reich and its disappearance in the flames of the final Gotterdämmerung, in dogmatic irrationality rising to the ultimate summits of history when history itself seemed to be interrupting, if not ending in the darkness of antihistory? For all is mystery acting in darkness, in 'great history' all is dogmatic irrationality at work.

And the bloody expulsion from historical temporality of the very Christian imperial dynasty of the Romanovs will not escape the rule of the mystery of dogmatic irrationality drowning out the visible course of 'great history'. On the contrary.

We shall preside serenely over the destinies of Our Empire, which from now on will be debated only between God and Us", was to declare Emperor Alexander III – the *Mirotvorets*, the "Peacemaker" – when he took power following the terrorist assassination of his father, Emperor Alexander II – the *Osvoboditel*, the "Liberator" – whose highly suspicious democratic inclinations were to lead him to end up, as we have seen, in an orgy of bloodshed and subaltern, manipulative, manipulated violence. The highly subversive machinery intended for the final liquidation of the Romanovs in power had already been reassembled in the eighteenth century: let us not conceal the fact that, in the shadow of their mystically inspired powers, Madame Krudener and her followers had been able to see rightly, and very prophetically, the terrible fire that was about to break out.

On the night of July 16–17, 1918, in Yekaterinburg, in the Urals, Emperor Nicholas II and his entire family were, on orders from Moscow – on orders from V. I. Lenin – bestially murdered by their guards. Was this a bloody but explicable conclusion to the ongoing Communist Revolution? This is what, since then, people on all sides have been trying to make us believe, with an increasingly revealing relentlessness which, instead of hiding, exalts what they want to conceal.

For it is not the case that Emperor Nicholas II and his family were massacred as a necessarily predictable, fateful episode of the Communist Revolution at its most critical, paroxysmal inner moment, but rather that it is the Communist Revolution that – all things considered, in the shadows, obstinately gives itself away as unspeakable – should be seen today as an episode in the subversive battle begun, since the 18th century, against the Romanovs, should rather be looked at, today, as an episode of the battle subversively started, since the XVIIIth century, against the Romanovs, and against the historically established states of the imperial and royal idea in Europe, an idea fundamentally Christological.

The inner workings of the 'special turmoil'

In his *Exile Diary*, Leon Trotsky wrote: "It was not only urgent, but necessary to take the decision to kill the imperial family. The severity of this summary justice showed the world that we would continue our struggle without mercy and stop at nothing. It was necessary to execute the tsar and his family to frighten, horrify and disgust the enemy, but also to shake up our own troops and show them that there was no turning back and that total victory or total destruction lay ahead. But is this really true? Is this how it was supposed to be? No. No, it is absolutely not true, and it is absolutely not the way things had actually happened. Today, after the internal collapse of the Soviet Union and seventy years of communism in Russia and in the world, this change of perspective finally provides the keys to the deep and decisive, final intelligence of the process which had already begun with the so-called French Revolution and which was to lead, after the First World War, to the dismantling of the last three Christian Empires of Europe: the German Empire, the Austrian Empire and the Russian Empire. For it was necessary at all costs to de-Christianise world history, which, in its march, was arriving at the threshold before it had to stop trying to make the suprahistorical light of the Victorious Cross its own.

Who, then, and why? And, on the other hand, how is it that the British Empire was not also swept away by the same "special" turmoil? Apart from the fact that the time for the liquidation of the British Empire is now approaching, it must also be said that if the "special turmoil" which was to bring down the European royalties of divine right – these, as a whole, being heirs to the Roman Empire through the Holy Roman Empire – the British Empire, as well as the deviated, turned around, totally alienated British royalty, had been charged with a very special mission: a mission of high treason and crime, of subversion and perjury, for which they must now, at last, pay the just price, and the terrifying interests that go with it, occult, confidentially hellish. What mission?

None of us, none of those who are engaged in the camp opposed to that of the "Mystery of Iniquity", can ignore what was the infernal game of the Court of St. James in the subterranean setting in motion of the so-called French Revolution and the liquidation in extreme opprobrium and blood of the Bourbons of France, of which London had so well – so badly, one must hear – tried to support the last soubresauts with the only aim of better pushing them back towards the swirling darkness which already held them.

Just as the de facto, direct and total, decisive responsibility for the massacre of the last Romanovs belongs to the liberal scumbag David Lloyd George (1863–1944), who was also the architect of the infernal trap that was the Treaty of Versailles, David Lloyd George who ended up *taking back* – cancelling – the right of political asylum granted – for the sake of form – to the Romanovs, a political asylum negotiated by Kerenski, and who brought the victims of the Yekaterinburg massacre freedom from Communist Russia, freedom, life. It all fits together. Didn't Ramsay McDonald, another despicable scumbag, publicly call Emperor Nicholas II a "blood-stained creature" and even a "common criminal"?

Since the battle of Naseby and the advent of the subversive criminal power following the assassination of King Charles ^{I} (1649), a criminal power exemplified, at that time, by Olivier Cromwell (1599–1658), Britain is indeed nothing but its own corpse, a living corpse, half-living and surviving, but non-living, babbling corpse in the service of the powers of perdition that have chosen to set up their base of occult action there, and which constantly intervenes to nip in the bud any hint of revival, of spiritual and national liberation in Britain on the domestic level, as was seen with the sordid conspiracy knot that forced King Edward VIII to abdicate in 1936 and, even today, by the increasingly intense obstructionism opposed to Prince Charles' ascension to the throne.

The extinction of the Romanov race had a 'precise objective'.

After seventy years of communist terror at home and relentless revolutionary political warfare abroad, after the unexpected – and itself extraordinarily mysterious – collapse of the Soviet Union and the ongoing global conspiracy of communism, that Russia, in its own reality, has remained the same, in terms of geopolitical awareness of its own destiny and at the final level of world history in progress, is a kind of miracle, the communist nightmare now appearing as an increasingly incomprehensible, useless and fundamentally perverse episode, belonging to an otherworldly, other-reality, other-historical place, devoid of any intelligible meaning in the whole of history currently in progress.

For geopolitics, the vital projection of being, will always prevail over the aberrant alienations that non-being and its powers of intervention, of active and secret subversion, will try, until the end, to impose on history, on 'great history'. History can sometimes be alienated. Geopolitics never does.

Does the hallucinatory genocide of the Russian people, inaugurated and as if announced by the massacre of Nicholas II and his followers, thus become, in the end, the immense holy holocaust through which the Russian people succeeded in warding off the forces of chaos and nothingness which, coming – called, invoked, summoned – from outside Russia and outside this world itself, had been able to subversively install themselves within it – as had already happened, perhaps on another level, as we have just said? from outside Russia and from outside this world itself, had been able to subversively install themselves in its midst-as had already been done, perhaps on another level, as we've just said, in Great Britain since the assassination of King Charles ^{I} in the 17th century-to make it lose itself, and thus make it the thing through which the whole world would have to lose itself. But the plan failed: there was finally something stronger than the protocol implemented by the instances of subversive action outside this world and its history, by the elusive designers of this hidden plan, and now the great backlash will soon come, which will sweep away everything, and irrevocably, so that justice will be done and being and life, restored to their ontologically regal rights, will be able to give themselves another historical beginning. It was through Russia that everything was almost lost; it is also through Russia that everything will be called to new life after the fading of the existing darkness.

The mystery of the communist massacre of Emperor Nicholas II and those of his blood, the last of the Russian imperial stock, should be placed in this apocalyptic and vigilante perspective. Mystery? What mystery? Everything in it seems to be certain, and certain even of the facts that are now fully known- or that have been arranged to be held as such-of the massacre that took place on the night of July 15–16, 1918, on the ground floor of the "house of special purpose" in Yekaterinburg. But, as far as we can tell, nothing is less certain.

Thus, revelations must and will be made about the abysmal implications that shed a spectral, infinitely disturbing light on all the undertakings that presided over the relentless, careful and concerted pursuit of the plans to liquidate the Russian Imperial family, in its last reigning nucleus and also in the perpetuation of certain immediate blood ties or significant relationships. Revelations destined to completely change the angle from which the facts of the horror that bloodied the walls of the mysterious Ypatiev house in Yekaterinburg for ever – beyond space, beyond time – must be considered.

Pierre Lorrain, in *L'assassinat de Nicolas II*, Éditions Fleuve Noir, Paris, 1994: "On 18 July, the day after the Yekaterinburg tragedy, in Alapaievsk, the Grand Duchess Ella, the sister of the Empress, the Grand Duke Serge Mikhailovich, and the Princes John, Constantine and Igor, three of the sons of the Grand Duke Constantine, were murdered in a horrible manner. They were thrown alive into a well where some grenades were thrown. Not all of them died on the spot. The agony of the survivors lasted several days."

As Pierre Lorrain so aptly put it, *the extermination of the imperial house had a precise objective.*

Terrifyingly, the house of the engineer Nicolas Ypatiev, in Yekaterinburg, requisitioned and converted, on the orders of V. I. Lenin, into a "house of special destination" – and we have seen what this "special destination" was, the liquidation on the spot, and the supposedly definitive end, of the Yekaterinburg family. Lenin, into a "house with a special purpose" – and we have seen what this "special purpose" was, the liquidation on the spot, and the supposedly definitive end, of the Romanov dynasty by the physical elimination of its last reigning representatives – bore the same name, and was it not in fact for a decided purpose, of a secretly symbolic nature, as another Ipatiev house, which, in 1613, had housed the birth of the Romanov dynasty.

It was in the Ipatiev Monastery in Kostroma – a town near the confluence of the Kostroma and Volga rivers – that Mikhail Feodorovich Romanov was crowned Emperor of all the Russias in 1613. However, it is worth noting that only five years before the bloody events in the "house of special purpose" in Yekaterinburg, within the walls of the Ypatiev House, Emperor Nicholas II and the entire imperial family had taken part in the solemn ceremonies in the Ypatiev Monastery in Kostorama to mark the three hundredth anniversary of the birth of the Romanov dynasty.

But things are getting out of hand. From Tobolsk, Emperor Nicholas II and Empress Alexandra Feodorovna, already prisoners, arrived in Yekaterinburg and were immediately taken to the "house of special destination" on 30 April 1918. A month later, they were joined by Tsarevich Alexis and the four grand duchesses, Olga, Tatiana, Marie and Anastasia, aged twenty-two, twenty-one, nineteen and seventeen respectively. The imperial family was accompanied by Doctor Botkin and three servants (Troup, the Emperor's footman, Demidova, the Empress's maid, and Kharitonov, the cook).

Prince Vasily Delgoruki, the Emperor's aide-de-camp, had not even been taken to the "house of special destination". Separated from the group of the imperial family on arrival at the Yekaterinburg station, he was led out of the city by the Chekist Grigory Nikulin and shot in the back of the head. Other members of the imperial family were later to be liquidated in a similar manner.

The special operational arrangements personally set up under cover by V. I. Lenin included, in Moscow itself, Jacob Sverdlov, Chairman of the Executive Committee of the Soviets, and the confidential liaison officer Alexei Akimov, attached to V. I. Lenin in the Kremlin. On site in Yekaterinburg, the permanent surveillance group assigned to guard the imperial family housed in the Ypatiev house included the Ural military commissar and member of the Bolshevik Presidium of the region Isaiah Goloshchekin, alias "Filip", Jacob Jurovski, deputy head of the Ural Cheka and commander of the "house of special destination", Piotr Ermakov, military commissar of the city of Yekaterinburg, as well as the basic Chekists Mikhail Medvedev, Serguei Lioukhanov, Grigori Nikouline, Pavel Medvedev and Alexei Kabanov (the latter, a former close guard of the Emperor). Eight other Chekists were to be part of the firing squad, including six foreign deserters, so-called "Latvians" (among them, it is still claimed, the Hungarian Imre Nagy, future Prime Minister of post-war communist Hungary in 1945, who was himself executed after the anti-Soviet uprising in 1956).

Nine of the victims were thrown into a disused mine shaft at the place called the Four Brothers and then de-identified with acid, buried permanently in a pit, covered with railway ties. Separated from the group, the tsarevitch Alexei and one of the grand duchesses – presumably Anastasia – were to be cremated, and their ashes scattered in the mud.

It was also carefully concealed that, on the fatal night, the four young duchesses had been raped while still alive by their murderers, and that, once dead, their remains had undergone a number of specific mutilations. These profanations were at once singularly bestial and highly learned, and in addition to their criminal obscenity, they also had a very obvious ritual dimension, implying the direct instructions, if not the presence in the shadows, of a higher necromantic responsibility, with a non-human and certainly anti-human duplicity. One dares not imagine what must have happened there that *night*. Dreaded black cosmic invocations, *arrivals*.

The report on the massacre of the imperial family reached Moscow on the evening of 17 July, and V. I. Lenin was informed of it immediately in the Kremlin, in the middle of the Council of Ministers, which he had interrupted for a few moments so that Jacob Sverdlov could briefly announce the news. Then V. I. Lenin demanded that the work on the school inoculations in the Moscow region be resumed as if nothing had happened, since the news of the Emperor's physical destruction – the fate of his family was still being concealed – was in fact no longer of any importance.

When, in fact, it was, for V. I. Lenin, the very moment of his *supreme realisation*. His great subterranean necromantic mission, his entire life as a marout, a living dead inhabited by an occult entity, the reason why he himself had been foretold of the task, removed from the living, plunged into the mystery of the series of abysmal metamorphoses leading him to become progressively something more and more non-human, an entity lodging its centre of gravity in a reality outside of this world, directly dependent on the Superiors Outside.

The nocturnal powers, absolutely unmentionable, forbidden to any discursive citation, that lead the world and the history through the uninterrupted sequences of criminal overcompensations, of which, mysteriously, *something* nevertheless manages to show through on the sometimes thinned surface of things, did not stop to make all the opprobrium of the immense communist criminology concentrate on the person – the character of I.V. Stalin, and on him alone, while fighting to promote to the full the imbecilic, scabrous and diversionist mythology of the "integrity", the revolutionary "purity" of V.I. Lenin, whereas it is indeed the latter who constituted – and still constitutes, probably not for much longer – the supreme infernal pole of the gigantic rise of acting darkness, of "dead bark", of *klippoth* introducing itself into the world through the Soviet communist revolution, its apparatuses of world subversion and their doubles in the invisible. For, at this level, nothing exists except by duplication in the invisible.

It is therefore high time that V. I. Lenin was definitively unmasked as a high initiate of certain negative, fundamentally infernal, suprahistorical, non-human and supremely anti-human instances, outside this world but invited to act in it by groups of ontological deviants, of which to date perhaps only H. P. Lovecraft has been able to give a somewhat appropriate image, and still.

The living dead, a corpse animated by the effective presence in him of an occult, anti-human entity, indebted only to active demonology, V. I. Lenin directed by secret infernal delegation the final collapse of Western and European history, attacked in its very core, and this during the decisive decade preceding his own death by the failure of the Soviet Union. Lenin directed, by secret infernal delegation, the final collapse of Western and European history, attacked in its very lifeblood, and this during the decisive decade preceding his own death by the unforeseen, premature failure of his body – the body he had at his disposal – which, in the end, was nothing but a decaying carrion, too much solicited from within by the exorbitant thrusts of forces passing through it.

A certain Clemenceau Georges, a kind of French politician, made himself famous in his time by declaring from the rostrum of the Palais Bourbon that the *Revolution is a block*. But shouldn't we answer that the *Counter-Revolution is a block* too? A block that will remain standing as long as the secret domination and permanent threats of the vast revolutionary conspiracy in place since 1789 persist?

In this connection, let us remember that in *The Hut in the Vines*, Ernst Jünger reports that, on the day of the Japanese attack on Pearl Harbour, the Japanese ambassador in Rome made a special visit to Prof. Johan von Leers – Johan von Leers, Johan von Leers, the brilliant editor of the *Nordische Welt* magazine and of certain other superior but secret metapolitical bodies, who was himself staying in Rome at the time, in order to be able to announce the 'great news' to him personally, had found, in order to do so, this absolutely dazzling formulation: *It is the revenge of 1789!*

For everything we do, those of us who are faithful, of uninterrupted counter-revolutionary continuity, is, in fact, only a revenge for 1789. And everything that the ontological enemy of what we do not want to cease to be, finds its ardent model and even its substance in the outbursts of bloody darkness of 1789.

It is therefore not so surprising to prove that the identity of the most criminal and ignoble subversive procedures, procedures of false denigration, of false and shameless moral destitution of the victims of the revolutionary butchery, the debasement and the unheard-of insults made to Queen Marie-Antoinette, resurface, and correspond – practically exactly the same, to the point of repeating almost the same expressions, the same dirty and filthy words, the same breath of inferior, bestial, subhuman insanity – to what was thrown in the face of the empress Alexandra Feodorovna at the very moment of her spectacular, hallucinated death, and even long afterwards. There is no limit to the degradation, to the unconscious, exalted and dirty negation of human nature itself. One can recognise the bloody signature of a monstrous claw, which is not of this world.

Both – Queen Marie Antoinette and Empress Alexandra Feodorovna – had been called, above all, the "foreigner", the "German", both accused of high treason, of being "sold out in the service of Germany". In both cases, the relentless, obsessive use of a process of sexual over-cultivation pushed further and further will go to the ultimate depths of the unspeakable, of opprobrium and concerted defilement. Queen Marie-Antoinette was accused – on the basis of bogus testimonies which can only be remembered with the utmost disgust – of having had filthy relations with the Dauphin, herself and her sister-in-law together, of having led the Dauphin astray and of having repeatedly "masturbated him to death". Just as much, if not more so, as she was convinced, through official writings and backroom testimonies, that she had performed the same criminal acts on the person of the Tsarevitch Alexis, herself and the Grand Duchesses, and that she had also forced the latter to submit to Rasputin's assaults. For having taken "fresh blood baths" in the company of Virubova, complex and crazy orgies, frightening, in which the Grand Duchesses were incessantly forced to participate. The "popular unconscious" had in fact been unleashed to the point of total insanity, to complete or even "justify" – the torture and rapes, the insane profanations that the Grand Duchesses had to undergo, whose angelic natural beauty, great youth, purity, the rectitude of heart and the intact imperial honour acted on the dregs of the sub-humans at work like the fire of an unbearable excitement, demanding the immediate rupture of all restraints, of the last dykes, leaving the way free to the surges, to the most inconceivable psychopathological appetites, to the ultimate *infernal spills*. That night was the night of the appearance of the Red Star.

The time had come

The Tibetan horoscope of Tsrevitch Alexis, drawn up by Badmaiev himself, prefigured a highly providential destiny, since he was supposed to accomplish historically what Emperor Alexander [1] had not been able to achieve during his lifetime, a Europe – the Greater Europe – having pulled itself together counter-revolutionarily, and thereby capable of stopping the surge in this world of the negative metastases of the Dark Power and the vast revolutionary conspiracy which was subject to it. Able, too, and Russia, then, in the front line, to set up, to constitute, in terms of high spiritual strategy, that *force* of *retention* – the *Kata-Exon* – which, according to the Apostle of the Gentiles, remained, at the end of time, the only instance in a state to be able to contain, to forbid the coming, the direct historical emergence, the birth and the appearance of the one called the Antichrist.

In a certain sense, "the time had come", and the mission of the Tsarevitch Alexis was precisely to oppose personally the appearance, the "coming" of the Antichrist. And this is precisely what the Dark Power had to prevent at all costs, to thwart at any cost. And this is also what happened, V. I. Lenin having been able to carry out his very occult necromantic mission, to sweep aside the anticipated advancement of the Antichrist as a real political possibility, in the process of being accomplished if not already accomplished.

Bishop Ioan of St. Petersburg: *God has destined us to become contemporaries of the 'last times'. The Antichrist, as a real political possibility of our time, is already beyond doubt.*

Taking place in the invisible, outside of visible history and against it, one can be emboldened to envisage the history of communism in Russia and in the world as an occult trial of strength, in the shadow of the Antichrist himself, between V. I. Lenin and Tsarevich Alexis, a trial whose final conclusion will not be seen until long after their deaths. Now it would seem that the omnipotence of V.I. Lenin, of his revolution in Russia and of its projection on a planetary scale, has already been forced to yield to the divine weakness of the predestined child from Above, to the eternally supplicated figure of the Tsarevich Alexis, that it is not the Red Star that has won.

Concerning the apocalyptic symbol of the Red Star, I would like to remind you that, towards the end of 1918, a group of very high ranking Russian military and religious personalities from the national anti-Bolshevik camp had compiled a reserved ultra-confidential file, listed under the conventional title of *Krasnaya Zvezda*, which was initially intended to be used for the planned investigation of the great trial for high national treason and the crime of regicide, as well as, more confidentially, for satanic activities, a trial that the White Armies had undertaken to bring to trial, was to be used for the planned investigation of the great trial for high national treason and the crime of regicide, as well as, more confidentially, for satanic activities, a trial which the White Armies had undertaken to bring, behind closed doors, after the final victory, against those responsible, visible or hidden, for the bloody events of Yekaterinburg, against the leaders in the shadows of the "Camp of the Antichrist".

However, in view of the negative turn of events, the *Krasnaya Zvezda* file was later entrusted to the custody of the military honour of King Alexander I of Yugoslavia. After the entry of the Wermacht into Yugoslavia, the *Krasnaya Zvezda* file was intercepted by the Abwehr in the secret archives of the monarchy, in the cellars of a monastery near Belgrade. Question: for what incomprehensible reason – but, after all, not so incomprehensible a reason, when one knows some of the high treasonous activities of which the *Abwehr was* constantly guilty at that time – did *the Abwehr* in Belgrade not send this file to Berlin? In 1945, it was Tito's political-military services that in turn seized it from one of the Belgrade *Abwehr's* pending caches, only for it to resurface ten years later, as a result of who knows what obscure transactions or exchanges, at the *Foreign Office* in London, where it must still be sitting, unattainable (though, of course, it is).

On the other hand, I was able to obtain some very valuable – albeit unfortunately rather incomplete – revelations on the *Krasnaya Zvezda* file during my stay in the *Dalmatinska Uliça* special political prison in Belgrade, 1948–1949, where, in the armoured cell number 15 (and later 4 and 6), I received the confidences of a former senior Abwehr officer in Belgrade – who had previously been posted in Paris – detained in connection with his activities there just before the end of the war, I had received the confidences of a former senior *Abwehr* officer from Belgrade – before that he had been stationed in Paris – detained in connection with his activities there just before the end of the war, and probably destined to be executed (let me quote his name, von Ditges).

Revelations concerning the darkest part, strictly speaking given as intrinsically incommunicable, and even - still - dangerous to mention, concerning the other side of the conspiracy set up by V. I. Lenin-and behind him, by the close non-human delegations of the Outer Entities at work-for the physical liquidation of the Romanovs, the vile, truly dreadful manipulations of the grand duchesses. Lenin-and behind him, by the close non-human delegations of the External Entities at work-for the physical liquidation of the Romanovs, the ignoble, truly appalling manipulations of the grand duchesses, as well as the very extraordinary Western complicities-English and French, above all, but German too, and even some others-in the conspiratorial march of the plans aiming at, and in what profoundly depraved manner, the execution of the Bolshevik plans for the annihilation of the "obstacle" constituted by the Romanovs - and by the Russian Empire - in the announced advent of a world and a history entirely subject to the direct intervention of the "Mystery of Iniquity", and all of this having to undergo an extreme operative acceleration due to the predestined presence - already there, and ready to manifest itself in its hour - of the Tsarevich Alexis, the "Saviour".

The visionaries of the great disaster announced, of the immense turmoil prepared underground

Unjustly ignored in Europe, a great Russian writer, a brilliant visionary, a high-flying initiate, André Biély, had, in - among others - two of his prophetic writings, *The Silver Dove*, and *Saint Petersburg*, openly delivered the keys to the complete mastery of the "other side", the "forbidden side", occult, plunged into the darkness of the unspeakable, even the unknowable, of what was going to be - only a few years later - the communist revolution of 1917 in its Leninist drift, thus proving, in a way that no longer bears the slightest doubt, that this one had only been on the surface, apparently and by strategic diversionism of high subversive science, a "materialist revolution", governed by dialectical and historical materialism, and pushed forward by V.I. Lenin, we know with what unprecedented force and efficiency. And that, in fact, the communist revolution - in its precedents, in its unsuspected future - had been the exact opposite of what V. I. Lenin had said, deceitfully. Lenin:i.e., in reality, a planetary revolution of identity and nominal sign, of intimate substance, of secret philosophy, of suprahistorical inspiration and fundamentally infernal, "satanic" goals, entirely subjugated to the Power of Darkness, to the "Mystery of Iniquity", and to its agents engaged in the field; and, therefore, anything but a "materialist" revolution, "founded in reason", "heir to the Enlightenment", "committed to the cutting edge of progress", etc. Its fundamental anti-spirituality was not materialism, but an inverted, deviant, *demented* form of spirituality. And its agents in action, plunged, of course, deeply, in a way that was sure to be undetectable, into the swarming, anonymous, faceless, inhuman mass, and following its obscure tumults, the real leaders never being those who were given as such, with the exception undoubtedly of V. I. Lenin himself, whose activist figure as well as the other one, the nocturnal, hidden figure, could never really be known, grasped, intercepted in an effective way, only when the security devices originally attached to him weakened, the time allotted to their functioning having vanished, so that only now certain things have just begun to become clear, to begin to *show* through the "dead husks" assigned to their protection.

In *La Colombe d'Argent*, André Biély sets out to reveal - to denounce - the demonological underpinnings of the work undertaken over a long period of time precisely within the "little people", the living soil of life, of Russian reality, by the nebulous - secretly centrifuged - sects which, under the guise of a kind of deviated Christianity, subversively give shelter to influences, to infernal identity presences, overactivated, and already in a position to take over to act on the level of history in progress, whose decisive instances they subterraneously invest. André Biély's *La Colombe d'Argent* is an invaluable document for exposing the subtle, nocturnal reasons behind the mysterious unravelling, the obscure social upheavals that made possible the sudden apocalyptic reversal of the 1918s and, finally, the liquidation of the Russian Empire, a fortress reputed to be impregnable for the just Orthodox faith and its Christological, Eucharistic and paraclete certainties. *The Silver Dove, an* inverted, demonic figure of the Holy Paraclete.

In André Biély's *Saint Petersburg*, however, something incredibly mysterious and terrible happens. On the wall of a clandestine room, a sort of spasmodic, pernicious blister appears, like a sort of shield that is self-constituting due to the very substance of the wall being put to work, and in its centre this blister produces a "diabolical face", coming from beyond the world, which André Biély calls "the Chinese", but which, in reality, is nothing other than a mediumistic representation of V. I. Lenin, a decisive prophetic excrescence of the "nightmare of my life".I. Lenin, a decisive prophetic outgrowth of the "Mongolian nightmare" that haunts the abysmal Russian unconscious.

I've already asked myself many times whether this episode of the "face in the wall" in André Biély's novel was not, in fact, the central, original prophetic figure of the entire Communist Revolution that was to come, at its double Russian and planetary level.

With his extraordinary occultist novel *Walkers* - in French *Démences*, published by Presses de la Cité, Paris, in 1991 - Graham Masterton provides an illustration as terrifying as it is close to the most secret reality of things as they sometimes allow themselves to be surprised. I myself have investigated at length the trial of Graham Masterton's *Walkers* and, among other things, I refer you to the text I gave to the *Unknown World* in September 1991, under the title *Is the Ancient Religion of Earth and Fire Coming Back?* Now, in a certain sense, everything is already said there. It is enough to know how to approach it from a correct angle, or to read between the lines. Take the spectral tangent.

I would add that the occult of the highest level, with cosmic pretensions, has always known how to handle the procedures of wall transreverberation, which - as in André Biély's *St. Petersburg*, and Graham Masterton's *Walkers* - comes out half, and even entirely, of evil walls, rocks, ancient dirt surfaces. Like moving, convulsive, grimacing reliefs, overflowing with hatred, foaming. Sometimes figures are recognisable, all of which belong to the demonologies of the underground world of darkness.

Towards the middle of the first millennium, an immense migratory whirlwind was born, and *born as if from nothing*, which, having caught the innumerable Mongolian peoples of the Yellow Continent, had then violently propelled them forward, from East to West, from deep Asia towards Europe, This historical cataclysm has forever marked the abysmal unconsciousness of the Russian and European peoples, and its obscure after-effects have remained subterranean until the middle of the second millennium and even, in a certain sense, until now.

In front of the ruins of Samarkand destroyed, reduced to ashes by the Mongol hordes, in front of the endless fields of piles, of pyramids of skulls dripping with blood, the Arab historian Ibn al Azir testified: 'Since the creation of the world, there has been no worse catastrophe for humanity, and nothing like it will happen until the end of the world'.

Only the magical implementation of an active demonology of the vastest dimensions could possibly explain the mobilisation, the migratory upheaval, the enlightened fanaticism, the demented, spasmodic, inflamed will of the Mongolian Hordes on the march, their power of duration and blind persistence to the task, their unquenchable thirst for blood and destruction, their seemingly superhuman irresistibility on the crest of the mystagogic impetus, their constitution of non-human mass. Brought back from what infernos of chaos, darkness and outer emptiness by the magical action of the Great Shamans of the Race standing in the shelter of their immemorial cities, buried in the mystagogic sands of Central Asia, the powers of High Demonology that acted through the Mongolian migrations remained, however, in abeyance, in the near invisible, during the historical extinction of the original magical impulse of the Carrying Horde, to be once again re-actualised, mobilised and put back to work, this time on an almost exclusively metapsychic level, by the groupings of infernal obedience having chosen to invest V. I. Lenin to prepare the Final Act incumbent upon the delegates of power of the "Mystery of Iniquity".

It is only in the mediumistic opening of this different science of world history that one can realise to what extent the figure of the 'Chinese in the wall' used by André Biely in his *St. Petersburg* is gratifying, carrying the last revelatory keys. This vision of André Biély is in fact a black, infernal announcement of the imminent return of ancient demonic unleashes (and, as we have seen, this is how things happened a few years later).

At this level, however, a level situated beyond that of simple facts, the bloody darkness of the nightmare of the Mongol invasions of the past will have been only the visible part of the great black ceremonial in progress, whose symbolic, prophetic and heralding part was implicitly concealed behind its manifest part, and concerned precisely the "second wave" of the investment of the Eurasian space by the darkness of non-being, namely the Communist Revolution of Russia. But on each occasion - during the Mongol invasions, during the Russian Communist Revolution - nothing could have been done without the occult mobilisation of immense black metapsychic powers and their operative setting in motion by powerhouses powerfully instructed for this purpose.

Russia's recovery

In the few years remaining until the end of the millennium, which is almost over, in the first ten years of the next millennium, a gigantic internal change in Eurasian grandcontinental European history will have to renew its own identity and even its very destiny - its historical destiny and, above all, its spiritual destiny, its new spiritual destiny – and this renewal will be driven, above all, by the imperial return of Russia to the European community, a return made possible – and imperatively necessary – by Russia, And this renewal is driven, above all, by the imperial return of Russia to the European community, a return made possible – and imperatively necessary - by the collapse of communism in Russia and throughout Eastern Europe. Through Russia, Europe is now once again finding its earlier Eurasian destiny. Didn't Aleksandr Dugin say that *Russia is Europe's bridge to India?*

In a certain sense, it is precisely Russia's return to history, its final uprooting from the anti-history of which it had made itself the active vanguard during the time of its forced subjugation to the world conspiracy of communism, that is now constituting the new foundations - the living refoundations - of the new Eurasian history of the world, which is already underway, a history that is still to come in all its availabilities, but which, at the level of the principles, is already there: Without Russia nothing was possible, with Russia everything is possible again.

As Guido Giannettini observed in one of his pioneering geopolitical essays, for the first time since undefined times, since the end of the Neolithic perhaps, men of the same blood and belonging to the same fundamental vision of being and of the world, to the same profound civilisation, are once again together, ready to integrate the ancient unity of their common predestination, from the Atlantic to the Pacific.

Russia, however, must above all be able to find itself, in the depths and at the most perilous level of its present immediate history, which is in a state of total crisis. Overcoming, overcoming this crisis.

Now, for Russia to find itself again, two dogmatic conditions seem to me to be necessary: to exorcise, abysmally, annihilate the spectre of V. I. Lenin and what he means, all that he means, and to appease the reviled shadows, still inconsolable and inconsolable, of the imperial stock of the Romanovs so ignobly devastated in 1918, in Yekaterinburg.

Following this dialectic of redemption and mystagogic reparation of a depraved historical reality, excommunicated from the avowed order of the world, will the mummy of V. I. Lenin have to be reduced to ashes and these ashes scattered, neutralised according to the ancient secret laws of expropriation and forcible expulsion from the legal limits of this world? Lenin's mummy must be reduced to ashes and these ashes scattered, neutralised according to the ancient secret laws of expropriation and forcible expulsion from the legal limits of this world of what had infiltrated it from elsewhere, and with hostile intentions, as well as of all traces of occult influences, indefinitely harmful and persistent, attached to this mummy and its shadow double - or shadow doubles - dependent on this mummy or on the states of its spectral stagnation still in reverberation, and able to respond to renewed solicitations, wherever they may come from, including from the intermediate nothingness of the worlds and of the antiontological infra-worlds of a spectral nature that certain elements instructed by the ultra-secret group of ( ), or in its persistent following in Great Britain, have been able to glimpse.

This work of cosmic exorcism must be entrusted to the Dalai Lama personally, who alone today has the equipment, the human and superhuman aggregations still capable of irrevocably carrying on, even in the "outer spaces", an operation of this kind and of this cosmic importance, capable of breaking up the demonological aggregates that have been at work for so long.

As for the appeasement of the Romanovs, who were supplicated and desecrated on purpose in Yekaterinburg, it should be possible to achieve, in order for what needs to be done in this regard to be done properly and quite effectively, a state of mobilisation, of total Russian national ecumenicity on this project, integrating in the same deep and holy impulse, the return of the entire nation to its former sentiment, as well as their regular canonisation by the Orthodox Church of Russia and, eventually, by the Church of Rome as well. For the supplicated shadows of the Romanovs must charitably accept the immense ordeal of bloodshed and suffering that was the ordeal of the Russian people caught in the trap of communism, and the Russian people must come to consciously identify with the final, metasymbolic ordeal, as the tens of millions of innocent victims, Russians and non-Russians alike, silently testify, liturgical and cosmically signified torture of the Romanovs themselves, and that the two holocausts be thus offered, together, to God for redemption and transfiguration, for divine assumption and exaltation, for their loving and thaboric integration into the Mountain of Suffering, into the Black Carmel built by communism for ends finally turned against itself, losing, thus, in the last instance, by the very secret nocturnal dialectic of Divine Providence in action, always watching over.

On the other hand, on the sidereal level, where only the intersigns produced by the divinity itself appear and act, a high ritual procedure would still have to be accomplished: that the "red star" of V. I. Lenin be replaced on the Kremlin's roof by a representation of Our Lady of the Assumption. Did not Saint Maximilian Kolbe predict, before the last war, that the day would come when the glorious figure of Mary the Immaculate would illuminate the earth and the heavens from the ultimate summit of the Kremlin?

Now, let us not forget that the original Church of the Kremlin, the work of Ridolfo Fioravanti, is dedicated to Our Lady of the Dormition, in other words to Our Lady of the Assumption, to *Maria in cœlo assumpta*.

The Marian coronation of the Kremlin is worth infinitely more than a symbol of the return to the ancestral faith of Orthodox Russia, so long degraded, because an abysmal mystery has its ontological foundation in it: The always inexplicable liberation of Russia from communism, such as it had to take place, as if in the space of a dream, in what unreal way, was it not the result of a direct intervention of Mary the Immaculate in the present history of the world, an intervention announced conditionally during the Marian apparitions of Fatima, This intervention was conditionally announced during the Marian apparitions at Fatima in 1917, and was to be accomplished only under the formal commitment of the consecration of Russia to the Immaculate Heart of Mary, a consecration to be proclaimed by the Sovereign Pontiff reigning in Rome, "in close and profound communion of vow with all his Bishops"?

It was thus very miraculously that Russia's liberation from Communism took place shortly after Pope John Paul II's proclamation of Russia's consecration to the Immaculate Heart of Mary, despite and above what those in Germany and Russia who were at that time secretly mobilised in their anti-Soviet conspiracy work might have believed, and whatever the part of their action in the field in the shadows, the part of their special, underground political action, the inconceivable miracle of the liberation of Russia from Communism having been - it must be recognised absolutely - the direct, personal work of the Immaculate Heart of Mary, of the very one whom Saint Maximilian Kolbe called the Immaculate. The Marian *coronation* of *the* Kremlin would then become, first and foremost, a Thanksgiving, the charismatic gesture of thanksgiving by Russia to its Divine Liberator and to her Immaculate Heart.

Thus the present and future developments of the symbol of the Marian coronation of the Kremlin, visionarily glimpsed and announced by St. Maximilian Kolbe, become more important than the fact of this symbol itself, which is already opening up at the present time, under the sun of the mysterious Marian plan in progress, like a bud which successively delivers the secret of its implicit transformations, foreseen, present in it before it has to open, and which will only become known by being accomplished in the full light of day, in the last state of its metamorphosis.

Where is the great saving plan of the Immaculate Heart of Mary heading, and what will be its supra-historical, unheard-of conclusion, when the time comes and in view of what has already been done up to now?

A testimony from the current Russian political power

However, for reasons of conscience, I was also keen to know a point of view opposite to my own as to the new paths that Russia should, in my opinion, take in order to meet without further delay its ultimate revolutionary destinies in Europe and Eurasia. So that it can become the "New Russia" for which so much is expected.

Thus, having shared the grid of these revolutionary eschatological instructions, which seem to me to be urgently needed, with someone who had recently held, and still holds, very high special political functions in Moscow - someone who could have been Oleg Lobov, or Yuri Skokov, etc. – and whose intimate convictions, under their layer of diversionary circumventions, of circumstantial precautions, seem to me to be the same, in the end, as ours. - and whose intimate convictions, under the layer of their diversionary circumvolutions, of circumstantial precautions, seem to me to be the same, in the end, as ours, I have drawn the following overall response. Here it is:

I do not deny that at a certain level, the spiritual and religious, even mystical, considerations that you are telling us about can have their importance, no doubt, somewhere, a more or less decisive importance, capable of changing the face of things entirely, in the present and, above all, in the future. But it is no less certain that your point of view - to which, once again, I personally subscribe, without reservation, but only personally - can in no way be of real, immediate operational use in today's Russia. Russia's most vital problems are at present - and will be increasingly so for a long time to come - exclusively material problems, economic and social problems of a gravity that no one in the West can at present have the slightest idea of. The band of traitors and degenerate morons who have been entrusted with leading the revolutionary process of pulling Russia out of communism have brought us, in three years, to the brink of a catastrophe without any known or even *conceivable* precedent, a catastrophe that is perhaps already *irremediable,* as if it were enclosed in itself and that could now go as far as forms of insanity, of collective suicide, and that is ready to draw the whole world into the terrible apocalyptic whirlwind of its final spasm. The original nuclear endowment of Russia - of the Soviet Union - remains in principle as operational as more or less intact, let us not forget this at any time. I am telling you this so that you know it, and so that you know it precisely from me, and so that you cannot claim, later on, that you were not warned about it when there was still time for you to react, to prevent the inconceivable. Material-financial, economic, industrial, supervisory and educational aid, technological and cultural relief-supported, massive, strategically concerted, planned over years, operational support, a real presence, of appropriate dimensions, such as President Richard Nixon had advocated, could perhaps have saved what could still be saved, but I believe-we fear very much-that by now it was already *too late for all that*. In this situation, talking about the magical neutralisation of Lenin's mummy by the Dalai Lama, the canonisation of the last Romanovs massacred in 1918, the crowning of the Kremlin with a votive statue of Our Lady of the Assumption, is - I'm sorry to have to tell you this so openly – a form of hallucination that, at best, will not be of interest to anyone, at best, will only be able to interest – or even mobilise - marginal groupings, or revolutionary elitist fractions of the kind that are currently being formed around personalities of special Western influence, such as Alexander Dugin and some of his close comrades in arms. So we are still far, very far from what you yourself call the "state of inner ecumenicity" of all the peoples of Russia. But, who knows, I myself may be tragically wrong in my own analysis of the situation. At the point we have reached, in this state of absolute despair, without any remission, everything suddenly becomes possible – everything becomes possible again, and *above all impossible:* we will have to see on the spot, in real circumstances, to sleepwalk forward, to take no account of anything. I don't know anymore, I really don't know. After all, I know as well as you do: it is the spiritual that commands the material, the superior that commands the inferior, and not vice versa. But, on the other hand, you have no knowledge of what the present situation of Russia means, I mean what the present social decline of the Russian people means in *fact*, and of the increasingly irreversible exhaustion of their own self-consciousness, their shame and despair, their impotence, their state of inner dismantling.

But it is also because of this very fact that, as you dare to predict, a reversal has now miraculously become possible. And even, how can I put it, the "Great Reversal". Let's wait, let's do what we can still do and, in any case, your lights, I confess in all sincerity, are really, extraordinarily precious to us. Save us, I tell you, so that we in turn can save you. Between Europe and Russia, there is now, secretly, an absolutely tragic community of fate. It is suicidal to ignore it.

A few days later, in the presence of Robert Steuckers and Christopher Gérard, and also of Alexander Douguin, I had to speak about the inspired obligation of the symbolic crowning of the Kremlin with a figure of Our Lady of the Assumption, even asking him to take upon himself the recourse to the adventurous dialectic of the fait accompli, that, thanks to a coup de main enjoying certain unofficial complicities within the Kremlin's current security apparatus, a statue of Our Lady of the Assumption was brought in to replace the "Red Star" of communism on its heights.

I believe that it is difficult to conceive of an identity of views more perfectly arranged than that of the positions of Aleksandr Dugin and his followers and of our own overall metahistorical positions, at all levels and on all the subjects of our current struggles, and above all as regards the direct political orientations of our common grandcontinental action already underway, concerning the ''Eurasian line'' and the planned outcome of this, namely our project of the ''Eurasian Empire of the End''.

Now, the reticence produced by Alexander Dugin with regard to the "Ultimate Spiritual Act", the crowning of the Kremlin by Our Lady of the Assumption, seemed to me, at the time, to be produced above all by his rootedness in his ancestral Orthodox convictions, immobilised by the very weight of their current survivals, over-activated, no doubt, by the changes in the situation underway, by the return of Russian Orthodoxy to power and perhaps also by certain Catholic interventionist attempts on the spot. For, it would seem, Rome has no intention of adopting a passive attitude towards the process of the fiery reawakening of Christianity in Russia.

Thus, Alexander Dugin's more or less avowed impediments to the vision of St. Maximilian Kolbe and its urgent, crucial realization in practice have nothing to do with the *affirmation of the principle* of the greatest spiritual war that we are waging, but with the Catholic implications of this affirmation, and only with them. For the affirmation of principle, the cornerstone of our present great spiritual war, is indeed that of the "Ultimate Spiritual Act", the crowning of the Kremlin by Our Lady of the Assumption in place of the "Red Star" of Communism.

Thus we can see that it is the confrontation on the ground, and on the ground more than doctrinally, between Catholicism and Orthodoxy that will constitute, in the years of black turmoil and vertigo that are to come, the insurmountable obstacle to the implementation of a true grand-continental policy of total European integration. So what can be done? This is certainly not the place to talk about it, nor to decide anything about it. But I am convinced that it is on this line of confrontation, on this supremely decisive tectonic fault, that the real leap forward over the void will have to take place, so that we can all find a way to return to the counter-revolutionary vision of the Mystic Emperor, the great Alexander [1], and the Holy Alliance of the Three Christian Empires, the German Empire, the Austrian Empire and the Russian Empire, which amounts to the eventual integration of Catholicism and Orthodoxy into a single imperial instance of presence and witness of life within a single imperial Church structure. Resistance to this project of the imperial reintegration of a single grandcontinental religion, whether from within Catholicism or within Orthodoxy, understandably, and it is time to say so, will have to be forcibly broken down, annihilated. And there is absolutely no question of going back on this.

We will thus find the final meaning of Möller van den Bruck's definition when he says that "there is only one Reich as there is only one Church". It is here, then, that the great battles of the Spirit are to be fought, the decisive battles of the coming New Spirit, the Spirit of Renewal, which will be both the New Spirit and the Spirit of the End.

Is this not also what Pope John Paul II is working on at the moment, through his great projects of religious meetings and new beginnings on the horizon of the closing of the millennium that is ending, on the threshold of the millennium that is coming?

Thus, the two great gaping wounds of the holy Pontificate of John Paul II were, on the one hand, the betrayal of the Bishops towards the Roman Power, that theological AIDS infiltrated, within the Church, by the Second Vatican Council, and the positions of intractable refusal that Orthodoxy opposes to Rome's nuptial approaches.

There is therefore no longer any question of concealing it from ourselves: the sly, relentless, intractable resistance, the dark resistance from wherever it comes, to the reintegration of the present European Churches - Catholic and Orthodox - can only be, in any case only manifestations of the conspiracy of the power of darkness at work, opposing the only force of revival and living charismatic presence that can block the unceasing advance of the Anti-Reign serving the "Mystery of Iniquity".

Taking all necessary counter-intervention measures to reduce the forces of resistance and blockage to the reintegration of the present European churches is a decisive counter-strategic mission of the Eurasian Great Continental Liberation Front of us, the "guardians of the threshold".

Samuel Huntington, and the Eurasian grand-continental vision

Samuel Huntington's main theses are well known, and I myself would substantially subscribe to them, with the only difference being that I would place serious emphasis not on the concepts of culture or civilisation, but on the concept of religion, which constitutes the basis of them.

—The clash of civilisations will dominate world politics. The fault lines between civilisations will be the front lines of the future". And also: "Conflicts between civilisations will be the latest phase in the evolution of conflicts in the modern world".

—"The fault lines between civilisations are replacing the political and ideological borders of the Cold War as sources of crises and bloody conflicts.

The Cold War began when the Iron Curtain divided Europe politically and ideologically. It ended with the lifting of the Iron Curtain. With the ideological division of Europe gone, the cultural division of Europe between Western Christianity on the one hand and Orthodox Christianity and Islam on the other reappeared. As William Wallace has suggested, the line that most significantly separates Eastern and Western Europe may well be the eastern border of Western Christendom in the year 1500. This line passes over the borders that now separate Russia from Finland and the Baltic States, cuts through Belarus and Ukraine, separating the Catholic-heavy western Ukraine from the Orthodox eastern Ukraine, detours west to separate Transylvania from the rest of Romania, and then crosses into Yugoslavia, following almost exactly the line that now separates Croatia and Slovenia from the rest of Yugoslavia. In the Balkans, this line naturally coincides with the historical border between the Habsburg and Ottoman empires.

The great geopolitical project of Eurasian imperial integration in the near future, the resumption, therefore, and the revaluation in its exacerbated, final dimensions, of the concept of *Kontinentalblock* defined - revealed - by Karl Haushofer, The fundamental geopolitical project of which we are now making the very revolutionary basis of our 'Eurasian line', which should lead to the politico-historical institution of the 'Eurasian Empire of the End', our entire present and future struggle thus risks being defeated, within our own camp, by the current irreducibility between the positions of the Catholic European bloc and the Orthodox European bloc: To overcome this irreducibility, which is coming back, fateful, appears, from now on, as the essential revolutionary goal of our Eurasian imperial enterprise.

Now, things being what they are becoming and, above all, what they have already become, only the fundamental concept of *the Imperium is* still in a position to take on the task of this suprahistorical overcoming: to go back to the times when Roman imperial unity had not yet had to experience the separation between West and East, the *Imperium* being situated in a transcendental manner above all divisions, historical, religious, or otherwise.

Now, today, once again, the transcendental, suprahistorical concept of the "Eurasian Empire of the End" surpasses, integrates, reconducts, assumes and assumptively exalts all the successive, circumstantial imperial conceptions of separational path, inscribed in history, between *the Imperium* of the Beginnings and *the Imperium* of the End. There is only one Reich as there is only one Church'', wrote Möller van den Bruck, and, he added, the ''Third Reich will be eternal''.

And not only must it be understood that Mœller van den Bruck is not at all talking, in this case, about the "Third Reich" in its later National Socialist sense, a passing, alienating sense that is all the more prophetically rooted in the visionary fact that the Hitlerian Third Reich did not yet exist at the time he wrote his great essay on the Third Reich, but which, in fact, in the ultimate fullness of its own transcendental and assumptive demand, concerns, in reality, the final, eschatological, suprahistorical and divine imperial concept of the Fourth Reich, *the* crowning *Imperium* of history after history, the advent of the *Millenium Christi:* The real Third Reich is not the Third Reich. The real Third Reich is the Fourth Reich.

Thus it appeared, at an apparently political level and as if exclusively political, circumstantial, barely symbolic, but as if in the shadows, that a European - or even Eurasian, in the final analysis - imperial overcoming could be immediately conceivable, over and above any ideological, religious or other border, when, during the German-Soviet Pact, from 1939 to 1941, a superior political concept, implicitly Eurasian, and in fact if not in law of grand-continental imperial dimensions, had succeeded in uniting the double grand-continental German and Soviet political petition under the aegis of a single Act.

The time has therefore come for the rest of us to no longer shrink from the formal recognition that the concept of the "Eurasian Empire of the End" is providentially bound to embody very precisely the Fourth Reich, the transcendental *Imperium* of history from beyond history, where the religiously open confrontation between Catholicism and Orthodoxy will find its final Eurasian imperial resolution.

For, if there is no New Empire, no *Novum Imperium, and* even less an Empire of the End, *an Imperium Ultimum,* without a new imperial religion, the "Eurasian Empire of the End" will have to lead, above all, to an imperial religious renewal of its own, and that this imperial religious renewal of the end, beyond history, be confirmed by a new divine intervention in history, by a new living and acting incarnation of the *Principium* of the whole cycle that has passed and is about to begin again.

The transcendental suprahistorical foundation of every new Imperium is contained in the new historical incarnation of its own *Principium.* This may mean that we are now moving towards the Reign of the Holy Spirit, towards the historical incarnation of the Paraclete, towards the establishment of a Sophianic history of the world at its end, and this founded in the liberation of the Hagia Sophia of Constantinople, the ancestral mission of the Russian Empire, the present mission of the "New Russia" which is announcing itself on the revolutionary horizon of our near future history, and which, secretly, is undoubtedly already there.

The great imperial secret of Nicholas II

On the other hand, certain considerations of a higher political order must also intervene, and in a way that will eventually appear to be quite enlightening, in the in-depth approach that we must try to make to the hitherto indecipherable personality of Nicholas II. The time has come to reveal his deeply hidden identity, in every way out of reach, corresponding to his state of "absolute concept" in the continuity of a pantocratic, sacred lineage, of an original superhuman predestination, of a secretly transcendental, eschatological ministry, leading beyond history and which will at the same time finally draw history as a whole *into it*, the history of a world itself approaching its end, and thus imposing on it its ultimate sacred, assumptional dimension. For the bloody, fundamentally sacrificial end of Nicholas II will directly challenge the whole of Eurasian grand-continental history, on which it will leave *its burning mark*, the spectral cipher of its passage. And of what remains of it. For something will remain of him, which with each passing day will come even closer to his imperishable figure, the figure of his sacrificial self-giving.

The great imperial secret of Nicholas II will have been, as it seems to me, that of his unconditional attachment to the Eurasian grand-continental mission of Russia as the pivot and privileged instrument of a preconceived providential plan, of Russia eucharistically crucified - offered, torn apart – between Europe and Asia at the very time of the separation of Europe closed in on itself and Asia plunged into its dogmatic slumber, and which, at the very heart of this separation, was not to finish installing – or attempting to do so – the final imperial integration of the two sides, the European and the Asian, as the Romanov Eagle hermetically proves - in the living body of the Third Assumptional Term, Eurasia, the "Great Continent" recovering its previous historical identity and pursuing its fulfilment in this "Eurasian Empire of the End" which must constitute its historical and suprahistorical coronation.

The secret geopolitical vision of Nicholas II was turned, as we now know, towards Greater Asia and towards the planetary opening to the Pacific Ocean, his horizon of vision including the political march of Europe towards Iran, Iraq, Palestine and the whole of the Middle East, Central Asia, Afghanistan, India, Tibet, Korea, Japan and the Pacific Islands, and this is precisely what Nicholas II seems to me to have been the inspired, visionary precursor of all our great geopolitical struggles today, all of which concern the establishment of a final Eurasian imperial planning involving a final revolutionary overvaluation, doctrinally and on the ground, of the conceptions established, in the same sense, by Karl Haushofer. "Every unbiased man is obliged to recognise that Korea must and will be Russian", wrote the German Emperor William II to his cousin Nicholas II. William II, who considered himself the "Emperor of the Atlantic", called Nicholas II the "Emperor of the Pacific". This is what Nicholas II had tried to be all his life, the "Emperor of the Pacific". The "Emperor of the Pacific", but in the name of Europe, with all of Europe behind him, from the "Atlantic to the Pacific".

The imperial counter-strategic secret service of Nicholas II had already pushed their field research and their level of definition of the Eurasian mainland geopolitical situation very far in view of Russia's "imperial missions" and direct conspiratorial investigation, confidential staking out of the space concerned and the establishment of high-range subversive irradiation sites. By 1917, all plans were ready for Russia's investment in Tibet, and its taking over as an imperial Russian protectorate.

It must be admitted that the reign of Nicholas II had marked the return of Russia to Asia, to *Asia Mysteriosa*, the mystical effort of the "Emperor of the Pacific" towards the living heart of the latter taking precedence over all the other deep concerns of the regime. In this perspective, which is still confidential, but whose counter-lighting will bring out many things, many new situations, the war that Russia had just lost to Japan - this marriage of iron and fire, which continued underground - takes on a completely different *meaning*, from which all negative dimensions disappear. A sacrificial and liturgical meaning, following the living prophetic dimension, ensured in and through blood, whose communion of the two parties at stake, the Russian and the Japanese, in death and through the overcoming of death, will make it, in the invisible, the common initiatory test opening the way to another state of heroic, sanctifying, imperial communion in the most ontological sense of the term.

A testimony by Karl Haushofer

Thus Karl Haushofer was not at all misled when, in a text of invaluable visionary significance, dated 1940, a text printed but not distributed, entitled *The Central European-Eurasian-Japanese Continental Bloc,* he tried to give its true meaning to the joint Russian-Japanese funeral ceremonies which, in the pre-war period 1929–1945, had liturgically celebrated the raising of the bodies of the combatants who had fallen during the five months of deadly confrontations in Mongolia between the Soviet intervention forces and the Japanese, in the pre-war period of 1929–1945, had liturgically celebrated the raising of the bodies of combatants who had fallen during the five months of deadly confrontations in Mongolia between the Soviet and Japanese intervention forces.

Karl Haushofer: ''Then both fighting parties received at the same time, one from Moscow, the other from Tokyo, the call to end this struggle. This was then done in a grandiose scene in which, in a truly Japanese manner, a joint death ceremony for the souls of the dead warriors was performed on the ground in the previously disputed area; despite the religious character of the ceremony and although it must not be easy for him ideologically, Soviet General Potapow attended the ceremony in perfect dress. These celebrations as organised by the Japanese are of considerable psychological importance. At the head of the troops marching with flags unfurled on the altar grounds is an elderly general, who walks towards the altar of the dead. Every Japanese is firmly convinced that the souls of the dead warriors are really present around this altar to receive the message from the emperor. It is a testament to the remarkable adaptability of the Soviet general and his officers that they attended this very long ceremony in an impeccable manner. As it is not permissible to turn one's back on spirits, all participants in the ceremony had to walk a long distance backwards with their faces turned towards the altar. It would be sacrilege to turn one's back on the spirits of the ancestors who are considered to be present. This ceremony, imbued with absolute religiosity, is very interesting and convincing from the point of view of the psychology of the people; it also made a deep impression on men who, with a wealth of experience gathered from all over the world, were allowed to attend such a ceremony and who could say to themselves: here is a whole people who firmly believe in the migration of souls. They believe that during the brief earthly existence one can by means of meritorious deeds for the fatherland acquire a high place in that hereafter, or that in case of failure one falls to the bottom. The feeling that, with the exception of a few freethinkers who tend to hide their personal impressions, a whole people is ardently animated by this conviction, gives this people enormous strength, cohesion and readiness to sacrifice.

The last word, the 'appearance of the final saviour

The fate of Europe and the present fate of the world depend on Russia, on Russia's final recovery. A recovery with the meaning and importance of a true rebirth, of a return to its former being, to its original predestination, to its ultimate eschatological imperial mission, and thus able to give the decisive impetus to the revolutionary movement of the total politico-historical integration of the Eurasian great-continent Europe. A revolutionary movement which alone would still be capable of changing the face of the world today, of stopping the forward march of world history towards the final, irreversible crisis, towards total dehumanisation and the totalitarian dictatorship of non-being, towards the Anti-Empire of the End, when the almighty power of the "Mystery of Iniquity" will be called upon to manifest itself.

We have seen what is the cluster of conditions necessary for the salvific recovery of Russia. But we have not yet mentioned the most important of these, on which everything else depends, namely the appearance of the "man of the greatest destiny", the "saviour of the end".

For it is the "appearance" of the latter that will signify the acceptance of Divine Providence as to the abysmal recovery of Russia, and as to the final salvific mission with which it will thus be charged.

It is thus the "appearance of the final saviour" who will say that *the time has come,* that the reversal of the present situation is already taking place. For it will begin by taking place in secret, and will then break out into the open.

Conference held by Jean Parvulesco before the ''inner circle of the ''Société Philosophique Jean Parvulesco'', in Neuilly, on 20 December 1994

Orthodoxy and Catholicism, the Great Restart?

The end, and the beginning of a great cycle

What happens between the beginning and the end of a great historical cycle is, so to speak, of no importance: at the end, or rather beyond the end, the beginning of the cycle will be intact, exalted by the achievement of the complete manifestation of its own historicity, whose secret figure will appear in what will then be its already eternal conclusion and true end. I am the Alpha and the Omega", says the veiled Lord of the Apocalypse, "the offspring of the race of David, the radiant Morning Star" (Apoc. , XXII, 16).

Undeniable signs - *signs of the times* - indicate that a great cycle in the history of Christology is about to come to an end. The cycle that has had to contain, to endure the historical times of the separation, in Europe, of the Churches of the West and the East, the terrifying mystery of the tunic of Jesus, torn not torn, buried, for a time, in darkness. This is what enveloped Christ, which in this time will strip him.

Yet the same signs also give us the certainty that the eschatological end of this cycle will have to find, reappropriate, once again, the times of its previous unity, reactualised by its projection into this beyond of its end, which will constitute its exhaustive recapitulation at the same time as its assumptive, suprahistorical end.

The horizon within which the future of the final destinies of the Orthodox and Catholic Churches is currently inscribed is the prophetic horizon of their future reunion in the updated times of their original unity, prior to the crucifying catastrophe of their separation in 1054, This is before the crucifying catastrophe of their separation in 1054, before their being put on the cross on the abysmal vertigo of their separation, which is now providentially being converted into a fiery wedding, into a nuptial recommencement, which bears in itself the sign of the end of the times of dereliction and trial.

For the mysterious movement of deep reconciliation between the Churches of Western and Eastern Europe, set in motion by John Paul II, will now be unstoppable. The Roman, reconciling, final and pacifying vision of Vladimir Soloviev, in the end - and here we are - will prevail over the antagonistic work, over the subversive and separating permanence of darkness in its action of death, and of the occult perpetuation of death. A *subversive permanence* whose lines of force have been reactivated in recent times, even at the level of immediate history, of "visible history". In the shadows, today as in the past, the same obscure powers act with impunity. But not for much longer this time: now other times are coming.

The anti-continental strategy of the Orthodox-Catholic divide

Since the dismantling of the Berlin Wall, the reunification of Germany and the end of the Cold War, the extreme danger represented for the United States by the irresistible rise of a movement from the depths leading all the European nations towards their integration, in the near future, into a single grand continental imperial unit, The United States was thus put on notice to react, in an immediate as well as total and concealed manner, to stop and neutralise, to prevent at all costs that this movement of imperial integration of the whole of Europe could not continue, nor reach the stage of a suprahistorical identity that was already under way. Indeed, the politico-historical advent of a "Eurasian Empire of the End" comprising Western Europe, Eastern Europe, Russia and Greater Siberia, India and Japan, would destroy without recourse the current imperialist hegemonic projects of what Bill Clinton has just called the US Planetary Superpower.

Hence - among many other measures of prevention envisaged by the United States, integrated into a vast operational device that is both manifest and completely hidden - the strategy of subversive exacerbation of the internal fracture line between the Orthodox half of Europe and its Catholic half. This strategy of subversive exacerbation found its major geopolitical expression in Samuel Huntington's doctrine of the 'clash of civilisations', and its politico-military implementation in the US military coup in South-East Europe, where the aggression against Serbia serves as an introduction to the establishment of a strategic continental base in South-East Europe under total US control. Albania, the "Greater Albania", including Kosovo, having in South-East Europe the special destination that the United States could not manage to impose on Vietnam in South-East Asia.

Bosnia and "Greater Albania" were thus intended to establish the continuity, under the direct and integral control of the United States, of a line of American politico-strategic presence in Europe which would link up with Turkey - another fundamental zone of influence of the United States in Europe - and, through Turkey, with the chain of ex-Soviet Muslim republics, with Afghanistan and Pakistan, thus destabilising the southern flank of the Eurasian "Great Continent", where the only area of grandcontinental counter-strategic presence would remain that of the Indian sub-continent. We will thus understand what is the particular mission of India in the framework of the intercontinental conflagration between the Planetary Superpower of the United States and the imperial emergence of the Great Eurasian Continent: India appears, from now on, as the axis of the great continental imperial resistance to the planetary conspiracy of the United States, as the decisive geopolitical space where the fate of the suprahistorical conflagration in the process of final definition will be played out. But it is from within that India will be assaulted.

The paraclete spirit of John Paul II's pilgrimage to Romania

The Protestant conspiracy of the Anglo-Saxons and their American Planetary Superpower, controlled in the shadows by the occult, unavowable powers that we know, a conspiracy directed against Catholic and Orthodox Europe communing in the cult of Mary, would it not be, In the end, then, is it not a hidden, clandestine conspiracy against the nuptial, transcendental figure of the Virgin, an aggression that dares not speak its name against the ever-living foundation of the European faith in the divine person of Mary, our supreme reference?

Obviously, behind the immediately visible part of things, other powers, other unspeakable influences, other superior, supra-human instances enter into the picture, secretly modifying the contributions of the forces at work in this struggle, whose developments determine the present course of history.

Thus it is that the American attempt to reactivate, to subversively exacerbate the internal dividing line of Europe between its Orthodox and Catholic halves has just suffered a resounding failure, the backlash of its own affirmation having finally reversed the terms. For not only has the politico-military aggression of the United States and its Western followers - either total betrayal or blindness, total unconsciousness on the part of these teeth - not at all had the effect of reinforcing the antagonism in principle between the two halves of Europe, On the contrary, it has finally succeeded in strengthening the previously rather weakened ties between them, and even in bringing them back, in a rather mysterious way, to their former unity, before the rupture between the Orthodox and the Catholic Churches.

John Paul II's pilgrimage to Romania-the second largest Orthodox country in the world, after Russia, with its 20 million Orthodox believers-a pilgrimage that took place from May 9 to 11, 1999-at the height of the American aggression in South-East Europe, in Serbia-meant, by confirming it, the providential reversal of a situation that could have been taken for granted, closed in on the fact of its own disaster, with no way out. The great paracletetic breath of John Paul II's pilgrimage to Romania suddenly revealed that the situation was not at all what we thought it was on the basis of the facts alone, that a secret meaning was entirely modifying the course of events, that an authority superior to events was working to change their direction. That the apparent defeat of our people was not a defeat. Too often we come to forget that every reality in this world has a meaning according to the world, and a hidden meaning, the result of the invisible work of the Spirit, which never ceases to act, whose living and burning fire is always there.

For it is necessary to understand the meaning - the whole meaning - of this Pilgrimage of John Paul II to Romania, as well as the hidden and gigantic extent of his active witness, a Pilgrimage with completely unexpected results, which are, strictly speaking, of a miraculous, directly providential nature.

Romanian Orthodoxy is already in a state of unity with Rome, and it is now certain that the other European Orthodoxies will follow the same path in the near future: the Greater Europe cannot fail to be created, and it is imperative that it rediscovers the mystery of its previous unity, of its original communion, the one not going without the other.

The attention of the Romanian Orthodoxy towards Rome is already part of the habits of the national religiosity. The anti-separationist attitude of Romanian religiosity is notorious. The two leaders of the Iron Guard, Cornelius Codreanu and Horia Sima, both Orthodox, did not cease to show a certain inclination towards Catholicism and, in spite of the "Orthodox line" of the Movement, they always refused to make the slightest difference between the Orthodox, the Uniates and the Catholics within it. Two of the most important leaders of the Movement, Ionel Motza and Vasiàe Marin, both Orthodox, went to give their lives in Spain, a fundamentally Catholic land, where they died bearing witness with their blood for the Face of Christ outraged by the bands of communist murderers. For Cornéliu Codreanu, as for Horia Sima, the only thing that mattered was fidelity, a deep and unconditional personal commitment to the Living Christ, the Risen Christ. They both felt the split between the two Churches of Europe as an intolerable wound.

The Western media-press, radio, television-which are totally subjugated to the enemy within, to the ontological enemy of all that we are, those of the imperial, grand-continental Europe of the end, those of the *Regnum Sanctum*, very deliberately did not let anything filter out of the formidable wave of mystical enthusiasm, The providential, paraclete impact of John Paul II's Pilgrimage to Romania, the real earthquake that had miraculously been unleashed at that time, a mystical earthquake, a collective, ecstatic illumination, set ablaze by a fire from beyond the world, had left its mark on the Romanian masses mobilised by a mysterious renewal of Faith, as sudden as it was fervent. No, no one knew about this, nor did they want to say so. Which is also a sign. *I have come to contemplate the Face of Christ engraved in the mystery of your Church. Thank you, thank you, brothers in Christ, for the gift of this Pilgrimage, which has allowed me to strengthen my own faith through contact with your faith, so lively, so fervent,"* said John Paul II in Bucharest.

John Paul II's pilgrimage to Romania - which took place at the darkest moment of Europe's impotent submission to the commands of the war waged on it by the Planetary Superpower of the United States - represents, however, a climactic, prophetic and significant moment for those who know how to see ahead, the fact of the irrevocable reversal of the resigning and separatist tendency of Europe, the recommencement of its reunification, the pledge of the future grand-continental imperial elevation of suprahistorical, transcendental dimensions, whose ultimate name will be, precisely, that of *Regnum Sanctum*. For this is what it is all about, and what could be more overwhelming than this unheard-of hope emerging from the very darkness of our apparent defeat of the moment.

Working in the shadows of the 'fiery spiritual heights'.

Even though it is undeniable that the immense negative weight of the Dead Bark from the dark misguidance of the past continues to poison, actively pollute, and contradict the present efforts for a definitive reconciliation, it should not be forgotten that the only things that count here are the attempts to bring the two Churches closer together, the attempts to bring the two Churches closer together by certain ardent spiritual summits of Orthodoxy and Catholicism, acting occultly, ''ardent spiritual summits'' which are the only ones entitled to carry the fire, to seek ahead, to join the burning waves of the *Incendium Amoris*, which has once again begun to move forward, circularly.

But what is meant by the radiance, by the living communion of what I have just called the 'burning spiritual summits' of Orthodoxy and Catholicism? What are these intervention groups with a hidden identity, always keeping themselves in the shadows?

Within both Orthodoxy and Catholicism, there are groups of special action, confidential and even occult nuclei, completely hidden from outside attention, which teach a direct and personal experience of Faith, These groups share a direct and personal experience of Faith, Hope and Charity that has nothing in common with current religious practices, and that rise to levels of presence, knowledge and experience that are close to sanctification and, at times, even beyond sanctity, with the immediate experience of divinisation, and even of divinity itself.

At present, however, it is through the very secret work of bringing together these 'ardent spiritual summits' of Orthodoxy and Catholicism that the future definitive reunification of the two separate Churches is being forged in the invisible. Without wasting a single moment, the urgencies are now becoming quite extreme.

In other words, it is the hidden elites who carry out the work which, when the day comes, will appear in the open, and it is indeed on the work of these spiritual elites that the choices, the advances, the decisions belonging to the visible march of the Churches are based. It is the contacts between these 'burning spiritual summits' of Orthodoxy and Catholicism that establish the over-fertilised and increasingly extensive territory of future decisive communions, which are constantly reducing the divide between the Churches of Western and Eastern Europe. The incandescent archipelago of these mysterious 'burning spiritual summits' is the starry night of our present distress, of our hourless waiting, of our dark helplessness in the face of encircling darkness. Thus we survive.

The birth, and the shedding of blood, of the 'Burning Bush' group

If, as I think, "everything is coming back into the zone of the supreme attention", it would be of considerable interest, therefore, if I were to provide here the operative definition, the historial proper, the secret of the active structures that had been its own in the field, the spiritual genealogy and the goals of the final eschatological struggle that had animated one of the groups that had, within the most recent Romanian Orthodoxy, the status recognised, and verified by integral martyrdom, by the ritual of the shedding of blood, the status, I say, of "ardent spiritual summit" if it is the "Group of the Convent", the status recognised and verified by the integral martyrdom, by the ritual of the shedding of blood, the status, I say, of "ardent spiritual summit" if we are talking about the "Group of the Antim Convent", which had acted, confidentially, in the fifties in Bucharest - the great years of the Red Terror - and which had ended up being annihilated by the communist political security in the terrible summer of 1958.

Through the analysis of the journey of the "Antim Convent Group", the secret identity of all the other "ardent spiritual summits" currently active will be revealed in a spectral way, because, at this level, every group is the same group.

In fact, the history-or rather the prehistory-of the "Antim Convent Group" begins in 1941, when the Romanian armies advancing into Soviet territory took the city of Rostov on the Don. In a hidden concentration camp, Bishop Nicholas, Metropolitan of Rostov, and Father Ioaa Culighin, his confessor, were found. As soon as they were liberated and their rights and powers restored, Bishop Nicholas and Father Ban Culighin were to accompany the Romanian armies in their retreat from the great Soviet counter-offensive of 1943, as far as Romania, where they settled in exile, integrating the community of the convent of Cernica, near Bucharest. Bishop Nicholas died there, and Father ban Culighin began his dazzling spiritual career there, which was to end in 1946, when he was arrested by the military police of the Soviet occupation forces, tried and sent to a Siberian concentration camp, where he disappeared without a trace. Ban Culighin's entire life was one long visit to the Living Fire of the Holy Spirit, and it was in the fire that he disappeared.

Father Ban Culighin, who, in order to act clandestinely in Romania, was to take the initiatory name of Ivan Strannik - John the Stranger – concealed, behind the changes of a life of adventurous wanderings and permanent occultation, the secret identity – strictly speaking unavowable, absolutely unavowable – of someone who had very early reached the supreme stage of divinising impersonality, totally transparent to the work of the Church, the secret identity – strictly speaking *unavowable,* absolutely unavowable - of someone who had very early on reached the supreme stage of divinising impersonality, totally transparent to the work of the Holy Spirit within him, having definitively found asylum in the bosom of the Holy Trinity. His words sprang from the heart of a silence that participated in the mystery of the age to come, of the age after the ages, while the words he used were like those of the present age, of our own lives', it has been said of him.

Now, as such, Father John the Stranger was to serve as the occult leaven for the constitution, rise and brief flowering of what was to be the "Antim Convent Group", which in its inner circles called itself by the secret name of the "Burning Bush". This, knowing that the orthodox doctrine of the beginnings held the "Burning Bush" to be a hidden prophetic figure belonging to the Virgin Mary's own theology, who, just as the Burning Bush received, in it, unharmed, unconsumed, the terrible fire of the Living God, she too would have to give asylum, in her human, earthly body, to the Living Logos, without this being destroyed, *rubus arderet et non comburetur.* Seek, above all, communion with those who are inhabited by the same mystery as you'', Isaac the Syrian taught his peers, the Brothers of the Desert, established in the intimate knowledge of certain ''divine secrets''. The ''Group of the Antim Convent'', sitting in the Bucharest convent of the same name, was made up of roughly equal numbers of monks from the Antim Convent and certain intellectuals belonging to Bucharest's high society – university professors, senior civil servants, John the Stranger, pursued a goal of total sanctification, of "liberation in life", having dared to make his own the word in continuity of the ancient Desert Fathers: Those who, in the name of God alone, will know how to endure everything, to the end and beyond, will be changed into active powers, and will receive wings like eagles, they will follow their work without knowing fatigue, will walk before them without hunger weakening them, rising from height to height, and God will show Himself to them in the Zion of His most secret wisdom and visions that stand on the supreme peaks.

By its mere presence there, by the very fact of its hidden spiritual influence, the "Antim Convent Group" considered that it was going to be able to influence, even change the political-historical situation of Romania, which was then preparing to slip under the dreadful leaden blanket of the fifty years of communism that were going to fall so fatally on it. An extraordinary spiritual and charismatic work had nevertheless been carried out in the meantime by the Antim Group, the ultimate fruits of which were undoubtedly still to come.

Until the fatal summer of 1938, when the political security of the communist regime in place would strike, to destroy, in one blow, the "Group of the Antim Convent": in the space of three days, the "Burning Bush" would be definitively dismantled, destroyed. All its members would be arrested, beastly tortured, condemned to long years of detention, or – like Sandu Tudor, the main leader of the 'Antim Group', executed in the prison of Aiud, disappeared without a trace – massacred, thrown into mass graves. The holocaust was the necessary conclusion.

The circuit of the high spiritual and mystical predestination of the "Group of the Convent of Antim", an exemplary figure of so many other "ardent spiritual summits", could not indeed close on itself otherwise than by the shedding of blood in common, by the bloody liturgy of martyrdom for Christ, in Christ. So it was.

In addition to sources which, for understandable reasons, are still highly confidential, the most important part of the information concerning the bloody spiritual journey of the "Group of the Antim Convent" of Bucharest, of the "Burning Bush", comes from a book published in Bucharest in 1996 by Mgr André Scrima, *Rugul Aprins, "The Burning Bush"*.

The person of Monsignor André Scrima is an existential space of sign and eschatological predestination.

Miraculously surviving the holocaust of the "Antim Convent Group", to which, in the immediate vicinity of Father John the Stranger, he had belonged in his own right, Mgr, André Scrima, after an important stay in India, was appointed plenipotentiary representative of the Ecumenical Patriarch of Constantinople, Athenagoras, to the Vatican and, as such, he had to carry out a number of decisive missions for the underground movement of rapprochement between Catholicism and Orthodoxy.

But was it not necessary that the surviving witness of the "Antim Convent Group" and its final holocaust, Monsignor Andre Scrima, should appear, even in his own existence, to be made in the disturbing image of the very thing whose sacrificial journey and mystery he has taken upon himself to revive? For it must be said that Monsignor Andre Scrima is a man of mystery, whose powers, which are undoubtedly much greater than one might think, are manifested only in the shadows, and whose personal journey will mark, in the shadows, the future of this century full of shadows that will never be deciphered.

Fulgens Corona

Certainly, revelations concerning the existence and very special activities, within Orthodoxy as well as Catholicism, of what I have just called 'ardent spiritual summits' could be multiplied, if one were so inclined; but this is not the purpose of the present work. It is sufficient, if it is to serve symbolically to evoke the whole of these centres of high reverberation of the Faith confidentially at work everywhere in living Christendom, that a consequent definition of these 'burning spiritual summits' be given, as has just been done, through the brief history of what had been, in Bucharest, under the communist terror, this mysterious "Group of the Antim Convent" which met the bloody end that is now known, and whose memory still shines in the darkness.

But time is short, very short. The new strategic commands of the coming new hour imply the urgency of an accelerated, sustained, and intensified work of those "burning spiritual summits" which represent, as in the past, the supernaturally moving part of the secret community of the living in the Risen Christ.

For, at the paroxysmically final moment of the conspiratorial domination of darkness – of the "Mystery of Iniquity" of which St. Paul speaks in his Second Epistle to the Thessalonians – over the history of the world at its end and over the subjugated ensemble of human consciousnesses in the process of irreversible alienation, It is the hidden work of the reviving archipelago of the "burning spiritual summits" that constitutes the last living barricade, the last apparatus of resistance to the fundamental manoeuvres of the subversion of non-being that is in the process of seizing total power, of being able to make its Anti-Church and its Anti-Empire of infernal substance rise up in front of the world.

Thus we know perfectly well what remains for us to do if the ultimate designs of the dark powers are to be thwarted, and what must be done we will do. The secret doctrine and strategies of our present action, of our future action, have been revealed to us, and we shall hold to them until the end.

Just as history is the visible tool of suprahistory, of history beyond history, and the visible the means of affirmation of the invisible, so the mystery of the Incarnation must appear to us as that by which the omnipotence in act of the Uncreated Logos is offered to us: It is the *Regnum Sanctum*, the historically established Final Empire of Christendom, which controls that which in the last instance stands in opposition to the Anti-Church and Anti-Empire in which the regressive powers of negation and chaos gather and find shelter.

Have things now become clear enough for us to be able to take the direction of our future revolutionary imperial steps, of our future commitments to total rupture and total recommencement, from this very clarity?

To institute the Empire of the End also implies the abysmal renewal of the Church, the advent of the Church of the End, within which only that which is most highly situated on the ascent of the prophetic spiral of the advancing Holy Spirit, namely the "already saved" destined to assume the salvation and deliverance of the "not yet saved", can command. In the saving action of the Church and her Sacraments, her own secret nucleus, her "burning spiritual summits", is today leading the decisive battle for the establishment of her new living hierarchies, of the new active ontology of her own identity to come, in the century and beyond. The supreme heroicity of the Faith lies in the heroic courage of its self-renewal.

And if this is so - as has already been said at the beginning of this research – then on both sides of the line of the present separation of the Churches the task of conforming, perfecting and finally openly declaring the unity to be regained – the regained unity - of the Churches of Western and Eastern Europe, to their own 'ardent spiritual summits', so that the former community of the two Churches - Orthodox and Catholic - thus reconstituted may serve as a living foundation for the *Regnum Sanctum,* to the "Eurasian Empire of the End", it appears from this that the supreme revolutionary task of the "great times that are coming again" is none other than that fundamentally incumbent upon the work of the "ardent spiritual summits", already long engaged in the front line, which have never pursued but one goal, that of preparing the parousal integration of this world and the other world, the "descent of the Heavenly Jerusalem". An essentially apocalyptic goal.

In any case, what appears to be absolutely certain from the more than advanced conclusions we have reached in our research is that the general horizon of everything that must happen and that will happen now, of everything we dare to expect and invoke, of what we even use ourselves to try to *provoke*, can only be, from now on, an apocalyptic horizon, or even the horizon of the Apocalypse. One way or another, "we are there".

The great lines of convergence, the great strategic orientations of combat that will have to be, in common, those of the "ardent spiritual summits" as a whole will therefore be, for the next few years, exclusively of an apocalyptic order.

Now the central character of the Apocalypse is, according to the canonical Apocalypse of Saint John, that of Mary'': ''A great sign appeared in heaven, a Woman clothed with the sun, the moon under her feet and twelve stars crowning her head; she is with child and cries out in the pains and travails of childbirth''. Hence, too, the mysterious apocalyptic motto of John Paul II, *de labore solis.*

The centre of gravity of the great avant-garde spiritual works in charge of the "ardent spiritual summits" will therefore have to be shifted to the divine person of Mary. All the work will be done on Mary, in Mary, for Mary and with Mary.

The "ardent spiritual summits" will thus have the primary mission of fighting, from within the Church itself - from the Orthodox and Catholic Churches and, subsequently, from within the reconciled Church, and reunited within the same final suprahistorical identity - so that the proclamation of the dogma of the Coronation of Mary Sovereign can take place in the shortest and, by that very fact, most *significant* time, with all that this implies at the level of the theological and dogmatic, even sacramental, renewal of the Church of the End, a truly abysmal renewal. But was it not said by Mary herself that *nondum erant abyssi et ego concepta eram*?

Now, following certain prophetic views of St. Maximilian Kolbe, is it not also on the lightning figure of Mary - the *Fu/gens Corona* of our great Pius XII - that, finally, the Catholic and imperial reversal of India and Japan within the "Eurasian Empire of the End", within the *Regnum Sanctum, will take place*?

For, as Mœller van den Bruck said, 'there is only one Empire, as there is only one Church'.

The cause for which we fight is inscribed in the highest heaven.

WE ARE THE CHURCH OF THE END

> *When, from the bosom of Being, God manifests Himself through the living Word, fused in the crucible of the heart of certain beings who have accepted the radicality of the ultimate test which leads them from kenosis to deification,*
>
> *It is suspended, in a gesture of Love, in the breath of the one who receives it, so that the Ineffable is coloured by the Voice of the beloved and gives Him the flesh that is lacking in his passion for incorporation.*
>
> *The Word, eternally in love, is consumed with his passion to embrace beings, especially men, in whom He reflects Himself – and finds Himself, by finding us, more Himself than Himself, after the Kiss of Fire.*
>
> Marikka Devoucoux

History as a fighting Mariology

The ontological advent of the Marian supernatural in the history of the world, which was intended from the very beginning to develop through the mystery of the Immaculate Conception, should therefore lead, according to the unfathomable plans of Divine Providence, to the mystery of the Assumption of Mary, dogmatically defined and established by our holy Pope Pius XII, from Rome, on November [1,] 1950, and it is the entire adventure of the Incarnation and its Christological procession in history that unfolds between the two mysteriosophic times of the Immaculate Conception and the Assumption of Mary, pivotal times. And it is the fiery wake of Christology in history, or rather of history as Christology in progress, which will reveal in continuation, in a manner that is as lively as it is uninterrupted, the flaming face of the Church and her terrifying mystery of love, and it is Mary who is the Church, because it is Mary who has been desired, willed the Bride of God, of whom Mary - and more especially the Immaculate Heart of Mary - is the mirror of the loving nuptial duplication which makes her, too, the Crowned Empress, alongside God, of all that has been, is and will be, eternally.

Jesus Christ, in whom Love and Charity are identified, and in what an incendiary manner, and more especially in the imperial mystery of his Sacred Burning Heart, in the *Incendium Amoris*, thus appears as Emperor in the eternity of the *Regnum Sanctum*, in whom the visible and the invisible, history and eternity, equally Christological, are called to identify themselves unceasingly, and to reveal themselves in the very act of their apocalyptic espousal, when the hour comes.

However, was it not also said: 'As for the date of that day, or the hour, no one knows it, not the Angels in heaven, not the Son, no one but God', Mark, XIII, 32.

Everything is therefore breath held back, ecstatic waiting, our history is nothing more than a history suspended by the secret expectation of its parousial completion.

We, in fact, must hold that the history of the world and of men - of humanity - has ceased to be a history that can be accounted for objectively: everything in it is totally changed from the direct intervention of the divine in its bosom, in its becoming, from its investment by the divine in the terms of the mystery of the Incarnation of the Word, et verbum caro factum est. An event that made everything - and history in the first place - become Christology, and its very principle and following the visible and invisible developments of this principle now in action.

Thus, considered in the sole Marian horizon of its most secret future developments, with the proclamation of the dogma of the Assumption, history will cease to be history, in order to become, in itself, in its most intimate becoming, the time after history, a time at once veiled, sovereign and sacred, whose only opening will henceforth be turned towards the end of history and its apocalyptic conclusion, namely the Second Coming of the Risen One, our only Saviour.

Now, what this final apocalyptic conclusion of history, or of the post-history of the Assumption, subject to Mary, is going to be - or already is - no one, it seems to me, has yet been able to say it with as much living power as our holy Pope Pius XII in his very dazzling Roman address on Easter morning 1957. May these brief prophetic quotations, these invocations charged with a power as formidable as it is immediate, make their own way into us and into the world today:

It is necessary to remove the tombstone with which truth and goodness have been locked up in the sepulchre; it is necessary to raise Jesus from the dead; from a true resurrection, which no longer admits any domination of death: "The Lord is truly risen" (Luke XXIV, 34). Death will have no more power over Him. (Rom.VI, 9).

Come, Lord Jesus!

Mankind does not have the strength to remove the obstacle which it has created by seeking to prevent your return. Send your Angel, O Lord, and make our night bright as day.

How many hearts, O Lord, are waiting for You! How many souls are being consumed to hasten the day when You will live and reign alone in our hearts! Come, Lord Jesus!

There are signs that your Return is not far off!

Lodged, as we are now by our visionary faith, in the Marian horizon of history, we are already, and will be until the end, in the times of the aftermath of history, of the history after history at its end, the times of Mary's Cosmic Kingship, when Mary is called to carry out her fight, her great final fight against the Mystery of Iniquity, a fight whose inner secrets appear transparently in chapters XII and XIII of the Apocalypse of St. John: "A great sign appeared in the heavens a woman whom the Sun enveloped, the Moon under her feet, and twelve Stars crowning her head: she was with child, and cried out in the pains and travail of childbirth. Then a second sign appeared: a huge Dragon, red with fire" (John XII, 1–3).

The proper space of our historical actuality to come will thus be shown to be the very interior space of Marian history after history, the post-assumptional historical temporality and space destined to bear the marks, both mournful and ardent, of Mary's assumptional departure from the womb of our history, Mary who at the same time finds herself in charge of clandestinely leading, from the invisible, the foundational struggles of both our own present action, of the apocalyptic end line of history after history, and also of what will come to us with the ultimate Christological conclusion of the latter, namely the Second Coming of Our Lord.

Everything is thus suspended in advance from the succession of stages, events and cosmic combats of Mary in the invisible. Everything is henceforth decided, defined by the very march of our Marian combat in the visible, where, "for a certain time", Mary will be supported only by the Archangel Michael: the absolutely fundamental task of our own theological consciousness illuminating, from within, this new Marian metahistoricity actively underway, a metahistoricity of both cosmic and immediately, historically combative dimensions, thus appears to be that of dogmatic framing and elucidation, of the definitive dogmatic definition by Rome of this new combative identity of Mary. This Roman dogmatic definition alone will be able to establish the new fields of reality, of proper tension, and also to make it come to be posited in terms of consciousness, to become the very being of our new theological - theological – and cosmic consciousness of ourselves and of history – the new Marian historicity in action - insofar as this will be invited to be accomplished according to the still occult designs of Divine Providence.

For our goal, as we have understood, is none other than that of the irrevocable subjection of civil society and of all historical or transcendental power to the Immaculate Heart of Mary, such as this revolutionary subjection could well be conceived, even today, and openly proclaimed by the visionary faith of an Irene Pivetti and of those who stand beside her in the rediscovered light of the ancient Fede Santa.

The dogma of the Cosmic Coronation of Mary

Such, then, are the abysmal, providential, immediately divine reasons for the imperial, cosmic, and supremely loving sovereignty of Mary, a dogmatic sovereignty whose consciousness is theologically supplied to us, and at the same time ontologically armed, by the new Catholic dogma to come, which we will bring about, the dogma of the Cosmic Coronation of Mary.

Dogma, too, of her Nuptial Coronation. The dogma of Mary's cosmic Coronation, whose serious emphasis will be dialectically placed on her nuptial identity, not on the Nativity, on her maternal identity as Mother of the Saviour, but on Mary as Spouse of the Only Father, or Saint Sophia lovingly facing the Holy Spirit. And, as such, as Sovereign Mistress of the entire universe, of consciousnesses and beings nuptially at work within the Mystery of Charity, a mystery nourishing the totality of being and of the divine and loving consciousness of being. An ontological totality that maintains, as Living Love, the burning eternity of *the Incendium Amoris*, and that will exacerbate it from its very centre, from the Immaculate Heart of Mary, with an exacerbation that exalts itself, within itself, following an infinite spiral. The spiral of the One Desire.

Thus, in laying the foundations of the Roman liturgical feast of the Sovereignty of Mary on [1] November 1954, our holy Pope Pius XII forcefully recalled the terms of his encyclical *Ad Cadi Reginam*, dated 11 October of that year, and hailed Mary as "Queen and Mistress of Heaven and Earth", as "Our Queen and Our Lady".

And I would also point out that the Marian appellations used, on this particular occasion, by our holy Pope Pius XII, namely "Sovereign of the whole Universe", "Mistress of Heaven and Earth", "Our Queen and Our Lady", were merely a repetition of the very titulary that had been used, with regard to Mary, within the ultra-secret initiatory organisations of the Sophianic, suprahistoric and supra-temporal movement, mobilised by the *Fede Santa*, or by its *Fedeli d'Amore*, whose very reserved teaching our great Dante Alighieri had been given the task of expressing "externally", of perpetuating its spiritual fires through the vehicle of the encrypted poetic creation that was his and his peers'.

On the other hand, and I am not the only one who can - or should – testify to this, in the last months of his life, our holy Pope Pius XII sensed very imperiously, in the terms of a living and certain interior inspiration, inescapable, that the Church would soon find herself invited to enter the times – the Great Times – of her Final Renewal, the cosmic times of what the secret – initiatory – Roman tradition – I mean the high occult initiatory tradition of the *Roma Aeterna* - had already known how to call the 'Great Summer'.

The winter, the dark winter, has already passed, Jam hiems trasiit'' (Cant. , II, 11), cried our holy Pope Pius XII on 19 March 1958. And, he added, on the same day and with the very words of St. Matthew the Apostle, Prope est Aestas, the Summer is near, the Great Summer'' (Mat. , XXIV, 32).

And also, on the same day:

A great Call to Renewal is passing through the world: will you listen to it? Do you want to make it yours too? ''

Seized as if by the revelation of a lightning inspiration, Pius XII did not fail to affirm that this Renewal should be understood as a Revival. And even more, that "everything in the world is an Awakening", the ultimate paroxysmal moment of the Christological vision of history and of the world considered as a resurrectional unity ontologically founded and made alive by the Risen One himself in his double identity, Eucharistic and to come, the expectation of the Second Coming constituting the very secret - and the salvific, vivifying, unceasingly foundational mystery – of the interference of the Fede Santa in the present and final history – in the Christological history - of the world. A world whose appearances, whatever they may be, already conceal a devastating, unquenchable fire, the very fire of the Awakening. I have come to cast fire on the earth, and how I wish it were already kindled" (Luke, XII, 51).

Now it already seems obvious to me that this immense interior Renewal of Catholicity and of the world on the march with Catholicity, a Renewal foreseen and announced by our holy Pope Pius XII, will concern above all the fact of the present entry of history into the times of "history after history", where the salvific power of Mary alone will henceforth be exercised, and that this Renewal will also be the result of our own awakening to the consciousness of the final change of cosmic jurisdiction, manifesting Mary's invisible sovereignty "in heaven and on earth", which is the change whose hopscotch, strategic structures and unconditional revolutionary impetus it is for us to govern.

A sovereignty that is above all a fighting sovereignty, a heroic and loving sovereignty, because Mary's tears are the vanguard tears of Love, and of Charity, which receives the very clear surplus tumultuously.

Under the heroic and loving sovereignty of Mary, that which was Disunited, ontologically founded - or defounded - by separation, and by separation alone, will come to be lovingly reunited again, sicut erant in principium. The cosmic season of Disunion will thus be revolutionarily replaced by the great cosmic season of Reunion under the incendiary aegis of the mirror of the Immaculate Heart of Mary and its new special protections, far more hidden but also far more surging than the old. For such is the law of the renewal of the same Love, ever higher, ever more ardent. Ever closer to the Immaculate Heart of Mary, ever more hidden on the upward spiral of her eternal nuptial virginity ever more exacerbated by the fires of the One Desire.

The end of communism and the reunification of the Great Continent

On the other hand, are we going to have to ask ourselves how, and to what ontological depth, these immense spiritual changes of Marian sign announced by the visionary figure of the Renewal, which had so intensely burned the end of the life of our holy Pope Pius XII, are going to have to reverberate at the level of the "great Western and planetary history" in progress? History has reached the end of a final cycle of increasingly twilight cycles, and it was intended that we ourselves should be chosen in advance as immobile witnesses, out of reach, but witnesses in arms, and we ourselves - as a Miguel Serrano might have said - sacrificed there, by our very testimony, where the founding sacrifice had to be made and had been made, totally. Witnesses in arms, at the same time as being tragically held entirely responsible for what was done, for everything that was done, for what was not done and, above all, for what will be done in the end, definitively *in aeternum*. To be in arms is not to be, forever, at the centre, at the absolute centre?

And everything that will now have to be done will be done under the sign of the final reintegration of the cycle whose historical march through time had been constituted, affirmed in advance by the sole disintegration of its own virginal unity of origins: to the Immaculate Conception of the origins will have to respond, once the present cycle is entirely over, and it is in the process of being so, the Immaculate Conception of the End.

Thus the Virgin of the End will be the same as the Virgin of the Beginnings, the Virgin of Disintegration will be the same as the Virgin of Reintegration, the Virgin of Destruction, the same as the Virgin of Salvation and Deliverance, the same as the Virgin of Final Liberation, for *Una est Columba Mea*.

However, since the higher, invisible world, the world of principles and nuptial changes in the divine, is reflected in the visible world, in the phenomenal world of events and history in progress, the advent of a new apocalyptic Marian disposition in the heavens cannot fail to be translated, on earth, in visible history, by an analogous movement of virginal return to original unity within what is currently in the state of separation - of disunion - specific to the ends of the cycle, and all the more so to the ends of a final set of cycle ends.

Thus, with the miraculous, providential collapse of communism, and the return of Russia and Eastern Europe under communist rule to the Western, European world, the original unity, spiritual, historical unity, unity of a new geopolitical consciousness and a new historical consciousness of the Eurasian great-continental space will find itself, for the first time in twelve millennia or more, once again reconstituted, or ready to be reconstituted, revolutionarily. As in its beginnings, the original unity is being reconstituted, is being remade in Mary, Virgin of Beginnings, *nondum orant abyssi et ego concepta eram.*

At the previous origins of the great cosmic cycle, which is now almost over, there was only one sacred blood, only one polar and solar race, surya vamça, only one consciousness of the superhuman predestination, providential of the latter, divine, only one living and acting religion, only one open history, heroically, tragically stretched forward:at the end of this same cycle and beyond this end, the unity of the previous origins of what we were, of what we are ontologically, in the occult, abysmal part, currently guarded by and concealed by immemory, of our unchanging, but crucifying and crucified identity, torn apart on the wheel, will find itself again as before, reconstituted, promised to the ardent mystery of its final assumption, presumed to be eternal.

The new revolutionary geopolitical consciousness that today is that of the coming imperial unity of the Great Eurasian Continent, and of what some are already calling the Great Eurasian Empire of the End, thus only translates at an immediate, direct historical and political level the deepest transcendental consciousness of the final recovery of the previous unity, of the original unity of the world and of the Western consciousness of the world and of history.

All consciousness of the final accomplishment of the world and of world history goes, leads, ends up in the accomplished West of consciousness and, by that very fact, in the Western consciousness of the end, of all ends: absolute consciousness is only the absolute West of consciousness accomplished by its ultimate nuptials with itself, and by its assumptive elevation and secret crowning as a loving junction with the supreme Marian mystery, with its *Fu/gens Corona.*

Today, in Western Europe, Eastern Europe and all the Russias are one again. And this new geopolitical unity, which is great European in its foundation, is also identified, within the new final Eurasian consciousness of history, which is already ours, with the North Asian spatiality of Greater Siberia, and also with India and Japan, as well as with the sacred lands of Central Asia, polarised by their inner fortress Tibet. Thus the ancient and still very secret Eurasian grandcontinental vision of Emperor Nicholas II of Russia, prophetically dubbed, by Emperor Wilhelm II of Germany, who knew far more than was known about him, "the Emperor of the Pacific", will be verified. From the Atlantic to the Pacific, once again and finally, one and the same imperial unit, alive, polar, radiant. Now we know, the Great Times are returning, and the Great Summer.

There is no New Empire without a renewed religion

What, however, founds every new imperial establishment in history is the prior advent of a new religion, of a new rise of the sacred taking its living foundations, and incarnating itself in the very becoming of history thus begun anew: the Empire, *the Imperium Novum*, is each time a new religion in the making, or renewed from its ultimate depths, which will demand its advent, the *Religio Novissima*. And the new advent of the being implied by this new nativity and its occult immaculate conception will always carry the inspirational signs of the *Religio Novissima* which, by this very fact, also become, and each time, the decisional signs of the *Imperium Novum*.

Today, the rise of a new imperial geopolitical consciousness of destiny, of grand-continental and Eurasian dimensions, must appear to us above all as a sign of the very secret religious nativity in progress, of the advent, still only implicit, of a new religious and spiritual state of the world and of history reclaimed by the abyssal breath of the sacred, And this is precisely what our holy Pope Pius XII so prophetically foresaw in the form of this Renewal, this Revival, whose irresistible salvific imminence he announced, and which we have identified as being the fact of the apocalyptic times to which the final ontological and cosmic kingship of Mary, "Our Queen and Our Lady" (Pius XII), calls.

For us, those of the Revival foreseen by Pius XII, it is the Roman proclamation of the dogma of the Cosmic Coronation of Mary which will have to constitute the occult, abysmal foundations of the future great Eurasian Empire of the End.

The failure of Rome in Western Europe

The time limits of the plans of Divine Providence are not inscribed in time, in the immediate times of human expectation, in profane and illusory times, but in the impenetrable temporality of the Holy Spirit, who is on the march following the spiral of his endless ascent, and who alone animates the One Desire: What the great prophetic pontificate of our holy Pope Pius XII had allowed us to foresee, to glimpse from the dogmatic foundations that were both new and absolutely decisive that he had been able to give himself in the accomplishment of his own mission, the revolutionary pontificate of our great John Paul II will be destined to realise it in history by imposing the formidable advent of the fact on the burning hinge of two millennia, one not yet fully finished and the other not yet begun, a hinge that appears, at the same time, as the line of interior tearing and exterior affirmation of our own generation. A tragic generation, if ever there was one. For we now know that the Third Millennium must be that of the *Regnum Dei*, and that it is up to us to ensure its arrival in a revolutionary way, with arms in hand.

John Paul II, who took as his pontifical motto the rallying cry and Marian service of *Totus Tuum*, began by succeeding in the inconceivable, by defeating the planetary conspiracy and the subversive dominations of communism by exclusively supernatural means, of an exclusively spiritual and mystical order. Indeed, it is by succeeding in consecrating - and this despite the diversionary and criminal obstinacy of the greater part of the world Catholic episcopate under Masonic and Marxist influence, fiercely opposed to the Marian vow of Fatima and to the cosmic imperialism of the Immaculate Heart of Mary - to consecrate, I say, by a sort of veiled power grab, to consecrate Russia to the Immaculate Heart of Mary that, miraculously, John Paul II reduced communism to defeat from within, "as if by itself", in Russia and in the whole of Eastern Europe under Soviet domination.

On the other hand, when, at the end of the 1980s, John Paul II tried to transfer to Western Europe what had been so decisively successful in Eastern Europe, the local resistance of episcopal subversion and of the terrifying zones of necrosis installed more or less clandestinely on the very body of the Western Catholic people, resistance which was assertive, The pontifical initiative for a "new evangelisation of Europe" was cut short and the counter-strategic actions of the East-West Continental Synod were annihilated before they could really manifest themselves. Here, obviously, the trial of strength between John Paul II and the FriendChurch of Darkness acting against him and his people from within his own Church, was to result in a total and significant defeat for the Roman positions, and which, moreover, almost cost him his life (and this, whether one knew it or not, already on several occasions; as I personally feel duty-bound to show later). Moreover, John Paul II only resigned himself to suspend his great project for a "new evangelisation of Western Europe" in the face of the threat of a declared rupture with the Church of Western Europe, or rather with its Episcopal Conferences, which were already saying - in a barely confidential manner - that they were ready to place themselves in a state of rebellion, of open insubordination towards the Sovereign Pontiff, towards Rome.

It is difficult to imagine a more significantly intolerable disappointment for a Pontiff reigning from Rome than that of the ostentatious refusal, both fierce and disdainful, of the so-called Roman Catholic episcopate of the Church of Western Europe – of the "Western world" – to accept the clearly expressed and defined desire of John Paul II to proceed with the traditional recovery of Western Catholicism, devastated from within by two centuries of apostasy, including a century of infiltrations, reversals, and Marxist infiltration, pushed in depth, of the Catholic hierarchies which had become the priority target of the special communist apparatuses everywhere in Europe.

Nevertheless, let us emphasise that John Paul II knew perfectly well how to acknowledge the blow, how to turn around a fundamentally negative situation to give it another direction of dialectical grasp, another sense of final commitment, and this one posing itself, from the outset, beyond the de facto acceptance of the disappointment suffered, and assumed. Acceptance of a defeat which, integrated as such into another project of action, was thus dialectically integrated, positively reassumed, to become the very fulcrum of its own present and future overcoming, of its resumption, of its recovery already at work and, on a powerfully enlarged level, seized in its final limits.

Subversively aborted, therefore, by the very people who should have supported the immense counter-strategic charge on the ground with heroism and fervour, the project thus postponed of the traditional Catholic takeover of Western Europe responding to the return of Eastern Europe to combat Christianity after the providential collapse of communism and its even blacker supports in the shadows, John Paul II provisionally suspended its execution so that, without further delay and as a single movement, he could begin the transition to the implementation of his 'great final plan', his planetary superproject of which Rome has become the sole representative, without further delay and as if in one and the same movement, he began the passage towards the implementation of his "great final plan", of his planetary superproject, of which Rome has made itself the underground metastrategic pole already in action, namely the superproject of planetary integration - of the bringing together - to be worked on, by Rome, of the whole front of present-day human spirituality, and this on the transcendental horizon of the passage to the Third Millennium

The passage to the third millennium should be considered, in advance, as a transcendental opening to the world and to history, through the implementation of this Roman Catholic super-project which we are going to call, from now on, precisely the conventional name of the Third Millennium Project, and which, for its part, Rome at the moment designates as the Sinai Project, or the Mount Sinai Project.

Now, if it is quite certain that, for the moment, Rome is clearly refusing to take any position, to make any exhaustive or truly revealing statement on the true final content of the Mount Sinai Project, it is no less true that, at the same time, the rumour is growing and growing with insistence that, coming, always, from Rome, it is already trying to explain the general meaning.

This would therefore propose, on the horizon of the third millennium, a founding gathering that would have its first foundations on Mount Sinai, in Palestine, a gathering that would concern, in principle and above all, the current religions of Abrahamic origin in their major components, Catholic, Orthodox, Jewish and Muslim, to which would be added, perhaps, Mahayan Buddhism, with a view to bringing about a traditional - even traditionalist – convergence of the great spiritualities that mobilise humanity at a time when prophetically, and in the light of the new millennium, it would be possible to bring together the major religions of the world, This gathering would, in principle and above all, involve the present Abrahamic religions in their major components, Catholic, Orthodox, Jewish and Muslim, to which Mahayan Buddhism would perhaps be added, with a view to bringing about a traditional – indeed, traditionalist - convergence of the great spiritualities that mobilise humanity at a time when, prophetically, and in a way that is already implicitly apocalyptic, the immense changes that we know and sense in the visible and invisible destinies of the human race are being announced.

Changes from above, the rise of which we had long since foreseen, and which is now becoming more and more imperious and irresistible. And which we have just spoken about at length here, in the immense shadow of Mary.

The Two Standards: Tradition versus Anti-Tradition

In fact, it is a question of bringing together the living forces of Tradition, in the Guenonian and sempiternal sense of the term, in the face of the plans for the criminal takeover and total domination of the world and its present and future history by the already active and almost victorious powers of the Anti-Tradition and the Mystery of Iniquity standing behind it. This foreseeable, imminent confrontation of Tradition and Anti-Tradition - already half a century ago, Pius XII had come to exclaim that the conflict between Christ and Antichrist is taking gigantic forms - will thus have to decide the ultimate meaning, the definitive form of the relationship of the human race with its own becoming, with the irrevocable outcome of the latter: The superman, Christologically divinised with the traditional, Catholic and polar line of Tradition, or the subman bestialized with the infernal line of Anti-Tradition. Thus, we find the active figure of the fundamental apocalyptic meditation of Saint Ignatius of Loyola, which has so fascinated our people, the figure of the meditation of the Two Standards.

Already, with the announced end of ideologies, history – "great history" - was coming under the providential jurisdiction of active theology, and history itself was already becoming theology with the birth, within it, of the movement of the depths which wanted to give theology – I mean Catholicism - the missions of a supreme intervener in the final course of history, The very acceleration of this movement, in its race towards a kind of conclusion that was still inconceivable but already presaged, revealed to those who could see the imminence of what we are now being asked to face at the risk of more than life, at the very risk of the supernatural condition of humanity saved by the bloody sacrifice of its only God.

Thus, following the new metahistorical perspective opened up before us today by the first announcements of the Third Millennium Project, many Catholic initiatives of the fairly recent past take on a revealing, full, immediately decisive significance, becoming clearer from within.

Let us be clear. The Movement for a Better World (MMM) of Pius XII, which had wanted to make Catholicism, openly mobilised in the vanguard of history, like another Order of the Temple, a supranatural battle force against the front of the devastating interference of the Dark Power secretly in the front line at the end of the planetary war of 1939–1945 and holding in its power the gigantic criminal apparatus of the communist masses and their hierarchies of supervision and clandestine warfare; as well as the very extraordinary body of highly inspired eschatological-indeed, apocalyptic-teachings that the same Pius XII was able to mobilise and proclaim in the darkest hour, so that they might serve to reinforce and arm what he himself called, at the time, the mystery of the forthcoming inner, resurrectional and cosmic Renewal of the Church, and the coming to term of this mysterious Awakening which was to find in it its immediate supra-historical fulfilment, and its Reign; just as, later, under other pontificates, the profound upheavals preceding the vertiginous event of the Second Vatican Council - unfortunately diverted from its primary, supernatural aims, and even in its very identity, by the infernal forces negatively at work of the Anti-Church acting within the Church itself - and of what the Second Vatican Council could have been if it had been possible to salvage what could not be saved. All these initiatives, and many others, better concealed no doubt, were, as we can now understand, and understand it actively, so many preliminary attempts, so many successive approaches to the subterranean work continually accomplished by the Holy Spirit with the aim of making the apocalyptic figure of the direct mission of the Church in history emerge at the end, culminating and dazzling. For in this end, which is almost beyond all ends, the Church - I mean the Church as such - will have to act, impose her own revolutionary will and her own revelations, her own dialectic of total overthrow, within the history of the world as such, at the end of the history of this world as such. Here we are, the time has come.

However, and precisely because of all this, a formidable work of surveillance and direct spiritual and counter-strategic control, at all times, is becoming more necessary than ever, a matter of life and death, a matter of eternal life and eternal death, on the part of the living forces invited to respond to the unconditional mobilisation that a traditionalist enterprise of planetary, immediately meta-historical dimensions, such as that of the Third Millennium Project, is already requiring. And this one draws everything to itself.

For, already, a vast disinformation structure is being put in place, seeking its diversionary and accelerated encirclement marks in relation to the pre-announced positions of the Third Millennium Project.

Paradoxically enough, the first line of attack against the Third Millennium Project comes from certain fundamentalist circles - in the fundamentalist sense of the word - which work using arguments, essentially fundamentalist "denunciations", which set in motion circles, organisations and bodies of openly fundamentalist influence. Thus the claim, put into circulation through certain more or less specialised agencies, and even more so by giving vent to successive waves of oriented rumours, that the Third Millennium Project is being used by John Paul II in order to clandestinely bring about the final abdication of traditional Catholicism without return, without return, of traditional Catholicism in the dark waters of an irremissible ecumenism, aiming to deviate, to dissolve the Catholic deposit of our Faith by the vitriol of a globalism of higher Masonic manipulation, or something else.

Feigning not to understand – or really blinded by who, in this case, blinds, manipulates them shamelessly and mercilessly, "leads them to the slaughterhouse" - the proponents of this disinformative thesis confuse, or purposely pretend to confuse, an operation of putting in convergence the active metahistorical aspirations of the spiritual forces presently invested in the world – among which Catholicism - invited, and very precisely by Catholicism, to face, together, a final apocalyptic challenge, the Supreme Challenge of the Power of Darkness, and I don't know what operation of subjugation, of I don't know what project of alienation, of dissolution of Catholicism in a state of larval ecumenism which, in any case, would represent a fraudulent, irremissible liquidation.

This amalgam is essentially criminal, and must be treated as such, without the slightest complacency aroused by the traditionalist pretensions of its peddlers, even if they are masked for the ambiguous needs of their cause, which, moreover, conceals another, more obscure one.

As far as we are concerned, things could not be clearer. What Rome wants to achieve through its Third Millennium Project - or Mount Sinai Project - in accordance with the fighting dialectic of the Two Standards, is that a transcendental inventory be drawn up as a matter of urgency of those who, in the coming hour, will be under the White Standard, the standard of the Camp of Rome.

Same Faith identifications

Certainly, the Holy Spirit, who is God, can do everything. Spiritual convergence to the point of total identification of certain religious bodies, so that in the end they become one, is always possible, but any process of identification that has to go all the way to the end can only bring into a unifying - or reunifying - presence parts that were already unifying beforehand, and identical and secretly united by the mystery of their pre-ontological belonging, and whose separations in the century were ordered only from the outside and for the outside, by the manoeuvres of the secret agents of the century and of the decays of the century which, in itself, is nothing but a lying and impotent illusion, nothing in the face of the truth inhabiting the inhabitants of the truth.

Thus, Orthodoxy, for which a man of the extraordinary providential stature of Bishop Ioannos, Metropolitan of St. Petersburg and Ladoga, is currently bearing witness, can and must at all costs meet, without further delay, and meet in terms of a nuptial reunification, of a great return, the living and active faith that is currently that of Rome under the leadership of John Paul II. And this will be the part of the miraculous fruition given by addition to the profound mystery which, whatever else may be the case, is immutably at the base of the convergences already under way, which the Third Millennium Project is in charge of.

From now on, as we can see, it is only at the edge of the abyss, and what an abyss it is, that those who seemed to have lost their way meet again, and it is indeed at the edge of the abyss that I myself will take up, today, here, to make our spiritual bread, the statements of Bishop Ioannos about the struggle that is common to us: "God has destined us to become contemporaries of the 'last times'. The Antichrist, as a real political possibility of our time, is no *longer in* doubt".

And what is true for Orthodox Traditionalism, by which I mean the spiritually intact part of it, or rather the part that has not yet been obscured, as in Greece, Serbia and elsewhere, by the nocturnal infiltrations of Masonic anti-Catholicism, can just as well be true for other instances of the Living Tradition that are still in action. For it is time for the battle of Tradition against the planetary front of the forces of Anti-Tradition exasperated, in the invisible, by the conjuration of Aquarius, a front into which are integrated all the fundamentalisms bearing Dead Bark, and themselves reduced to the state of Klipphoth, whatever side they supposedly were on. And this is all the more true since the present great wave of fundamentalisms has been deliberately created only to oppose them, when the time comes, to the positions of the Living Tradition. This moment, which, among other things, also represents for us, the terrible final revenge of René Guénon's teaching, which has been rejected, despised and denigrated, especially by the wretched Catholic or assimilated fundamentalisms, which have never been anything but dismal impostures, subject, like all fundamentalists, to the black horror of the Dead Letter, is now being activated.

In any case, this century of inconceivable spiritual depravity and of terrifying and dark trials for Faith, Hope and Charity, will also have benefited from the truly providential charism of the series of three sovereign Pontiffs of visionary, eschatological commitment, Pius X, Pius XII and John Paul II, undoubtedly, in the very measure of the great peril that overhangs us, the most holy, the most awakened of the whole history of the Church.

And we also know that the eschatological and fighting pope, the military pope that is our John Paul II, gave his life in advance as a high expiatory and foundational sacrifice so that the Third Millennium Project could be carried out perfectly and within the foreseen time. An oath and a sacrifice that we must take as accepted by Heaven.

The oath of John Paul II

John Paul II has therefore, in a way, pledged himself, offered himself as a holocaust so that the Third Millennium Project might succeed, and so that he might see this success with his own eyes after having led us there himself, through the darkness, from battle to battle.

And yet, will John Paul II manage to remain, unshakeable, awake, at the head of the armies of his faithful for the twelve years or so that would be required for the full realisation of this final eschatological programme of the Church? The present state of his health, already so severely tested by the pitfalls that we know and do not even suspect - for the attack in St Peter's Square would ultimately have been only the tip of the iceberg - means that this may indeed seem difficult to envisage without the direct intervention of divine power.

In the meantime, while preparing to announce the opening of the next Holy Year of the year 2000 with an apostolic writing entitled *Tertium Millenium Adveniente, a* text which should also constitute his "spiritual testament", John Paul II has repeatedly let the certainty shine through, mystically inspired by his visionary faith, but also by confirmations from the other world, about the personal deferment of life that would be granted to him by heaven so that he could hope to be able to carry out his mission concerning the entry of the Church into the Third Millennium.

On 29 May 1994, on leaving hospital, John Paul II made some very advanced statements: 'In these days, I have found beside me the great figure of Primate Wyszynski, who died thirteen years ago. At the beginning of my pontificate, he said to me: 'If the Lord has called you, you must lead the Church into the Third Millennium'. I understand now that this road is one of suffering. ''

Moreover, Roman confidences whose spiritual validity cannot be doubted also refer recently and insistently to an extraordinary apparition - no doubt Marian – intended to strengthen John Paul II's assurance of the certain grace granted to him so that the Third Millennium Project – the Mount Sinai Project - would be completed, and his planetary imperial vision fulfilled, on schedule.

But is it not the Mystery of Faith which, of all the Christological mysteries at work in today's history and beyond, is still the greatest? Thus, the new Christological and Marian undertakings for which we have to assume active responsibility will all be operative through the Mystery of Faith above all. What we believe will be.

We are the Church of the End

As has already been said, vast new political and power gatherings are being prepared, revolutionarily, on a planetary level, gatherings that will be justified more and more by religious professions of faith.

Through the Third Millennium Project, Rome is committed to building, at the highest level of the rapprochement that can be envisaged by the new metahistorical convergences underway, what will have to be its own camp, the camp of the Freedom of the Spirit. A great light will be made there, new, sunny, virginal, the light of Mary, the same light which, projecting itself on the fiery-red background of the heavens, will fight and strike down the Negative Entity, the envelope of darkness of the Mystery of iniquity. It is the light of Mary that will be the bearer of the new imperial salvation of the heavens and the world, and will illuminate the apocalyptic consciousness of our people from within. Our consciences will be changed according to the changes from Above. Within the Church itself, the choices and the activist gathering of those who will go to salvation and its battles of final spiritual liberation under the white standard of Mary will henceforth be made on the apocalyptic criterion of holiness, of the ardent Faith of those who will have known how to make the heroic sacrifice of themselves in advance.

We are the Church of the end, the Church of *Regnum Mariae*. In the proper temporality of the history after the end of the history, which is the limpid and ardent temporality of the Regnum Mariae, we will be called to live, with the Imperium, in the century of all our fights of holiness to come, and, with the *Regnum Mariae*, out of the century: the marriage of the Kingdom and the Empire we shall live ecstatically in ourselves, for every mystery of power and life is a mystery concerning the Inner Kingdom, the Kingdom of the Fiery Sacred Heart of Jesus, whose figure Marguerite-Marie Alacoque rightly asked to be placed on the Standards of France, which is itself the Inner Kingdom.

Having said all this, it is nonetheless certain that it is the immediate and direct political commitment that is currently ours that is most important for us to identify in the perspective of the planetary imperial vision of the Mount Sinai Project. For there is a politics of eternity, the aims of which are aimed at the installation of the Empire of the End, towards which world history is currently moving, in the shadows, and our task is precisely that of ensuring that the direction that the history of this world is going to take at its present great apocalyptic turning point is that of the final eschatological imperial horizon that it has providentially been given to us to sense, to glimpse before us. We know where we must go, our decision comes to us from beyond this world. This is the ultimate secret of our generation, a predestined generation if ever there was one. Even if there are only a few of us left, the *last*.

RUSSIA'S EUROPEAN MAINLAND MISSIONS

*Karl Haushofer
Subha Chandra Bose
in memoriam*

The Franco-German axis is a World Revolution

In the geopolitical circles of Gaullism, I mean within its highly confidential "geopolitical groups", whose action, whatever one may say, continues in the shadows, one is more convinced than ever of the vital, ontological necessity of a great Franco-German continental policy.

For, while keeping a very low profile in relation to the commitments that the official Gaullist movement has contracted, currently in France, through the governmental experiment pursued by Edouard Balladur and Charles Pasqua, the 'geopolitical groups' are nonetheless keeping a close eye on the increasingly worrying evolution of the general political situation in Europe.

Now, for the "Gaullism of the end", for the Gaullism in the process of final accomplishment, which is ours alone, the more European politics finds itself in difficulty, in relation to itself as well as on its external, planetary fronts of affirmation, the more it is necessary that the Franco-German rapprochement intensifies, and that it even ends up resolving itself in a decisive federal integration, going as far as total identification. A final identification destined to change, as if by seismic reverberation, from within and irreversibly, the entire continental political situation.

Gaullism, the greatest Gaullism, was, is, whatever one may say and do to the contrary, and will have to be visionary until the end, a geopolitical concept centred on the integration of the entire Eurasian continent from the central Franco-German revolutionary core. For General de Gaulle, the immediate establishment of a Franco-German community of destiny was, both in terms of becoming and in terms of final completion, a World Revolution. This founding unitary consciousness, this superior, agonising Gaullist intelligence of the Franco-German problem has its origins in the tragic, fiery and chaotic years at the end of the last European civil war, in the fateful winter of 1944.

Let us recall that, in his *Memoirs*, General de Gaulle quotes, without any comment but exhaustively, the personal letter that had reached him in 1945, through special channels, from Heinrich Himmler, when the latter was already being caught up in the darkness. In this letter, Heinrich Himmler made a prophetic appeal for the constitution of a future Franco-German community of destiny, for which he strongly invited General de Gaulle to take immediate and active political responsibility. In truth, the only path that can lead your people to greatness and independence is that of agreement with defeated Germany. Proclaim it at once! Make contact, without delay, with those men in the Reich who still have de facto power and who want to lead their country in a new direction. They are ready for it. If you overcome the spirit of revenge, if you seize the opportunity that history is offering you today, you will be the greatest man of all time', Heinrich Himmler once wrote.

Now, as early as 1945, General de Gaulle's very first and fundamental concern had been to distinguish and then to mobilise, within a devastated, politically and socially annihilated Germany, the resources of life that had not yet been damaged, the "ultimate part", mysteriously preserved against all odds, so that another beginning of history could find its foundations, the immediate opening of all its future developments, an opening that was, moreover, foreseen in advance. What General de Gaulle was going to ask of Germany was, he said, to rebuild, with France, "our Europe and our West".

Speaking of this dramatic turning point in the new European history - rising from its own ashes - General de Gaulle noted in his *Memoirs:*

Freiburg, in the Black Forest, groups together to receive de Gaulle all those who are representative of the regions occupied by us on the right bank of the Rhine. On 4 October, Dr. Wohleb introduced me to the personalities of Baden. On the morning of the 5th, Mr. Carlo Schmitt introduced those from Württemberg. The Archbishop of Freiburg, Mgr Grœber, as well as Mgr Fisher of the diocese of Rotthausen, are among the visitors. Then, these men of quality, trembling with goodwill, gathered to hear me evoke "the links that once brought together the French and the Germans of the South and that must now reappear to serve to build our Europe and our West".

On the subject of this visionary will of General de Gaulle, anxious to start again, as soon as the war was over, the interrupted Western history, to build, forward, the greatest European history to come by founding it on the French-German ontological axis, Dominique de Roux wrote, in his revolutionary book on General de Gaulle, these lines which will remain, *definitively*

It is in this sense that we should certainly understand General de Gaulle's statement, speaking of the Franco-German rapprochement, when he said in June 1963, in the Charentes region, that after immense misfortunes, having concluded peace between them and having united for a common destiny, Germany and France have accomplished, together, a World Revolution'.

Blessed are the Pacifics

However, it is no less obvious that the "Franco-German Axis" could not have any direct and active political and historical reality if it was not supported by its geopolitical duplication in the East, by what, in 1994, the Minister of Foreign Affairs of Moscow, Andrei Kozyrev, did not hesitate to call the "German-Russian Axis".

We see how the suprahistorical destiny of the Eurasian great-continental political community of the years to come is revolutionarily identified with the current political destiny of the Paris-Berlin-Moscow great-European axis, the raison d'être already in action, the foundation of the greater Europe in which our generation is called to meet its destiny and the decisive test of it, its supreme test. For now, "everything is again in the zone of supreme attention".

Thus it becomes more than urgent, thus it becomes vital that we remember, today, the fact that the grand-continental thesis of the Paris-Berlin-Moscow axis – at the present time, let us repeat, a fundamental counter-strategic thesis of the "geopolitical groups" acting within the Gaullist movement in place – appears to have a much more distant origin than that of the first attempts to project it, to make it directly embodied in the course of ''great history'' that General de Gaulle, then in power in Paris as President of the Republic, had undertaken in a more or less subterranean way in the 1960s, and which had failed at that time only because of the very suspicious - of the more than suspicious - incomprehension of the Bonn government.

The thesis of the Paris-Berlin-Moscow great-continental axis was not, in fact, originally, as one would be tempted to believe today, of exclusively Gaullist genesis, but came from certain French ideological-doctrinal adjustments made, during the last years of the war, in Paris, to the body of advanced geopolitical positions supported, doctrinally reinforced by Karl Haushofer's vision of the *Kontinentalblock*, of the ''Continental Bloc''. It was then a question of doctrinal development work that originated within certain secret groups of influence and penetration that acted in Paris under the responsibility of Georges Soulès – better known, later on, as the "Continental Bloc". Later known as the novelist Raymond Abellio – within, and from within, the upper echelons of the Mouvement Social Révolutionnaire (MSR), while maintaining close relations - not without the support, in the shadows, of certain higher German political services - with a certain fraction of the Gaullist politico-military resistance under the orders, in clandestinity, of the future General de Bénouville.

In his first novel, *Heureux les Pacifiques*, published in Paris in 1950, Raymond Abellio lifts a corner of the veil by having one of his characters - one of his doubles - talk about the fact, hitherto kept secret, that there were ''socialists everywhere'', national-revolutionary socialists, in all the opposing camps in those years, and even up to the paroxysm of the last years of the war, after 1942, because there is also - there was, and there will be more and more at work in the future - an underground, clandestine international of national and imperial revolutionary socialism, a grand-continental, "Eurasian" socialism. Raymond Abellio: "There are," he says, "socialists everywhere: they would like to see the creation of a Franco-German-Russian bloc, a Paris-

Berlin-Moscow axis that would free the West from the tutelage and contradictions of the Anglo-Saxon economy".

For *those who know*, the primary forces ontologically present in history in progress will always remain the same, absolutely unchanged. Yesterday as today, there was, there is only one enemy of that which endlessly returns to the attack to impose the cosmic order of its own polar identity of origins, the Imperium beyond the reach of those who, "from the stars" through the Junction of Venus, had established, on earth, the first hyperborean station of the high beginnings, and controlled all the subsequent transmigration stations and their successive ontological descents further and further away from being – what Heidegger calls the "being of being" – and therefore more and more obscured, nocturnal, oblivious of all anteriority, closer and closer to the abyss of the Ultimate South. Yet, in any case, once the Ultimate South has been reached, it will provoke - I mean, provoke - as of itself the Final Righting, the "Great Reversal", what the seers of Vedic times had called *Paravrtti*.

Now, at the present time, the polar camp of European national-revolutionary socialism of grand-continental opening is once again directly mobilised on the barricades of the fight for the immediate political and historical reconstitution of the Paris-Berlin-Moscow axis. It is there, and only there, that all the vanguard struggles are now being waged, it is there that the inner, abysmal renewal of the "great history" is taking place tectonically.

At the centre of Europe, thus challenged by its new destiny, Germany will find itself torn apart by the double attraction and by the double petition of encounter that contradicts this attraction while making it come true, an attraction that is being exerted on it, France and Germany, the West and the East of the Great Eurasian Continent, already caught up in the vertiginous final vortex of the great continental reintegration in the process of being carried out under the ardent and polar auspices of the *Imperium Ultimum*.

Immense negative powers, hidden

This is precisely the reason why immense secret negative powers, concealed, oppose today the definitive integration of France and Germany, just as immense secret negative powers will oppose, also, and at the same time, the definitive integration of Germany and Russia: yet in both cases, these negative powers, occultly and always subject to non-being and to the original chaos in its nocturnal, concealed persistence, will prove to be the same. If we have thus remained the same, the ontological enemy of all that we are and have been, of all that we will be again, has also remained the same, unconditionally identical to itself and to its missions ordered by the "outer darkness".

The danger is also to be invoked, and there with the sharpest clarity, of the powerful manoeuvres of delay, of "anti-fascist blocking", of permanent destabilisation that the Socialist International and those who predetermine it, silently, hidden in the nocturnal background of our own history in progress, are pursuing against us, both in broad daylight and completely in the shadows. It is therefore a question of forcefully denouncing the Marxist and cosmopolitan socialism, anti-national and anti-European, subversively conveyed by the Socialist Parties of Portugal, Spain, France, Italy, Belgium, Germany, refuges and hardened activist bases of the apparently self-neutralised Communist Parties, which have passed to the tactical stage of "previous presuppositions". The case of the Italian PDS remains the most flagrant, which, with its electoral masses, cadres, parallel organisations and leaders, led by Achille Occhetto, is nothing other than the PCI reinforced by the alluvial sludge of a "popular front" otherwise engineered, and all the more dangerous.

On the other hand, the situation remains particularly critical in Germany, where the possible arrival in power in the next legislative elections of the PSD, reinforced by the leftist candidacy of Rudolf Scharping, whose shadowy political thinking and subversive relations with underground alternative formations are notorious, would provoke a political catastrophe of European dimensions, and probably much more. This will have to be prevented by all means, including, as the other said, "by the most legal means".

We shall therefore place ourselves immediately and unconditionally at the side of Chancellor Helmut Kohl, the hero of the complete reunification of Germany and of Germany's definitive reunion with itself, as well as of the new beginning of the Greater Europe, which stems directly from this. May Chancellor Helmut Kohl count on us, who, for our part, will always know who is who.

Thus, as we can see, all the forces in confrontation, in the visible and the invisible, are already in a state of maximum alert, lined up in their pre-established places, ready for anything.

The time for the great earthquake is approaching, which will once again shake everything. So I am going to quote this terrible prophetic word of Chancellor Helmut Kohl, a prophetic word whose topicality is accelerating, and which we must understand at its double level: *What we sowed in May, we shall reap in October.*

The movements of Middle-earth

Changes are happening everywhere, and they all point in the same direction, in the direction of the total renewal that is coming, and whose tumultuous line it will be up to us to master one day.

But the situation is now also becoming clearer in the depths.

If, in relation to the German "Middle Kingdom", in relation to the "Immutable Lands" of the polar centrality, out of reach, embodied, in these times of the end, by Germany, France, for its part, represents, today, and brings to it - for such is its predestined mission - the whole of the Western Great European camp, The West, therefore, of the Great Eurasian Continent and, more visibly, the Western imperial base Madrid-Rome-Brussels, Russia, as far as it is concerned, represents, and brings to it, principally, the East of the Great Eurasian Continent, including "the Greater India" and "the Greater Japan".

However, as I already had the opportunity to show in my study on *"the foundations of the secret geopolitics of Gaullism"*, the concept of *"heartland"*, of *"middle land"*, fundamental geopolitical equivalent of the "Immutable Lands" of Taoism, concept of *"heartland"* already defined in terms of active geopolitics by Sir Halford Mackinder, and to which Karl Haushofer had also fully subscribed in his work, is a concept destined to move within the central space that constitutes its own continental area of presence and action, its movements following the spiral that carries forward and manifests the great cosmic cycle in progress.

Thus, whoever holds the secret of the paths foreseen in advance, inscribed in advance on the spiral governing the displacements of the *heartland* of the Great Eurasian Continent, also holds, by this very fact, the secret of the becoming of the inner power of the *Imperium*, and of the visible historiai of the latter in history on the march towards its ultimate conclusion, towards this *Imperium Ultimum* where history will be called upon to identify itself assumptively with the beyond of history.

The fundamental counter-strategic project of ours, on the very eve of our greatest suprahistoric and revolutionary battles at the end, must therefore know how to find the necessary audacity to go out and meet what appears to us as the secret already in action of the future ontological displacement of the geopolitical centre of gravity of the Great Continent, of its next imperial and polar recentrification. We must know how to make the very inevitability of history our decisive suprahistorical weapon, the current that carries our highest power of historical and political intervention in the future.

For our people, and at this time more than ever, the profound choices of destiny are, in advance, as if 'inscribed in the stars'.

Thus it is that if, during the season of our present preliminaries to the conceptual, principled setting up of the Great Eurasian Empire of the End, the ontological location of the "middle-earth" is still situated in Germany, once the grand-continental imperial process has been revolutionarily initiated at the level of direct historical and political action, and directly inscribed in the ongoing history, the *heartland*, the *principium of* the Middle Lands, will have to move - as planned – to Russia, in order to reach its place, planned since ever, and planned also to last *until the end,* during the whole millennium – or the ten millennia of our previous legend - of the next temporal projection, immediately historical, which will be that of the *Imperium Ultimum.*

Moreover, anyone whose gaze is accustomed - or rather entitled – to catching the essence of the historical future beneath the apparent, obscure and troubled course of his own contingencies at work, must have already understood, as if by himself, that the centre of gravity of the new Western history of the world is currently shifting towards Russia, whose attraction is becoming more and more irresistible, and whose deepest heart has undoubtedly already started beating – to beat again - *somewhere*. Thus the 'polar rise' of Russia, the predestined territory of the next emergence of the 'Middle Lands', is taking place, and going on.

On the other hand, no one can ignore the fact that Russia, at the present time, is trapped in an apparently hopeless situation, in the grip of extraordinary and quite dark, destabilising difficulties, in a situation even darker than that of Germany in 1945, because the disaster of Germany in 1945 could not fail to find in itself something to start the process of a future recovery, whereas the suspicious vertigo into which Russia seems to be sinking at the moment is designed to be self-intensifying and unable to extricate itself from the fatality of death that has been invested in it on purpose. For there is a vast design at work to prevent Russia from emerging on its own from the trap of annihilation that surrounds it everywhere and tries to suffocate it, that keeps it crucified on the inconceivable shame of its current ontological reduction to misery, to economic and social dismantling, without any major help, and this conspiracy conceived, from outside *and inside*, preventively, to rob it of its miraculous liberation from communism and to forbid it to join the new transcendental and suprahistorical, polar destiny which is now its own, despite everything.

The comparison of the situation of total distress that is currently Russia's of the interregnum, of the post-communist transition, and that of Germany's historical catastrophe in 1945 concerns only the visible, external and immediate face of things.

For if Germany was defeated in 1945, Russia was not. On the contrary. Russia has been *saved*. *Whatever* Russia's current situation may be, Russia has risen from the dead. And this resurrection, now, tells us its present path, and its future path.

The Marian horizon of the New Russia

Now, miraculously delivered, without internal civil war or external military defeat, from the bloody and unfailing nightmare of seventy years of darkness and shame, of total powerlessness in the face of the Communist grip and of what was hidden behind Communism, Russia was only delivered by the work of the Immaculate Heart of Mary, Today, as I have just said, Russia is a country that has risen from the dead and bears in its very being, and for ever, the stigmata of an inconceivable miracle, like so many Eucharistic incisions, ablaze with life, already radiant, salvific, inextinguishable.

So Russia must now find, above all, the most appropriate way of giving thanks, of thanking her Divine Saviour for the unheard-of and very high victory, for the abysmal intervention which her Immaculate Heart has so well known for, as if in a dream, as if nothing had happened in between.

We remember the prediction of St. Maximilian Kolbe, the mystic who was tortured in Auschwitz: that the day will come, he said, when the statue of Mary will replace the infernal whirlwind of the "Red Star" at the top of the Kremlin. So everything must be set in motion, and right away, so that this symbolic change can take place in a formal, nuptial way. Before that, nothing will be done that must be done for the imperial promotion of the New Russia called to the transcendental vanguard for the final battles of our *Imperium Ultimum*.

And, in this circumstance, it is quite impossible for me not to reproduce here, because that is how it should be done, the conclusions of my recent Catholic and Marian interview with Eric Vatré, an interview that has since been published in a group work entitled *La droite du Père*.

So I began the last part of this long interview with a quote from Pius XII. A fragment of the extraordinary speech that Pius XII made in Rome at Christmas 1942. At the very heart of the supremely decisive winter, just at the moment when everything was about to tip over into the darkness of misguidance and defeat, and for so long and from then on without any respite.

Should it not rather be,' said Pius XII, 'that on the ruins of a public order which has given such tragic proof of its inability to ensure the good of the people, all upright and magnanimous hearts should unite in the solemn vow to give themselves no rest until in all the peoples and all the nations of the earth, become legion the company of those who, determined to bring society back to the unshakeable centre of gravity of the divine law, aspire to devote themselves to the salvation of the human person and his community ennobled in God?

Humanity owes this vow to the countless dead buried on the battlefields; the sacrifice of their lives in the performance of their duty is the holocaust offered for the new social order to come, which will be different''.

And I myself added this comment, which took up again, and brought up to date, the fighting line of Pius XII: "Having laid the visible and invisible foundations in blood, in the heroic and mystical sacrifice of those who gave their lives for the future and the tragic honour of their faith, the new continental unity desired by Rome is on the march, and nothing will stop it. The sun of Rome is rising again in the West of the world; Europe, brought to the dimensions of the Great Eurasian Continent, is once again becoming a transcendental idea''. And then: "My message will be addressed exclusively to those who are already involved, or who will be involved, in the terrible spiritual and nuptial conspiracy of the mystery of the *Incendium Amoris*.

How *does* the *Incendium Amoris* conspiracy operate, what are its ultimate goals and the ultimate horizon of its conflagration? The answer to this question concerns us in the most direct way: "Beyond their future historical incarnations and what will be involved in them, thus, processionally, in the times carried towards the final assumption of the *Regnum Sanctum*, of *the Imperium Sanctum*, the great events to come and which will all have, in their totality, Rome as their polar centre and the metahistorical light of Rome as their horizon of return, also call, henceforth, and with an increasingly passionate violence, for a final, decisive, coronary, Marian incarnation." And in an even more precise, and therefore more perilous, manner: "Mary must ensure with her testimonial and loving coming the return of Europe - of the greater Europe - to the being of the renewed Catholic faith, just as it is through the proclamation of the dogma of the Coronation of Mary that Rome must supernaturally arm its present final counter-strategic offensive for the Catholic recovery of the Great Eurasian Continent". And finally, very dangerously, and very deliberately so, the Book of Baruch, III 38, saying, as he spoke of Wisdom: *Then she appeared on earth, and lived among men.*

Will the circle of continental geopolitical assumptions close on the coronary petition of an assumption of solar elevation, of a communional spiritual ascent "to the sun", confirmed cosmically by the very coming of the Sun-clothed Bride, the most virginal *Sponsa Soli*?

Acting on history, we also act on the beyond of history, every major, foundational, decisive geopolitical vision also implies its own geotheological - even geotheological - coronation, for, as Möller van den Bruck wrote, 'there is only one Reich as there is only one Church'.

On the scale of the ultimate horizons of Western history on the way to the fulfilment of its most hidden predestination, ontologically hidden, the goal of 'great geopolitics', of what some of us, and in the first place myself, have already taken to calling, among ourselves, 'transcendental geopolitics', is none other than that which will have to be incarnated – which is already lovingly incarnated in the cosmic dogma of the Coronation of Mary.

Nevertheless, for the time being, the order of emergencies on the ground appears to be different.

The tasks of the missions that are ours, at the present time, challenge the most visible and tragic part of immediate history, rediscover the political and activist dimensions of our struggles and engage in them with all the intensity, with all the violence of those who, in the very becoming of contingencies, intercept, from within, the living light of the perpetual call, within them, of the previous polar base.

The order of emergencies

For the moment, the order of counter-strategic emergencies on the ground requires that everything necessary be done to ensure that Germany - the

Germany of the German-Russian axis desired by Andrei Kozyrev - can provide Russia, in due course, with the support required for its restoration and its political and economic-industrial maintenance at the level of a planetary superpower, a level which, in principle, absolutely cannot not yet be its own.

In the final struggle for the greater Eurasian continental Europe, we are concerned only with Russia in its identity as a planetary superpower available to the demands of its suprahistorical imperial predestination.

Yet, from now on, the only planetary continental superpower able to confront the United States and the oceanic and other conspiracies of the de facto *Imperium* maintained by the United States at the level of its own global pretensions and contingencies, appears to be the Greater Europe, governed by the Paris-Berlin-Moscow axis and which is already preparing to rise by itself to the level of the future great Eurasian Empire of the End, of our *Imperium Ultimum*.

We argue that the world political moment is therefore most propitious for an immanent operational grid to be established for our own purposes, producing counter-strategic and, subsequently, in a second stage, strategic and defensive theses, intended to mobilise, according to the deadlines of a first overall grand-continental imperial set-up, the doctrinal and direct action structures at the disposal of the fundamental Paris-Berlin-Moscow axis and of the basic revolutionary projects pursued by it.

Thus our latest analyses of the situation in charge at its overall grand-continental imperial level lead us to respond to the challenges that emerge from this very situation with an immanent grid of seven operational theses, four counter-strategic theses of direct continental engagement, and three offensive strategic theses on a planetary revolutionary level. The battles inside and outside the *Kontinentalblock* constitute, however, a single front. One front, one command.

Counter-offensive inside, offensive outside of Karl Haushofer's *Kontinentalblock*, the Continental Block on which the polar influences, the higher powers of what we serve, soldiers of a single Absolute Concept, are exercised.

Thus, this immanent grid of seven basic operational theses intended to promote the fundamental geopolitical axis Paris-Berlin-Moscow on the ground at its imperial avant-garde level, at its Eurasian grandcontinental level, appears to us to be, at the present time and in view of our profound situation, most certainly definable in the following manner, and which we make our own entirely:

(1) It is in the depths of herself, of her conceived, willed history, engaged in her active totality, of her most occult spiritual predestination, that Russia- that new Russia which is ours-must try to assume towards herself the superhuman effort of finding-returning to-her own polar centre of gravity, her own pole of living transcendental unity, For it is from this moment of inner Eucharistic conflagration, and only from this moment, that Russia, renewed in itself from its very solar centre, will be able to conceive of itself as being really in a state to assume the suprahistorical imperial tasks that are its own, from all times and until the end of everything, apocalyptically.

(2) For, to what the Greater Europe, currently challenged by its Paris-Berlin-Moscow axis of mobilisation, can and must urgently do for the political and economic-industrial re-establishment of the New Russia, Russia, the New Russia, must be able to respond by implementing, on its own responsibility, the spiritual and charismatic revolutionary renewal that must raise up, set on fire in conscience and irrationally, the whole of Europe and the Great Continent: It is from Russia, as we no longer ignore, that the *new Incendium Amoris* must now come to us, which will change everything.

(3) For the Paris-Berlin-Moscow counter-strategic axis, the absolutely priority economic and industrial objective on a grand-continental European scale remains, at the present time, and before any other combat option, whatever it may be that of starting the confidential projects concerning the joint revolutionary development of Siberia, at all available levels, with the full support of Japan and excluding in advance any participation or right of review by non-continental powers such as the United States or the movement under cover of which the United States follows.

On the other hand, it is becoming clear that the immediate, direct and full participation of Japan in the Great Siberian Continental Project (GSCP) will constitute, in fact, the founding act, the original wish of the entry - of the re-entry - of the "Greater Japan" into the advanced continental integration camp of the future Eurasian Empire of the End, and that the rest will follow. A bold will, a will both abrupt and new, will find its ways, and all its ways, including those, prophetic and sacred, of the "pass to the West".

Through its commitments to the Greater Siberia Continental Project (GCP), Japan is turning westward, joining the *Kontinentalblock*.

When Karl Haushofer says that he understands the Chinese as a race from the North migrating southwards and the Japanese as a race from the South migrating northwards, he also defines the demographic cyclone from which Japan can only free itself by exchanging the negative weight of China in its immediate oceanic environment for the positive counterweight of the *Kontinentalblock* without its large, global environment. Japan's integration into the *Kontinentalhlock*, its reorientation towards the West, represents, for Japan, its accession to what Taoism calls "the pass of the West".

But "the pass of the West" – such will have been, in the end, the "great secret" of Taoism – represents, in reality, the obligatory passage, the only "way of passage" towards the North, the very path of the Junction of Venus. For the Junction of Venus, see again, from its most secret operational angle, *The Star of the Invisible Empire*.

Now it is New Russia that is expected to lead Japan along the perilous paths of the "Western Pass", in its final return to the North and the "zone of supreme attention" of its most occult polar gratifications, in the high glacial paths of the "Polar Steel".

For it is in relation to the start-up of the Greater Siberia Continental Project (GCP) that the new German-Russian axis envisaged by Andrei Kozyrev will be able to give its full measure, Germany being, in this precise and quite decisive case, the prime contractor and central mobilising power of the great continental ensemble called upon to take part in this project, the first "great continental project" of the planetary superpower represented by the Greater Europe. In a certain sense, everything will have to happen, from now on, in the operational environment of the Greater Siberia Continental Project (GCP), and the higher implications of its implementation.

(4) Ultimately, what else are we, in these times of vertigo and secret decision, other than the visionary consciousness of our own revolutionary action in the field, present action and, above all, action to come?

In other circumstances, we have already written: "Carrying the powers of being and of revolutionary change that are its own, the visionary consciousness of the near and more distant future of Greater Europe and its imperial Eurasian destinies is already approaching, and increasingly so, immediate history, and this approaching march is in itself already increasingly organisational, in the deep, fractal and cosmogonic sense of the term. Does the organisational interpellation of history change its course?". This last question subversively justifies and founds all our present and future action, and gives us the right to claim a transcendental power of control over the greatest history, a power of control that we will have to take away from those who hold the hidden keys today. Keys that are not, moreover, those of history, but of the dark anti-history that, for a short time to come, will serve as their history, as the pretense of history.

Thus, "a first geopolitical grand continental consultative assembly will have to be set up by us, which will bring together, in view of later consultations, which can already be envisaged in their major lines, representatives of all the countries or significant regions of the Eurasian Continent, from Japan to Iceland, a Provisional Continental Government (PCG) being called upon to emerge thereafter. And, also, a president for life emerging from the Imperial Entity of the End, elected in a manner identical to that which still decides the Roman Devolution, and having the full ontological powers belonging to the state of his secret imperial predestination, but which will manifest in due course, *signed data*. A president for *life* of the Eurasian Imperial Entity of the End elevated by dogmatic irrationality to the state and titles of an absolute concept, and this "absolute concept" being itself, then, only the last state of dogmatic irrationality in action.

(5) The first offensive strategic task, the first "external task" of the Paris-Berlin-Moscow axis will then be that of providing for the establishment - the re-establishment - of ontological identity states, of being and of destiny, with the highlands of Latin America, an outpost of planetary combat against the global imperialist of the North American subversive power plant and those who manipulate it occultly, and, at the same time, a space of cosmic renewal in direct relation to the forthcoming return to strength of the Pleiades. Under cover, the Horbigerian legacy in the Andes still holds. We shall return to it, according to our plans. Thus we have taken note, in the meantime, and with the utmost activist attention, of the planetary combat article by Dr. Carlos A. Dissandro, of La Plata, in the United States. Dissandro, from La Plata, Bolivia, *Global invasion y defensa cultural, etnica, telurica, published in Ciudad de los Césares*, Vina del Mar, Chile, March-April 1993.

(6) The Paris-Berlin-Moscow continental axis will also have to assume-reassume, reactivate and redeploy, above all the politico-strategic tasks on the ground, all the missions of offensive revolutionary intervention which had already been those of "great Gaullism", of the Gaullism of the 1960s - with General de Gaulle in power - towards Quebec, Canada and that part of the United States which, on the borders of Louisiana, still retains the subterranean memory of its European and French origins, a cultural and politico-strategic bridgehead for our future actions of liberation and recovery of our former Northern Lands, of "North America".

(7) The final integration of all the currents of higher spirituality that have arisen in the grand-continental space of the first hyperborean processions will come to be constituted under the active protection of the imperial geopolitical reunion that marks the end of the present cosmic cycle, The Eurasian Empire of the End will thus be brought to be, for the Marian and paraclete Christologies of the End, what Rome had already been, once, for the historical ensemble of nascent Christianity, for the 'new religion' called to arise in the West.

And so it will be in the polar spaces of the last Middle-earth, in Russia and in what will then be the New Russia, that the scattered descendants of the great Anterior Light will come together, whose Last Rome will only complete the suprahistoric process of inner reunion and the ultimate Divine Identity, "Mary of the End".

And, why not say it, the high work of gathering, of polar resourcing currently being carried out from Moscow by Aleksandr Dugin and the groups of watchers close to him who are already at work there, are maintaining, on the spot, the preliminaries already confidentially begun of what, later, will lead to the Great Return.

Now, just as the reintegration of the great-continental camp of the future Eurasian Empire of the End will have to be done, for Japan, for the "greater Japan", by the means of its fundamental, ontological participation in the Great

Siberian Continental Project (GSCP), India, the "greater India", will join the same imperial metahistorical space by bringing to ours, as if from within, that which, even if only in an abysmally occult way, in the depths of Hindu and Tibetan spirituality, cannot fail to still subsist from the immense Anterior Light, from the "bright light" of the Vedic and hyperborean, polar times, even before the Vedic times.

Thus the double mission of the New Russia to the East of the Great Eurasian Continent will soon be put into effect, a double mission that concerns and engages, as we have already seen, the ontological, profound reunion of the fundamental geopolitical axis Paris-Berlin-Moscow, and of the whole of the Great Continent mobilised by this axis, with the 'Greatest India' and with the 'Greatest Japan'. Raymond Abellio, *there will then be unprecedented marriages.*

For what at that moment will have to come together, constituting the East of the Great Continent and of its supreme Imperial Project, will come together through the intermediary of the New Russia, conceived metahistorically so that it receives, at the same time and as if by the same movement, the West of the same Continental Bloc mobilised by the fundamental Paris-Berlin-Moscow axis.

At the end of the cycle, and here we are, Karl Raushofer's *Kontinentalblock* will have its polar centre of imperial geopolitical affirmation somewhere in the spaces that are currently Russia's, and it is in the very heart of our New Russia that the new "Middle Lands" and their inaccessible inner spaces of imperial virginity stand lovingly, nuptially at the service of the Ultimate Mary and *the Imperium Ultimum* that will surround her in the invisible and, also, in the visible. For, at this predestined and most secret moment, let us remember, as we must, the fundamental prophetic word, the *verbum novissimum* of Baruch, *then she appeared on earth, and lived among men.*

This seems to me to be the order of urgency that commands the fundamental line of our current struggles and the immanent grid of operational theses intended to promote their deployment on the ground, the *passage to direct action.*

THE COUNTER-GLOBALIST STRATEGY OF THE PARIS-BERLIN-MOSCOW AXIS

In his resounding speech on 12 May 2000 at Berlin's Humboldt University, Joschka Fischer, Germany's current Foreign Minister, called for a federal Europe based on the Franco-German core, on the "Carolingian Pole" of a federal union of France and Germany, which should thus constitute, together, the inner framework, the central island of support and permanent mobilisation of a politically enlarged Europe, of what will undoubtedly be the future "Greater Europe". Joschka Fischer's return to the federalism of the Franco-German core undoubtedly represents a major attempt to revive the political concept of a "Greater Europe", which is emerging on the open horizon of the next few years of the new millennium.

Wolfgang Schauble, the former president of the CDU, the German Christian Democracy, and Hans Dietrich Genscher, Fischer's predecessor at the head of the German Foreign Ministry, were quick to declare themselves to be in full agreement with the federal European proposals that the current German Foreign Minister had just made in Berlin. Thus, a deep consensus seems to be emerging in Germany, encompassing the entire arc of the current German political reality, in favour of the federalist grand European theses put forward by Joschka Fischer. And what this would mean in the longer term.

Thus, in an interview with *Le Figaro,* dated 20 May 2000, Hans Dietrich Genscher perfectly framed the sum of problems raised by Joschka Fischer's statements:

(1) ''Fischer's intention is now to strengthen the European Union in view of its enlargement. The aim is to make it an effective player in the new world order''.

(2) ''The bipolar world of the Cold War has been replaced by a multipolar world. The United States, Russia, China and, at some distance, Japan, have already taken their place. India is about to join the club. Europe should not be left behind. The new German government had left the foreign policy field somewhat untouched at the beginning. This Fischer plan gives it a European face in the background of globalisation. Fisher has a long view. He will have opponents, but he is on the right track.

Of course, that the current German Foreign Minister has felt strongly, and for once has been able to say clearly and loudly, the need for a significant strengthening of the political links already uniting France and Germany within Europe, This strengthening is intended to go as far as the immediate establishment of a federal relationship between the two countries, a special federal relationship, intended to serve as an incentive, as a pole of attraction and as an open site for other available European countries in the race for political integration, what could be more normal?

But what appears to be completely abnormal at the same time is the inconceivable omission of Russia from Joschka Fischer's proposal for a federalist "central island" to become the heart of the future Greater Europe. For what is the mutilated Europe of Russia now? Nothing, a vague fiction, one more social-democratic decoy, designed to preventively block the paths of the revolutionary project of the Paris-Berlin-Moscow axis, which alone can ensure a decisive political-historical reality for the greater Europe, for the suprahistorically unified, but *reunified* Eurasian "Great Continent". For it is indeed a *final suprahistorical reunification* that is at stake here, and if one has not understood this, one has understood nothing.

Is it possible, then, that the political blindness - undoubtedly, moreover, quite voluntary - of German social democracy with regard to the real political-historical situation of present-day Europe, which is violently undergoing the permanent political-strategic aggression of the globalist conspiracy led by the "Planetary Superpower of the United States"? as well as with regard to the new imperial mission of Russia in relation to the Europe of today and, above all, of tomorrow, can reach such dimensions of dangerous inconsequence, rich already in what future disasters?

In the present European political conjuncture, whose decisive characteristic is that of the preventive installation on the spot of a vast social-democratic conspiracy everywhere in power in the present European political space, a social-democratic conspiracy subversively put in place and directed, in the shadows, by the "Planetary Superpower of the United States", the struggles for the liberation of Europe can only be, today, underground struggles, the desperate struggles of an underground resistance. For there is an underground front for the liberation of Europe, which remains, at present, the last chance for a new European politico-historical freedom in the face of the globalist conspiracy that wants its end, *that fights* for the end of Europe, and of its imperial and supra-historical geopolitical freedom.

The very fact that the political leaders of today's social-democratic Europe ignore or pretend to ignore the existence, the great predestination of Russia, whereas it is now thanks exclusively to Russia that Europe, the Greater Europe, the Eurasian grand-continental Europe, can already claim its future existence, gives the right measure of the ideological and, finally, the immense political and historical betrayal of European social democracy in the service not of the freedom of conscience of Europe and much less of its underground, clandestine struggles for liberation, Finally, the immense political and historical betrayal of European social democracy in the service not of Europe's freedom of conscience and even less of its liberation struggles, underground, clandestine, desperate struggles, but of its subversive subjugation to the interests, to the goals of imperialist control of the globalist conspiracy in action. All the social-democratic regimes currently in power in Europe-and, for that matter, all over the world-are nothing more than auxiliary regimes, harki regimes at the disposal of the US globalist occupation force acting in the shadows.

Western Europe, America's geostrategic 'bridgehead' in Eurasia, entitles Alexandre del Valle a chapter of his book *Guerres contre l'Europe. Bosnia-Kosovo-Tchétchénie*, published by Pierre Guillaume de Roux at Éditions des Syrtes, Paris, 2000.

A fundamental work, a visionary work, a work of immediate counter-strategic use if ever there was one. And it provides the confidential keys to the battle plans for the ontological encirclement of Europe, for the globalist conspiracy that can only achieve its ultimate planetary objectives by preventing the creation of a Eurasian imperial Greater Europe. Through its military-political aggression against Serbia, the US globalist conspiracy has directly attacked Europe, *the intercontinental war of the end has begun.*

I quote from Alexandre del Valle's book, *Guerres contre l'Europe. Bosnia-Kosovo-chechnya*, which fully confirms our own theses.

(1) ''Aware that a strong and independent Europe would be able to overtake America in *all* areas of power, especially economic, American strategists want *at all costs* to prevent the slightest awakening, to nip in the bud the slightest hint of European autonomy, in the event that clear-sighted leaders decide to set up a Greater Continental Europe, reconciling its "two lungs", Orthodox and Western. Hence the American desire to weaken and dilute the European continent by including - in the name of NATO – Turkey in the European Union and by consequently distancing it a little more from Russia, so that the constitution of an independent and strong continental Greater Europe, likely to compete with the United States – but thus rendered impossible - would never see the light of day.

(2) ''With regard to Eastern Europe, the United States is thus pursuing a twofold policy consisting of: firstly, *extending NATO to the gates of Russia*, by integrating into the ''Western world'' the anti-Russian nations of the former Soviet Bloc in the process of industrialisation, of Catholic-Protestant culture (Hungary, Poland, former Czechoslovakia, etc.) and Islamic culture (Turkey, Muslim republics of Central Asia, Bosnia, Albania-Kosovo, etc.); secondly, weakening Russia, ''pushing it back'' towards the West.Secondly, to *weaken* Russia, "push it back" towards Asia and cut it off from Western Europe. The aim is to *split* the European continent in two, reactivating a "new Cold War" between a post-Byzantine ex-Soviet-Communist East and an Americanised West, a new "geo-civilisational clash" between the "two Europes" opposed to each other around the strategic stumbling blocks of Islam-Westernism and socio-economics.

(3) ''The United States' "global" strategic doctrine is clearly reflected in the new American concept of "national security strategy", the content of which was revealed to the general public when a version of the Pentagon's *Defence Planning Guidance*, drawn up in conjunction with the National Security Council (NSA), America's highest authority on security and international policy, was published in the *New York Times* on 8 March 1992. It states that the United States of America must do everything possible to 'deter potential rivals among advanced and industrialised countries from challenging our dominance, even if only to aspire to a greater global or regional role (...) The United States' mission will be to ensure that no rival power is allowed to emerge in Western Europe, Asia, or the territory of the CIS'. In short, it is nothing less than to prevent Europe and Japan, relatively docile 'allies', as well as the weakened but still formidable Russia, from ever raising their heads and casting a shadow on Washington's 'benevolent hegemony', in fact on the formidable American economic and commercial machine. US foreign policy must aim to convince potential rivals that they do not need to play a big role. Our unique superpower status must be perpetuated by sufficient military strength to deter any nation or group of nations from challenging US supremacy, and from seeking to undermine the established economic and political order... We must prevent the emergence of an exclusively European security system that could destabilise NATO. In the Far East, we must remain alert to the risks of destabilisation that would come from an increased role for our allies, in particular Japan'', explains the *Defence Planning Guidance*. (Pages 10, 11, 161, 162).

These documents, in fact, make any commentary unnecessary, as they themselves shed a singularly worrying light on the times of the next American-European confrontations, which are now fatal.

In other words, it must be recognised that, at the present time, total political-subversive war is secretly declared between the globalist conspiracy governed by the "Planetary Superpower of the United States", and Europe - Western Europe, and Eastern Europe, already together on the front line - which is seeking its own ways of revolutionary self-liberation. The *salvific rift*.

As for the encirclement, *the encirclement* - the strategy of the anaconda, which Karl Haushofer identified as the natural, unconscious, instinctive strategy of America - currently being carried out by the globalist conspiracy towards Europe, which is more or less already on the defensive, it is definitely certain that all the political-strategic work subversively pursued by Washington's secret services over the last ten years in Europe and against Europe had, as we have just seen, only one final goal, that of the totalitarian implantation of the social-democratic regimes in their service, in order over the last ten years, in Europe and against Europe, had, as we have just seen, only one final goal, that of the totalitarian implantation of the social-democratic regimes at their service, to prevent, thus, any return of Europe to its previous identity, to the being of its own total historical freedom. However, for their part, the living, hidden forces of the European resistance, having chosen clandestinity, have only the unconditional forward commitment to a revolutionary counter-strategy of already continental dimensions before them to survive the task. To the current internal and external aggression of which it is the object of the globalist conspiracy at work, Europe can only oppose, with its back to the wall, its inspired will for an imperial integration with a suprahistorical, transcendental, eschatological aim, the Eurasian grandcontinental integration of the end. Playing the whole thing for all it's worth, and all at once.

In the current state of affairs, the Eurasian grand-continental integration of Europe must imperatively take the obligatory passage of the Paris-Berlin-Moscow axis, which represents, in effect, the *salvific fault line* for ours.

This amounts to demanding the double mobilisation of our people, on the one hand, to put an end, by all means, to the subversive stranglehold of social democracy and its conspiracies everywhere at work, everywhere in power in Europe and, on the other hand, to achieve a decisive revolutionary implantation in the European collective consciousness of an overactivated representation of the absolute and immediate necessity of grandcontinental integration, whose first operational phase will have to be that of the political setting in train of the Paris-Berlin-Moscow axis. The final battle for the liberation of Europe will therefore be a battle that will have to be fought in terms of consciousness, the battle for its final awareness of itself and of its great polar predestination of the origins.

Thus the double test of the dismantling in force of the social-democratic stranglehold on the whole of the present European political power, and at the same time of the accession of Europe as a whole to the revolutionary consciousness of its own pre-ontological unity, of its Eurasian imperial predisposition, constitutes *the very line of passage* from the Europe currently in a state of non-being to the Europe once again capable of revolutionary mastery of its own politico-historical destinies, once more conscious of its final suprahistorical mission.

History, however, never gives gifts, all the objectives belonging to the active definition of the great politico-historical predestinations to be accomplished must be won, always, with great struggle, tragically, heroically. This, then, appears to be the task of our generation, the generation dedicated to the decisive revolutionary mission of salvation and liberation of the Greater Europe from its present subjection to the globalist conspiracy governed by the "Planetary Superpower of the United States".

Now it is the very circumstantial future of the present world history, at the fatal hour of the accomplishment of a secret destiny already inescapably in motion, that makes us find ourselves called today before a commandment of immediate and total action: it is *now or never* that we must act, and that by acting we win the game.

As has been repeated over and over again, the transition to direct revolutionary action by underground Europe, by Europe already clandestinely engaged in the fight for its liberation, can and must be made only from the politico-historical trail of the Paris-Berlin-Moscow axis.

Unfortunately, neither France nor Germany is currently in a position to take the political initiative on the Paris-Berlin-Moscow axis.

Only Russia could do this, but it would be necessary for the "providential man" to appear beforehand, the "man of the greatest destiny", who alone could take it upon himself to engage Russia in the great Eurasian imperial adventure presupposed as necessarily consecutive to the establishment of the Paris-Berlin-Moscow axis, which is only the original pivot, the ontological bunker of the beginning.

For, in any case, Europe will be Eurasian grand-continental, or it will not be.

In fact, the Franco-German federal core proposed today by Joschka Fischer already represents nothing: the Europe he calls for is not Europe, but a sort of spectral, ectoplasmic apparition of it. The real Greater Europe is *the Imperium* that will emerge around the Paris-Berlin-Moscow axis, once this has become the Madrid-Paris-Rome-Berlin-Moscow-New Delhi-Tokyo axis.

Thus, the only interest of Joschka Fischer's federal project lies in the fact that, by proposing a hard Franco-German federal core, to which the other European countries envisaged would subsequently join and be federalised as well, he was overstepping the most formal prohibitions of the American globalist conspiracy, which will not tolerate at all the emergence of a Federal Europe, even if it is reduced to its reduced, mutilated expression, even if it has a social-democratic orientation, in the European space under its control. What exactly does this attempt by Joschka Fischer amount to, one wonders? Is Germany finally planning to embark on a parallel political manoeuvre, taking considerable risks? Is Berlin thus embarking on who knows what political blackmail, who knows what obscure showdown with Washington, or are Berlin and Washington together playing an as yet indecipherable game, pushing forward a new phase of the secret American game of incumbent Social Democracy?

As for the rest of us, we can already venture to say that the decisive political battle for the implementation of the Paris-Berlin-Moscow axis project has now begun, and that it is in Moscow itself that we have chosen to set up the operational centre for its immediate start.

If it is up to Moscow to take the initiative, it is in Moscow that we will have to start putting pressure, trying to create the great groundswell of revolutionary enthusiasm towards the collective supramental representation of the Paris-Berlin-Moscow axis project. It is Moscow that, as it is said, will have to give the signal to start, a mysterious ritual requires it.

Therefore, we must concentrate all our agitation, influence and intervention capacities in order to incandesce *the abysmal interest of* our ideological-revolutionary structures of presence and supervision acting on the spot, in Moscow, so that when the time comes, they can determine, from the depths, the entry into action of the media and the large groups of political, cultural and even religious influence, as well as, finally, of the active governmental bodies, in order to promote, to demand a decisive political initiative from Moscow in favour of the project of the Paris-Berlin-Moscow axis. An initiative from Moscow to which we commit ourselves to obtain the expected responses from Paris and Berlin.

It will therefore be necessary that at the same time we urgently undertake a double analogous movement of awakening, of exacerbation, in Paris and Berlin, by putting to the test in an extremely intensive way the "geopolitical groups" which we have, on the spot, at the moment, so that the mobilising figure of the project of the Paris-Berlin-Moscow axis is present there, and acts according to our plans.

This implies-we will be obliged to do so-that the "geopolitical groups" will come out of their semi-clandestinity to act in the open, a new situation that will surely entail quite serious dangers. But it is no less certain that, by this very fact, the political control of the so-called social democracy over the whole of the political power in place will be violently challenged, and that, in any case, we will have to go to the test of strength.

And it is not even impossible that the trial of strength between the social democracy in power and the forces of protest which will then rise up against the *state of affairs* could immediately take on the appearance of a civil war, They have not yet openly declared their existence, and therefore show no relation with what is called, no doubt by derision, the "national opposition" – so-called "Gaullist", and other formations of the same show-off, which are shamefully complicit in the imitation of the current power – "national opposition", whose posted positions openly pledge allegiance to the slogans of the globalist conspiracy, which is present in the shadow.

On the other hand, it will also be necessary for the start of the campaign in Moscow in favour of the Paris-Berlin-Moscow axis project to coincide in some way with the sudden appearance and assumption of presidential power by the "providential man", by "the one we are waiting for", so that we can be certain of the Russian government's attitude on this subject. The Moscow government should then, in fact, seize upon the current petition for the Paris-Berlin-Moscow axis project to make it its own battle horse, at the level of "grand politics". The matter should ultimately be dealt with on a state-to-state basis between Russia, France and Germany.

Moreover, if the "providential man" who will have to take over the presidential power in Moscow is identical to the visionary, prophetic figure of "the one we are waiting for", he will have to have already thought, by himself, about the fundamental revolutionary problem of the Paris-Berlin-Moscow axis, which is the absolutely priority problem of the "new power" in Moscow, whoever it will be.

The project of the Paris-Berlin-Moscow axis will be ready to be immediately activated at the moment when the revolutionary national powers of the French, German and Russian elites and masses, overactivated by our care, will meet and espouse, on their very rise, the triple will of the state of France, Germany and Russia, because it is indeed this meeting that is called upon to found, to abysmally renew Asian Grand European history.

And it is not at all that one would try to conceal, now, what at that moment cannot but be the fierce opposition of the American globalist conspiracy to the emergence, in Europe, of the Paris-Berlin-Moscow axis – the liberation of Europe will then have already been accepted, the political encirclement and all the politico-strategic prohibitions opposed by the American globalist conspiracy to the emerging Greater Europe smashed, swept away, annihilated by the uprising of the European national forces of revolutionary liberation. For, in the present state of affairs, it is in fact impossible for the Paris-Berlin-Moscow axis to be installed before the total political liberation of Europe is declared, and it is precisely the declaration of the installation, of the setting up of the Paris-Berlin-Moscow axis that will mark the advent of the Greater Europe on the march, the revolutionary wrenching away of this Europe from the subjugating grip of the "Planetary Superpower of the United States".

The ideological war of the Paris-Berlin-Moscow axis will be waged by the great battles of consciousness to come, and it is we who will then hold the supreme command of these battles. The fundamental reversal of the home front of the decisive battle for the liberation of European consciousness will mean that the American globalist conspiracy will be reduced to the defensive, and that it is we who will lead the offensive of the dismantling and final assertion of our own grand European positions, which will have won.

At a recent group meeting, someone had made the very accurate observation that the Paris-Berlin-Moscow axis project brings with it a powerful ancestral, sacred *shamanic presence.* Now there is nothing unexpected here, nothing very surprising: the profound change in the history of a vast grouping of populations that are essentially identical in terms of their hidden being but different on the surface must always secretly set in motion colossal subterranean spiritual powers, the implementation of which undoubtedly comes from certain occult, unavowable identities of a transcendental order. Supernatural, faceless identities.

Whether we like it or not, this point of view is likely to prevail in the end. Magically. And all the more so because this same point of view represents a profound constant of the European spirit in its subterranean timelessness.

Let us conclude this brief combat article on the counter-strategic project, currently underway, of the Paris-Berlin-Moscow axis, by quoting what Ernst Robert Curtius called, in his monumental *Balzac* of 1933, the author of the

Conspiracy of the Thirteen's "allusion" to a certain "Europe as a mystery", to this *great continental family, whose every effort tends towards some mystery of civilisation.*

Now this great continental family of which Balzac had in his time the visionary prescience is, in fact, precisely that of this permanent conspiracy which, from century to century, subterraneanly perpetuates the will of final imperial integration of the Eurasian 'Great Continent' and the realisation of its occult eschatological goals, a conspiracy which constitutes what Balzac called, in such a genial way, a *mystery of civilisation.* An imposing march that nothing can stop, because 'it is God's will that is being carried out, it is his thought that is being realised', he said (quoted by Ernst Robert Curtius in his *Balzac).*

Thus we see that the Eurasian grand-continental obsession of a certain secretly imperial European revolutionary consciousness is not new, that it has existed in continuity since time immemorial; that this obsession constitutes a real "mystery of civilisation".

Far from representing a simple circumstantial politico-historical emergence, the project of the Paris-Berlin-Moscow axis for which we are already fighting appears as the immediately visible face of a profound supratemporal actuality of the European consciousness, of this "great continental family" envisaged by Balzac considered in its ultimate Eurasian, imperial and revolutionary dimensions.

The globalist conspiracy can certainly claim, at the present time, to be in a position to lock everything down, to neutralise any vestige of European resistance, this claim being posed in the very terms of the offensive dialectic of its own overall interests, of its own designs, henceforth in the open, for planetary domination. The globalist conspiracy *already believes itself to be there.*

But history is absolutely not the sum of its circumstances: on the contrary, it is history that decides, invents and irrationally imposes the circumstances of its own forward march. Historical circumstances are never more than the effects of an abysmal cause, the very cause of that 'mystery of civilisation' of which Balzac spoke and which is the hidden key to all 'great politics' in continental Europe and Eurasia.

The current proponents of the globalist conspiracy command the circumstantial effects of visible history. We, who are on the side of "Europe as mystery", command the causes, because it is the causes that command us, directly. The invisible, abysmal, eschatological and providential causes, the "first causes". To the terror of totalitarian democratic reason, we oppose the front line of the dogmatic irrationality of history itself.

Thus it is that despite the state of the present unconditional grip of the globalist conspiracy on the whole political structures of social democracy, history, of itself, moves forward by forcing its own decision spiral, its own substantive changes and its own forms of renewal over the de facto circumstances and hegemonic designs of US democratic imperialism subversively at work within the space of its permanent European aim: mysteriously, things are being done that should not be done, things that are both irrevocable and secretly fundamental. It is as if history is constantly escaping from the grip of globalist subversion on the emerging Europe, from all the shenanigans in the shadows. As we have seen, the ultimate objective of the current and future grand political strategy of the globalist conspiracy is and will be to prevent by all means **the** imperial emergence of the Greater Europe: in spite of this, by the very inner movement of history on the march, the Greater Europe never ceases to progress, ineluctably. And it is from within the European social-democratic power that initiatives concerning this forward march of Europe, such as that of Joschka Fischer, arise, while the social-democratic power is only there to prevent its affirmation, its effective implementation. Jacques Chirac's astonishing European performance on 27 June 2000 in Berlin, in front of the full Reichstag, belongs to the same kind of operation unconsciously imposed by the proper march of history, history that follows the commands of its own dogmatic irrationality. Whatever they do, it is only what must be done that will be done.

For the history that reveals itself in its own choices will always be stronger than the history that reveals the choices we try to impose on it.

Irrational historical forces are fighting underground, supporting our own fight for the Paris-Berlin-Moscow axis. The objective appearances of the situation are against us. But in the end, only the counter-objective certainties emanating from the very march of history, the *abysmal part*, count.

THE MYSTERIOUS RISE OF VLADIMIR PUTIN

(1) Vladimir Putin, the end of a cycle

We knew it, but what is most important is that it continues, without interruption, until now: Russia, by its very nature, by its original historical predestination, by its very becoming is, and remains, a mystery. And the indecipherable personality of its new President, Vladimir Putin, only confirms this certainty of fact. In his book *La mystérieuse ascension de Vladimir Poutine,* Pierre Lorrain writes: "The personality of this man with the borrowed allure, the dull physique and the reserved appearance of a civil servant without stature contrasts so much with his meteoric rise to the summit of power, that it is difficult not to conceive the suspicion of a great mystery, immediately corroborated by his sulphurous past as a secret agent".

Although Pierre Lorrain's book does not contain any major revelations about Vladimir Putin, it does reconstruct, in exchange, in an exhaustive and very precise manner, the underground current which, within the occult arrangements of the Soviet power in place, had prepared for Vladimir Putin's rise to power, an event which was both prefabricated in the shadows and inscribed in the very destiny of the forces actively involved. Forces that were secretly divergent and often even antagonistic. But the result could not but end up conforming to what was dialectically inscribed in it from the beginning of the great historical cycle in progress.

The spectral horizon, dark and tormented, tragic, within which we passed from Stalin to Kruschev, from Kruschev to Brezhnev, from Brezhnev to Andropov, from Andropov to Gorbachev and from Gorbachev to Yeltsin, is indeed clearly deconspired by Pierre Lorrain, reduced to the dialectic of the passage of power within a device maintained as it is, unchanged through the very series of changes that have historically traversed it but never undone it.

The ontologically definitive break with the ideological-political structure set up by Stalin only took place with the advent to power of Vladimir Putin, and in this perspective, the whole political development of Russia, from Stalin to Boris Yeltsin, was in fact a long secret path leading to, and having led to Vladimir Putin. Who himself represents the return to what had been so tragically interrupted by the "Red October" of 1917, the massacre of Nicholas II and the entire imperial family, and by the birth of the USSR. And the advent of Vladimir Putin to final power was dialectically foreseen, which was to mark the conclusion of the cycle, the *recommencement,* and thus the overcoming of what had ended in blood, the hallucinatory violence of the Soviet course, and the building of the USSR on this blood and violence, inexpressible, but at the same time foundational.

Pierre Lorrain shows perfectly that the appearance of the occult political current which, through the action of dismantling and dismantling undertaken by Gorbachev from within the Soviet power apparatus, had its origin in the overall action set up underground by Andropov, since his accession to the leadership of the KGB and, subsequently, to the general secretariat of the party. It is not for nothing that Vladimir Putin, as soon as he arrived in the Kremlin, had a golden plaque put up in homage to the memory of Yuri Andropov, *the one who started it all.*

It was not Andropov's accumulated power as head of the KGB, writes Pierre Lorrain, that opened the way to the General Secretariat, but his place in the hierarchy. By the time Souslov died, Andrei Kjrilenko, who was close to Brezhnev, was already in a semi-disgrace. The balance of power required a leader in the number two position who could counterbalance the Brezhnevs. Andropov was that person. At the plenum of the Central Committee in May 1982, he was appointed Secretary of Ideology, which meant giving up the presidency of the KGB. So he left Lubyanka Square and moved five hundred metres away to Souslov's office in the Central Committee headquarters on the Old Square.

It was therefore in the capacity of number two that he became General Secretary on 12 November, at the end of a "conclave" which surprised everyone by its brevity. In fact, collegiality imposed the nomination of Andropov, even if some members of the apparatus would have preferred Konstantin Chernenko. The same unwritten rules made Chernenko, Brezhnev's heir and Andropov's rival, the new Secretary of Ideology, which *ipso facto* made him the second most important person in the hierarchy. At the same time, one of Andropov's closest personalities, Mikhail Gorbachev, was moving up the ranks to become number three. He quickly formed an embryonic clan based on Kirilenko's former protégés who had been "orphaned" by his dismissal and who had become close to Andropov. This group of specialists in heavy industry and planning, all from the Sverdlovsk region in the Urals, included Nikolai Ryjkov, the future prime minister, and a certain Boris Yeltsin who would later become very famous.

Thus, in a few lines, Pierre Lorrain draws up the prehistoric figure of the knot of forces in motion constituting the origin of the final seismic shift, which will lead to the disappearance of the USSR and the advent to power of Vladimir Putin, the one by which what was no longer was going to be able to start again, the new emergence of the "Anterior Russia" nevertheless assuming the dramatic heritage of the USSR. Beyond the Empire of the Romanovs and the imperialism of the "world communist revolution", the Third Russia, the "New Russia", bearer of Vladimir Putin's great Eurasian imperial design and the geopolitical imperial current of which he is the representative. But Pierre Lorrain refrains from talking about all this, at least for the moment.

(2) The secret services in power

The subterranean history of the last fifty years in Russia is in fact the history of the 'power shift' from the 'total political power of the party' to the 'total political-administrative power of the special services'. This "transition of power" culminated in the advent of President Vladimir Putin, who represents the supreme degree of the qualitative assumption of the "special services", the ultimate summit incarnation of their own historical evolution.

So the total revolutionary reversal of Russia's current history from the imperialist totalitarian state of Stalin to the orthodox imperial "transcendental" state of Vladimir Putin is really only the external projection of the "internal revolution" of the Russian special services in their occult march towards final power, towards total power.

In a private conversation with Pierre Lorrain, former Prime Minister Sergei Stepashin said: 'In the Soviet era, the KGB gathered the country's elite: college graduates, with a good education and a "clean bill of health" as they used to say. Many intellectuals.

This is, in fact, the real big secret of the collapse of the USSR and of Soviet-style communism throughout Eastern Europe. For it was the over-concentration of the active elites of the communist countries mobilised within the political special services, in the front line, that had provoked, ensured the setting up of the great final anti-communist conspiracy emanating from within their own security services. To whom the elevation of the consciousness of its senior cadres and leading active elements was fatal to the primary, anticivilisational and anti-spiritual ideology of Marxist aberration and dialectical materialism, to the unbearable Stalinist and post-Stalinist straitjacket that was in principle imposed on them by the party. The awareness of the operational elites of the Soviet-line communist regimes was ultimately fatal to the regimes themselves, as the consciousness of consciousness won out, in the end, over the Marxist alienation of consciousness: freedom is the foundation of being, and the consciousness of being will win out, in the end, against all the conspiracies of non-being. The proof is what happened in the USSR, and in all of Eastern Europe under Soviet rule. In the end, we had to *give in to reality.*

But what is the *ultimate meaning* that must be given to this assumptional overthrow of the political special services of Russia and Eastern Europe, in what *ultimate perspective* must we situate what has happened? Let's say that in order to answer this twofold question, we have to resort to an eschatological explanation, which is not possible in an article like this one, where space is extremely limited. I will leave that for another occasion.

(3) Vladimir Putin, the predestined

On the subject of Vladimir Putin himself, however, Pierre Lorrain will provide information that I believe to be quite considerable. Vladimir Putin's family," writes Pierre Lorrain, "comes from Pokrovskoie, in western Siberia, an obscure village on the Tobol River, between Tyumen and Tobolsk, whose main claim to fame is that it was the birthplace of one of the country's most controversial figures, Grigori Rasputin, the infamous *starets* ("holy man") whose influence on Empress Alexandra Feodorovna contributed to the discrediting of Tsar Nicholas II and the monarchy on the eve of the 1917 revolution. According to our source, some members of the family, anxious to distance themselves from such a politically troublesome relative, abbreviated their surname, deleting the first syllable. It has to be said that this no (which can be translated as "Debauched") is not very easy to bear, even if the nationalist writer Vadim Rasputin, a champion of Siberia and an apostle of rural life, has given it some credibility in the eyes of Russians. Is Mr Putin the great-nephew or a distant cousin of the *starets?* ". And Pierre Lorrain adds: "A family link, even if tenuous, between Mr Putin and Rasputin would explain the curious physical resemblance, minus the beard, that can be seen between the current president and the man who was nicknamed the 'mad monk' abroad, even though he was neither a monk nor mad.

Pierre Lorrain also provides us with other particularly substantial information on Vladimir Putin's stay in East Germany, in Dresden, on his distant and more recent biography, on the stages and twists and turns of his known career. But the man remains elusive, distant, fundamentally secret. As if he belonged to another reality, another world. Which, by the way, seems to be precisely the case.

(4) Geopolitical views

It remains to approach - to unveil, one might even say - what must be called Vladimir Putin's Eurasian Great Continent imperial geopolitics, as it currently emerges from the doctrines put forward by the geopolitical groups in Moscow that closely surround, protect and exalt him, which foresee the imperial integration of the Eurasian "Great Continent" - Western Europe, Eastern Europe, Russia and Greater Siberia, Tibet, India, and Japan - into a "Eurasian Empire of the End", the latest state of Karl Haushofer's geopolitical doctrines and his fundamental operational concept of *Kontinetalblock.*

And knowing that there is no new Empire without a renewed great imperial religion, Vladimir Putin, himself a deep, mystical believer, is fundamentally siding with Orthodoxy, while counting, in the long run, on a continental reunion between Orthodoxy and Catholicism involving a suprahistorical return to the 'previous religion', from 'before the separation'.

It is also thanks to Vladimir Putin's Orthodox commitment that the canonisation of the martyred Emperor Nicholas II and his family, witnesses of blood, massacred on the orders of Lenin, has taken place and that "Great Orthodoxy" has practically become the state religion of the "New Russia". Vladimir Putin's secret meeting in Rome with John Paul II has a prophetic significance, the decisive meaning of which only the future can tell us.

In his book, Pierre Lorrain tries to warn us against what he calls the "millenarian and messianic" fads of Vladimir Putin. But in doing so, he is dramatically mistaken, because it is there, in fact, that the greatness of Putin lies, his hidden prophetic identity and his final predestination, which we can still consider unpredictable but which we already know is that of a secret election, manipulated from above, from the invisible. An election in every respect *decisive*.

In this spectral hour when world history is on the verge of reaching the moment of inner rupture from which there is no turning back, let alone a possible march forward, and when what the Hindu tradition calls the *Paravrtti*, the "Great Reversal" can be unleashed at any moment, the problem of the present history of the Great Eurasian Continent comes to be posed in the very precise terms of the choice offered to Russia of seeing or not seeing the emergence in its midst of the "providential man", the "man of the greatest destiny". For, once again and in any case, it is in Russia that - obviously, given the current final politico-historical configuration of the Great Continent - the future destinies of the last great European history of the world will be decided today.

Twenty-four years ago, I published an article in *"Correspondance Européenne"* which, at the time, caused quite a stir, and which has often been quoted since. Even R. V. Nikolski had mentioned it in his clandestine manuscript, which I have discussed at length elsewhere in very approving terms. An article dealing with the secret - and more than secret – duplication of the Soviet Union by a certain Counter-Russia acting underground, in the shadows, at all levels of the political-administrative apparatus of the Soviet State, including – and perhaps especially - at the "inner levels" of the Party itself, and in which I wrote, in conclusion, this:

History, the great history, is never what those who suffer it think, blinded by its occult leaders. The active secret of history must be sought in the living reasons of those who make and unmake it, in the silence and darkness of the underworld, far from the gaze and attention of the masses, and they know that history moves forward or backward, that it lights up or darkens, each time, according to the inner workings of a will that maintains itself beyond the course of history, a transhistorical will'. This is an unconventional perspective on the course of history, what Julius Evola called the 'fourth dimension' of history. And, in the same article, I continued: "It is in the light of this interiorising conception of history that we must know - *know in advance*, everything is there – who, in the Soviet Union, will end up winning, at the desired time, over the other side, implacably, in order to immediately commit to changing – in one direction or another - the direction and even the very face of world history. Today, as in the past, this is the sole purpose: to change the face of the world.

However, in the perspective of the *single goal,* which of the two camps will prevail over the other? The one that will be able to let the will of destiny of the providential man appear within it, who will also be the man of the last battle. When will he come? Inevitably, at the appointed time" *("Correspondance Européenne",* February 1977).

Now there are a few of us who have already understood that, in the present circumstances and, from now on, definitively, because, in the visible as well as in the invisible, these *present circumstances* are also *final circumstances,* this man who is expected, the "providential man", the man "of the greatest destiny and of the final battle", cannot be other than the present President of Russia, Vladimir Putin.

A deep, inspired intuition, as well as an absolutely obvious certainty when we know what we know, Vladimir Putin is already, for some of us, the man of the great revolutionary, "imperial" and "eschatological" recovery of the "New Russia", and therefore the one on whom the fight for the ultimate recovery and assumption of Europe and the geopolitical and suprahistorical whole of the Eurasian "Great Continent" in its final dimensions is also based at the decisive moment.

The secret visionary, the "man of the last battle" who is thus called upon to lead, historically and suprahistorically, the forward march of the "New Russia", the land, since time immemorial, of great messianic, "eschatological" visions, appeared precisely where it had to appear because the greatest destiny had to speak, and so it spoke, even if it has not yet been heard by the "few" of the revolutionary vanguard watchmen, the "midnight harvesters". But what had to be done was done, "ineluctably, at the appointed time".

Of course, I am not unaware of the tragic politico-revolutionary responsibilities that are incumbent upon us, those who have understood that, in the final analysis, there is only one way out of this formidable final politico-historical crisis that is Europe's current crisis in the face of the total counter-strategic offensive of the globalist conspiracy underway: namely, the urgent setting in motion - of the utmost urgency - of the process of Eurasian grand-continental imperial integration, of which President Vladimir Putin is at present the only European political leader who not only understands all the tragic stakes, but is already fully committed to the "last battle" of the "greatest destiny" that appears to be, at present, already for us and for the greater Europe, the battle for the revolutionary establishment of the "Eurasian Empire of the End".

The "Eurasian Empire of the End" - as we keep saying - will consist of the total federal political integration of Western and Eastern Europe, Russia and

Greater Siberia, Tibet, India and Japan, the last state of Karl Haushofer's fundamental geopolitical concept, the *Kontinentalblock* concept.

Having thought that I should add a few details to Pierre Lorrain's book, *The Mysterious Rise of Vladimir Putin,* of which he had in fact only given us a rather external, overly conventional portrait, I don't know if at the same time I didn't go too far in my revelations about the implicit commitments and avant-garde political-strategic choices of the current host of the Kremlin. This is particularly true with regard to what Pierre Lorrain calls the "millenarian and messianic infatuations" of the President of Russia, in whom, as far as we are concerned, we do not hide the fact that we have recognised the "man of the last battle" and of the "greatest destiny" of Europe and, consequently, of the Eurasian "Great Continent".

However, trying to show President Vladimir Putin in the true light, in the sharpest light of his highest political identity, present and future, can only reinforce, it seems to me, the awareness of rupture that one can, that one must have from now on, in Western Europe, and more particularly in France, of the mission, of the suprahistoric, religious and eschatological predestination, of which he must be credited. For, if it is only by relying on France that President Vladimir Putin will be able to influence and change the final direction of the new European history of the world, it is certain that a very mysterious lack of influence, a very flagrant lack of interest in him, is manifesting itself today in France, with a strange obstinacy maintained in the shadows by occult nuclei of special action, overactivated.

It is therefore high time to denounce, with the utmost violence, the subversive enterprise currently underway in France with regard to the militant figure of Vladimir Putin, an enterprise that is the direct product of a concerted machination aimed at preventing him from being recognised for *what he really is*. A machination directed by the same nocturnal, unmentionable and, above all, for the time being *unnameable* forces, which continue to implement the increasingly advanced alienation of the profound being of France, of its own history and of what France means beyond history.

Through our immediate, visible political struggle, it is in reality the power of darkness that we are fighting, today as yesterday, *until the end*.

WHAT EUROPE EXPECTS OF VLADIMIR PUTIN THE ESCHATOLOGICAL DESTINIES OF THE NEW RUSSIA

(1) The Seventh Seal

The decisive years are returning. The vertiginous whirlwind of a final reversal of abysmal dimensions of ongoing world history now prevails over the obscure stagnation of the times of resigned decay from which we are emerging and in which we had already almost lost ourselves. Everything is now entering the zone of supreme attention''.

For that is how it is: at the very moment when Vladimir Putin had assumed presidential power in Moscow, an immense reversal was taking place in the invisible backstage of "great world history" in progress. Not only was the century-long interregnum of the bloody dictatorship of darkness of Marxism-Leninism really coming to an end, but the very sense of history that had allowed this to happen was being reversed, giving way to the revolutionary resumption of a different identity of Russian historical reality, to the revival of the eschatological predestination of the "previous Russia", of Russia as the "absolute concept" of world history conceived as the controlled development of a secret "grand design" of Divine Providence.

Thus, in the Christological vision of the world and its history, the terrible bloody sacrifice of the crucifixion of Russia and its captive peoples in the world conspiracy of Soviet communism will not have been in vain: for it is only through the liturgical paths of the mystery of the Cross that the occult, final path of the supreme, active mystery of the Resurrection passes.

Now, in spite of these first equivocal and heart-rending times that mark the return to life after the long processional descent through the black chasms of death, it is indeed the bright morning of the Resurrection that Russia, that Vladimir Putin's "New Russia" is called to experience today, even if it is perhaps not yet fully aware of its new state, which is essentially a state of grace.

For a certain counter-current of impediment, of ontological torpor and slowing down, marks, subterraneanly, at the present time, everything in Russia and in the whole world that testifies to the return to being, already incipient, everything that shares the current incipient resurrectional thrust: what is no longer there is not yet replaced by what is not quite there yet.

So let us not be fooled by deceptive appearances, doctored on purpose: this dreadful general torpor, this increasingly unbearable hypnotic impotence, this slowing down of everything, which seems to have taken hold of everything that wants to move forward in recent years, is, in spite of everything, and must be-for those who really know how to see, beyond the simple fact of seeing-the sign of the setting up, difficult, very difficult for the moment, but absolutely inescapable in the long run of a change in the ontological state of the world and its present history, the very sign of the "great reversal" that has taken place, that is in the process of taking place on your "line of passage" towards the Third Millennium.

So it is no longer so much the fact that, because of the very course of things, we must constantly free ourselves from the dead weight of the past that forces us to move forward in spite of everything, but already the irrational call within us of an irresistible new, revolutionary impulse, of a different renewal, implying the leap forward over the precipices of your end of the previous regime of things, the *leap over the void:* for we have indeed reached this point, and there is no turning back.

In the meantime, we have to face every day the mystery of what is still constantly slipping away from us, of what seems never to be able to find its fulfilment, of what sinks indefinitely into the vague and dirty mud, very dirty indeed, of its own impossibility of being: This invasion of what rises from the most nocturnal depths of the abysses at the hour of the truly final suspension of the breath of being, is indeed the part that is ours today in a world struck by the prohibition of being subversively signified to all the forces of life, of renewal, of recommencement. But let us also know that all this can only be, in reality, *essentially temporary.* And when the Lamb opened the seventh seal, there was silence in heaven for about half an hour'', we read in the Apocalypse of Saint John. These, then, are the times of the extreme ambiguities of the non-being in power and the temporary degradation of the powers of being, the dark times of the ultimate exaltation of abjection, the times of the ending interregnum of the illegal rule of the abject.

This is the reason why the double subversion of social-democrats and liberal-democrats - which will always be the regimes of equivocation, alienating diversion and concealed passage to the enemy - have prevailed, and are still illegally holding on to power in the three main countries of Western Europe, Britain, France and Germany, in the very heart of the battlefield where everything is going to happen. And this, until the renewal in the depths comes to revolutionarily overwhelm, to cross the "crossing of the line" to impose revolutionarily, with Vladimir Putin and with what Vladimir Putin symbolically means at the present time, his law of total, irreversible change, the law of the great "Final Reversal", of the *Paravrtti.*

In itself, the interregnum is never anything other than the guarantee of the exit from the interregnum.

(2) Vladimir Putin's eschatological imperial 'grand design

So what are the magnetic lines of force that could be called, if not Vladimir Putin's governmental doctrine, at least his fundamental project of politico-strategic action in the near and more distant future?

First of all, to return Russia to itself, in a revolutionary, total, unconditional way. To immediately reconnect with the great suprahistorical predestination of Russia, an eschatological predestination to be rediscovered, to be taken up again precisely where the Soviet revolution interrupted it, in the framework of an occult suprahistorical conspiracy whose dimensions far exceeded the destiny of Russia alone.

This was precisely because, by continuing the work of his predecessors, Nicholas II, whom his cousin Kaiser Wilhelm II had called the "Emperor of the Pacific", was about to make Russia the world's superpower "from the Atlantic to the Pacific", and thus finally set in motion the "secret plan" of his own supra-historical imperial and continental predestination.

For it was to prevent Russia from imposing its own eschatological imperial will on current world history "from the Atlantic to the Pacific" that Russia was slaughtered, forcibly dislodged from the history it had chosen to carry forward to its final transcendental outcome, which would have been that of its imperial Christological transfiguration. To develop, therefore, the conceptions of the Holy Alliance to its ultimate planetary and historical dimensions, to the realization of its decisive suprahistorical identity.

This is what the nocturnal powers representing, in the forbidden backstage of "great history", the abysmal occult identity of what the traditional Christological doctrine calls the "Mystery of Iniquity" at work until the "Second Coming", could not allow to be accomplished. Hence the worldwide conspiracy of the powers of darkness to dismantle the Russian Empire in its eschatological identity, which was then secretly already activated and about to enter the stream of history, through internal and external complicities that remain unknown and *unrecognisable to* this day.

But, at the present time, it is this same eschatological imperial design of Russia that is once again on the agenda of Vladimir Putin, who intends to bring Russia back to itself, relying for this on his "New Russia" and on the "great Russian and East European Orthodoxy". But at the same time, despite and beyond the resistance of Orthodoxy, and whatever its intransigence and concerted refusal to accept, it will also rely on Rome and traditional Roman Catholicism. And this, as he had shown-and demonstrated-on his first trip abroad as the newly elected President of Russia, when he had very significantly insisted that it take place in Italy, and with John Paul II, with whom he had the long confidential interview that we know. We will talk about Vladimir Putin's special relationship with Rome and Roman Catholicism later in this article, Vladimir Putin being a fervent reader of Vladimir Soloviev. This clarifies many things.

Thus, it seems quite obvious that for this to really happen, Vladimir Putin must first of all succeed in forging the politico-strategic tool of planetary revolutionary action that can really give course to his visionary designs, namely a Russian state with the weight of a planetary superpower, and leading the bloc of a European grandcontinental imperial political concentration of transcendental and polar identity. And this one also turned in its ultimate revolutionary instances, towards the trans-continental mobilisation of Latin America, also a Catholic continent, as well as of the United States itself, rid of its enemies, of its nocturnal subjection to the Protestant illuminist subversion and above all to that which, since the beginning, has been spectrally hidden behind it, and whose name we dare not say nor attempt to unveil its face of darkness.

Vladimir Putin's fundamental struggle will be, in these conditions, that of the internal liberation of Russia from the formidable negative burdens that continue to encumber - still – the miracle of its political resurrection, and the setting in motion of its administrative, economic and military renewal, which should lead to its recovering, in due course, its status – already twice lost - of imperial planetary superpower (a status lost, first, in 1917, and then with the liquidation of the Soviet Union). What appears in perspective, therefore, is the renewed figure of a Third Russia, which should also want to be, finally, a Third Rome.

The real internal liberation of Russia includes, in the current state of urgency of the situation, a grid of priorities that must be solved dramatically, at any price, immediately and completely, each one for its part and all at once. And this from effectively derisory means, the most certain of which appears to be, in this case, that of Vladimir Putin's accession to supreme presidential power. We have to deal with it.

A number of recovery tasks await Vladimir Putin at the turn of an infinitely perilous destiny, a perilous destiny to which, in addition to Vladimir Putin's personal charisma, recognised in great depth by the current Russian national community, one can only oppose, in fact, his own icy calm, his unshakeable decision, and the active confidence in his visionary predispositions, his confidence in his "secret star". Is it little? Is it a lot, the future will decide. But some of us are already convinced that the future is already on Vladimir Putin's side, that the future already belongs to Vladimir Putin.

And above all his awareness of having the healthy, living structures of the nation at his side. *I am close to the Army, I am close to the Fleet, I am close to the people,"* he declared during the dramatic events following the fatal accident of the nuclear submarine *Kursk*.

(3) What recovery tasks?

The games therefore appear tight, to say the least. The dramatic 'tasks of recovery' that Vladimir Putin must urgently face would appear to be, in their entirety at the moment, the following.

(1) The liquidation of the oligarchic and economic-social-political command structures, of interference and blackmail, inherited from the situation invented by the chaotic, rotten and rotting regime of Boris Yeltsin's "family", feudalities in place with exorbitant weight, which must be put down at any price and with the utmost urgency. The outrageously cosmopolitan arrogance of Boris Berezovsky, Vladimir Gusinsky, and their entire Interlopian smalia of anti-Russian hyenas, must be severely punished, and we must once again resort to cleaning up with a vacuum. For it is a fact: the shameless and quite criminal plundering of Russian national assets during the great denationalisations at the end of the USSR is, in fact, equivalent to a veritable economic cataclysm for Russia, to a gigantic, conspiratorially concerted operation of fraudulent appropriation of the whole of Russia's "great economy" by those oligarchic groups of dubious origin, aims and identity, to say the least, having acted with more than suspicious means, which now appear to have been those of an anti-Russian offensive conducted secretly from outside. As long as the continuing blemish of the current oligarchic conspiracy still in place and its teeming subversive metastases are not wiped out, the national economy of the "New Russia" cannot get off to a truly decisive start.

(2) To give back to the Armed Forces, without further delay, the means of their power - of their super-strategic power of continental and planetary dimensions, as well as the surface of decisive politico-social affirmation which must imperatively be theirs in the process of fundamental renewal – refoundation - of the State. The revolutionary restructuring of the state must necessarily pass through the militarisation of work, education, and the social, cultural and religious organisation of the whole nation. An organisation that is entirely oriented towards a single saving goal of transcendental, supra-historical, "religious" self-deprivation. This is an overall process in which the driving, pedagogical and in-depth supervisory role of the Armed Forces will prove to be the backbone of the nation's life, as it had already been under the Tsars: Russia will never be anything other than what its Armed Forces make of it, and Vladimir Putin is, above all, the man of the Armed Forces. For, just as the Roman Empire was, Russia is fundamentally an imperial nation, by its very nature, by its secret predestination. All its previous history proves this.

In the final analysis and fundamentally, Vladimir Putin's "New Russia" will only be able to achieve its goal of the salvific renewal of present-day Russian history if the national-revolutionary consciousness of its Armed Forces can truly assume full control of the renewal process already underway, and ultimately lead it to its goal. The fate of Vladimir Putin's "New Russia" and thus the very fate of the emerging Greater National-Revolutionary Europe thus depends in a closely decisive way, in the present circumstances, on the present awakening, on the present evolution of the revolutionary consciousness of the Russian Armed Forces and on their role in the awakening, in the grand-continental European consciousness of Russia, in other words, on the return of Russia to its previous eschatological predestination. Vladimir Putin's map is the map of the Armed Forces. The doctrines of Marshal Nicolai Ogarkov have thus finally prevailed. For the national-revolutionary process that Vladimir Putin is now engaged in does not date from today, it has a long subterranean path behind it.

(3) The establishment of a new secret politico-strategic apparatus of over-activated ideological protection, intelligence and special intervention, with extensive powers, designed to ensure the internal security of the entire imperial revolutionary enterprise of Russia and the Eurasian Great Continent bloc of its externally active movement.

This is the revolutionary counter-strategic vanguard apparatus that will be responsible for erecting a permanent barrier of impediment to attempts at negative enemy interference from outside, and to the internal failings of the Eurasian grand-continental camp as a whole. Much could be said about this, but certainly not here.

(4) As well as the definition of a coherent, total, thorough metaphysical, geopolitical and theological state doctrine and, let us specify, of a new Great European, Orthodox and Catholic imperial Christological theology. Vladimir Putin knows that there is no new imperial emergence without the appearance of a new imperial religion, and he must also be aware of the prophetically decisive words of Möller van den Bruck according to which *there is only one Reich as there is only one Church.*

The 'Great Orthodoxy' resurrected by Vladimir Putin and traditional Roman Catholicism will have to be reunited, together, by the very force of action of the Empire, of *the 'Imperium Ultimum'*, in the movement bringing them back to their own former unity, and thereby carrying them forward to the Third State of the reunified European grand-continental imperial religion.

(5) To re-establish, to revive the intimate, vital connective tissue, the profound radiant unity of Russian society as a whole, which should be able to regain faith in itself, and in its own national and supranational destinies, which are naturally its own, its own foundational predestination, its own archaic, abysmal origins; of its eschatological imperial missions, of its immediate revolutionary tasks, of the formidable effort of ontological and politico-historical self-righting demanded of it, at the present time, by the very march of world history which is arriving at a tragically irreversible turn.

(6) It is also up to Moscow itself to support very effectively the efforts of the "geopolitical groupings" currently emerging all over Europe, indeed all

over the world, and which follow the Eurasian grand-continental political line of Karl Haushofer's fundamental geopolitical concept, the *Kontinentalblock* concept.

For Moscow must become the over-activated hub of all counter-strategic networks now mobilising in the vanguard of the revolutionary concentration movement fighting for the Greater Continental Europe, for the "Great Eurasian Empire of the End".

(7) The definitive control and counter control of the political administration of the internal regions of Russia, which were almost as a whole on a dangerous centrifugal spiral, tending to self control, to "self sufficiency", a situation implicitly opposed to the centralising principle of Moscow, and at any moment could be exploited by clandestine interference from outside, by manipulations belonging to the camp of the globalist subversion in action Replace the exquisitely elected governors with safe military ones.

(8) To destroy all the structures of organised crime, the social subversion of the existing mafias and the unbearable permanent insecurity of the current Russian society, which is reaching dangerously critical limits and which can also be seized upon by external interference for destabilisation purposes and attempts at clandestine appropriation of certain sectors of civil society that are more exposed than others to this kind of covert manoeuvre

(9) In addition to the obligation that it should make itself provide, on its side, by all the means at its disposal, for the over-activating promotion of the Franco-German Carolingian Pole, the founding base of the Greater Eurasian Continental Europe, It should be remembered that General de Gaulle affirmed that it constituted, on its own, a "World Revolution", Russia must also take on the task of opening up the continent of Europe towards India, the revolutionary hub of European presence and action in Asia. Didn't Alexander Dugin say that *Russia is the bridge from Europe to India, and through India to Greater Asia*? The visit of President Vladimir Putin to India last year and the launch of a vast Russian-Indian grandcontinental counter-strategic plan should therefore be placed in this perspective. The real significance of President Vladimir Putin's recent visit to Japan, where the confidential foundations of certain common line agreements were put in place on that occasion, must be placed in the same Eurasian and Greater European perspective. Like Russia, France is also attentive to the absolutely decisive rapprochement of Greater Europe with India and Japan, which appears to be a most significant Franco-Russian convergence, a *secret* sign of destiny.

(10) I deliberately wanted to deal last with the problem of the revolutionary Islamist destabilisation of Chechnya and the abscess of anti-Russian and anti-European subversion that is being artificially maintained in the region in a state of acute crisis by the bodies behind the current globalist offensive.

For today's Russia, putting out the Wahabi fire in Chechnya is a matter of life and death: If the fire is not extinguished in time, the entire southern flank of the Great Eurasian Continent will be set ablaze in the short term, from Pakistan to the chain of Islamic republics of the former USSR, to the south-east of the European continent, where Bosnia and Albania, including Kosovo, serve as relays both for revolutionary Islam on the spot and for the subversive, clandestine manoeuvres of Washington's special services, who intensively maintain imported revolutionary Islamist terrorism there, with the aim of destabilising Europe, the emerging Greater Europe and the 'European geopolitical line' that is currently asserting itself at the level of its new emerging history, a new Eurasian grand-continental history.

Will the counter-fire lit by President Putin at the meeting of the "Shanghai Group" in July 2000 in Dushanbe (Russia, China, Tajikistan, Kyrgyzstan, Kazakhstan) last much longer in the face of the irresistible push of the Islamist militias? Through the intermediary of Turkey and Israel underground, the globalist conspiracy of the United States - and what stands behind it, in the shadows - is fanning the flames of Fundamentalist Islam, while installing the politico-strategic milestones of its future takeover of the subversive transcontinental geopolitical line Tirana-Sarajevo-Grozny-Kabul-Islamabad.

Russia and South-East Europe are now once again in the front line of the revolutionary offensive of fundamentalist Islam, and it must be realised that this is a long sacrificial tradition of resistance, as Russia and South-East Europe have had to block the Islamist offensive towards the centre of Europe for centuries. Islam is used by the US globalist conspiracy as a strategic diversionary and blocking force in its clandestine war on Europe, and as such Islam enjoys considerable secret support, politically and strategically, thus becoming more and more an extreme threat to the emerging Greater Europe, both externally and internally, with Islamist emigration to Europe acting as an advanced bridgehead into the European lines of resistance.

Chechnya is the lock on Europe's southern front, and in Chechnya it is on behalf of Europe that Vladimir Putin has engaged Russia in a decisive battle.

Any move against Russia's involvement in Chechnya is an act of high treason against the unity and freedom of the emerging Greater Europe.

(4) The Paris-Berlin-Moscow axis

It would seem that Paris, Berlin and Moscow - but, in the present circumstances, Moscow above all - should understand that large-scale European integration inevitably requires the prior establishment of a Paris-Berlin-Moscow axis.

At present, the initiative for the Paris-Berlin-Moscow Axis can only come from Moscow.

In fact, if Berlin remains somewhat indecisive, suspicious and cautious about this project, Paris, on the other hand, and as incomprehensible as this may seem when one considers the positions previously taken by the Gaullist government on this very subject, is putting the brakes on and preventing - not to say sabotaging - with a morose, unavowed obstinacy, any initiative that goes in the direction of this transcontinental European axis project.

It is that in Paris, the extreme negative pressures that are constantly maintained and exacerbated, concerning the concept of the Great Eurasian Continental Europe, and even more currently concerning the project of the Paris-Berlin Axis, certain occult influences subversively in action in the service of the globalist conspiracy, have just reached a state of paroxysm that is truly ultimate, absolutely intolerable, and perhaps already unstoppable, for some at least, that we know only too well. This requires an urgent counter-reaction, as hard as it is exhaustive, on the part of the still healthy forces of the nation, reduced by the conspiracy in place to a final state of paralysis and daze, of increasingly tragic impotence; where it is intended that France, finally, be banned from Europe, that the heritage of General de Gaulle's revolutionary vision of the Grand Europe be annulled. But they do not know what awaits them. The backlash that will come will indeed be absolutely terrifying.

Since things are now as they have become, it is up to Moscow to take it upon itself to begin the preliminaries to the implementation of the Paris-Berlin-Moscow Axis project, relying also, and perhaps above all, in this case, on the work of agitation and penetration of the "geopolitical groups", which are ready to launch themselves into the ideological and politico-strategic battle of the creation of broad and deep currents of support for this fundamental European project.

This will be an opportunity for Moscow to act directly on the European political front, at the immediate level of the new European consciousness that is being revolutionarily asserted.

(5) Serbia, and South East Europe

Yugoslavia's intelligence services had long known that Kosovar Islamic subversion was planning to attack Macedonia as well. In October 2000, the President of Yugoslavia convened a general conference in Skopje, Macedonia, to which he invited the heads of state and government of Albania, Bulgaria, Greece, Macedonia, Bosnia, Romania and Croatia. Under the pretext of the implementation of a 'stability pact' for the whole of the Balkans, President Vojislav Kostunica was in fact planning to produce and personally support a project, which is still very confidential, concerning the short-term political and economic integration of all the states of South-East Europe, with the aim of being able to put up a common front in the dialogue with the European Union, before which Eastern Europe, still destabilised by the after-effects of communism, is currently in a situation of inferiority that is difficult to accept. This situation had to be remedied.

Certainly, Russia's European presence must fundamentally rely on Serbia-first and foremost-and the other Orthodox states of Eastern Europe, as Serbia is already engaged alongside Russia in the latter's current counter-strategic battle against Islamic revolutionary terrorism. At the same time, Serbia is also the first European state to have directly suffered the anti-continental aggression of the globalist conspiracy governed by the "Planetary Superpower of the United States": the total mobilisation of the entire Serbian nation in the face of NATO's politico-military aggression makes it today the country in Europe with the most awakened political consciousness with regard to the conspiratorial shenanigans of NATO and the ongoing globalist offensive.

In any case, South-East Europe still remains the critical zone where the investment is still maintained from the European continent by the politico-military advance of NATO engaged in the service of the globalist conspiracy of the "Planetary Superpower of the USA" and, as such, South-East Europe must permanently mobilise the counter-offensive attention of the European grand-continental whole, and this over and above the fact that the current social-democratic liberal-democratic power in power in the European continent is still in power, South-East Europe must permanently mobilise the counter-offensive attention of the whole of continental Europe, and this over and above the fact that the present social-democratic liberal-democratic power in power in the whole of Western Europe participates in the politico-military exactions of the anti-European occupation forces of NATO. But it is not the surface betrayal that counts: it is the profound options of captive nations, subversively silenced, gagged, victims of foreign alienation from them, nations as the living dead, nations made zombies by media voodoo specialists. And a certain degeneracy of the masses also has a lot to do with it.

(6) The four Christological invitations

Vladimir Putin's presidential tasks emerge dialectically from the encounter - the marriage, one might even say - between the fundamental concept of the suprahistorical and eschatological imperial predestination of Russia, of the "New Russia" of today and of Russia of all time, and the real conditions, such as they are, of the current political, social, economic and administrative situation in Russia today. In other words: something must be done, and will undoubtedly be done, under the conditions that actually exist at the time when this obligation is to be fulfilled, given to be, projected into the current of history in progress. And what must be done in this way is now the historic task of President Vladimir Putin.

Now, if we have just tried to review what constitutes, precisely, the real conditions for the recovery of Russia's present situation, we still have to determine the actual content of the transcendental reverse side of the situation, what should be done now in order to re-establish, also, Russia's predestined eschatological identity, its own suprahistorical mission, which has been imposed on it since the beginning of its history, and even before.

Thus, four invitations to immediate Christological action emerge from the current situation in Russia, as follows:

(1) To obtain the elevation to the altar, the official canonisation of Nicholas II and the entire imperial family, as well as of a symbolically significant number of witnesses of the Faith who fell during the persecutions, the bloody massacres of the years of Leninist and Stalinist terror, during the "years of darkness".

This is the fundamental act of the *reversal of the times*, and this fundamental act has just been effectively accomplished by the Patriarch of Moscow Alexy II, in the presence and on the special personal arrangements of President Vladimir Putin.

(2) It is well known that the liberation of Russia from the domination of the bloody darkness of communism was only made possible by the direct supernatural intervention of the Immaculate Conception, a liberation that took place from the moment when, following her own sacramental vow formulated in 1917, Russia was consecrated to her Immaculate Heart by the reigning Pontiff, in profound communion with the whole of the Church, following its own sacramental vow formulated as early as 1917, Russia found itself consecrated to her Immaculate Heart by the reigning Supreme Pontiff, in profound communion with the entire episcopal body of the world.

Now there is a prophetic vision of St. Maximilian Kolbe, the Catholic hero of Auschwitz, according to which the Red Star of Communism will one day be replaced in the Kremlin by the statue of the Immaculate Conception, and that on that day a new stage in the history of Russia will begin, the final, decisive stage of its entire history and of its secret suprahistoric mission.

It should be remembered that there is a statue of the Immaculate Conception in the Catholic Church of the Immaculate Conception in Moscow, on Malala Grouzinskaia Street, which is considered to be precisely the one that should be present and radiant on the summit of the Kremlin: All that remains is to order its placement on the summit of the Kremlin, in place of the Red Star, and this is what President Vladimir Putin must now do, because he has *no* choice.

The great provisions of Divine Providence are never significant on the scale of human appreciation. A simple fact such as the erection of the statue of the Immaculate Conception on the summit of the Kremlin can have incalculable repercussions, immense political and historical consequences. In the same way, the non-execution of these same provisions can provoke unforeseeable, definitive impediments or even catastrophes.

The status of the elevation of the statue of the Immaculate Conception on the summit of the Kremlin is that of a providential request of the same nature as that which Saint Margaret Mary Alacoque had made known to Louis XIV in the name of heaven, namely that he mark all the standards of the Kingdom with the arms of the Sacred Heart of Jesus. Louis XIV, not having thought it necessary to give effect to the invitation thus made to him by heaven, caused France to incur a negative debt which she is still far from having finished paying.

We must therefore make sure that the same tragic misadventure does not occur with regard to the order from above concerning the location of the statue of the Immaculate Conception on the summit of the Kremlin. Let there be no misunderstanding.

(3) As has already been said here, if Russia is to be a full participant in the historical and supra-historical advent of a "Great Eurasian Empire of the End", comprising Western Europe, Eastern Europe, Russia and Greater Siberia, Tibet, India and Japan, and since there can be no new Empire without a renewal of the Empire's own religion, it is therefore up to President Vladimir Putin to bring about the reintegration of Russian and Eastern European "Great Orthodoxy" and traditional Roman Catholicism into a "third state", it is therefore up to President Vladimir Putin to bring about the reintegration of Russian and Eastern European 'Great Orthodoxy' and traditional Roman Catholicism into a de facto 'third state', where the two great European religions would regain their original unity, renewed by their integration within the newly established imperial identity 'from the Atlantic to the Pacific'.

Vladimir Putin must risk playing "Great Orthodoxy" against itself for itself, knowing how to impose the necessary choices, all the necessary choices, in the name of Russia's greatest imperial destiny. The intransigent fortress of "great orthodoxy", only Vladimir Putin can today manoeuvre it to bring it back to the reason of the changing history.

(4) The only fundamental gesture that can mark the moment when the great-continental European history will prevail over its own anti-history, the moment of the *reversal of times,* is that of the politico-historical and religious liberation of the imperial Basilica of Saint Sophia in Constantinople and its glorious restoration to the cult of the time before the collapse of the Eastern Empire submerged by the irresistible and chaotic tide of Islam. For the end of the abysmal mourning of Western world history must supernaturally coincide with the liberation of the sanctuary of the Basilica of the Hagia Sophia, whose destitution had precisely marked the beginning of the mourning of our own, and of the whole of our history since.

Thus, the mobilising myth of the vanguard of the new revolutionary rise of the Great Continental Europe of Eurasian dimensions, which today represents the predestined eschatological task of Vladimir Putin's "New Russia", cannot be other than that of the liberation of the Hagia Sophia, the fundamental vow and oath of the new beginning of the history of Russia, delivered from the darkness of communism and thus returned to its own previous destiny, to its own archaic, abysmal identity of the origins.

The liberation of the Hagia Sophia, the supreme symbolic task of the imperial revival of Russian history marked by Vladimir Putin's providential rise to power, the supreme symbolic task, too, of Vladimir Putin's own destiny.

Russia's confrontation with Islam is not, therefore, a crisis instance in the current historical development of Greater Europe, a mere crisis instance, but the very ontological substance of what Russia is called to do in the final course of its own history, where *everything is now being decided.*

In this sense, the political-strategic war currently being waged by Russia in Chechnya against the revolutionary terrorism of fundamentalist Islam is in fact only a dialectical instance of the great final symbolic battle for the liberation of the Hagia Sophia.

In February 2001, in Munich, the Secretary of the Security Council of the Russian Federation, Sergei Ivanov, declared: *Russia is in the front line in the fight against international terrorism to save the civilised world in the same way that it saved Europe from the Tartar-Mongol invasion in the 13th century, at the cost of immense suffering and sacrifice.* Sergei Ivanov had made these statements in direct relation to Russia's political-strategic struggle in Chechnya, which was the background to his speech.

(7) "The Spirit is born and grows".

A double objective thus presents itself to the rest of us: not to cease reminding the revolutionary elites of the "New Russia" of the urgency of their own missions in relation to the current future of the new European imperial, grand-continental, Eurasian history, and to reveal, to make the European revolutionary elites of the West understand the meaning and the acting reality of the current imperial eschatological turn that the historical evolution in progress of the "New Russia" of President Vladimir Putin is taking.

For it is indeed from this double movement of permanent visionary recall with regard to the "New Russia", and of active doctrinal revelation in Western Europe that the new revolutionary European grand-continental history currently in progress is constituted. And it is through us that the history of the Great Continental Europe with a Eurasian horizon is being made, exclusively through us.

For our goals of total ideological warfare are now above all the goals of the new revolutionary consciousness of a predestined generation, which is in the process of constituting itself as such and accessing its own new revolutionary consciousness. And what we ourselves have understood and what we are in the process of making our people understand is the extraordinary historical and suprahistorical importance of the current emergence of the "absolute concept"

Vladimir Putin in Russia and thus at the very heart of the new European grand-continental history of the world, which is now asserting itself in terms of immediate revolutionary consciousness and in terms of immediate revolutionary action.

Today, there are a few of us who are the bearers of this new revolutionary consciousness, and we must not cease to make it known to all those whom we know to be among us. This is what Raymond Abellio - who at that time was still called Georges Soulès - had already understood in 1943, when he wrote, in his fundamental prophetic book, *The End of Nihilism,* that the "Spirit is born, and it is developing". For, in fact, what can the new revolutionary history of the world be but the secret history of the development of the New Spirit, already in action? Is history anything other than the place of the visible and invisible manifestation of the Holy Spirit? And what are we, in the final analysis, if not the secret agents of the Holy Spirit in action in history in progress, the secret agents of the revolutionary conspiracy of the Holy Spirit?

We know what is at stake today: whether the final European civilisation will survive or perish. And that this now depends exclusively on us, we also know this. The fact that the geopolitical centre of gravity of the current great-continental European history has shifted eastwards, towards Vladimir Putin's 'New Russia', towards South-East Europe under the ideological-political influence of Vojislav Kostunica, represents today a historical change that is as unforeseen as it is absolutely decisive, as profound as it is fundamentally committed to the renewal of the final destiny that will henceforth inevitably be ours.

For the final revolutionary decision, the 'leap over the precipice' to which the end of the world's history is now inevitably leading, which is also, whether we like it or not, our history and our world, is now up to us. Are we equal to the situation? That is what we shall see.

In any case, we are the few who are supposed to take upon ourselves the de facto responsibility for the present revolutionary turn of the new great-continental European history emerging into the light of day, and we already know each other, all of us, from Moscow to Dublin, from the "Atlantic to the Pacific", each of us where we are now. The "front line" we hold without interruption.

Everything is already in place. What we are waiting for is the signal that will carry us to the revolutionary assault of our own history engaged in the battle against the positions of its own anti-history currently in power throughout Western Europe: the war of liberation from under the current domination of the ruling Western anti-history will be the final war of liberation of the eternal West of the world, of which we represent today the suprahistorically active consciousness, the revolutionary consciousness of the first line.

VLADIMIR PUTIN AND THE EURASIAN EMPIRE OF THE END

Whatever we may or may not be aware of, we now find ourselves on the watershed of 'great history', suddenly close to its end: something is coming to a definitive end, and something else is about to happen, abysmally, something absolutely new.

The underhand and degrading terror exercised, on a planetary scale, by the overactivated subversion of the globalist conspiracy, which arms, justifies and never stops imposing its doctrine of so-called democratic "political correctness", reaches, at the present time, the ultimate limits of the unbearable, of the permanent and total nightmare. Arriving, thus, at these extremes, at this final paroxysm of the active affirmation, of the subversive and totalitarian impositions of the globalist conspiracy in place and of its incapacitating democratic terror, world history seems to have momentarily stopped in its march, as if self-immobilised in the expectation of the fatal moment when it will have to tip over, ineluctably, into a state absolutely contrary to that of its current total negative blockage, to change its direction entirely.

For a new specific form of change has now appeared in the visible becoming of world history, a new ontological form of direct action in the immediate course of history, which implies and decides, in the long run, when *the time comes*, the total and instantaneous self-destruction, without the slightest external intervention, of any fundamentally constituted power situation, politically asserting itself and seemingly impregnable in its foundations of the moment: What seemed to last indefinitely will then disappear in a mysterious and sudden way, without a trace, forever erased from the stream of history; as if nothing had happened.

This is because, at the time of its great changes, at the time of its great, decisive, unforeseeable, sudden turning points, history is forced to change, to transform itself by the very mystery of its own irrational depths, a mystery in action that is only led, from the invisible, by the occult revolutionary decisions of Divine Providence, which is always there, always hidden behind the immediately visible events. To understand history in its march is not to penetrate its objective reasons, which are never more than arranged appearances, but not to ignore the abysmal identity of what really drives it and makes it move forward, from below, according to a providentially conceived plan conducted from outside time.

So it was with the abrupt end of Soviet communism and all its subversive conspiracies of planetary dimensions: without any visible intervention from outside what was happening at the decisive moment, for absolutely no objective reason, at the appointed hour-and which nobody expected, because it was an occult hour, suprahistorical hour-it was like a sudden total collapse, from within it, like a sudden black lightning bolt, cancelling everything, and the greatest political-military power in the world ceased to exist, was sucked into the nothingness that it secretly carried within it, instantly. And quite definitively, without pause or recourse.

Now this same new ontological structure of instantaneous self-destruction, mysterious in its appearances, has also struck the whole of the current European political situation. The all-powerful Italian and German Christian democracies have disappeared into the nothingness of their own self-destruction, just as the great European imperial dream of "tin Gaullism" seems to have vanished, and in France, too, the vast movement of popular mobilisation that the National Front had set up, as well as the Communist Party itself, shattered into disparate pieces from within. While, under the very appearances of their power, still unconditionally in place at the moment - in France, in Germany, in Italy - the social democracy, local subcontractor of the globalist conspiracy, installed everywhere in Europe, as well as in Great Britain, finds itself, in spite of everything, from now on, at the mercy of the sudden seismic movement of the depths which is going to send it, from one moment to the next, back to its black hole of origin. Thus, from Bucharest to Lisbon, an immense empty, charred, dull, immobile desert, 'oozing with secret, unpredictable evil', stretches out at the height of desolation, at the height of powerlessness. Europe's democratic history is dead, and it is becoming its own common grave.

But it is above this decaying mass grave that the immense fire whirlwind of the great European revolutionary enterprise of salvation and liberation will soon have to rise, and in what unexpected way, to put in place, politically and historically, what is already called the Eurasian Empire of the End.

For if, from now on, in these times of interregnum, without time or hope or any legitimate expectation, when the evidence of the political abdication of Europe functions as a final scattering field, there is still only the risk of the ontology of the instantaneous self-destruction of this political ensemble in a terminal situation, as was already seen with the political self-destruction of the Soviet Union, or with the mysterious fading of the European Christian democracies – it is no less certain that the dialectically opposite movement, that of an ontology of total reversal and abysmal reconstitution, of a sudden paroxysmal rise of original being, of an emergence of absolute reversal and absolute recommencement of a situation apparently closed without recourse, can also take place at any moment. And turn everything upside down, all at once.

Today, everywhere, in the inner space of the Greater Europe, of Europe as the revolutionary vanguard of the Great Eurasian Continent, the fire of the return to being, of the revolutionary political recovery of the whole continent, is smouldering underground, and is being kept clandestinely available against all odds, waiting for that "emergence of absolute overthrow and absolute beginning again" which must mark the next tipping of the present European political situation into its own opposite. This is the active dialectic of the new form of ontological intervention in history that demands it, through its double commandment of the self-destruction of the past, of the condemned forms that have already passed away, and of the abysmal mobilisation of what will suddenly be called upon to give a new face to the future that is already, secretly, under way.

In conclusion to a politico-revolutionary research work that I published in 1976 under the title *The geopolitical line of the USSR* and the "fundamental oceanic project" of Admiral *G. S.* Gorshkov, I had prophetically placed the following lines, whose topicality seems to me to be quite striking, more than ever immediately operational:

It is in the light of this internalizing conception of history that it will be necessary to know - to know in advance – everything that, in the Soviet Union, will eventually prevail, at the desired time, over the other side, relentlessly, in order to commit itself immediately to changing – in one direction or the other - the direction and even the very face of world history. Today, as in the past, this is the single goal: to change the face of the world. However, in the perspective of the *single goal,* which of the two camps will win over the other? The one that will be able to let the will of the providential man appear within it, who will also be the man of the last battle. When will he come? Inevitably, at the appointed time.

Now it is precisely the appearance - the advent - of what I called, at the time, the "providential man" that, now that the times are ready, will have to provoke the final tipping of the immediate European political actuality in the direction of its revolutionary return to being, to provide-beyond its current disaster-its decisive ontological form to another total recommencement of European history and political consciousness, of their own structures of affirmation and active presence, renewed from their rediscovered original depths.

For it is a fact: the final revolutionary explosion is now ready to break out. All over Europe, "geopolitical groups" of consciousness and clandestine imperial political intervention in the Greater Europe, already operating on Eurasian continental dimensions, are on the lookout for the imminent change of history near its end, a change that is beginning to take place underground and of which these "geopolitical groups" mobilised on the spot constitute the explosive mass, to which the appearance of the "providential man", the new "absolute concept" of history reaching its supreme critical point, will provide the predestined detonator.

The ideological-doctrinal definition of this announced change can be found, exhaustively defined, in a recent document emanating from one of the operational centres at work, in a semi-landestine manner, of this vast subterranean political movement, of which this one represents one of the current decisive instances of immediate revolutionary affirmation. Of this ideological-doctrinal definition, here is the document that states its basic operational project, a document known more or less confidentially under the title of "Eurasian Imperial Pact". I quote, verbatim.

A foundational document, "The Eurasian Imperial Pact

It is from the confrontation of our imperial and Catholic doctrines with the present, direct, politico-historical reality, to which they are revolutionarily addressed, that the final emergence of the Great Catholic Empire, which constitutes our ultimate goal, *the Imperium Ultimum*, of the *Regnum Sanctum*, will dialectically result.

The first of these three operational stages, that of **the** very act of putting the final imperial project on the track, will concern the creation of the Paris-Berlin-Moscow axis, the future imperial grand-continental European pole. Since it will not involve the political integration of France, Germany and Russia, the Paris-Berlin-Moscow axis will only have a first function of bringing into definitive and total convergence the communion of destiny-of predestination-of the three countries of the great-continental founding pole mobilised forward by the same irrevocable imperial vision, by the decision of the Fundamental Pact.

The second of the three operational stages of *the Imperium Ultimum* will see the effective realisation of the Eurasian Empire of the End, constituted by the total political-historical integration of Western and Eastern Europe, Russia and Greater Siberia, India and Japan.

As for the third operational stage of the Catholic imperial revolutionary construction of this world and its final history, it will have to include, also, after the definitive reduction of the democratic globalist conspiracy led by the "Planetary Superpower of the United States" and its revolutionary liberation, the double integrated geopolitical instance of the two Americas, South America and North America. The third imperial stage of final world history will be the appearance of the unified Planetary Archipelago, a suprahistorical, transcendental entity, placed under the revealing, parousial light of the *Regnum Sanctum*.

Thus the globalist conspiracy of the Planetary Superpower of the United States will have to come to an end by self-destructing, in the terms of a continental civil war that will be a repetition in reverse of the American Civil War, of its own original founding act (1861–1865).

In this second Civil War, it will be the oppressed national majority of the Planetary Superpower of the United States, its "southern" majority, traditional and spiritualist, Catholic, of European heritage in continuity, which will have to prevail, irreversibly, over the "northern", anti-traditional, leftist and materialistic part of the North American continent.

And it will be the predestined mission of South America, which in the meantime, under the revolutionary impulse of Argentina and Chile, will have already been able to accomplish its own continental integration, to support, politically and strategically, the effort of the national, "southern" majority of the United States in its enterprise of the final revolutionary cleansing of the North American continent during its second Civil War.

And so, at the end of the present history of this world and beyond, the Planetary Archipelago in its geopolitically integral totality will find itself identified, in a transcendental, suprahistorical way, with the acting concept of the Great Catholic Empire of the End, with the *Regnum Sanctum*. It is in this, too, that we recognise, and loudly affirm, the mission, the transcendental revolutionary predestination of our own chosen generation to take upon itself the task of accomplishing the apocalyptic change of this world, according to a design conceived in the invisible.

The 'sign of departure': the appearance of a new 'absolute concept', a new 'providential man'

It is thus the "geopolitical groups" of the subterranean Great European revolutionary ensemble that constitute, at the present time, the emergence device, already in place, of the future seismic tilting movement, of the future ontological reversal of the meaning of current history at its final end. A reversal that will mark the new revolutionary beginning of the new world history that is about to make its sudden appearance. The latter, in order to *appear,* is only waiting for the "starting signal" of its new destiny, *the fundamental event that will be the advent of the "absolute concept", of the "providential man"*, in which it is asked to incarnate so that it can act on the level of visible history, to suddenly crystallise, to over-actively polarise its new revolutionary identity to come, or rather, which is already coming.

Now, with the accession of Vladimir Putin to the supreme political magistracy of the "New Russia", the "absolute concept" of the new world history already subterraneanly in progress, the "providential man" of the abysmal recommencement of it, has just mysteriously appeared in the light of day, and by this very fact, everything is suddenly thrown forward towards this *Total Weltrevolution* of which we have all been secretly waiting, for so long, for the definitive coming, the "polar affirmation of the end".

But who is, in fact, Vladimir Putin? Vladimir Putin is first and foremost and very essentially the direct emanation of the permanent revolutionary secret councils of the Armed Forces of the Soviet Union, which were looking for themselves, and which were waiting for the opportunity to surface, to cross the line into visible, active history, since the years 1948–1952, when there were the first significant manifestations of their action, of their fighting presence, of their will to assert themselves politically, not against the Soviet state, but confidentially within its own power structures. It is since then that one could speak of an immanent national revolutionary doctrine of the Armed Forces of the Soviet Union, a doctrine which became more and more precise and decisive from the sixties, and whose basic geopolitical theses were confidentially supported by L.I. Brejnev and, thereafter, openly-or almost-openly by Y.V. Andropov.

Two military personalities of the first rank are considered to have been, and still remain, emblematic representatives of the immanent politico-military doctrine of the Soviet Armed Forces, a global doctrine, semi-clandestine, or rather implicit, but, in its time, more and more active and overactive where it managed to act, and which, today, is in the process of becoming, effectively, and quite openly this time, the official geopolitical doctrine of the "New Russia". These two Soviet military personalities are the former head of the GRU and, later, of the General Staff of the USSR Armed Forces, as well as the later Commander-in-Chief of the Warsaw Pact forces, General-Colonel S. M. Chtemenko, and Marshal N. V. Ogarkov, who, like General-Colonel S. M. Chtemenko, was to become head of the General Staff of the Soviet Armed Forces a few years later. It was as head of the General Staff of the USSR Armed Forces that Marshal N. V. Ogarkov had attempted, and almost succeeded, in taking total control of the political leadership of the USSR by the Armed Forces, which finally failed because of the rival counter-conspiracy, which was to bring Mikhail Gorbachev to power through the General Secretariat of the Communist Party, leading, in the last instance, to the irreversible political self-destruction of the former Soviet Union.

In his capital book, which definitely counted for a whole generation of researchers, *GRU, le plus secret des services soviétiques, 1918-1988*, Stock, Paris, 1988, Pierre de Villemarest called General-Colonel S.M. Chtemenko "one of the first geopoliticians of the USSR, perhaps even the first of all". Also, on General-Colonel S. M. Chtemenko, Pierre de Villemarest wrote that he "belongs to a clan of senior officers, certainly 'Soviet', but above all Great Russian in spirit, and perfectly expansionist". And also: "For this caste, the USSR is an empire destined to dominate the Eurasian continent, not only from the Urals to Brest, but from the Urals to Mongolia, from Central Asia to the Mediterranean". And then: "On this last point, Chtemenko is indeed the man who invented, from 1948 to 1952, not the eventual invasion of Afghanistan, but its slow absorption by continuous economic interpenetration, with accompanying subversion. And, at the same time, the irruption of the USSR in the Arab capitals, in Beirut, Damascus, Cairo and Algiers. At the end of 1948, he already explained that, at the intersection of the East and Asia, Afghanistan offered a strategic means of covering the fleets that Admiral Serge Gorschkov - one of his personal friends - was beginning to develop in order to reach the Mediterranean from the Black Sea. The visionary power of the avant-garde geopolitics of General-Colonel S.M. Chtemenko still nourishes, today, the active approach of the geopolitical positions arming the revolutionary ideological bases of the "New Russia" of which Vladimir Putin embodies, and assumes the destinies, of the Eurasian grand-continental imperial project and the final eschatological mission.

Thus, going to the heart of the matter, it can be argued that, over and above the de facto state of the Soviet regime in place, and yet from within it, the immanent politico-military doctrine of the USSR Armed Forces included a double internal operational perspective, both geopolitical and transcendental. Its geopolitical doctrine included the fundamental project of a final, "total", "imperial" political integration of the great Eurasian continent as a whole, while its transcendental doctrine merely reiterated and renewed the great suprahistorical objectives of tsarism and of a certain eschatological, "polar" visionary conception of the final, "apocalyptic", saving spiritual predestination of the Greater Russia.

Thus, when, towards the end of the sixties, Marshal N. V. Ogarkov, then Chief of the General Staff of the USSR, launched the call and attempted to impose the doctrine of "integral militarisation" and "total militarisation" on the USSR. Ogarkov, then chief of the General Staff of the USSR, launched the appeal and tried to impose the doctrine of the "integral militarisation" and the "general and permanent mobilisation" of the industrial production apparatus and the Soviet economy as a whole, the very small number of those who are said to be "aware of things that must not be known" – a "very small group" at present - and confidentially at work in the USSR as well as in Eastern and Western Europe – were not aware of this, and confidentially at work in the USSR as well as in Eastern and Western Europe - had not failed to understand that the "Secret Order" was about to go on the final, decisive offensive, the "Secret Order" of the great immanent conspiracy of the Soviet Armed Forces in place, acting at the very heart of the Soviet power, which they intended to change from within. Hence, then, almost on the spot, the dismissal of Marshal N.V. Ogarkov, who temporarily-but should we not rather say subversively-returned to the shadows, waiting for what would happen next. Because the time, one would have to believe, had not yet come for this "final offensive" nor, above all, for what it would have implied and, as a result, made irreversible on the still untouched plan of the great Soviet politico-military strategies renewed by the open resumption of the Eurasian grand-continental line.

Now, if all this could not have been done at that time, it is most certainly now that it will have to be done, through everything that the seizure of power in Moscow by Vladimir Putin and the great revolutionary overthrow that this implies from the depths.

This evidence is fundamental to what is really at stake here: the immediately operational thesis of the total mobilisation, the "revolutionary mobilisation" of the political-administrative, social and cultural, even religious structures of Russia in view of a suprahistorical "grand design", constituted the central core of the immanent revolutionary doctrine of the Russian Armed Forces of yesterday and today, thus rediscovering the super-activating principles of the Russian Empire of the origins, according to its missionary, "Roman, imperial" identity, of its first beginnings in arms, according to its "abyssal, occult", "polar" identity.

It is indeed this visionary politico-historical vision and its great geopolitical and transcendental operational theses that Vladimir Putin is, today, the heir, the direct bearer, the "providential man" called to a predestined task, which it will be up to him to carry through to the end.

And it is in the revolutionary light of this vision that we must now situate the true meaning, the whole meaning of Vladimir Putin's recent declarations concerning the predestined mission of the Russian Armed Forces in the work of recovery and revolutionary salvation of Russia and therefore of the whole of the great Eurasian continent as the Eurasian Empire of the End, which he, Vladimir Putin, knows that he must assume, in an inspired manner, and without further delay. For the doors of destiny have closed on him, and he will have to do what he must now do. Without the slightest hesitation.

Indeed, Vladimir Putin, the "Russian de Gaulle", recently declared that the recovery of Russian society, "currently on the brink of the abyss", requires, for him, a general, in-depth reorganisation of the country as a whole, centred on the urgent priority given to the Armed Forces and their model of organisation and structural functioning, which must become the organisational backbone of the revolutionary renewal of the "New Russia", the active core of the very birth of the "new times", the expression "new times" being in the process of appearing as an obsessive refrain of the upheavals in progress or to come, the new password. And this to such an extent that the future industrial recovery of Russia will have to be supported, in the first instance, by the sustained and intensive exploitation of the fund of 'special avant-garde technologies' currently available to the Armed Forces. Thus, the protective shadow of the Armed Forces is once again extending over the whole of Russian society: Vladimir Putin's "new times" have just brought back the formal obligation of military training at school, followed closely by mass appointments of military personnel to key positions, to strategic positions for the renewal and reorganisation of the political-administrative, social, economic and industrial situation of Russia, which is thus being pushed into the era of accelerated change, towards its abrupt "normalisation". Reconstituting the State, rebuilding and imposing continuity, a will, a haughty, "Roman" conception of the State, such would seem to be the main and immediate goal of Vladimir Putin, who, moreover, maintains the cult of secrecy, of not revealing his action plans *(a cult of secrecy* revealing an old Russian imperial habit, taken up again in continuity by the Soviet power)

On the other hand, we are not unaware of the direct and profound influence exerted on the circles close to Vladimir Putin's personal politico-military command group by Alexander Dugin's "manual of imperial geopolitics",

Great European, Eurasian and "transcendental", "polar", political advisor to the President of the Russian National Assembly, in charge of the active management of the "geopolitical cell" of the latter, an entity responsible for the definition of the major current and future geopolitical lines of force of this "nascent Russia" whose new revolutionary destiny Vladimir Putin intends to forge.

Therefore, the importance that Aleksandr Dugin and his Eurasian imperial geopolitical conceptions are currently gaining among Vladimir Putin's political-military command group appears to be extremely significant, full of future promise, because the thinking of our comrade Aleksandr Dugin is the same as that of our "geopolitical groups" currently in action, precisely, of the whole of our "geopolitical groups" currently in action, the combat positions and the operational theses of Alexander Dugin the same as those advanced by the "Eurasian Imperial Pact" already quoted in the current article. Here, a loop is closed, which will deeply mark the future political-spiritual destinies of the Eurasian continent, and more particularly of the Greater Europe.

It is also certain that if Vladimir Putin chose to focus his own political power on the problem of a complete and definitive settlement of the conflict in Chechnya, he understood perfectly well that to give in Chechnya would mean having to give in later, in the face of the permanent conspiracy created by the globalist conspiracy, through Turkey and behind the shenanigans of Fundamentalist Islamism, on the southern flank of the Eurasian continent, all along the chain of instability of the Islamic republics of the former Soviet Union. *In my heart I decided that my mission, my historic mission, would be to solve the problem of the North Caucasus,"* Vladimir Putin said in an interview with the Moscow-based magazine Kommersant.

Now, if, as he keeps saying, for Vladimir Putin the war in Chechnya, a war of destabilisation and infiltration with essentially subversive objectives, represents the line of opposition between Islam and Christianity, he could not fail to understand that, in a war of religions, it is a question of the irreducible confrontation of two religions which can only end by the abdication of one of these religions before the other, and consequently of a *total war*.

But this is certainly not the only reason why Vladimir Putin keeps emphasising the need for the full integration of Orthodoxy into the current block of the revolutionary heritage of the "New Russia": he knows at the same time that there is no Empire without a religion of Empire, that the founding act of the creation - or renewal - of an Empire can only be of an exclusively religious nature. And that the great final eschatological mission of the "New Russia" must be, in the final analysis, a religious mission.

In the above-mentioned interview with the magazine *Kommersant*, Vladimir Putin also stated that, a few years after the death of his mother, who had had him baptized secretly in the Orthodox religion, she had given him his baptismal cross so that, during a trip he had to make to Israel, he could have it blessed "at the tomb of Christ". And, he adds, 'so as not to lose it, I put it around my neck. And I have kept it there ever since''.

In any case, the "New Russia" must always remember that it owes the inconceivable miracle of its sudden liberation from communism, "as if by magic", to the fact that, in communion with all the bishops of the world, Pope John Paul II consecrated Russia to the Immaculate Heart of Mary, following the vow and conditional promise made by the Virgin Mary in her apparition at Fatima, Portugal, in 1917, the same year that Russia was sinking into the hallucinatory nightmare of seventy years of communist terror.

But there is more. According to the prophecy of St. Maximilian Kolbe, the martyr of charity at Auschwitz, if the "New Russia" is to be truly on the verge of its planned reunion with its greatest future destiny, the Red Star on the highest tower of the Kremlin must be replaced by a votive statue of the Virgin Mary, a symbol announcing the *Regnum Mariae*. It is only a symbol, but it is undoubtedly on this symbol that the eschatological future of Russia and therefore of the imperial whole of the great Eurasian continent depends entirely. I don't know if Vladimir Putin knows this. But he should be made aware of it.

For the time being, the maximum amount of effort to be deployed by the "geopolitical groups", and by the European political formations that they could influence, must concern the setting up of the Paris-Berlin-Moscow axis. At the same time, if the Greater Europe is now, because of Russia, both Catholic and Orthodox, it will be necessary to hasten the reintegration of the two religions, Catholic and Orthodox, going back to the times when their separation had not been consummated. What now seems impossible, a transcendental will will do, supported by certain occult powerhouses at work, and by *holiness*.

WHAT IS THE "BIG SECRET" LINKING VLADIMIR PUTIN TO JOHN PAUL II?

The long political-ideological speech given by Vladimir Putin in Berlin on 24 September 2001 before the entire Bundestag served first and foremost to define the nature of the current political and historical relations between Russia and Germany, as they stand at present. Namely, according to Vladimir Putin, Germany is both the European country with which Russia currently feels the closest in depth and through which Russia is establishing its openness to Western Europe. A de facto preference has thus been established, and affirmed as such, in a clear and apparently irreversible manner. However, behind this choice of destiny - or even predestination - it would seem to persist, for the truly alert and well-informed, that France has finally come to find itself excluded from the vital preferences of Russia and its great foreign policy, and this exclusion is not at all on the part of Russia, on the contrary, which could even recognize itself as a loser. But on the part of France, still and always a prisoner of its fateful slide into the power of the dark powers, of negative alienations in the service of regression and the darkness of non-being, from which it would seem that it can no longer free itself. These are the dark powers that are working underground to impose on France its incomprehensible refusal of present-day Russia, dictating to it its suicidal attitude with regard to its own political interests and those of the whole of Europe. And it would perhaps be up to the future Greater Europe to take it upon itself to fight, to the very end, for the liberation of this fundamental part of its own geopolitical, spiritual and cultural identity, which is France, so mysteriously decaying today, subjected to the manipulations of occult powers at work both from the outside, and from within itself. For France is forcibly held in the power of darkness, as we know.

Vladimir Putin's Roman inclination

The new turn in Russia's foreign policy is now defined by its rapprochement and its decisive availability towards Germany, and it is no less certain that another choice, perhaps no less significant, although in a different and, in any case, much more confidential way, seems to have marked Vladimir Putin's personal orientation, and continues to assert itself in continuity thereafter.

Indeed, it is well known that Vladimir Putin wanted his first foreign visit as the newly elected President of Russia to be to Italy, and it is also well known that he is exceptionally interested in the new Italian politics, especially since Silvia Berlusconi's abrupt liquidation of the socialist-communist conspiracy that had previously existed in Rome.

For Vladimir Putin, committed as he is at the moment to the still more or less confidential positions, but less and less confidential, of his vast Eurasian imperial project which should lead, in the long term, to the setting up of what is already called the "Eurasian Empire of the End", Italy-and Rome-represent, still and always-if only as a symbol of the future, to the setting up of what is already agreed to be called the "Eurasian Empire of the End", Italy-and Rome-represent, still and always-if only symbolically-the survival of this *Imperium Romanum on* which its own grand-continental Eurasian imperial visions are currently feeding.

Now, as one might have noticed, Vladimir Putin's visit to Rome was in a way exalted by his double reception at the Vatican by John Paul II, who received him twice. A first, official reception, followed by a second meeting, on a personal basis, if you will. It subsequently became known that during this second meeting between John Paul II and Vladimir Putin, problems were discussed and decisions were taken that directly concerned the ultimate historical and religious destiny of the greater Europe to come.

For Vladimir Putin, John Paul II is, above all, as Roman Pontiff, the heir in direct continuation, symbolically, but also really, of *the Imperium Romanum*, surviving himself as well as over and above, and outside of, history in progress. And that, at the same time and at the present time, John Paul II is also the supreme leader of one of the two great European continental religions, Catholicism, Orthodoxy being the second. And of which, as President of Russia, Vladimir Putin considers himself to be the political delegate. The pontifical doctrine of John Paul II concerning the "two lungs of the Church" - of one and the same Church - which in Europe are Catholicism and Orthodoxy, finds its perfect answer in the imperial doctrine of Vladimir Putin concerning the "two great European continental religions", whose destinies must be brought together once again. For if Vladimir Putin knows that there is no New Empire without a New Church, he also knows that without a New Church there can be no New Empire. Thus John Paul II and Vladimir Putin are united in identical positions concerning the need for a unification-reunification, in fact-of the two European continental religions, Catholicism and Orthodoxy, in a Third Church, which would in fact be the First Church, the one before the separation of Catholicism and Orthodoxy, *the Ecclesia Una* of the first beginnings of the present European history.

How can this final reunification of Catholicism and Orthodoxy be achieved?

Thus, the reunification of these "two great European continental religions" appears to be a fundamental - and at the same time foundational - instance of the current European grandcontinental federal evolution, which is already underway and which, in the end, nothing will be able to resist.

The question that now arises is how to achieve this final reunification of the "two European continental religions".

The answer is that there are three operational structures that can be mobilised at the same time and that have already been mobilised at three different levels of action, and that for the time being must also remain secret or at least confidential. These will have to be, as it seems, the following.

(1) The basic action, in the first place, of the "ardent spiritual summits", of those occult foci of faith and conscience lovingly active, of high theological foresight also, inspired, which, both within Catholicism and within Orthodoxy, work today in dispersed order. And whose secretly nuptial, trans-religious dialogue will have to constitute the connective tissue of the new Catholic-Orthodox reality in the rise of the reunification, in the long run, of the "two great European continental religions" in a single instance of life supernaturally sustained by the mystery of the Eucharistic Fire.

The secret reunion of the "two great European continental religions" must therefore be continued at the level of the summit elites already at work, on both sides of the invisible barricade that has been erected and subversively maintained, this barricade of darkness, to prevent them from coming together, to keep them apart again and again, but which we must eventually overcome. And this is what our "ardent spiritual summits" are now working on. Moreover, all that can be revealed about these, about the 'burning spiritual summits' at work both within present-day Catholicism and within Orthodoxy, I have already said in a previous chapter of this same book, 'Orthodoxy and Catholicism, the Great Beginning? ''.

(2) The second of the three structures acting in support of the ongoing process of reunification of the "two great European continental religions" appears to be precisely that of the path of work that John Paul II and Vladimir Putin are currently pursuing, each on his own side and both together. They are also confronted with the fierce resistance to the work of reunification that has already begun on the part of the higher ecclesiastical hierarchies of both sides (the higher ecclesiastical hierarchies of the Vatican and of Catholicism, as well as the higher ecclesiastical hierarchies of the Church of Russia, which is currently under the singularly negative leadership of the Patriarch of Moscow, Alexis II).

If, as far as Orthodoxy is concerned, the current, seemingly insurmountable resistance of the higher ecclesiastical hierarchies to the process of reunification of the "two great European continental religions" can be explained by a mistrust of a possible expropriation of their acquired privileges, To this could be added the petrification in the dark, the self-stifling of a centuries-old self-enclosure, while Catholicism's refusal of the same process would be the result of an incoherence of the Catholic Church, The refusal of Catholicism to accept the same process would be the result of immeasurable pride, the measure of appearances and acquired certainties, both in terms of faith and in terms of social recognition, and of a no less immeasurable indifference to the living reality of Orthodox spirituality, it would also remain, of course, that in both cases the basis of this double refusal is in any case the subterranean work of the Power of Darkness itself. And this I must dare to affirm, despite the extreme difficulties that there would be, in the present state of European consciousness, in making it heard by anyone other than those who are already initiatively aware of it all.

It will therefore be against their own camp that John Paul II and Vladimir Putin will have to fight, first of all, to complete the work in progress of the final reunification of the "two great European continental religions". This situation is, in fact, a most revealing sign of the times.

This would mean that both John Paul II and Vladimir Putin are already, at the present time, under the urgent obligation to confidentially set up apparatuses of direct strategic action intended, on the one hand, to slow down and then completely neutralise the front of negative reactions of their own subversive clerics and, on the other hand, to provide for the accelerated and more thorough creation of favourable currents, of instances of spiritual, mystical and intellectual support, even political, for the offensive march of the new imperial theology, on the other hand, to provide for the accelerated and increasingly thorough creation of favourable currents, of instances of spiritual, mystical and intellectual, and even political, support for the offensive march of the new imperial theology aimed at the final reunification of the two European continental religions. To give themselves the weapons of their own struggle.

As for providing further details here on the status of these semi-clandestine counter-strategic apparatuses designed to come into action in the current battles for the reunification of the two European religions, I think I really cannot venture to do so without thereby putting their already ongoing action at foreseeable risk. Serious risks.

The present masses of both Catholic and Orthodox believers would certainly be willing to follow John Paul II and Vladimir Putin in their visionary exhortations about the final reunification of the two European religions. It is, however, only the intermediate ecclesial hierarchies that resist, sabotage and prevent this from happening. It is therefore a question of setting up absolutely new structures in the front line, making it possible to have immediate trade between the tops of the Catholic and Orthodox hierarchies concerned, over and above these hierarchies, and those who must follow them in the revolutionary task of reunifying the two European religions. This would be a return to the structures of dialectical combat already used by the Maoist "cultural revolution". We are inevitably heading towards a general "cultural revolution" of European religions in their ongoing struggle for reunification, which can only be an imperial reunification.

(3) Finally, it is obvious that we cannot fail to count, at the same time, and as if beyond the efforts made by our own, whatever they may be, on the exclusively supernatural dimension that we must introduce into the data of the visible and invisible battle underway, I mean on the action, both direct and occult, of Divine Providence itself, working so that the "two great European continental religions" may eventually find themselves reunited in the imperial identity of the same Church, the "One Church of the End", which will be the same One Church as that of the beginnings of the present historical cycle of our civilisation in terminal crisis. Our efforts may fail, but Divine Providence does not. Hence the extreme topicality of John Paul II's cry, "Do not be afraid!"

The current disasters of the Catholic Church

However, it should also be noted that it is not only the subversive resistance of the greater part of the higher Catholic hierarchies to the pontifical will to reunify the two European continental religions that makes it so difficult for the latter to act on the ground at present, but also the inconceivable state of decay of the faith and of the inner unity of the Catholic Church itself, and of Catholicism in Europe. This is the result of two centuries of external and internal siege by nocturnal, anti-spiritual and anti-Catholic powers working underground according to the outlines of a predetermined plan of action, with the aim of rotting and alienating, of dismantling the living Church, of putting an end to her pretensions to remain identical to herself beyond time, above the very march of history.

The present state, *the final state of* this now accomplished putrefaction of the European Catholic Church and religion, was prophetically foretold in the middle of the nineteenth century by the voice of the Virgin Mary herself at La Salette, and again at the beginning of the twentieth century by the Virgin Mary at Fatima. The unprecedented seriousness of what the Virgin Mary had said about what was going to happen to the Catholic Church even forced the latter to try to conceal the Marian message about the dark alienations of its final disaster, and even, recently, to misleadingly divert its content.

And what had managed to remain more or less standing, the Second Vatican Council ended up completely tearing down. The national bishops' conferences remain in a state of permanent insubordination to the Supreme Pontiff, some bishops have even come to openly doubt the divinity of Christ, his Resurrection and his Real Presence in the Eucharist, the Mass has been dismantled, and as it were replaced by the abject kyri of "repentances".

What still remains in the depths is the simple and ancient Faith of the people, of the little people, and the irreducible islands of certain religious orders - or of certain parts of certain orders - still conforming to the Rule. Holiness has become occult, as has true religion. The last Catholics are returning to the primitive way of the catacombs, at least on a social level. The heavens seem to have closed over us. Without the direct intervention of Divine Providence, it is now impossible to go back up the slope. But this final, supremely nocturnal ordeal will pass, because Christ has said that the "Gates of Hell will not prevail against his Church".

But at the same time, the problem of the Church's inner self-devastation remains totally unknown in Eastern Europe, as if the long years under the bloody terror of Soviet communism have actually only preserved and secretly strengthened the Faith, through the direct experience of martyrdom, through bloodshed in abundance, and through the seeming omnipotence of darkness.

Now the all too obvious abyss of this non-conformity of the present ontological states of the two great European continental religions will also work against the march of what might be called the imperial conspiracy of John Paul II and Vladimir Putin for the reunification of these into one Same Church of the End, having regained the unity of its own former states. This makes the work undertaken and pursued in this direction by those whom Divine Providence has chosen to do it, and to carry it out to the end, all the more supernaturally heroic. Against all odds and all things.

However, one must believe that John Paul II was able to place some of his most trusted men in Russia on the front lines of the battlefield. At the same time, it must be taken for granted that Vladimir Putin will not swallow the bitter affront inflicted on him by the Patriarch of Moscow, Alexy II, who refused to accept that John Paul II could make an official visit to Russia. And in so doing, suspending the official invitation that had been personally extended to John Paul II by Vladimir Putin himself, during his private meeting with the latter at the Vatican, and then stubbornly maintaining this same refusal, not taking into account the confidential pressure he had been subjected to by the President of Russia; who is not used to not giving in to his will.

But we must trust Vladimir Putin: Just as he was able to prevail, at the right time, over the fortified, reputedly impregnable line of the stateless oligarchies at work, from within, against the new Russian national power, against the "New Russia", when the time comes he will find the irresistible dialectic of force that will allow him to finally impose his point of view on the eschatological problem of the final reunification of the two European religions, which are, for the time being, seemingly antagonistic. The presidential will, today, in Russia, is already, secretly, an imperial will.

If the Church, beyond the reach of its supra-temporal, divine identity, is entrusted in the century to the care of the Empire, it is obvious that *the latter* has the supernatural *duty* to put the Church back on the right path when it goes astray.

Thus, in a supernaturally existing human-or even superhuman-society such as an Order society, order appears to be the real presence of God: Order is to the Empire what the Eucharist is to the Church.

Now, in Vladimir Putin's 'New Russia', everything today is about the re-establishment of the original, 'archaic' order, the reestablishment of the previous order, which is at the same time the revolutionary order to come, an order that Heidegger would have called, with one of his most mysterious concepts, 'unprepensable', *unvordenklich.*

The duty of a predestined generation

We, therefore, who have taken upon ourselves the superhuman task of brutally rectifying, in terms of the sharpest violence, a dying historical cycle, clearly know where we stand with regard to our secret mission of subterranean politico-strategic investment of the still intact or less irreparably damaged structures of a society whose internal order has been dragged far into disorder in the space of only two generations, until the present terminal chaotic anti-order, which we will have to begin by totally devastating, destroying and destroying, in the space of only two generations, the inner order has *been* dragged far into disorder until the present chaotic terminal anti-order, which we will have to start by totally devastating, destroying until, as Dostoyevsky said, "not one stone remains of it".

The third millennium will be that of the great planetary battles C: religion, and of the races that carry these religions, the battles of the reappearance of God. For, as Martin Heidegger said, 'only a God will save us', a *God* who never stops hinting at his next advent, which will also mark the next and new advent of being, or rather the 'return of being'.

It is within this final spiritual and religious conflagration that the current struggles for the final reunification of the 'two great European continental religions', Catholicism and Orthodoxy1, take on their full apocalyptic significance, bringing into the open the 'great secret' linking John Paul II and Vladimir Putin, a secret whose inner dialectic and revolutionary suprahistorical affirmation we now know.

The two halves of Europe, which history in its apparently irrational march had separated, are now preparing to meet again in the *eschaton of* their double imperial exaltation, which will also be a unifying assumption of that of which they are still the sacrificial symbol.

The Return of the Great Times

At the human level, the immense, almost unavowable task that John Paul II and Vladimir Putin have set themselves seems out of reach, we must admit. But it is not at the human level that the problem of this task is really posed, which only gains its true place in an exclusively providential perspective, where everything is possible, even, and especially, the inconceivable. What do we want, what is the founding secret of this revolutionary suprahistorical enterprise? We now know the answer to this question, as we have seen: the secret of a great saving conspiracy. And, in a certain sense, the secret in action of this conspiracy is the imminence of the salvation and final politico-historical deliverance of the European continent, the advent - the return, one might even say - of the imperial and transcendental unity of the Eurasian "Big Island".

And something else is also certain. If religion, the invisible but living and permanent contact with the "supreme sacred", constitutes the infrastructure of all accomplished civilisation, the present battle for the final reunification of the "two great European continental religions" will be seen as being, albeit somewhat hidden, that of the return to the horizon of their common origin, which will then also be that of their ultimate suprahistoric achievement, the "Return of the Great Times", the "Return of the Holy Days", the "Return of the Great Cultures", that of the return to the horizon of their common origin, which will then also be that of their ultimate suprahistorical achievement, the "Return of the Great Times", the sudden advent there of the fascinating Heideggerian *wieder*, the "new absolute" redeploying the dialectic of its regained omnipotence, definitively.

And here, I suppose, one might ask why I have made a point of quoting so many times in the course of this chapter the master of veiled philosophy, the thinker of "roads to nowhere". The answer is simple. But it must be found.

As is the response to the relentless obstructionism that Alexis II, the Patriarch of Moscow, is constantly raising against John Paul II's planned visit to Moscow. For it is a fact. There is no reason to doubt that Vladimir Putin will succeed in forcibly reducing the resistance to his personal plans by the Patriarch of Moscow. The problem is already solved.

On the other hand, it is no less certain that in the case of a sudden disappearance of John Paul II, it is hardly conceivable that Vladimir Putin would be able to find a Roman pontifical interlocutor in the same providential dispositions as John Paul II regarding their current "saving conspiracy".

In this connection, it is not uninteresting to learn of a confidential rumour circulating in certain circles of the great Roman Catholic aristocracy, according to which, during a particular *vision of* the Virgin Mary, John Paul II received the promise that he would live until his project for the reunification of the "two European continental religions" was effectively realised, "until he was able to go openly, on an official visit, to Moscow and Russia". But hasn't John Paul

II's life been on hold since the attack on St Peter's Square on 3 May 1981? Hasn't his life been on hold since that day?

The situation of Catholics in Russia today is defined as follows by Father Stanislas Opiéla, General Secretary of the Russian Catholic Bishops' Conference: 'In Orthodoxy, there are those who are open to dialogue with Catholics, but are frowned upon by the hierarchy. And those who refuse all dialogue, claiming that the truth of Christianity is to be found only in Orthodoxy''.

At present, there are about a hundred Catholic parishes in Russia, grouped into four apostolic administrations in Moscow, Saratov, Irkutsk and Novosibirsk, whose difficulties are endless.

But I cannot conclude this chapter without mentioning the extraordinarily significant figure of the Apostolic Administrator of Moscow, Archbishop Tadeusz Kondrusiewicz, the highest hierarchical authority in Russian Catholicism, who represents the most advanced point of the tormented block of John Paul II's more or less unavowable expectations of Russia, the burning thorn in the side of his pontificate.

In fact, it is Bishop Tadeusz Kondrusiewicz who has the task of watching over the silent progress of the project for the reunification of the two religions, the 'saving conspiracy', whose fires he must keep burning, whose breath he must control, whose still secret developments he must direct, and whose paths, hidden from the eyes of the hostile environment in which he must move, must avoid clashes, pitfalls and crises, and must assert himself as far as possible. A measure that must certainly be considered more than small. Within the area directly concerned, everything rests on Mgr Tadeusz Kondrusiewicz, who clandestinely perpetuates the active shadow of Rome.

What exactly was the action of Bishop Tadeusz Kondrusiewicz on the spot, history, the "great history", will say later. Or it will keep quiet, as it should.

For a First Eurasian Continental Conference on the Greater Siberia Project

The time has clearly come when, beyond certain appearances that are still negative, the problem of the accelerated construction of a large continental Europe with a Eurasian horizon and dimension must be considered by the political leaders in place in an immediately operational manner.

Thus, Western and Eastern Europe, Russia, Tibet, India and Japan must, without wasting a single moment, mobilise all their efforts in depth to integrate, around a First Eurasian Continental Conference on the "Great Siberia Project", the over-activated whole of their current, their future Eurasian grand-continental imperial politico-historical availability: There is here a knot of destiny that has just been constituted at the very level of the facts, the political opportunity of which we must imperatively seize and the direction of march that it imposes on us by indicating it in the open, without any strategic dissimulation.

President Vladimir Putin for Russia, Chancellor Gerhard Schröder for Europe, the Dalai Lama for Tibet, Prime Minister Atal Behari Vajpayee for India, and Japan's new Prime Minister Junichiro Koizurni, are to meet urgently, somewhere in the middle of the ''Great Continent'' - in Berlin or St. Petersburg - for a First Eurasian Conference, at which the lines of force for the future development and joint exploitation of the fundamental geopolitical space of Greater Siberia should be drawn up. François Mitterrand: ''The territories of Greater Siberia are home to 80% of the world's energy reserves'', and that says it all, quite soberly.

The fact that Europe is to be represented at this First Eurasian Continental Conference by Chancellor Gerhard Schröder, the socialist head of a social democratic state, while all the social democratic and liberal regimes in Europe are currently being subjugated, and subversively subjugated, in a total way by the driving forces of the US-led globalist conspiracy, cannot fail to be a problem.

But since things are now only what they have become, should we not, from now on, stick exclusively to the level of the facts, and the facts alone, which currently carry a meaning that goes in a new direction of history, which appears to be precisely that of our own avowed, and even the most unavowable, wishes?

In fact, Chancellor Gerhard Schröder, who today embodies the return of German central political power to Berlin, is pursuing a twofold policy towards Europe - towards Greater Europe - the two fundamental elements of which are currently, on the one hand, his personal project of a final European Federation and, on the other hand, his unconditional support for Russia's participation, as a full participant, in the current process of building the future continental Greater Europe with a Eurasian horizon. Thus, on the subject of President Vladimir Putin's "New Russia", Chancellor Gerhard Schröder declared in June 2000 in Berlin that "there will be no lasting peace in Europe without Russia", adding immediately afterwards that "we must integrate Russia into Europe on all levels, both from the economic and political point of view and in terms of security and defence". To which President Vladimir Putin replied, in a definitive and clear perspective, that "Germany is and will remain Russia's most important partner, in Europe and in the world".

In Germany, geopolitics has once again - subterraneanly, but decisively - prevailed over the subaltern dialectic of ideological choices, which are only the purposely exhibited face of the occult suprahistorical options at stake in the abysmal march of world history: in history, geopolitics is the part of truth itself, this bare-faced truth, both primary and ultimate, which, in the wake of Heideggerian thought, represents the fundamental freedom of being, that which makes being and non-being.

However, it is no less true that, if one were to stick to the original perspective of the political future of today's Europe, it is indeed France – the France of "great Gaullism" – that should have represented Europe within this First Eurasian Continental Conference on Greater Siberia, which was already being prepared in confidence.

Indeed, the project of the Paris-Berlin-Moscow Axis - which is at the origin of the very vision of the Greater Continental Europe - had been, at its first beginnings, a French visionary option, since it had been launched, in 1943, from Paris, by Raymond Abellio and the clandestine parallel bodies of the Mouvement Social Révolutionnaire (MSR), a movement of which Raymond Abellio had just taken over the secretariat-general, while the current final geopolitical vision of the Greater Continental Europe with a Eurasian horizon, defined in the first place by Karl Haushofer through his fundamental - or rather founding - political concept of the *Kontinentalblock*, had been taken up and brought to its present state by General de Gaulle who, by reinstalling in the history of Western Europe the Franco-German Carolingian Pole, to which he recognised, already in 1946, the status, importance and destiny of a "World Revolution", was laying the immediately activated foundations of our future "Eurasian Empire of the End". For, in a way, everything was already decided in the immediate post-war period, in the mysteriously decisive years 1945–1946. While all seemed lost, in reality things were only secretly beginning again.

It is in the terms of a highly symbolic figure of the final reversal of things, the providential work of the secret self-management of history, that the criminal betrayal of the Bundestag which, in 1964, demolished the de Gaulle-Adenauer state agreements advocating the immediate setting in motion of the "total political union" of France and Germany, is today redeemed, and the debt of the past emptied of its black substance by the revolutionary avant-garde choice through which Chancellor Gerhard Schröder is forcing the doors of destiny, of the great destiny of continental Europe, by affirming in a politically decisive manner the fact of Russia's ontological presence within Greater Europe, thus laying the foundations of the future great-continental European federation of Eurasian dimensions, horizon and destiny. Thus, the same Germany which, in 1964, under the hidden influence of Washington, blocked the de Gaulle-Adenauer project of "total political union" of France and Germany, thus preventing the construction of the Greater Europe, is today giving its decisive chance to the effective realisation of the same continental Greater Europe by bringing Russia into its midst and, behind Russia, India, Tibet and Japan. For this is, in fact, Russia's true mission, and its deepest predestination.

And if Germany is obliged to take the place of France in the conduct of the high political and suprahistorical manoeuvres of the construction of the Great Continental Europe, it is because France is at present incapable, from within, of facing up to her own original destiny, This is because of the final catastrophe of her present political reality, a catastrophe to which she has been led, on the one hand, by the criminal action, subversively concerted and followed by the dark forces, subterraneanly at work in her heart since 1968, and, on the other hand, by the politico-historical self-destruction of the Gaullist national movement. No living country can resist for too long the immense metastasis of the cancer of negative ideologies.

The current reversal of Europe's political axis

At the same time, however, the unconditional subjugation of Western social democracy and "liberalism" to the globalist investment of Europe was criminally and self-subversively exposed - especially in Great Britain, France and Germany – in the course of the political-military aggression of the US globalist conspiracy in South-East Europe, in Serbia, France and Germany - thus bringing down the masks, and Western Europe as a whole suddenly appearing for what it is, a space of US colonialist domination. A concealed but total political domination, coupled with an unwavering economic domination, which is advancing.

Nevertheless, the grand continental European reaction to the aggression of the globalist conspiracy against Serbia - and thus against Europe as a whole - and at the same time to the providential awakening of Vladimir Putin's "New Russia", still managed to mobilise, over the heads of the anti-continental high treason regimes everywhere in power in Western Europe, the front of the still healthy base of the European nations reduced to the mercy of the conspiracy to bring them to impotence, to total political unconsciousness, to the definitive enslavement and final alienation of their own beings, of their living and self-consciously affirmed identity. It was therefore the aggression of the United States' globalist conspiracy that provoked their recovery from the depths, and this recovery was confidentially supported by the sudden awakening of Russia, which was in the process of rediscovering itself, thanks to the appearance of a providential man, and whom it had immediately recognised as such. This was also a form of miracle.

Thus, the fact that the geopolitical centre of gravity of Europe has shifted from West to East, from Western Europe to Russia, and from North to South and South-East of the continent – to the emergence of the subversively destabilised zone of South-East Europe under temporary foreign dependence, is currently matched by the counter-emergence, in Italy, These are facts that must appear to us, fundamentally, as signs of the times, as signs of a profound seismic movement in progress, which announces a chain of transformations to come, or already underway, of supra-historical planetary dimensions: the polar axis of the earth's secret political identity is being reversed.

The current eclipse of France within the Franco-German founding couple being compensated for by the over-strengthening of Germany, the damage suffered by the "polar centrality", by the "immobile centre" of the Franco-German Carolingian pole, does not therefore have much consequence: the movement of profound political transformation of Western Europe that will follow the process of setting up the project of the Great Continental Europe with a Eurasian horizon will not fail to lead to the final liquidation of the subversive stranglehold that incapacitates France in the paths of its own interrupted destinies, subversively suspended in their current politico-historical march. If France does not save Europe, it is Europe that will save France: this is precisely what General de Gaulle said to André Malraux in his visionary book *"Les chênes que l'on abat"*.

And this, while not forgetting that the politico-strategic apparatuses of the device of underground action of the Gaullist movement – which, since its beginnings, has not for a single moment ceased to find itself duplicated by the clandestine counter-movement of the ''great Gaullism'', of the ''Gaullism of the end'' – can set in motion, at the desired moment a sudden and definitive internal collapse of the political foundations of the socialist-communist regime currently in power in France, which only remains in place thanks to certain circumstances illegally and subversively maintained, from the outside, by the globalist conspiracy of the United States and of what stands, in the shadows, behind the US. And these circumstances being, moreover, only the consequence of the in-depth infiltration by the special political services of Washington - and this already since the fifties - of the entire French trade unionist apparatus of non-communist line.

Towards the complete liberation of Western Europe

The fact that Italy, for its part, providentially liberated on 13 June from its subjection to the socialist-communist conspiracy in power, in place, in fact - over the head of the Christian democracy, or with the latter's underhanded complicity - since 1945, is now rushing to join the paths of its own great destiny, This is the first decisive concussive shock in the already ongoing shake-up of the European political status quo, a status quo constituted by the de facto submission of the whole of Western Europe to the politico-strategic investment devices of the US-led globalist conspiracy. The first major breach has been made.

In the short to medium term, France, and Germany too, will now have to free itself, following the over-activated example of Italy, from the socialist-communist dictatorship enslaved to the globalist conspiracy in place, and Belgium will follow, and the rest.

This is precisely why the time also seems to have come for the initiative - which could be Russian or Italian - of convening a First Eurasian Continental Conference on the "Great Siberia Project", for all the already emerging forces of the new Eurasian European revolutionary consciousness to manifest themselves and to succeed in imposing their point of view, in force, concerning the future of the Great Continental Europe that it is up to us to bring to the baptismal font of future history.

The "geopolitical combatant groups", which are present everywhere in Europe and Russia, will now have to raise their heads and engage in a sustained, immediate and long-term undertaking for the final assault on total political power, This enterprise would find its support in depth in the situation of the national revival of regime change in Italy, which is becoming the new centre of national revolutionary incitement in Europe and the radiating focus of the vast suprahistorical renewal in the process of being self-defined at the grand European level.

The decisive affirmation of the national-revolutionary revival in Italy, which, following the collapse of the socialist-communist dictatorship, is now smouldering under the ashes, must thus constitute the horizon within which the future national-revolutionary conflagration of mainland Europe will be declared. For, from now on, everything must happen in Italy for a long time to come.

However, the formidable immediate revolutionary effort that the great history in progress already requires, at the present time, of the Great Europe, of the "New Europe", which is coming, so that it can face

(1) to its new grand-continental destiny

(2) the political liberation from the subversive domination of the globalist conspiracy that is still in place, and

(3) the construction of the greater continental "Eurasian" Europe requires the support of a gigantic revolutionary economic infrastructure, which can only be assured by the Great Siberian Project: hence, the capital importance, for the present moment of its becoming, of the First Eurasian Continental Conference for the construction of the "Great Siberian Project", the fundamental common construction site of the future imperial great European continental economy. Just as at the beginning of the current great suprahistoric cycle, it is Greater Siberia that once again becomes the living heart of the "Eurasian Island", its final, secretly polar *heartland*, which Sir Halford Mackinder, the English double of Karl Haushofer, had foreseen.

The current moment in continental geopolitics

The fundamental ideological and operative weapon in the current struggle of Europe - of greater Europe - against the domination of the globalist conspiracy of the United States thus appears to be geopolitics, active geopolitics. For, in the final analysis, geopolitics will always be stronger than history: geopolitics commands history underground, and will currently oppose it insofar as it is through the subversive concealments of the present Western history that the globalist conspiracy of the United States lays down its bases of support in depth, and advances its positions of offensive investment within the European political space.

Considered from this special angle, what is the current geopolitical situation of the great continent of Europe in the process of finding itself?

In its eastern half, President Vladimir Putin's "New Russia" is committed to the revolutionary political line of the eventual imperial constitution of a Eurasian grand-continental federation of openly eschatological destinies, striving to push as far as possible a basic propositional dialogue with India, Tibet and Japan on the one hand, and with Eastern and Western Europe on the other. In this respect, President Vladimir Putin's active options are as clear as they are inexorable. Something has already been set in motion that will not stop.

In Europe, in the South of the continent, the absolutely decisive political event of the national liberation of Italy from the socialist-communist grip has just taken place, which, together with Spain, Austria and Serbia, is now in a position to set up the "blue belt" of a European continental zone torn from the grip of the globalist conspiracy of the United States, and ready to take the step towards the planned constitution of a grand-continental European federation.

At the same time, in the centre of the continent, despite its deep subjection to its own social-democratic regime, which is still in place, Germany, for its part, now appears to be determined - as has already been said - to participate fully in a great European continental federation based on Russia, Chancellor Gerhard Schröder is himself both the doctrinaire and the field craftsman, having to face, at least for the moment, the refusal of the other reluctant European democracies, still under the thumb of the globalist conspiracy. But this German breach in the existing globalist system is therefore of considerable importance. And this is all the more true since, for the rest, Chancellor Gerhard Schröder's subversive social-democratic positions remain unchanged, totally unacceptable, enemy positions. This obviously complicates matters considerably.

The present state of the globalist front's hold on Europe thus appears to be largely deficient, with Vladimir Putin's "New Russia" providing a super-base of revolutionary political and strategic support for the whole of the grandcontinental liberation movement currently being affirmed, a movement within which the "geopolitical groups" representing, especially in Western Europe, an offensive base that must be considered fully committed to the fight, and which will now be able to find a space of considerable political support in Italy, within the important Italian national revolutionary movement in full rise.

If. as shown in an important-very important-article in the left-wing Parisian daily *"Le Monde"* dated 6 June, President Vladimir Putin is currently acting as the providential charismatic leader of the "New Russia", relying, to do so, firstly on the Yearly Forces and, secondly, on civil society and, above all, on the proponents of the Russian "geopolitical line", including, on the cutting edge of geopolitical positions, Alexander Dugin, it is indeed the latter who is the most important, on civil society and, above all, on the proponents of the Russian "geopolitical line", among whom, on advanced geopolitical positions, Alexander Dugin, it is indeed the latter who is, in fact, the doctrinaire of the new Eurasian imperial regime in the process of installing itself in Moscow, the "new Lenin" of the "New Russia". Aleksandr Dugin, the "new Lenin" fighting for Christ the Pantocrator.

With inexorable continuity in the action he is pursuing, President Vladimir Putin is in the process of installing, through his state visits - and the political-strategic agreements that follow – the infrastructure – Tokyo, New Delhi and no doubt, soon, Tehran - of the future Eurasian grand-continental empire of which the "New Russia" wants to be the spearhead. The serious emphasis is currently on New Delhi and Tokyo. It is Russia that will open Asia to Europe.

For his part, on his return from Tokyo these last few days, where he had been officially received at the Ministry of Foreign Affairs as well as by other high-level political authorities, Aleksandr Dugin told me of his deep dismay at the discovery of the extraordinary interest currently shown by Japan's higher political spheres in the Eurasian project, which the latter had been maintaining. The Japanese diplomatic apparatus is also preparing to launch a campaign in European capitals in favour of the Paris-Berlin-Moscow Axis project, which it would like to extend to Tokyo. It is not for nothing that the Programme of the Eurasia Political-Social Movement explicitly foresees the final integration of Japan and Europe, the double strategic coastal spaces, East and West, "from the Atlantic to the Pacific", of the "Eurasian Island", into the imperial grand continental Eurasian project of the "New Russia" of Vladimir Putin. Karl Haushofer's original geopolitical thinking is thus still very much alive.

However, since 21 April, with the formation of the Eurasia politico-social movement in Moscow, with over-activated representations in seventeen of Russia's most important cities, led by Alexander Dugin, the "geopolitical line" proponents can act as a governing party in Russia, or at least as a parallel support to government action. Russia has a Eurasian future, or no future at all, says the Programme of the Eurasian Political-Social Movement. ''Vladimir Putin: ''The Russian nation is fundamentally a Eurasian nation''.

That the appearance on the Russian and European-planetary political scene of the charismatically providential Vladimir Putin could take place, and take place at the very moment when it was supposed to, remains, for many witnesses of the current emergence of the "New Russia" of eschatological imperial destinies, as a kind of miracle, which is obviously very likely to be the case.

And is it not at the same time another kind of miracle that, in the wake of Vladimir Putin, Alexander Dugin, the "new Lenin", was able, in the space of only a few years, to build up the gigantic doctrinal and ideological-strategic apparatus of Russia's Eurasian "geopolitical line" and the future "End Eurasian Empire", to set up the gigantic doctrinal and ideological-strategic apparatus of the Eurasian "geopolitical line" of Russia and of the future "Eurasian Empire of the End", a doctrinal apparatus which is already called upon to shape the present history, the final history of the "Great Continent"?

And where does the extraordinary sum of revolutionary intellectuals and political activists of the "geopolitical line" that have just appeared in the fighting ranks of the "New Russia" emerge from, one may ask? Where did they come from? How did they get there? What does this incredible rise to the forefront ultimately mean? This inexplicable rise to power of a generation already trained, already committed, already heroically on the barricades and already ready to sacrifice?

Where did the overactive mass of traditional intellectuals come from, too, which today in Italy constitutes the backbone of the national renewal movement in the process of direct and total revolutionary reaffirmation? Where were they before, where were they hiding, and in the terms of what mysterious strategy of secret, prophetic waiting for the necessary hour?

Where do the "geopolitical groups" that have swarmed in ardent semi-clandestinity in Western Europe since the early 1990s also come from? Who, or what, is behind the ongoing revolutionary bush-hammering of these "geopolitical groups" called to forge the revolutionary future of the "Greater Europe" of Eurasian imperial horizon? Who mobilised and organised them?

It is that a very deep subterranean movement of the "great history" in progress is now surfacing, which will take everything with it, before it, a revolutionary imperial current of Eurasian orientation, of final eschatological commitment, of which we are still far from being able to understand all the seismic implications, nor the terrible apocalyptic conflagrations of which it is the bearer.

In the invisible, the "Great Reversal", the *Paravrtti* of the Hindus, has already taken place. Non-being is now being replaced again, cosmically, by being, which is in the process of accelerating the reappropriation of its own hierarchies.

Now this will also have to be reflected in the visible. What has already been achieved in principle will be translated into action later on, and this is also the explanation for the upturn that can now be seen in European politics on the continent, where the grip of globalist subversion is suddenly in a position to retreat. And this process of liberation - of self-liberation - is now to be pursued more and more explicitly. Now other times are coming', said Cornelius Codreanu in his time.

The problem of the moment, as we have understood, is that of moving from doctrinal vision, from vision in principle, to political realisation on the ground, and in this respect the First Eurasian Continental Conference on the ''Greater Siberia Project'' is going to be an extremely significant test, because the heads of government approached for this decisive meeting - Vladimir Putin, Gerhard Schröder, the Dalai Lama, Atal Behari Vajpayee and Juinchiro Koizurni - all belong to the world of visible, front-line politics and, as such, represent the part of immediate politics, to the direct reality of history.

Thus, the First Eurasian Continental Conference on the "Greater Siberia Project" is called upon to act, to impose itself in the manner of an abscess of fixation in relation to all the great lines of force in action, of the current geopolitical convergences initiated by the revolutionary concept of the largest continental "Eurasian" Europe, the supreme figure of which already confesses to being that of a "Eurasian Empire of the End", comprising Western and Eastern Europe, Russia and Greater Siberia, Tibet, India and Japan: The 'Eurasian Island' having thus met its previous unity, and its own final destiny.

ON THE ULTIMATE PREDESTINATION OF ROMAN AMERICA

We all know that in his original vision of the immediate and more distant destinies of geopolitics, Karl Haushofer always refused to publish a 'fundamental manual of geopolitics', convinced that the research undertaken by himself personally or under his direct influence were only the 'waiting stones of a doctrinal edifice to come', which was to see the light of day only with the advent of that final planetary imperial history whose paths he himself tirelessly persisted in digging, and in having the paths dug ahead. Until the immediate approach of its implied imperial conclusion, a conclusion that was necessarily final, world history obliged geopolitical research, by its very course, to remain tragically open to the future, in the state of a petition of principle indefinitely called into question *while waiting for its time.*

Bausteine zur Geopolitik, "Building Stone for Geopolitics", was the title of a collection of geopolitical works published in 1927 by Karl Haushofer in collaboration with Lautenbach, Maull and Obst, by Kurt Vowinkel, in Berlin, a title that sends directly to this vision of geopolitics in progress, of an open and permanent research, which was essentially Karl Haushofer's, a research whose very incompleteness was meant to be an assurance of the implicitly suprahistorical conclusion of the geopolitical path and its mysterious arrangements of 'building blocks' constantly mobilised to the task.

This is also my own position in principle, and this is precisely the reason why I ask that my present research on *The Ultimate Predestination of Roman America* be considered only as an assembly in progress of simple operative notes trying to define the new horizons of the current planetary geopolitics grasped in its revolutionary avant-garde becoming. A "building stone", therefore, a "waiting stone" as Karl Haushofer would have said with another of his own expressions, a "waiting stone" in the perspective of a forthcoming imperial conclusion of planetary history now irrevocably marching towards its end. Operative notes, however, whose secretly fundamental, active intention is to intervene in the very march of history now underway, to impose a preconceived direction, a new, abrupt and total turn, corresponding to a great final revolutionary design.

It is therefore, in any case, a matter of research engaged in action and, by that very fact, doomed to be constantly overtaken by it, and thus given, in advance, for provisional in its intimate march, ready at any moment to be caught up in the irrational vertigo of history, in the impetuous, irresistible current of the dogmatic irrationality at work in the abysmal subterraneans of 'great history'. Risks will appear, which we will have to assume entirely.

The moment, however, has come, as it would seem, for us clandestine holders of a certain revolutionary vanguard consciousness of planetary geopolitics entering the truly final phase of world history, the moment has come, I say, when the problem of the suprahistorical destinies-of the implicit, as yet unrevealed predestination-of Roman America must be posed in a way that is both immediate and decisive, leading to an immediate and decisive solution of the problem, where the problem of the suprahistorical destiny-of the implicit predestination, not yet revealed-of Roman America must be posed in a way that is both immediate and decisive, leading to an exhaustive definition and at the same time fully engaged in the current historical future. A definition that carries a geopolitical concept of its own, definitive, transcendental, the very definition of the mission and future of Romance America at a time when everything is being decided at the level of the next ontological renewal of world history. A concept immediately usable in the suprahistorical struggle secretly already underway for the imperial domination of world history, for the emergence of the final imperial identity of history after the coming end of history.

Thus, in the planetary struggle that now pits the 'continental superpower' against the 'oceanic superpower', the Great Eurasian Continent, against the planetary hegemonic will of the United States and its concealed domination mechanism already at work, Will Romance America naturally find its place as the reactivated projection - and constantly to be reactivated - of the intervention forces of the Great Eurasian Continent virtually already mobilised to the south of the North American continent, offensively, whose geopolitical identity it duplicates by a politico-strategic counter-identity of a close presence, of a new historical assertion and of its own destiny, of another destiny: Roman America represents the most advanced transoceanic positions of the Eurasian great-continental superpower in the fundamental geopolitical neighbourhood of the imperialist oceanic superpower of North America.

At the same time, it is necessary to argue that the final geopolitical definition of the Eurasian grand-continental superpower today takes up, extending and strengthening it to its final historical and politico-strategic limits, the fundamental concept of the *Kontinentalblock* proposed by Karl Haushofer, thus integrating, in a single imperial unity of destiny Western Europe, Eastern Europe, Russia and Greater Siberia, India and Japan, a rediscovered unity of destiny that must eventually lead to the establishment of what we call the Eurasian Empire of the End, the starting point of *the Imperium Ultimum*, of what, at the end of history and beyond history, must be the *Regnum Sanctum*.

It is therefore quite certain and obvious that the transition of the Eurasian Empire of the End to the final stage of the Ultimate Empire, to the stage of the *Ultimum Imperium* of total planetary dimensions, requires that the Eurasian grand continental superpower unconditionally prevails over the imperialist superpower of the United States, so that the Atlantic and Pacific oceans attain the status of the "internal seas" of *the Ultimum Imperium*, of the "Total Empire of the End".

At present, it is China that, within the geopolitical space of the Great Eurasian Continent, represents the decisive metastrategic bridgehead of the US imperialist oceanic superpower, The recent visit of the President of the United States, Bill Clinton, to Beijing has just provided a confirmation that is as irrevocable as it is designed to evolve in the direction of an increasingly significant intensification, an open, undisguised, staggering confirmation of the new Sino-American planetary alliance that is called upon to define the setting up of another world history that is beginning.

Like China, Fundamentalist Islam, an anti-continental weapon of the United States

However, it should be pointed out that the new political-strategic blocking device currently being set in motion by the United States, through its recent - confidential - arrangements with China, against the Great Continent of Europe, is at the same time reinforced by the double American and Chinese support for the revolutionary cause of Islamic Fundamentalism, whose belt of active subversion set up by the Iran-Afghanistan-Pakistan political-strategic line, is already on the point of strategically circling the southern flank of the Great Eurasian Continent.

That the current nuclear advances - overt or covert – of Iran and Pakistan were made possible by the essential technological support that was – and still is - given to them under cover by China, is now a fact that is considered indisputable, just as the political support subversively given by the United States to the cause of Fundamentalist Islam in its planetary implantation undertakings appears to be equally certain, even in the Mediterranean, where Washington's support for the ultra-criminal activities, repeated massacres and indiscriminate devastation of the Algerian Islamists' clandestine combat organisations is now a known fact, and more than proven.

It is certainly essential that, in the present circumstances, we know how to discern the two complementary strategies set in motion by Washington, through the support, and the exacerbation provoked and maintained, in the shadows, of the revolutionary activism of fundamentalist Islam: On the one hand, this vast subversive operation aims at blocking, destabilising and maintaining in a permanent critical state, and which is constantly accentuating, advancing in the direction of irreparability, the southern front of the Great Eurasian Continent and, on the other hand, it weighs negatively on the relations of the great-continental European bloc with the Arab world as a whole, which is not religiously negative, "secular", including, in the first place, Iraq

This also explains the apparently incomprehensible relentlessness of Washington against Baghdad, as Saddam Hussein's national resistance regime represents the last Arab stream belonging to the old 'pro-Arab European line' that General de Gaulle had set up with a strategically offensive intention against the American positions and activities in the Middle East, Africa and Asia, which were essentially engaged against the French and European positions in place.

The antagonism between fundamentalist Islam and the "pro-Arab European line" of Gaullist France, a line that still persists, against all odds, is currently approaching the critical zone of an extreme rupture, in Iraq as well as in Algeria, Libya, Egypt and Palestine. The countdown has begun, and it will not stop without an overall strategic counter-action, which Europe would seem to be incapable of envisaging, either strategically or even politically. But we must not swear by anything, must we? We have seen, in politics, other incredible reversals of apparently even more desperate situations.

Thus, the United States is now playing the card of Islamic fundamentalism against Europe and the Eurasian great-continental bloc, just as it is playing the card of China with the same aim, at a metastrategically higher level. All of this forms, in a non-exhaustive way, a unitary set of actions armed, from below, with an extraordinary coherence, with a lucid and unfailing will, posing itself in the very terms of a certain conception of "total war" belonging to the dialectic of the planetary imperialism of the United States, which knows more than anything else how to act subterraneanly, in the shadows, sheltered from their so-called democratic principles.

On this subject, I make a point of pointing out here that a book has just been published in Paris by L'Âge d'Homme - *Islamisme et États-Unis Une alliance contre l'Europe,* by a young senior French civil servant, Alexandre del Valle - which constitutes, in itself, a formidable denunciation device, quite exhaustive and going into great depth, of the planetary conspiratorial strategy of the United States in its current manipulations of fundamentalist Islam.

Roman America, bridgehead and advanced metastrategic base of the Great Eurasian Continent

However, in the current state of affairs, what China is within the geopolitical space of the Great Eurasian Continent, the bridgehead and advanced fundamental base of the imperialist oceanic superpower of the United States, Roman America must also be, in counterpart, within the geopolitical space of the planetary oceanic superpower of North America: the bridgehead and advanced metastrategic base of the Great Eurasian Continent.

It is from and through Romance America that the Great Eurasian Continent will be able to intervene in the interior space of the North American oceanic superpower, because part of it remains - just as Romance America remained -

a suprahistorical projection of the previous Europe, of the ethos and civilisation, of the final predestination of a certain transcendental Europe.

For a new war of secession - a war of secession in reverse - will have to pit the United States against itself at the beginning of the next millennium, within which the Southern component of secretly European identity, the "original Vinland", will rise up to win against the subversive, anti-European, democratic and communist, "leftist" component that had the upper hand in the first domestic confrontation, during the first North American civil war, 1861–1865.

So, if the inner component of European substance, identity, ethos is to prevail over the other inner component of the United States, over its negative component, governed by the subterranean global conspiracy of the Dark Power, by the Mystery of Iniquity and its shadowy enforcers, it will only be with the metastrategic support of Romance America. With the support of Romance America, constituted as an advanced counter-strategic political base, as an offensive platform of the Eurasian grand-continental line of imperial and polar orientation, traditional, archaic, original, "anterior".

It is also clear that in the future political-strategic game of Latin America within the geopolitical space of the United States, the Hispanic community, which now has more than twenty-five million inhabitants living within the borders of North America, will also count in a singularly appropriate way.

Everything is indeed ready for the times to change, for the 'great times to return'. The time has come, therefore, when, at the call of its most occult predestination, Roman America will have to awaken from its long dogmatic sleep, to join the first outposts of the immense political and suprahistorical confrontation whose dividing line will soon break in two the history of a world at its end, in order to remake, afterwards, its most ancient unity, begun anew, with the virginal nativity of a new cycle, for the time being still inconceivable.

Six operative geopolitical theses

However, in order for Romance America to become, to impose itself and to be able to act as a concept with an immediate metahistorical and political-revolutionary double identity, a certain number of developmental conditions appear to be absolutely necessary, essentially the following six conditions, which are all operative geopolitical theses.

(1) That the historical, politico-strategic and economic integration of the whole of Romance America can be considered a fait accompli, or in the process of being definitively achieved.

(2) And that the final historical and politico-strategic integration - reintegration - of Romance America be done fundamentally in terms of an ontological return to its own previous origins, of an auroral renewal of its imperial Spanish and Catholic, Great European identity, and hence an abrupt and total revolutionary emergence due to a new awareness of its own continental destiny of planetary and imperial scope, as a decisive instance of the final imperial whole that places it on the continental meeting line of the two oceans, the Atlantic and the Pacific, considered as the "internal seas" of the *Imperium Ultimum.*

(3) That a new and total revolutionary and imperial consciousness should thus appear as both the starting point and the over-activated and over-activating conclusion of the historical and politico-revolutionary reintegration of the whole of Romance America, an identitarian consciousness capable of providing itself with the organisational means of its own historical establishment, of its own immediate political installation.

(4) That a first nucleus of immediate historical and politico-revolutionary integration should thus be constituted by the mobilisation of an original block of new beginnings and new foundations comprising Argentina, Chile, Peru, Bolivia and Paraguay, a nucleus from which the final process of total continental integration can be initiated, put to revolutionary use, to the end.

(5) The final process of the revolutionary continental reintegration of Romance America also implies a total ontological reconsideration of the present situation of Spain, for it is through Spain that the predestined participation of Romance America in the European grand-continental bloc will have to be manifested: In order to accede to the new European grand-continental mission which represents its own final predestination in the direction, once again, of Romance America, Spain will have to make its second national revolution, to take up again at a higher level of consciousness, will and revolutionary destiny the now outdated experience of its first national revolution born of the civil war of 1936–1939.

The great continental imperial revolution of Romance America must thus find its metahistorical foundations in the ontological recommencement of a new internal history of Spain that has rediscovered in itself its own previous origins, the project of a new Spanish history of the world. A gigantic task, like all the political-revolutionary tasks marking the historical beginnings of the third millennium.

(6) However, the imperial ontological turnaround of Romance America towards its own anterior origins will ultimately have to go abysmally beyond the level of visible history, in order to reach - to recover – the subterranean, metahistorical, transcendental foundations of its suprahistorical, occult, principial identity, to reach, therefore, the buried precommencements, of the present suprahistoric cycle, as these beginnings – precommencements - are defined by Horbiger's visionary cosmogony, and even deeper into the ultimate ontological layers of the abyssal planetary immemory, where the pre-original mystery of what Miguel Serrano calls the "reversal of the poles" is held.

The secretly so ardent nostalgia of Roman America-Argentina, Chile-for the South Pole being, in reality, the abysmal nostalgia for the North Pole before the pre-original reversal of the Poles: what transcendentally attracts Roman America to the South Pole revealing, to the initiatory gaze of sacred science, the hidden persistence of the previous immemory of the Original North.

Thus the true face of the historical and political-revolutionary reintegration of Romance America as a whole, in its deepest acting totality, appears in the double light of the occult cosmogonic doctrines of Horbiger and Miguel Serrano.

Roman America in a state of self-defeat

Indeed, it is only once these six operative geopolitical theses - these six resurrectional conditions - are brought together in the framework of a metahistorical and politico-revolutionary front of immediate, living and active coherence, having its own imperial centre of gravity within itself, that Romance America will be in a position to assume its predestined mission with regard to North America, in a state of being able to intervene in a fundamentally decisive way in the process of internal revolutionary conflagration of the United States, which is called upon to forge its new secessionary destiny, its "other destiny", foreseen by the final transcendental concept of the Imperium *Ultimum.*

Without forgetting, however, that the process of the reunion of Romance America with its own previous origins also involves Spain in its course, which will have to follow the paths of a similar abysmal reconditioning before it becomes the planned interlocking device of Romance America in the march of the final suprahistorical destinies of the Eurasian grandcontinental bloc: Once again, it is through Spain that Romance America will find itself engaged in the convergence of its own destinies - of its secret predestination - with the imperial revolutionary future of the great Eurasian Continent.

The providential secret of the "greatest history" is therefore currently challenging the historical future of Romance America at a level of self-defeat that must be considered heroic and transcendental, inviting it to ensure that, from the depths of its subterranean being, the resurrectional emergence of the ultimate, unsuspected and unsuspected figure of its suprahistorical and eschatological identity, a figure that has been hidden until now, is produced. For the figures of the ultimate margin of history must be hidden, always, until the very last hour.

The 'crossing of the line' into the third millennium draws upwards, exalts all the structures of action that are engaged in the task, forcing them into a state of self-exceeding that constitutes the very sign of what is already happening there that is miraculous, that is secretly predestined by the invisible beyond of history.

A decisive generation

Thus the question that will be very necessarily asked is the following: to this profound and tragic final interpellation of history addressed to Romance America, will there correspond, in due time, the answer and the advent of a new revolutionary generation, a predestined generation, bearer of a different and total metahistorical consciousness? A generation of activists capable of responding to what this supreme turning point in history will demand of them, capable of bringing to its ultimate completion the heroic and transcendental mission that is already theirs today, capable of facing without flinching, in all lucidity and in the terms of a resolute decision - Heidegger's mysterious *Entechlossenheit* - the formidable historical earthquake for which it is up to them to ensure the responsibilities and even the execution, *on the ground*?

The near future will tell, and it will confirm or deny our vision of a situation of final historical rupture, of a situation that is essentially eschatological: the end of one world is here, very close, and the beginning of another world is undoubtedly even closer.

The mobilisation of the decisive generation, bearer of a new planetary imperial destiny, will not happen by itself. An immense revolutionary work in depth will have to be tirelessly pursued, a work of ideological and organisational framing which, through the local action of the Geopolitical Groups, will have to lead to the emergence of the new metahistorical and revolutionary continental consciousness of Romance America, an integral part of the European-Eurasian grand-continental imperial front, rising up against the active pretensions of the planetary imperialist hegemony of the United States, of the planetary "oceanic superpower" engaged in the paths of its great design of subversive domination.

For the revolutionary work of the Geopolitical Groups, political-strategic work of vanguard, must be the same, in Roman America as well as in Europe, in India and in Japan, and even inside the own geopolitical space of the USA, where the Geopolitical Groups will support the rise of the counter-strategic consciousness of the structures of affirmation belonging to the anti-subversive, recessionist insurrectionary line, to the camp of the "Southern revenge" against the "politico-social alienation of the Northern domination".

And just as within the Eurasian grand-continental revolutionary front already in action, it is the Franco-German Carolingian Pole that constitutes the strong point, the founding polar identity of the whole, just as Russia constitutes the double European grand-continental bridge in the direction of India and, through Great Siberia, also in the direction of Japan, just as Spain constitutes the passage of development and European grand-continental imperial reverberation in the direction of Romance America, Roman America itself is called upon to duplicate geopolitically, from the South, the North American continent, within which it will have to intervene when the decisive time comes, the Andean Pole of Argentina and Chile playing the same founding role within the geopolitical space proper to Roman America as the Franco-German Carolingian Pole does within the original Great European space.

The immediately preceding historical reference to the Franco-German Carolingian Pole, the original nucleus and super-activating basis of the whole of European imperial grand-continental integration, remains General de Gaulle, as does the reference to the Andean Pole, and even more so, the project of the total integration of Romance America, which finds its backbone in the major charismatic figure of General Juan Domingo Perón.

In both cases, these are the representatives of the armed forces of their respective countries: it is the armed forces that, again and again, undo and redo history in the making. Will we see the same phenomenon repeated once again, with the same decisive consequences? Repetition, and the mystery of great destiny.

Let us remember General Juan Domingo Perón's speech at the National War College in November 1953:

Si subsistiesen los pequeñitos y débiles países, en un futuro no lejano podríamos ser territorio de conquista''.

Es esa circunstancia la que ha inducido nuestro gobernó a encarnar de frente la posibilidad de una unión real y efectiva de nuestros países, para encarnar una vida en común y para planear también una defensa en común.

Es indudable que desde el primer momento nosotros pensamos en esta, analizamos las circunstancias y observamos que, desde 1810 hasta nuestros días, nunca han faltado distintos intentas para agrupar esta zona del Continente en una unión de distintos tipos.

''Yo no quería pasar a la historia sin haber demostrado, por lo menos fehacientemente, que ponemos nuestra voluntad real, efectiva, al y sincera para que esta unión pueda realizarse en el Continente''.

Pienso yo que el año 2000 nos va sorprender o unidos o dominados.[1]

---

[1] *If the small and weak countries were to remain, in the not too distant future we could be a territory of conquest".*
It is this circumstance that has induced our government to face up to the possibility of a real and effective union of our countries, in order to create a common life and also to plan a common defence.
There is no doubt that from the first moment we thought of this, analysed the circumstances and observed that, from 1810 to the present day, there have never been any lack of different attempts to bring this part of the continent together in a union of various kinds.

You are in a state of total war, in the visible and in the invisible

But we must not let ourselves be fooled, nor must we let down our guard of permanent analytical vigilance, and always in advance of the affirmation of circumstances, of circumstances alone: What we are dealing with today is war, *total*, unconditional, profound and final *war*, war for the imperial domination of the world and of its history, which is reaching its end, war between two absolutely antagonistic ontologies, war between being and non-being, represented by the figure of the "Two Standards", the central instance of St. Ignatius of Loyola's "Meditations", the war of light besieged by the powers of darkness, the war of liberation of life encircled by the subversive conspiracy of the powers of resignation and death.

For the final war of liberation of the continental planetary superpower from its siege by the oceanic planetary superpower is itself none other than the war of liberation of being from the encirclement of non-being, the all-out war of the powers of light against the enveloping work of the power of darkness. Since the collapse of the USSR and the disappearance of communism, we have been in a state of total planetary revolutionary war against the imperialist hegemony of the US "oceanic superpower" and its supporting, contributing and interposing forces, primarily Britain.

On the other hand, we must also admit it, it is impossible not to do so now: we are not unaware of the fact that behind the visible facade of the planetary imperialism of the United States there is a conspiracy of essentially suprahistorical and occult dimensions and scope, which it is not possible for us, in the present state of affairs, to call by its true name, but of which the United States itself is a simple tool of penetration and domination in broad daylight. And where, on the other hand, the part of the invisible counts in a singularly decisive way, concerted, conducted and manipulated in the terms of a long guarded design, and developing in continuity to ends still concealed, but the most important of which-the primary end-remains that of putting an end to Catholicism once and for all, of putting an end once and for all to that 'light of being' which has always constituted the foundation of the intimate ethos and of Eurasian civilisation in its very becoming, and beyond all becoming, immutably.

In this connection, I am reminded of what Admiral Carrero Blanco said to me some twenty years ago: If our main enemy remains communism, we must not for a moment forget that behind communism stand socialism and

---

I did not want to go down in history without having demonstrated, at least in a reliable way, that we put our real, effective and sincere will to make this union possible on the continent".
I believe that the year 2000 will surprise us either united or dominated.

capitalism, that behind socialism and capitalism stand, in the shadow, Freemasonry, that behind Freemasonry stands a certain world conspiracy which has its secret and not-so-secret epicentre somewhere in the Middle East and which spreads underground throughout the world, and that behind it, finally, stands the Prince of this World himself, surrounded by his own "occult Sanhedrin", who is responsible for everything and who directs everything. For this is the ultimate truth of the situation.

This, what Admiral Carrero Blanco called the *ultimate truth*, had to be said, as I have just done. But let's not dwell on it too much, if only because everything about it is contained, exhaustively, in some of Miguel Serrano's visionary writings, and that's where you have to go to find it if you're really interested in this final zone of forbidden, dangerous problems that suddenly open up onto quite dark precipices.

On the other hand, what I think needs to be repeated is the fact that at the present time we are already in a state of total planetary revolutionary war against the imperialism of the United States and that which is hidden from the exacerbated hegemonic will - hegemonic will manifested on the triple level of politics, economics and culture - of the United States, the active centre of world subversion. In this sense, the defensive planetary war of the European imperial grand-continental unity against the subversive activities of the "oceanic superpower" of the United States is merely a continuation of the last world war, with Russia now on the grand-continental side of the ongoing confrontation. We must therefore assume the sacrificial weight of the countless European civilian victims of the US Air Force's terrorist raids, which plunged the European continent from Brest to Bucharest into mourning, while also taking into account the unheard-of massacres in Tokyo, Hiroshima and Nagasaki. Like a ritual of secret communion in death, where the future imperial identity of the great Eurasian continent is found to have been constituted in advance in darkness, awaiting the day, now approaching, when it will appear in full light, finally victorious in history and beyond history, in death and beyond death.

Because we have to face facts: for us, from now on, *having understood the situation* is a matter of life and death, of being or not being. We are on the line of passage between our own destiny, defined by the mystery of our occult predestination, and submission to the anti-destiny, to the sudden absence of any destiny, we are on the *line of fire*.

Now we have to choose, knowing that it is an absolutely irrevocable choice, a final choice.But what will our tasks be, assuming that we choose - but have we not already done so - the party of being, the *party of survival?*

For the moment, it will suffice to understand what is absolutely at stake in our present struggle, in our struggle to come: the emergence of a new imperial revolutionary consciousness, of a new continental and planetary consciousness of being, of the same consciousness acting within the whole of the Eurasian grand-continental geopolitical space, as well as within the final geopolitical space of Romance America. This is the fundamental condition for our salvation, our deliverance and our liberation. This is where everything else will have to come from, and where everything that has to be done will be done.

We dare to say that our combat strategies are completely up to date. However, we will not make any statement on this subject here: this would be to give the ontological enemy an unexpected gift, insofar as the present research is destined for a non-confidential audience.

Strategic secrecy belongs to combat.

Certainly, in the face of the all-pervasive planetary developments for which we must now credit the "oceanic superpower" of the United States, our own politico-strategic positions - the positions of the Eurasian great-continental camp in a state of encirclement - may appear to be tragically deficient, and they are. But, at the same time, this is not at all the way to pose the problem of the relations of forces in presence. Our revolutionary perspective changes everything, because it is based on the dialectic of *revolutionary overthrow, a* dialectic which is in itself this overthrow.

The dialectic of this same revolutionary reversal also holds the secret of the ultimate predestination of Roman America.

(Personal contribution to the *II Encuentro de la América Romanica de Politica y Cu/tura alternativas,* Santiago de Chile, September 1998)

JUNICHIRO KOIZUMI AND JAPAN'S GREAT AWAKENING

The formidable planetary trap set by the global conspiracy of the United States and what stands behind it in the shadows, gripping the nations of mainland Europe and Latin America in its steel jaws, including living freedom, has thus seemingly closed in on us once and for all, whose living freedom, eschatological destiny and final politico-historical integration could very effectively represent an absolutely critical peril, a *mortal peril* for the ongoing "grand design" of American hegemonic imperialism, whose preliminaries are already obscuring the horizon of near future world history.

However, while the still free nations of Western Europe would seem to have ceased to struggle under the alienating, devastating embrace of the globalist conspiracy at work, Eurasian mainland nations such as India and Japan have just freed themselves from it, by their own means, and are giving themselves - or are in the process of giving themselves - another destiny, based on their own regained freedom.

For what Atal Behari Vajpayee has succeeded in doing in India, Junichiro Koizumi is in the process of doing in Japan as well: both democratically brought to power by huge waves of revolutionary national consciousness, did not hesitate for a moment, once in power, to abruptly begin the process of liberating their country from the subversive external grip of the globalist conspiracy.

Thus it is that, just like Vladimir Putin's "New Russia", Atal Behari Vajpayee's India and Junichiro Koizumi's Japan, are currently together on the front line of the abysmal seismic upheaval pushing the Eurasian "Great Continent" to rediscover its own being and its original predestination, This upheaval is arousing, mobilising, securing and affirming the active foundations of the imperial liberation movement that is deeply involving the entire Eurasian "Great Continent", which is in the process of awakening and will ultimately prevail.

In a very important article entitled *Les relations récentes entre la Russie et l'Inde*, Gilles Troude, a researcher at the Sorbonne's DESC, writes in *Géostratégiques* (Paris) in March 2001

"... Faced with a unipolar world dominated by the overwhelming power of the United States, which no longer has any rivals not only in the economic sphere, but also in the military and political spheres, are we not slowly moving towards an India-China-Russia strategic triangle, the only one capable of competing with the superpower that wants to be the master of the world? ''

This is the fear of US international affairs experts, who have seen signs of increased cooperation between Russia, China and India, and a growing sense in all three countries, especially after NATO's bombing campaign in Yugoslavia in the spring of 1999, that US power must somehow be kept in check. Although these three countries are still a long way from merging into an anti-NATO Eurasian Axis, these analysts are concerned about the emergence of a potentially very serious threat: an alliance of some 2.5 billion people, formidable military power and an impressive stockpile of nuclear years - since India is now officially a nuclear power - the cement of this coalition being to counter America's global dominance.

It would be a disaster for the United States'.

If this web of relationships progresses,'' said Charles William Maynes, president of the Eurasia Foundation, a Washington-based *think tank*, ''then you have the continental *heartland* - 2 billion people in China and India - combined with the formidable technological power of Russia. That would be a disaster for the United States.

And yet, Gilles Troude, while misunderstanding the *final meaning of the* real political situation of China, present and future, of its preconceived line of destiny, which excludes it in advance from unity, from the imperial grand-continental Eurasian reintegration, strangely does not take into account, in his analyses, the "great national awakening" of Japan that is taking place at the present time. The role of Japan appears to be absolutely decisive in the ongoing mobilisation of a Eurasian grand-continental front of total politico-strategic opposition to the designs of the globalist conspiracy led by Washington.

In reality, it is the extraordinary innate, deep, secret vital power of the Japanese people that made possible, and was able to ensure, the coming to power, at the precise moment when it had to be done, of the providential man, the "absolute concept" that is Junichiro Koizumi, charismatic bearer of the new great destiny of Japan. Someone had to come, and the will of the Japanese people made him come.

With Junichiro Koizumi, the providential law is once again verified, which says that countries always end up finding the predestined leaders they deserve, and this is entirely certain also for Vladimir Putin and his "New Russia", as well as for Atal Behari Vajpayee and the "Terminal India" currently emerging in the face of history. It is therefore high time that we in Europe finally understood who Junichiro Koizumi really is, and what great revolutionary destiny he holds.

Junichiro Koizumi, bearer of a new destiny for Japan

Junichiro Koizumi is indeed the man charged by destiny - and by 75% of the Japanese - with the final reunion of today's Japan with the earlier history of "Great Japan", the man charged with reconnecting with Japan's timeless imperial identity, which had to be pretended to be suspended on 15 August 1945, the day of the "surrender".

For it is now well known that Junichiro Koizumi openly claims to be entirely faithful to the national, traditional and imperial line of his predecessor and master of thought, the former prime minister, also a member of the LDP, Yasuhiro Nakasone (1982–1987), who was the first to dare to break the democratic taboo concerning the Yasukuni Shinto temple in Tokyo by going there on a pilgrimage on 15 August 1985. This provoked a wave of violent protests in several Asian countries that had been under Japanese occupation, led by the political secret services of Communist China. For the Shinto Yasukuni temple in Yokyo is the highest shrine of Japanese national memory, the supreme symbol of its deep, untouched identity, which takes no account of the vast disinformation campaign mounted by the United States after the end of the last war about Japan's "guilt".

For his part, Junichiro Koizumi had already stated, on several occasions, his firm intention to go to the Yasukuni temple on 15 August 2001, the anniversary of the "surrender" of Japan in 1945, to participate in the religious ceremonies "in homage to the memory of the heroes who fell in defence of Japan". A gesture whose symbolic significance appears to be self-evident, and *decisively* so. And irreversible.

But, in fact, it was on 13 August that he went there, thus trying to relatively disinvest from the rising protests more or less artificially raised by his decision. For the combined forces of reaction and the red front had seized the opportunity to launch an intensive barrage against Prime Minister Junichiro Koizumi's decision to make an official pilgrimage to the Yasukuni temple. But nothing helped. Just as nothing could convince him to reverse his decree allowing - and encouraging - school history textbooks to adopt openly 'revisionist' positions on Japan's 'responsibilities' in the last war.

Located in the centre of Tokyo, near the Imperial Palace, on Kudan Hill, the Shinto Yasukuni temple is in fact dedicated to the memory of the 2.5 million Japanese combatants who fell in the face of ennemy, whose souls - including those of the thirteen war criminals – or so-called war criminals – hanged by the American occupation forces, including those of the thirteen war criminals – or so-called war criminals – hanged by the American occupation forces, led by General Hideki Tojo, Emperor Hirohito's Prime Minister - are gathered there, in the invisible, around the supremely sacred liturgical mirror which constitutes its cosmic pivot. Yasukuni is, in the invisible, an immense sea of souls in perpetual reverberation, watching over the Empire.

It is quite certain that a decisive majority of Japanese believe that their country was, during the last war, the victim of a concerted plot, of global dimensions, led by the United States, which aimed to prohibit the effective presence of Japan in Asia and the Pacific; in the face of which, Japan did nothing but fight for its survival, on the brink of extinction, in the terms of a battle that was both final and total. The apocalyptic conclusion of Hiroshima and Nagasaki is well known.

In the outbuildings of the Yasukuni temple, a museum dedicated to Japan's national memory is currently presenting a major official exhibition entitled "How We Fought" (in English, "Japan's War and Soldiers"), an exhibition whose fundamental testimony is centred on the memory of the thousands of kamikazes who offered their young lives to save the Empire. See you at Yasukuni! they cried as they flew to the ultimate sacrifice. In the film that shows their heroic, superhuman feats - *divinizing*, in Shinto terms - it is stated: "Many people think that, in the war of fifty years ago, Japan was gravely in the wrong: this is absolutely false. Thus the Tokyo Trial is null and void. The Commander-in-Chief of our Armed Forces, General Hideki Tojo, was accused of "crimes against humanity" and hanged by the Occupying Forces, with the United States alone demanding his death sentence. It is time for Japan to wake up! It is high time Japan recognised the true reality of its own history! Japan, wake up!

It is known that Junichiro Koizumi's doctrine of government is very close to the overall vision of Shintaro Ishihara, elected in 1999 as governor of Tokyo with an overwhelming majority, "by a quasi-plebiscitary vote", on ultranationalist, anti-American positions, openly in favour of the transformation of the "Defence Corps" into a new great Japanese Army, and author of a very successful book, "Japan that knows how to say no", as well as a novel with non-conformist theses, "The season of the sun" *(Tayô no kietsu).* It is also known that the group of young ideologists and intellectuals currently behind Junichiro Koizumi is led in the struggle by Professor Fujiuka Nobukatsu of the University of Tokyo, whose thinking is oriented towards a renewed, revolutionary search for the hidden foundations constituting the original predestination of Japan, the "Great Japan".

As for the train of totally disruptive reforms that Prime Minister Junichiro Koizumi intends to impose on Japan as a matter of urgency, the decisive formula belongs to University of Tokyo professor Yoshiro Tanaka, who recently declared that what is expected of him is "to make the 'Third Revolution', after those of the Meiji era and the post-war period of 1945". For, as Heizo Takenaka, the minister in charge of economic policy in the current government of Junichiro Koizumi, warns us, "…if we undertake the necessary reforms now, we will also have to accept the pain that will follow, which will be great; but, if we delay these reforms, it may lead us directly to death". For such is the immediate and most profound reality of the social and economic situation in Japan today, which is in fact on the brink of collapse. Contrary to all appearances, and this is what we must not ignore. For old, hidden burdens have now come to an end, and whatever the cost, we must *face up to them*.

The life-saving use of the Armed Forces

However, in addition to a series of reforms that will have to turn Japan's current political-administrative and economic infrastructures upside down, which amounts, in effect, to an internal rupture like the one that occurred during the Meiji era, Junichiro Koizumi also nourishes - and without doubt above all - the "grand design" of restoring the National Armed Forces to the place that should fundamentally be theirs, that is to say, the first place in the politico-historical configuration of a country that has regained its own centre of gravity within itself, outside of any subjection, outside of any foreign interference or domination.

Even if, for that, Junichiro Koizumi would have to succeed in revising the current Japanese Constitution, whose famous "Article 9" forbids Japan to have a "National Army". However, this is what Junichiro Koizumi is very firmly determined to achieve with his political action of government, the keystone of which is precisely the return of Japan to its previous politico-military identity, with all that this implies at the level of "great history", of the great historical and political decisions immediately to come, in Asia and in the Pacific and, also, within the framework of Japan's future choices in relation to the emerging Eurasian grand-continental unity.

In his return, which is not politically devoid of danger at the outset, but which he intends to pursue in a completely resolute manner, towards the urgent reconstitution of the National Armed Forces of Japan, Junichiro Koizumi rediscovers the fundamental movement of any revolutionary national salvation and liberation enterprise in the face of the subversive hold, alienating, globalist and social-leftist conspiracies of Trotskyite infrastructure – always "the reaction and the red front" – which today very effectively hold political, economic-social and cultural power all over the world. By turning, as he is doing, to the National Armed Forces of Japan, Junichiro Koizumi is doing, in his turn, what Vladimir Putin did in Russia, Atai Behari Vajpayee in India and Vojislav Kostuniça in Serbia, what Silvio Berlusconi is trying to do, underground, at the present time, in Italy: the recourse to the Armed Forces is, always, the very last chance of the persistent instances of being succumbing to the manoeuvres of encirclement, internal penetration and annihilation carried out by the agencies of investment and disappropriation of non-being on the way to the final establishment of the anti-world and the Anti-Empire from beyond the end.

And so Junichiro Koizumi's revolutionary national recovery enterprise, now underway, already belongs, in fact, to the vast Eurasian - and Latin American - grand-continental strategic front of now irreversible opposition to the accelerated anti-historical subversion enterprise pursued by the planetary "globalist" conspiracy in the service of the "Planetary Superpower" of the United States and what stands hidden behind it.

For, in any case, it must be understood that Junichiro Koizumi's return to the use of the Armed Forces also represents the implied - but now unavoidable – decision to distance himself from, and eventually break the implicit subjugation pact – both militarily, economically and ideologically/culturally – of Japan towards the United States, and, by the same token, its new fundamental orientation, on the one hand, towards Asia and the Pacific and, on the other, towards the United States, This also represents the implicit – but now unavoidable - decision to distance itself from and eventually break the implicit military, economic and ideological-cultural subjugation pact of Japan to the United States, and thus its new fundamental orientation towards Asia and the Pacific on the one hand, and towards the Eurasian "Great Continent" on the other, and towards its future membership - already decided - in the Paris-Berlin-Moscow Great Continental Axis.

I must also mention, in this respect, the confidences that Alexander Dugin has just made to me following his recent official information trip to Japan, where he was able to note the very exceptional attention with which the high political and administrative authorities of the Ministry of Foreign Affairs are following today the progress of certain European grand-continental projects concerning the setting up, in the first place, of the Paris-Berlin-Moscow Axis, projects to which Japan would be prepared to give unconditional and overactive political and diplomatic support: For Japan, the extension - and completion - of the European grand-continental Paris-Berlin-Moscow axis to New Delhi and Tokyo is already a self-evident necessity, ineluctably. In any case, however confidential they may be for the time being, Japan's active economic presence and politico-military assistance in India is now a reality that cannot be ignored in any significant way. Major decisive things are happening there, underground, between Tokyo and New Delhi, *the consequences of which will not be long in coming.* All of this is undoubtedly at the instigation, or at least with the active endorsement, of Moscow, with Vladimir Putin personally involved in the continuation of this shadowy enterprise: it is the great geopolitics, it must be understood, that constitutes the hidden foundations of history in the making. Today as in the past.

The mystical outline of our future struggles

Everything concurs, therefore, in proving that the use that Junichiro Koizumi intends to make of the power that has just been democratically entrusted to him by the Japanese people will be that of a total revolutionary politico-historical recovery of the profound destinies of the latter, openly recognised as such or only partially *held as secret.* For there is an occult eschatology of Japanese national history, whose inner horizons open up to a double intelligence, both suprahistorical and cosmic, of this world at its end and of its hidden afterlife: This is what constitutes Japan's true collective suprahistorical force, and it is also what makes Japan identify itself, totally, with the common transcendental consciousness of all the peoples of the "Great Continent" of Eurasia, united in the visionary, preontological certainty of the fundamentally eschatological dimension of history in its final whole. The common, abyssal archaic consciousness of the peoples of the Eurasian "Great Continent" considers history as the very place of suprahistorical salvation from the end of beyond the end, the supreme sanctity being, for these peoples, that of the heroism of the human and superhuman fighters who must lead to this end and beyond this end.

Thus, the political reunification - the *reintegration - of the* Eurasian grand-continent currently being promoted by the project of the Paris-Berlin-Moscow-New Delhi-Tokyo counter-strategic axis will have to be duplicated, in depth, by a new common awareness of the identity of the spiritual and polar predestination of all the peoples of the Eurasian imperial space. The advent of this spiritual awareness, both imperial and polar Eurasian, is what will constitute, from now on, the task of the ideological fighters for the Greater Europe and of their high-level political-historical commitments. A great fighting mystique has thus been born, which is now in the process of revolutionary development, "destined to change the face of the world".

In this ongoing development, the part played by the "geopolitical groups" will be most decisive: Indeed, if there is a new civilisational awareness of Eurasian grand-continental dimensions, it will be due in the first place to the "geopolitical groups", to their heroic commitments of the night period of the clandestine, to their work of agitation, their work of agitation, consolidation and overactive revolutionary affirmation that they will have to deliver, now, in broad daylight, once the doctrine of the great-continental liberation will be openly called to become the active will of the whole of the peoples belonging to the original space of the same community of polar being and of final eschatological destiny.

In the immense revolutionary battle that is coming for a new common historical consciousness of the Eurasian inner space, the "geopolitical groups" will thus be the basic cells of the rising tide of the living ethos, of the consciousness on the march towards total change, towards the final transfiguration of a civilisation with apocalyptic predestination: the great hour of the ''geopolitical groups'' will have come when the unity of being of the Eurasian grand-continental whole will be recognised as the supreme acting value of its own terminal history, at the same time as its own *restarted history.*

On the other hand, in a more concrete, more immediately objective way, it is quite certain that, in the present state of affairs, what we will need most is a certain number of study, research and documentation centres (CERDs) aimed at the depths and at the same time truly exhaustive as regards their own objectives, a certain number of 'centres of influence' at the service of our active knowledge, This is where all our efforts to bring together, to update our political and historical knowledge and to re-identify spiritually with these peoples who belong to the same community of profound destiny should be directed.

Moreover, the problem of continental Europe-Asia relations is not at all new. Already in 1940, in his fundamental and decisive geopolitical essay, *The Continental Block Central Europe-Eurasia-Japan*, "printed but not distributed", Karl Haushofer strongly deplored the flagrant, catastrophic absence of high-level European study and research centres on India, Japan and Eurasia in general. Haushofer could, however, congratulate himself on the existence and activities, in many respects exemplary, of the 'Institute for the Middle and Far East' in Mussolini's Italy, operating 'under the direction of Senator Gentile, Archduke Tucci, the Duke of Avarna, son of the former Italian ambassador to the Viennese court'.

In the special situation of emergence that we are in today, at least six such institutes for the Middle and Far East should be set up as a matter of urgency, two in France, two in Germany, one in Italy and one in Spain. Russia should be considered separately for the time being, where several such institutes already exist, and which should be reorganised, restructured and intensified in a newly significant way.

On the whole, however, the problem area concerning China must be studied separately, with an offensive, preventive counter-strategic mindset. For, situated within the Eurasian great-continental space, China represents, however, geopolitically, a bridgehead of the 'outside', 'oceanic' world. With an irreducibly self-centred vocation, China is therefore subject to the "external influence" of the United States and to anti-continental, "oceanic" globalist conspiracies to encircle and invest offensively in the Eurasian "Great Continent". China is preontologically committed to the enemy camp of the "Great Continent", to the "oceanic camp" of the Leviathan, of "non-being".

On the other hand, does not the final encounter between the profound spiritual destinies of Europe and certain still hidden predestinations of Asia, which remain in the shadows, find a specific field of junction through the living and ardent convergences that are imposed in matters of activated religion, of religion on the march? Is it not in the invisible that the great spiritual encounters take place, and does not the Fire of the Spirit reveal itself irrationally in the special visions of its secret chosen ones?

We know that Saint Maximilian Kolbe, the martyr of Auschwitz, had a visionary foresight of the dual path of India and Japan towards Catholicism. Having visited Japan himself, and in particular Hiroshima and Nagasaki - and we can thus better understand the reasons for the choice of these two cities as targets of nuclear fire in August 1945, when we know that they were the two Catholic cities of Japan - he had indeed acquired the inner certainty of the great Catholic future of Japan.

At the same time, without having been able to give real expression to his burning desire to go personally as a missionary to India, St. Maximilian Kolbe's personal relations with certain proponents of initiatory Hinduism had led him to think the same thing about India: not in terms of a concerted reasoning, but from the fundamentally irrational perspective of a spiritual vision of his own, of a grace of clairvoyance in this regard, to which he had had access as the bearer of a special, ulterior and *decisive* mission. An occultly prophetic mission.

As far as Japan is concerned, it is true that initiatory Shintoism lends itself to fairly flagrant doctrinal comparisons with the great mystical Catholicism. In the sunny figure of Amatarasu, could we not distinguish an enclosed prefiguration of the Immaculate Conception? Just as the three objects of the Shinto imperial cult – the "mirror", the "dagger" and the "jewel" – could also find extremely revealing correspondences in Catholicism. Thus the 'Mirror' - fundamentally present at Yasukuni - recalls the Mirror of the Immaculate Heart of Mary, while the 'Dagger' can be identified with the Sword of the Living Word. Then the godless one will be revealed, and the Lord will make him disappear with the breath of his mouth, and destroy him with the manifestation of his Coming", II Thes. II, 8. And as for the "Jewel", this polar, central figure leads to the supreme nuptial mystery of the *Aedificium Caritatis*. One must dare to *penetrate behind the veil*.

For it is in this ultimate spiritual horizon that we must situate the current revolutionary attempt undertaken and pursued by Junichiro Koizumi in Japan, a secret country if ever there was one. All his political and administrative initiatives involve an occult spiritual split, an immediate response on the invisible plane. It is *the other world* that is now acting in Japan for very high purposes.

"New missions"

If, in the inner darkness of history, China is reflected on Japan, Japan is not reflected on China, and it is precisely this situation that must now be remedied. For, as with Russia and India, Japan's main Eurasian mission at present concerns China, which must be prevented at all costs from gaining access to the 'great story', which it is supposed to divert from its course, to distort the race ahead. Blocking the rise of China is the most urgent "new mission" of the Japan of the "Great Awakening", the Japan of Junichiro Koizumi.

The dialectic of Japan's urgent rearmament in force, which will not only affect the Armed Forces, but also a profound renewal of its national consciousness, will therefore have to fundamentally change the situation in Asia, because Japan implicitly intends to return to its former positions of challenge and its own missions in Asia and the Pacific. Missions that it will now have to accomplish on behalf of the Eurasian grand-continental imperial community, and which places it in the front line against China.

The immense gravitational force of the new offensive geopolitics of the new Japan, the Japan of the "Great Awakening", will thus be able to influence China within its own borders. By creating new power relations and new cleavages within the Chinese central political power, it will thus have to make a new pole of revolutionary politico-historical affirmation emerge, that of the "Northern China", This was a new pole of revolutionary political-historical affirmation, that of "Northern China", bringing together all the Ural-Altaic and Manchu components of the latter, as well as its Mongolian parts, against "Southern China", which Guido Giannettini calls "Oceanic China", belonging to the sphere of influence of Insulindia and the South Pacific. This internal secession of China should lead to the integration of its northern, "European" part into the Eurasian grand-continental camp of the new imperial movement revolutionarily carried forward by Russia and the emerging "Greater Europe".

This, in the same movement, will cause the politico-historical relations of Junichiro Koizumi's "Great Awakening" Japan and Vladimir Putin's "New Russia" to reach a paroxysmal level, the repercussions of which will be felt, in great depth, within the entire Eurasian imperial community. This is how the shift of the geopolitical centre of gravity of Greater Europe towards the East will find its maximum deviation, which will provoke in Western Europe a state of extreme politico-historical, even ontological weakening, the first signs of which can already be felt.

This is what will make a total revolutionary reconsideration of the current situation in the West inevitable, leading to the Final Reversal, *our goal*.

TO BLOCK THE PARIS-BERLIN-MOSCOW-NEW DELHI-TOKYO EURASIAN AXIS: THE US WILL OCCUPY AFGHANISTAN AND PAKISTAN

It is impossible not to recognise that the major terrorist action by Al Qaeda in New York on 11 September has completely changed the current identity of world history, and not only on the surface. Thus the new global political-strategic conjuncture, while continuing to sustain within it the increasingly active opposition of two fundamentally antagonistic geopolitical situations - namely, the opposition of the US globalist conspiracy, and the currently emerging unity of Eurasian grandcontinental imperial integration - is at the same time being brought to bear, At the present time, it is also undergoing the dangerous solicitation of a convergence obligation that claims to mobilise the two fundamental geopolitical antagonisms facing each other at the planetary level, but *neutralised*, into a common counter-strategic front called to block the way to Islamic terrorism.

This induces a terminal, ambiguous and catastrophic overhang within ongoing world history. An advanced crisis device. I think it is important to talk about all this. From now on, everything depends on it.

Nevertheless, if the established and politically over-activated bloc of the US globalist conspiracy is facing and opposing, under cover, the bloc of the Eurasian grand-continental space, the "Eurasian Island", this one, for the moment, has an effective existence only on the doctrinal level of the revolutionary geopolitics which, while being born and already developing, shows itself to be far from being able to claim a mobilisation power, a power in action really present on the front line according to its own final availability, while being born, and already developing, shows itself to be far from being able to claim a power of mobilisation, a power in action really present on the front line according to its own final availability, as it is indeed the case, at the present time, for the globalist bloc. If the globalist conspiracy is posed in terms of political power, the Eurasian imperial unity facing it can only be defined for the moment in terms of doctrinal power, having only a dialectical existence.

And yet, this face-off constitutes, in fact, the very foundations of the current planetary political-strategic conjuncture as a whole, in its current forward march.

But if the globalist bloc is thus symmetrically opposed to the Eurasian continental bloc in the perspective of the struggle already begun for the final domination of history at its end and of the world, it is no less certain that a profound dissymmetry is manifested, at the same time, between the self-consciousness of the two antagonistic geopolitical instances that are the foundation of current world history.

For the US globalist conspiracy bloc happens to be fully aware - through its all-controlling, occult central command bodies in Washington - of its own political identity, destiny and will to destiny, of a planetary hegemonic destiny in the making. Concealed behind its structures of cover and strategic diversion, the globalist conspiracy moves forward with full knowledge of the facts, following a front of designs projected far ahead.

On the other hand, as a result of a long and profound internal and external work of subversive counter-identitarian alienation, the European continental bloc, for its part - apart from a few semi-clandestine foci of geopolitical consciousness and action – does not have, at the present time The European continental bloc, for its part – apart from a few semi-clandestine foci of geopolitical consciousness and action - does not, at present, have the slightest collective awareness of its own identity, its abysmal identity or its final destiny, or even of its current situation of subordination and impediment, of being placed subversively in inferiority in the face of the total mobilisation of the over-activated consciousness that is that of the globalist conspiracy of the United States.

However, if the occult powerhouses of Washington are acting, as it appears more and more to be the case, according to a profoundly, dramatically accomplished awareness of the ultimate stakes of the current conflagration for the final domination of history and the world, and according to extremely concerted overall politico-strategic plans, the only barrier to their planetary hegemonic designs remains, today, the presence, in their path, of the Eurasian "Great Continent" in the process of awakening to a revolutionary consciousness of its own identity and its secret suprahistorical predestination.

But, for its part, the Eurasian "Great Continent" can only oppose the hegemonic designs of the globalist conspiracy in action for the moment by virtue of the sole weight of world history itself, of world history in progress, whose inescapable objective realities - national, political, cultural, religious and economic realities – still hinder, slow down and prevent the underground politico-strategic operations, currently in a situation of covert, unavoidable and unacknowledged offensive, The unavoidable objective realities – national, politico-cultural, religious and economic realities - are still hindering, slowing down and preventing the underground politico-strategic activities of the United States and its shadowy backers, which are currently on the offensive, unavowed and unacknowledged as such.

To which we must add, of course, as we have already said, as working, in its turn, on this *slowdown*, the increasingly intensive action of the great European "resistance" of the "geopolitical groups" – the "geopolitical groups" of Robert Steuckers and his relatives – and of the powers supporting more or less their current avant-garde struggles. As it was already the case during the time of General de Gaulle's rule in France, and as it is today in the case of Vladimir Putin's Russia-the "New Russia"-which is undoubtedly bringing Germany into it as well.

It is in this mysterious factual slowdown, imposed and maintained - by the very weight of history, and by those who secretly exacerbate its claims - in the forward march of the offensive designs of the globalist conspiracy for its final takeover of Western Europe, that we Europeans now have our *last chance* to pull ourselves together before it is really too late. Now.

The East of the "Eurasian Island" is already liberated. But not yet the West

It is a fact, then, that the US-led globalist conspiracy, at least on the surface, is, in any case, at the present time, a politico-strategic offensive bloc fully aware of its present and future power, and fully committed to a vast final planetary hegemonic design.

Now, what is the situation of the continental bloc of the "Eurasian Island", which is called upon, in principle, to irreducibly oppose this planetary hegemonic action in full offensive, and which concerns it directly?

In the entrenched camp of the great Eurasian continent, only Vladimir Putin's 'New Russia' today represents a power - a superpower - that is geopolitically aware of its own identity and history, of its great Eurasian imperial suprahistorical predestination and of its final eschatological missions.

At the same time, the East of the Eurasian "Great Continent" is experiencing, through the India of Atal Behari Vajpayee and the Japan of Junichiro Koizumi, a groundswell of a return to freedom, which is in the process of ridding itself in force of the totalitarian constraints of globalist democracy to which it was subjected, thus emerging, once again, into the daylight of "great history" to join the camp of the "Eurasian Island" in the process of regaining its own political-historical centre of gravity. Thus we can say that the East of the "Eurasian Island" is already liberated.

While the western part of the "Eurasian Island" - Western and Eastern Europe - is still under the alienating domination of the globalist conspiracy which, through the social democratic regimes everywhere in power in Western Europe, maintains, in the terms of the ongoing democratic terror, the permanent counter-identitarian subjugation of the European nations still alive, but prevented, thus, from reaching the revolutionary consciousness of their own historical destinies and joining, by the same token, the part of the Eurasian Island that is still alive, the state of permanent counter-identitarian subjugation of the still living European nations, which are thus prevented from reaching the revolutionary consciousness of their own historical destiny and from joining the already liberated part of the "Eurasian Island", Russia, India and Japan; Tibet is still under Chinese occupation. It is therefore on Europe that the efforts of the politico-strategic liberation enterprise will have to be concentrated, from now on, in charge of the whole of the subterranean counter-offensive device of the great Eurasian continent mobilised, from the inside, by its final suprahistorical liberation movement. By the movement of its revolutionary self-appropriation of its own destiny, of its greatest ultimate, "archaic" destiny.

The fact is that in Europe today, only the "geopolitical groups" can claim to have a truly revolutionary awareness of the identity and final destiny – eschatological, "apocalyptic" – of the Greater Europe. The "geopolitical groups", and no other formation, which, through the updated doctrine of the great Eurasian continental axis Paris-Berlin-Moscow-New Delhi-Tokyo, perpetuate the fundamental geopolitical doctrine of Karl Haushofer, the doctrine of the *Kontinentalblock*, taken up, after 1945, by General de Gaulle and the Eurasian continental design of the "great Gaullism", of the "Gaullism of the end". The political-historical birth certificate of which had been constituted by the accelerated rapprochement of France and Germany and the creation of the Franco-German "Carolingian Pole" – the appearance of which had marked a true "World Revolution", according to General de Gaulle – the touchstone of the future Great European Federation, which nothing can prevent us from building in the terms, precisely, of a new World Revolution. For this is the task of our predestined generation.

Thus, what should no longer be ignored is that the Greater European Federation constituted by the final imperial integration of Western and Eastern Europe, Russia and Greater Siberia, Tibet, India and Japan, represents a block of billions of inhabitants, with immense religious, cultural and political, scientific, technical, industrial and economic resources, whose ultimate geopolitical importance would objectively relegate the United States and the entire hemisphere of immediate influence to the rank of a secondary power. But this is precisely what the United States refuses to accept, opposing it *by all means in its power, including the most risky ones.* This can take us a long way, to a foreseeable catastrophe, and we must already know how to internalise the threat and get used to it. In fact, it is a question of life and death, of being or not being.

On the vast globalist operation of strategic diversion underway

It is certain that we must be able to understand this immediately: the current politico-military takeover operation pursued by the globalist conspiracy of the United States over Central Asia, an enterprise of penetration and, in the long run, of de facto occupation of Afghanistan and Pakistan, is aimed at blocking the Eurasian grand-continental politico-strategic device of the Russia-India-Japan ensemble. In other words, the same operation - magnified - as the US takeover of South-East Europe during the open politico-military aggression against Serbia: The West and the East of the Eurasian "Greater Continent" will thus be taken over by the United States in the terms of a double political-military operation carried out under the cover of circumstantial pretexts, but which, in reality, represents the first phase of the future intercontinental war - in fact, already begun - of the United States against the Greater Europe.

Even during the dramatic events of September 11 in New York, just as in the Cuban war against Spain, or the arranged outbreak of the Civil War, or the mysterious torpedoing of the *Lusitania*, or Pearl Harbour, or the "Kosovo massacres", Washington has always been able to create the conditions necessary for a response marking their subversive interference in history in progress. Interference that the abysmal preconditioning of the American mentality can only conceive in terms of a clandestine provocation, carried out and controlled behind the diversionist façade of a defensive justification and moral requirement to be pushed forward.

This ultimately only hides the repeated scenario of a kind of original mystery of American collective overconditioning, and the politico-historical predestination of a singularly interloping, and as it were unconsciously very dirty, vocation.

All this said, of course, so that we would not, under any circumstances, be fooled as to the true meaning of the gigantic manipulation, in several successive relays, of the terrorist attack of last September 11 against New York, which served as a pretext for the current planetary politico-military deployments of the globalist conspiracy of the United States: if there was a conspiracy, of course, it is no less obvious that there was, behind this conspiracy, a conspiracy of the conspiracy, and even a conspiracy of the conspiracy. I hope that I am being heard, at least by those who cannot fail to understand me.

That we must, on the other hand and at the same time, agree - that we must all agree – on the fact that the time has indeed come to put an end once and for all to the movement – to all the movements - of global Islamic terrorism, is a certainty that we cannot fail to subscribe to, entirely. And without any ulterior motive. And right now. The whole of Europe has done so. And so has Russia.

But it is no less certain that we cannot accept that this can in any way deliberately conceal the state of progress of the intercontinental conflagration already begun, underground, by the occult supporters of the globalist conspiracy in the midst of an offensive against the continental Eurasian bloc. That a joint operation carried out in broad daylight may give shelter to a counter-operation carried out in the shadows between the very elements constituting this operation. For we know that there is a double game, and this double game forces us to refuse it unconditionally. Whatever it costs us. And in the very terms of the total and undoubtedly final political war that is being waged against us.

That Europe, that Russia, that India and Japan, that China itself can tactically lend itself to the game being played, in this case, by the globalist front in its current endeavour against global Islamic terrorism, may indeed represent a vast counter-dialectical movement of operational engagement. Posing a common politico-religious war aim. But in no case can it serve to support the suicidal deception of a full-scale engagement in the covert trap set by Washington for the emerging Eurasian Great Continent.

For "common combat front" should not mean a subversively controlled shift towards the neutralisation and enslavement of those who are engaged in it together, and even less the underground engagement of the power leading the game towards another form of secret political war within its own camp, dialectically more advanced and metapolitically infinitely more perverse and criminal, because it is directed towards ultimate, decisive, dead-end conjunctures. This is what is currently happening, and this is why we intend to react in force. For what is at stake here is the very fact of our survival in the near future.

But let it not be thought that, because of all this, we can forget for a single moment the immense holocaust that has been going on for years in Algeria, close to home, by the abominable local accomplices of Osama Bin Laden, who in the end will have to pay for everything, himself and his people. As well as those who supported them and still support them in the shadows. Islamic fundamentalist extremism is inherently perverse. Rabid dogs, who must be treated ruthlessly as such.

Europe's current dual positioning

Following the events of 11 September in New York, the "great planetary policy" of the European continental bloc will therefore have to be defined dialectically, at a double level of political and strategic action. This duplication bears the specific mark of the current planetary political situation, in which all significant decisions will henceforth be divided against themselves, confidentially. There will therefore be no action, decision or consciousness other than dialectical, and world history itself will become dialectical. Dialectical consciousness of history, dialectical history of European consciousness in the face of current strategic demands. This new dialectical confrontation must manifest itself on a double level of the present political-historical reality. A first level where, alongside the United States, Europe will find itself willing, by the very force of things, to participate fully in the effort to definitively eradicate global Islamic terrorism currently being undertaken by the United States. And a second, more internal level, where, behind the circumstantial political options concerning its current relations with the United States, relations placed under the urgency of the common commitment against Islamic terrorism, Europe would absolutely not know how to lower its guard, to cease being-or having to be-aware of what fundamentally opposes it to the planetary hegemonic designs of the United States, that is to say, its own Eurasian grand-continental imperial politico-strategic design.

Now, this double positioning of Europe with regard to the globalist conspiracy of the United States has been illustrated recently by two successive positions taken by President Vladimir Putin, positions that are apparently contradictory; but which, in terms of active, operational policy, do not contradict each other, situated as they will be, dialectically, at two different levels of the same political-strategic conjuncture in progress.

So there was the very important performance of President Vladimir Putin on 24 September in Berlin, in the presence of Chancellor Gerhard Schröder, the German government and the entire Bundestag, where the man from the Kremlin spoke in German for more than an hour, asserting, and strongly emphasising, the very decisive character of the deep link between Russia and Germany. Russia now sees Germany as its most important partner in Europe and in the world," he said. And from Germany onwards, Russia recognises a profound community of destiny with Western Europe, in line with the current Eurasian geopolitical grand-continental vision which, in the projection, therefore, of the Paris-Berlin-Moscow-New Delhi-Tokyo Eurasian axis project, is today that of President Vladimir Putin and his "New Russia" moving towards its new destiny.

Putin even attacked, reports Le *Figaro*'s Berlin correspondent Jean-Paul Picaper in an interview with the mass-circulation newspaper *Bild*, German intellectuals who are bogged down in self-accusation because of Hitler's past and recommend a low profile for their country. *No country can suffer eternally for the faults with which it has burdened itself in the course of history,"* he said.

As for Europe, Vladimir Putin also expressed himself very clearly during his speech in Berlin. I believe," he said, "that Europe will only be able to assert, in the long term, its own will to constitute an independent centre of power within the framework of current world politics, if it unifies its own resources with those of Russia, with the people, spaces and natural resources, with Russia's economic, cultural and defence potential.

Finally, with regard to the second of these dialectically linked - opposed – positions taken by President Vladimir Putin, its content will reveal the complete convergence of his views and those of George Bush manifested at the APEC Conference - the "Asia-Pacific Cooperation Forum" – which took place in Shanghai on 21 October and brought together, principally, the United States, Russia and China. Convergence of views on retaliation and on putting a definitive stop to the global activities of the terrorism of fundamentalist Islam, and more particularly of the Taliban in Afghanistan.

I think that the response envisaged by George Bush is measured and appropriate to the threat facing the United States," Vladimir Putin said in Shanghai. And then: "If we start this fight, we must know how to finish it.

Otherwise, the terrorists could have the impression that they are invulnerable. And in that case, their action will be more dangerous, more insolent, and will lead to even worse consequences". An unfailingly firm stance.

It would be hard to imagine a closer meeting of minds, which George Bush did not fail to note in an exceptionally warm and grateful manner. We will remember this act of friendship", said George Bush.

However, Vladimir Putin's statements in Berlin and Shanghai respectively manifest two dialectically contradictory positions. The point of view of the counter-strategy, the affirmation of the whole and defence of the Eurasian great-continental space, currently threatened by the globalist conspiracy of the United States on the offensive, whose current focus is the Europe-Russia rapprochement. At the same time, the current unconditional support of the United States in its global commitment against Islamic terrorism is opposed. We are therefore, at the same time, both against and for the United States in its double planetary offensive, the offensive of encirclement and investment of the geopolitical space of the "Eurasian Island", and the offensive against Islamic terrorism. Thus the current engagement of the "Eurasian Island" with the US globalist conspiracy is a fundamentally and actively dialectical engagement, we are fully engaged in a final planetary war which is a dialectical war. The times of dialectical war have arrived, the times of truly total war.

From Berlin to Shanghai, an immense gap has thus appeared in the uncertain skies of the current planetary politico-strategic conjuncture, the very gap of the final dialectical war already underway.

Current states of dialectical warfare

Vladimir Putin's present dual attitude towards the US globalist conspiracy represents the very dialectical structure of the fundamental choice that all of us, the "geopolitical groups" as a whole and all those who follow the Eurasian grand-continental "geopolitical line" must follow. This means: that while standing by the United States in its current planetary politico-strategic endeavours against Islamic terrorism in action, to keep intact, to constantly overactivate our counter-offensive vigilance against the subterranean manoeuvres of the US globalist bloc, currently in the process of storming the basic Eurasian grand-continental positions in Western Europe and Central Asia.

Vladimir Putin was therefore not at all mistaken when, the day after the Shanghai Conference, he went to the Russian General Command Headquarters for Central Asia in Dushanbe, the capital of Tajikistan, and convened a sort of counter-conference - also attended by General Sergei Ivanov, Minister of Defence, and General Nikolai Patrushev, head of the FSB - in order to state his own personal counter-strategic positions on the American commitment in Afghanistan. To wit:

(1) That by trying to get a "democratic fraction" of the Taliban to participate in the future peace process in Kabul, Washington was recklessly deviating from the current struggle, because there are no good and bad Taliban, only Taliban, which must either be destroyed to the last man, or lose everything again. Islamist terrorism always rises from its own ashes and only yields to cleansing by vacuum. Washington's weaknesses with regard to the subversive myth of the 'good Taliban' is only the result of the subterranean work of negative influence exerted on the current American executive power by the same nightly bodies in place in the obedience of the same spheres of occult action that gave birth to the original emergence of Islamist terrorism under control and of the Taliban themselves.

(2) The only way forward, then, is to support the Northern Alliance unconditionally, whose unconditional victory over the Taliban would truly be the beginning of the end for the entire planetary conspiracy of Islamist terrorism; Russia, for its part, would then undertake to do the rest in Central Asia, to take over the conclusion of the work.

It should not be forgotten that last March a Russian Antonov 154 secretly brought Commander Ahmed Shah Massoud from Dushanbe to Moscow, where he was discreetly housed in the former residence of Yuri Andropov in the capital. For four days, Commander Ahmed Shah Massoud was invited to work with senior officials from the Ministries of Defence and security bodies of Russia, Tajikistan, Uzbekistan, Iran and India on the theme of 'comprehensive political and strategic action against Islamist terrorism and extremism'. This initiative appears, today, to be singularly prophetic.

The elimination of Commander Ahmed Shah Massoud abruptly deprived Russia of the centrepiece of a field commander with high charismatic potential. But this has not neutralised Moscow's plans for the politico-strategic primacy of the Northern Alliance, nor even diminished its commitments to it. On the contrary, one might even say.

In any case, by its very nature, dialectical warfare will imply the absolute primacy of the weapon of political-strategic intelligence - cultural and religious as well - over all other weapons: dialectical warfare is fundamentally a war of teaching. This makes it a superior war, a war of inspired intelligences, which can be waged by small occult units of decision and combat in the shadows, in charge of an infrastructure of ultra-specialised, "initiatory" elites, of a very high level of commitment and competence. And which will also call for personal sacrifice pushed to its ultimate, 'mystical' limits.

Thus, the US globalist conspiracy will have to contend in the coming years with counter-conspiracies that are increasingly abstract, conceptual, covert, penetrating and elusive.

Without anyone really realising it, the centre of gravity of planetary power will have changed sides.

Yet, it must be acknowledged that all these changes stem, in fact, from the unexpected emergence of Vladimir Putin's 'New Russia'. Russia should not be considered as just another state, but as a special civilisation, as an original continent, as a strategic, cultural and spiritual continent'', declared the *Eurasian Platform* in 1999.

GEOPOLITICS OF A FINAL GLOBAL SITUATION

India has long claimed total hegemony in Southeast Asia.

Jiang Zemin, President of the People's Republic of China

With the five nuclear tests that Pakistan has just carried out in the Balochistan desert, South-East Asia is abruptly tipping over into 'big history'. The political-historical existence of nations is now defined only by their qualification for metastrategic nuclear deterrence.

Until now, the only real nuclear power in Asia has been China, and it is in relation to China that we must now try to estimate India's continental metastrategic importance and not, as one might be tempted to do, in relation to Pakistan.

The continental nuclear confrontation, at the moment, has implicitly become that of India and China, since Pakistan is neither developing nor engaging - despite its claims and the continued monitoring of its military technological efforts – in anything other than an additional diversionary mission, reinforcing – in principle - China's anti-continental camp, to which one could possibly also add, in continuity, North Korea.

It is, however, quite clear that in the years to come, a nuclear explanation would most certainly become a possibility between India and Pakistan, in the event of a paroxysmal escalation of their contentious interests over Kashmir, or in the event of a series of Pakistan-sponsored terrorist blunders, of subversive actions pursued by Islamist extremism within Indian territory.

The fact that a nuclear conflict between India and Pakistan would result in ten million deaths on the spot would not be a major factor: it would be the global ecological consequences that would be catastrophic, perhaps even irreparable.

Yet, sooner or later - but the situation is becoming increasingly urgent - India should manage to settle once and for all the fundamentally critical problem of Pakistan, which is directly linked to the terrifying, elusive nebula of Fundamentalist Islamism and its fevers in that part of the world, in permanent resonance with the two hundred million Indonesian Islamists.

Charles Tenet, the CIA chief: "A political vacuum in Indonesia could create fertile ground for international terrorist groups and Islamist activities".

In fact, our total geopolitics of the Great Eurasian Continent, a revolutionary geopolitics of avant-garde, which poses the ultimate imperial concept of the integration of Western Europe, Eastern Europe, Russia and Greater Siberia, Tibet, India and Japan, into the camp of the same original predestination, formally excludes China from the active definition of the emerging suprahistorical Eurasian grand-continental unity, which is ours today. It is in a way against China that the unity of the Great Continent is now being constituted, and that China is therefore polarising negatively on itself. Thus China represents the second oppositional political-strategic pole, after the United States, which is rising in the face of the emergence of the Eurasian grand-continental community: China as the negative pole of the Pacific, the United States as the negative pole of the Atlantic.

This means that, in the face of China, India is supported by the grand-continental nuclear potential of France and India, of Russia too, and even, in principle, of Great Britain. Grand continental unity is a dialectical unity.

On the other hand, the Sino-Indian nuclear confrontation in South-East Asia implies, in the more or less long term, the imperative obligation for Japan to revise its own nuclear strategy as completely as inexorably, tragically, which, once manifested, will add to the nuclear camp in the region polarised by India. This is despite Japan's national psychopathology against any form of nuclear weaponry. But times change, and mindsets evolve.

It is thus as if the story of the reunification - as if the imperial reintegration - of Eurasian history immediately ahead will be the story of the nuclear encirclement of China and the middle powers in its direct sphere of influence in South-East Asia, an encirclement ensured by the community of great-continental imperial powers belonging to the geopolitical line of the Paris-Berlin-Moscow-New Delhi-Tokyo axis.

As for the attitude of the United States towards this state of affairs, it is inscribed from the outset in the fundamental geopolitical data of the current planetary political conjuncture: not only because the decisive confrontation to come-and which, moreover, can already be considered as quite current-between the Great Eurasian Continent and the United States corresponds to the lines of force of the ontological antagonism between the "continental power" and the "oceanic power", a fundamental antagonism of planetary geopolitics in its basic permanence, but also because it is now a certainty that the political construction of the Greater Europe with a Eurasian horizon - whatever the permanent obstacles, delays and impediments that the negative powers working in the shadows are increasingly trying to put in its way - will nevertheless end up raising an impassable barrier to the final, effective realisation of the planetary hegemonic "grand design" of the United States.

Thus the full force penetration of the Greater Europe into the ongoing final dialectical game for planetary imperial domination, as we already know, will have the inescapable consequence of reducing the present primordial status of the United States – the "Planetary Superpower of the United States" – to that of a second-rate power, since the United States will not be able to cope at all with the formidable imperial potential of the "Eurasian Island", once the latter has come to be itself, unconditionally. This will certainly happen, but never without us.

It therefore appears to be a very obvious necessity for the United States to try to urgently unite, in the same offensive front, its own efforts to politically neutralise Greater Europe and China's desire to resist the attempts to encircle it by the great continental powers, Russia and India in the first place. This will inevitably lead to a great Beijing-Washington alliance, where China would offer the United States a major political and strategic bridgehead in the east of the Great Continent, enabling them to turn Greater Europe through the east, and where the United States would ensure China, if not a partnership, at least a significant participation in the planetary opening of its own economic and political power of imperial "Great Oceanic" dimensions

At the same time, the permanent anti-continental offensive action of the United States encounters, and does not refrain from using, within the geopolitical space of the Great Continent itself, a formidable strategic device of conspiracy and revolutionary reverberation, which is the emergence in force of Fundamentalist Islamism. It is now trying to take over the entire southern flank of the Great Continent, while intensifying the action of its terrorist sites in Western and Eastern Europe. The revolutionary strategic device of Fundamentalist Islam that Washington is now trying to couple to the focus of the anti-continental emergences of the geopolitical fortress of China, whose formidable negative radiation destabilises and blocks from within the Far Eastern critical limit zone of the Great Continent in front of Japan, which is thus forced to close in on itself.

The recent book by a French researcher, Alexandre Del Valle, *Islamisme et États-Unis. Une alliance contre l'Europe,* published by Éditions de l'Age d'Homme, Paris, 1998, says all that needs to be said at present about the problem of the offensive metastrategic use of Fundamentalist Islam by the United States in its ongoing struggle against the great-continental European revival at the present time of revolutionary imperial affirmation and self-definition.

In this final planetary conjuncture, the particular mission of France-or rather of the Great Continental Carolingian Pole politically instituted by Charles de Gaulle-would be that of the predestined power that must unite, polarise, both ideologically and in terms of a single revolutionary imperial destiny, the whole of the geopolitical elements of the Great Eurasian Continent in the face of the globalist challenge of the United States and China, and also in the face of the subversive use that the United States is currently making of

Fundamentalist Islam in its open battle against Western Europe, which is under siege from within its own borders. For we must recognise that Greater Europe must now face, on two fronts at once, the negative undertakings of the "Planetary Superpower of the United States": the *home front*, and the *foreign front*, undertaken by the United States and its ongoing globalist conspiracy against the Great Continental efforts at revolutionary imperial reintegration. With all that the war on two fronts implies of dramatic, perilous, dangerous; of lucid and desperate defiance of a ruthless destiny, where everything is put and put back into play.

The planetary pole of the Great Eurasian Continent, *with* its fundamentally spiritual orientation and *inspiration,* is thus openly opposed to the materialistic positions of the Washington-Beijing axis, as well as to the influence and commandments-manifested in the light of day - or completely concealed, occult - of the 'globalisation' propagated by the United States. Under the more or less phantasmatic disguise of the progress of their "planetary super-economy", they aspire, in reality, to the conversion, to the materialistic transmutation of the ontological civilisation of being that is ours, and to the final change of the human condition, of human consciousness itself, as understood by the traditional European, Hindu and Japanese conceptions that are faithful to the "mystery of being", to the "living light of being".

On the other hand, in the face of the current alienating politico-economic penetration of the United States behind the back lines of Greater Europe in Africa, Europe must urgently initiate an offensive counter-intervention in Latin America, which, geopolitically, is to the United States what Africa is to Europe, a continent of duplication and immediate politico-economic reverberation. From this operational perspective, we can consider that the European positions of politico-revolutionary intervention in Latin America are, at the present time, already assured in terms of their subsequent development, first and foremost Argentina and Chile, the two countries from which an initiative - even if it is of European origin – to begin with the offensive revolutionary integration – or self-integration - of the Latin American continent now appears to be immediately conceivable, and which can therefore be envisaged as being put into operation without further delay.

Nevertheless, it is the case that, in the final analysis, the problem of the next planetary identity of world history appears to be, at the present time and in the present state of openly competing world powers, the problem of France's readiness for its own hidden, abysmal predestination, which demands that France take it upon itself to lead the forward march of the grand-continental metastrategic integration currently underway, and that it succeed in bringing it to its ultimate imperial conclusion; that "what must be done is done".

But, for this to happen, it would be necessary for a new, completely new, unhoped-for French will to arise today in France, so that it can converge and over-activate the responsibilities of France's most secret providential revolutionary predestination, mobilising and polarising them in the direction of a total offensive recovery, of another beginning of the French history of Europe and of the Great Eurasian Continent as a whole. In other words, that a certain "Secret France" suddenly - and as if miraculously - rises up in the face of the evidence of the disaster of its current decline, to impose upon itself the saving breath of a new access to being, so that "everything returns to the zone of supreme attention". Nothing more, in the end, than what we have been waiting for, secretly, since the beginning of time: the advent of the final politico-historical power of this mysterious "Secret France" of which we speak while not speaking about it, "as if in a dream". For France has never been anything but the dream of another France, "which has been, and which will return".

An immense mystical and life sacrifice has been conceived, accomplished and deposited, secretly, very secretly, so that Divine Providence may grant to the defeated France of today the grace of a new suprahistorical beginning, of a new beginning of her greatest destiny. So that France may once again rise from her ashes, so that she may accomplish her final grandcontinental imperial mission, so that she may become the providential tool of the suprahistorical birth of the *Regnum*, of *the Imperium Ultimum*. According to what had already been said, for a long time, prophetically as well as in the terms of a vertiginous promise.

An abysmal relationship that is already in effect brings France and India together in the terms of the same occult eschatological mission, of conclusion and recommencement, of passage from one cycle to another, in which Russia is included and which directly concerns the current future of the "Eurasian Island".

For the suprahistorical mission of France is not a mission of domination, but a mission of foundational liturgical self-sacrifice. A Eucharistic mission. Just as India, whose very being of its own ministry is sacrifice, Puja, or Mahapuja. Historical sacrifice, cosmic sacrifice. Ontological sacrifice.

Did the President of the People's Republic of China, Jiang Zemin, just declare that *India has a long-standing claim to total political hegemony in Southeast Asia?* President Jiang Zemin is absolutely right. Indeed, India has long claimed total political hegemony in Southeast Asia. However, India does not have this claim on its own behalf, but on behalf of this great-continental imperial community, of which it is indeed a certain "Secret France" that today supports and maintains the living flame, the transcendental breath at work.

In fact, it is known that Russia refuses any in-depth political dialogue with France alone, just as it refuses any decisive dialogue with Germany alone, while finding itself more than willing to pursue and increasingly strengthen a political dialogue of a fundamental nature with the Franco-German axis considered as the active expression of Western Europe, This is also the official attitude of India, with, in addition, the confidential demand that Russia be added to its own grand-continental dialogue with the Franco-German axis.

The shift of the critical centre of gravity of current European continental geopolitics from the West to the East is today one of the fundamental characteristics of the current confidential metastrategic development, the significance of which may not be obvious at first glance, but is nonetheless absolutely decisive for any attempt to actively interpret this new version of the *Drang nach Osten*.

In the restricted geopolitical circles of "those in the know", it is taken for granted that every shift of the great continental centre of gravity towards the East announces and establishes, whenever it occurs, the beginning of a new great historical cycle, the "beginning of a world". And shouldn't the very fact that the disqualification of Russia, torn apart by the hallucinated and recalcitrant wreckage of its own Marxist-Leninist adventure, has come to an end with the end of the millennium, which is now almost over, appear as a major sign? As the *new threshold* of the great passages to come, of the unheard-of metamorphoses sliding towards us from the gaping depths of a future that is still unknowable, but which we know to be the bearer of the supernatural mystery of *Regnum*?

And isn't it also now clear that the great future destiny of Vladimir Putin's "New Russia" directly concerns all the political and historical developments on the Eurasian continent and that, in any case, Russia will continue to be, as Alexander Dugin said, "the bridge from Europe to Asia"?

The present and future grand-continental commitment of the Franco-German Carolingian Pole to India and Japan is therefore bound to pass through Russia – through President Vladimir Putin's 'New Russia' – because Russia's geopolitical identity is mobilised at its very centre by Sir Halford Mackinder's *heartland*, by the final *heartland* of the 'Great Continent'.

At the two extremities of the Great Eurasian Continent, India in the East and France in the West, together undergo the predestined attraction, the permanent geopolitical solicitation of the South, India in the direction of the Pacific Ocean and France in relation to the Atlantic. And more particularly for France in the direction of the South Atlantic, whose profoundly occult call that mobilises it will always be directed towards South America and the Antarctic. Because it is in Antarctica, as some have known for a long time, that the highest destiny, the "final destiny" of the Great Eurasian Continent, will have to be played out. This is one of the closed, ultimate secrets of transcendental geopolitics, a secret that we will have to deal with inexorably in the near future, some of the directions of which are still hidden, "forbidden".

The time has come, therefore, for France to free herself once and for all from the fateful persistence of her conventional history, so that she can open herself to her ultimate, greatest occult predestination, which is already under way.

And this is undoubtedly because world history is now reaching one of its decisive turning points, a turning point of ultimate conclusion and very high recommencement which, with the beginning of the third millennium, will mark its return to its own previous origins, a *final turning point: For* the first time in ten millennia, the peoples of the Great Eurasian Continent find themselves in a position to think about reconstituting the previous unity of their original identity of being, consciousness and destiny, from Eastern Europe to India and Japan, to India once again fully in control of her own destiny. A great cycle is in the process of completion, and in this very completion regaining the untouched mystery of its beginnings. Thus the end of one world brings the beginning of another.

Beyond the immediate political circumstances, which may undoubtedly seem most disappointing, if not quite catastrophic, the future integration of the Great Eurasian Continent as a whole is already transcendentally inscribed in the historical development underway, and nothing can stop it from now on.

With its final appropriation of the two Poles, the Arctic and Antarctic continents, the "Great Continent" will reach the definitive state of its own precision: the ontological domination of history and of the transcendental beyond of history, the Imperium *Ultimum*. And all of this is already in the making in the geopolitics of the present final planetary conjuncture, from which we ourselves are asked to control the immediate future developments. All is will, all is occult predestination, all is subterranean struggle; all is visionary penetration, all is heroic submission to the acting mystery of irrational dogmatism. The battle is on

Now all this has just become quite dangerously clear in terms of the facts, and the "nine days in China" at the end of June by the President of the United States, Bill Clinton, consecrate, in a most irrevocable manner, the de facto convergence, the organisational arrangement and the operational implementation of the counter-mechanism of the American offensive in Asia against the European grandcontinental front and against its present geopolitical positions.

The rather abrupt announcement of the next Sino-American combined naval manoeuvres, as well as other, more confidential, joint projects, clearly situate the urgency and the level of commitments, of the current politico-strategic demands underway between Washington and Beijing, while shedding light on the *hidden meaning* – behind a more or less misinformed cover of falsely justifying economic deals, and beyond the muddy "doctrinal" democratic exhibitionism concerning "human rights" – of President Clinton's recent visit to Beijing, an already substantial turning point in the current Sino-American rapprochement, and the operative complements that it is already working to conceal, with the secret clauses far outweighing what has been said officially. For, as usual, everything is once again happening in the shadows.

President Bill Clinton's "nine days in China" will go down in the secret history of the shadowy confrontation between the United States and the Greater Eurasian Continent as the foundational element of the vast subversive enterprise then being set up by Washington and Beijing, and which will be required to act-by the time it is ready-in the next three or four years: it was during President Bill Clinton's "nine days in China" that everything was decided in principle, conceptually.

It may be hard to believe, but this is undoubtedly the most important clandestine politico-strategic terrorist operation in recent world history, in which the leading role will have to be played by the planetary revolutionary terrorism of 'Islamic Fundamentalism', which has been created from scratch, and as it were virtually, for this very purpose.

Multiple parallel special services, supranational secret organisations with double, triple and even quadruple interchangeable identities, as well as occult political command centres sometimes opposing each other will be called upon to intervene, directly or indirectly, within the ongoing world history: the hour of the "planetary terrorist war" - at the same time total and totally anonymous - will soon be ringing. And it will be the very territory of the United States, and all the strategic lines of the United States' political presence in the world, that will serve as a target for the terrorist offensive at work, which will be, moreover, nothing but a huge campaign of agitation-provocation, of double or triple-stage manipulation and with objectives hidden behind the terrorist action itself (which, in fact, will be nothing but another diversionary decoy, manipulated, over-manipulated by the United States sheltering behind its situation as a victim of the terrorist offensive in progress).

And it seems to me that the operational hub of this entire terrorist movement will be Pakistan, whose linchpin will be the Pakistani politico-military secret service, the very ambiguous ISI.

At the same time, the ultra-secret global special services of a certain small, particularly offensive power, which it would be very unhealthy to mention here, will be hired by the United States to subcontract the entire operation, at least at its most confidential levels; unless, at a certain level of the action, *it is the other way around*, that it is the United States which, unconsciously, subcontracts for it (which in the final analysis would not be completely excluded; nothing is impossible, and I personally would lean towards this second prospective version).

As for the United States itself, it will obviously not be the shaky institutions, such as the CIA, etc., that will be called upon to act, but a certain number of ultra-secret, "non-existent" operational structures, obeying only the provisions of a "buried centre", totally unknown, "unknowable". *This would require a republican administration,* and singularly dangerous in-depth positions, requiring the operational mobilisation of a certain number of elements of an extremely high level (which would have to be found, motivated, instructed, organised, and effectively engaged in the task).

It is as if a terrorist conspiracy of disproportionate scope will have to be created and manipulated by a nameless and faceless "occult power centre", a terrorist conspiracy that will be called upon to act dialectically as a vast provocation-agitation device intended to trigger a geopolitical "earthquake", to set in motion revolutionary situations and events preconceived by the United States itself, victims in the first degree of the conspiracy, but of which it will itself be the hidden leader, with long-range, unavowable views, committed to a dialectic of final planetary hegemonic domination: One goal, to create the conditions for the effective prevention of the ultimate imperial integration of the great Eurasian Continent, of the establishment of the ''Eurasian Fortress''.

However, it is only in three or even four years that we will really be in a position to understand what I have just denounced here, if only to make a date. So we must not insist. It is not yet time.

We can thus observe that, at the present time, history in progress, the 'great history', is becoming more and more the object of a separation, of a very marked internal division, of an obligatory double crossing: for there is, on the one hand, the visible and acceptable, conventional, avowable history; and, on the other hand, the occult, abysmal history, resolutely forbidden to any unwise gaze, to any uninformed approach, which is in the process of totally prevailing over the other.

As a result, the 'great history' is increasingly a history closed in on itself, a history unconditionally encrypted, beyond the competence of the imbecilised masses, and whose own process is made intelligible only to the knowledge and power of a superelite of extraordinarily high consciousness and power, but extraordinarily small in number. The apocalyptic times of the "very few" are here, there can be no doubt about it.

Very old negative influences are resurfacing by refocusing in Pakistan. Excited from without, they intend to prevail over India, which represents, for them, the "awakened consciousness of being". However, the major negative epicentre reconstituted in Pakistan is about to be answered by the immense vertigo of darkness that secretly awaits in the Pacific, in Indonesia.

(Published, in Spanish, under the title *Geopolitica de una conyuntura planetaria final*, in *Ciudad de los Césares*, Santiago de Chile, September 1998)

INDIA, THE FUTURE POLAR CENTRE OF THE GLOBAL ARCHIPELAGO

For the moment, it seems that everything is happening in Asia. After the military coup in Pakistan, which will no doubt try to bring Islamist extremism to heel, China abruptly marks the opening of its new European continental policy with the visit to England and France of the head of state and of the Chinese Communist Party Jiang Zemin. In Lyon, where he was sumptuously received by Jacques Chirac and Raymond Barre, did Jiang Zemin find the tutelary shadow of Zhou Enlai, the doctrinaire of China's "European continental line"?

At the same time, the revolutionary national right won the parliamentary elections in India for the second time and is about to begin the process of the great Hindu National Revolution, a process in which the Armed Forces - the expected revenge of the former Chief of Naval Staff, Admiral Vishnu Bhagawat - are taking on an increasingly significant weight, especially since it is on the Armed Forces that the new Hindu nationalist government is relying in the accelerated pursuit of its strategic nuclear programmes.

In the perspective opened up by the new positions of power revealed to us by transcendental geopolitics, the planetary emergence of India appears as the great revolutionary event of the Third Millennium. What is this new perspective revealed by transcendental geopolitics, within which India is revolutionarily winning the decisive place that now seems to be hers, thus changing the future course of world history?

And what is the 'transcendental geopolitics' itself, which defines India according to its predestination as the 'new, last and supreme polar centre of the future Planetary Archipelago'?

To speak of transcendental geopolitics is above all to invoke the decisive dialectical weapon of the great planetary confrontations of the Third Millennium, the weapon that is called upon to decide the direction that future world history will take, and the very face that will be the world to come.

What is transcendental geopolitics?

The geopolitical approach of what Nietzsche already called the 'great history', being not rational, but passionate and inspired, posing itself in the existential terms of dogmatic irrationalism, geopolitics is absolutely not to be considered as a science, as the uninitiated would tend to do, from the outside, but as the initiatory awakening to a state of active, permanent and unitary consciousness: the visionary consciousness of the immutable confrontations and the great currents of the politico-historical powers in constant march towards the final planetary Empire, towards the *Imperium Ultimum.*

In a certain sense, geopolitics is also a dialectical materialism, insofar as it considers, in an implied way, that the hidden foundations of the history of the world in its becoming are unceasingly constituted, reactivated, by the predisposed configurations of the territories where its stakes are set and put back into play, and that these configurations must thus appear under the light of a preconceived, unchangeable, definitively there fatality. It is the profoundly immutable configurations of the territories of promotion of 'great history' that decide the final orientations of the latter, as geopolitics asserts.

Thus, one of the most important geopolitical thinkers of today, Guido Giannettini, writes in one of his recent studies, *The Oceanic Empires of the Steppes and Open Seas:* "The Ottoman Empire and, before it, that of the Seljuks, have been in contact with territories whose geopolitical value is specific and significant: the Danubian-Anatolian region and the Iranian region. These territories seem to require their masters to assume the same function as those assumed before them by the peoples who inhabited them. Especially in the Iranian case, which in a certain sense evoked the world of their origins.

Conventional geopolitics will therefore always be posed in terms of a fatality, charged as it is with revealing, precisely, the constants of the fundamental immutability governing the encounter, the marriage of history on the march and the territories where this march occurs.

Thus, predetermined by the configuration of the territories in which it is called upon to develop, history - the sum of the historical thrusts in action that make history - can in no way be posed in terms of freedom, history being closed in on itself by the fatalities predisposed before its march, watching over its own manifestation.

This is where the new conceptions of transcendental geopolitics come into play, introducing into the confrontation between history and the developments of its territorial manifestation the third term of revolutionary consciousness, which is supposed to be able to establish the changes ordered by a visionary will in a state of opposition to the objective fatalities of the places, of the preconceived configurations within the territories solicited by the march of history, and to their action on the spot, predestined.

Emerging, through the action in consciousness of transcendental geopolitics, directly into history, into the very field of exercise where the freedom of consciousness of what is as it should be manifests itself, the revolutionary will will ensure that this freedom can assert itself and act unconditionally, according to its own law, which is the very law of being if, as Martin Heidegger discovers, "freedom is the foundation of being".

The revolutionary freedom that transcendental geopolitics is supposed to ensure for the consciousness of being in history will never, however, go against the original configurations that predetermine its course: the foundational freedom of being being being exclusively what one is and not something else, the revolutionary will will therefore only be exercised, through transcendental geopolitics, to ensure forward the unimpeded free affirmation of being.

This is precisely why the proper domain of the exercise of transcendental geopolitics is that of the struggles for the liberation of the consciousness of being, for the revolutionary liberation of being from the constraints and state alienation imposed on it by the subversive dominations of non-being, when this happens, as it is happening now.

Thus, as the present times of world history are those of the present final dereliction of being and of its most extreme obscuration, of its dark distress now without truce or hope of any kind, the hour has by this very fact come for the final advent of transcendental geopolitics, whose total revolutionary intervention goes to the total change, to the total reversal of the present terms of world history at its end.

Transcendental geopolitics thus appears as the fundamental counter-strategic weapon of the final liberation of being and its historical projection currently under the subversive domination of non-being. Today, the imperial civilisations of being are historically opposed to the globalist counter-civilisations of the totalitarian merchant Anti-Empire through the intermediary of transcendental geopolitics and its occult units of counter-offensive protection already at work underground.

Therefore, the new consciousness of the freedom of being called upon to intervene, today, once again, in the course of history through the revolutionary interference of transcendental geopolitics mobilised to lead the struggle for the final liberation of being unconditionally subjected, as it is now, to the subversive dominations of non-being, can certainly be held to be the active consciousness of Divine Providence itself, which watches over the destinies and the advancement of being in history.

We must therefore understand that transcendental geopolitics is nothing other than the emergence, both concealed and undisguised, of Divine Providence in the revolutionary geopolitical consciousness currently engaged, with us, in the vanguard of the struggle for the liberation of being and of the decaying civilisations that give it shelter.

India, the future 'polar centre' of the Planetary Archipelago

The projection of the current general problematic of India in the perspective provided by transcendental geopolitics must be done, since this is the aim of our present research, according to its own operative structures, which are arranged according to a double level of successive approaches, the grand-continental level, or of the Great Continent, which Karl Haushofer had already explored through his central concept of *Kontinentalblock*, and the level of the final imperial closure of history, which is that of the Planetary Archipelago, of the global elevation of geopolitics to its ultimate planetary level. This double level of successive approaches also constitutes the active dialectic that installs and affirms the current foundations of transcendental geopolitics.

Considered, therefore, at the first level of the current transcendental geopolitical vision, that of its grand-continental opening, the general problematic of India will immediately be integrated into it, following the dialectic of its constitutional presence, already acquired, within the future imperial political unity of the Great Continent, alongside Western and Eastern Europe, Russia, Greater Siberia and Japan: It has its own, quite decisive, share in this, because its fundamental counter-strategic mission appears to be that of actively blocking China's continental positions, positions blocked, at the same time, passively, on its rear, by Japan.

India, therefore, is destined to be the fundamental strategic counterweight of the great-continental unity against China and, as such, India is the key to the imperial closure of the great-continental unity in its overall action in the face of the immense gap represented by China's non-integrability, in the face of offensive imperialist pretensions, The latter is confined to its project of a superpower predestined for a career of its own, with a unique direction, bearer of a "grand design", creator, on its own account, of a decisive, final, total and totalitarian planetary and suprahistorical civilisation, bearer of the mysterious *Pax Sinica* of the Taoists.

At the same time, India is called upon to cut off and neutralise the political-historical belt being formed on the southern flank of the Great Continent by the current conspiracy of Fundamentalist Islam and its points of support from Turkey and the Islamist republics of the former Soviet Empire, through Afghanistan and Pakistan, to Indonesia, which, with its 200 million inhabitants, its unique strategic positions and its formidable reserves of raw materials, is already on the verge of tilting entirely into the Islamic camp.

On the other hand, considering the current general problem of India in the perspective of the second level of approach proposed by transcendental geopolitics, the level of the global elevation of geopolitics to its ultimate planetary level, the level of the Planetary Archipelago, We will have to understand that the subcontinent gathers on itself, in order to project it into the oceanic zone of the Southern Hemisphere, of which, in principle, it thus possesses total control, all the geopolitical lines of force of the Great Continent. For the avant-garde conceptions that transcendental geopolitics is showing today about the Planetary Archipelago, whose oceanic identity prevails over all its continental parts, foresees that it is the oceanic domination of the Southern Hemisphere that will decide, in the future, the planetary domination.

However, because of its position at the leading edge of the Great Continent in the oceanic spaces of the Southern Hemisphere, and its control of both the continent and the ocean, India has the new polar identity of the world, the possession of the 'centre of the world' in its final identity.

When India re-enters history, it has been said, world history will be close to its end, and the Total Reversal of the end of history, the *Paravrtti* foreseen by the original Hindu tradition, will take place in the apocalyptic terms of a catastrophic end to history and the world.

For this is the basic constitutional thesis of the new transcendental geopolitics: that at the coming end of history and the great Total Reversal, the *Paravrtti* foreseen by the original Hindu tradition, the axis of the world will be tilted entirely, the present Southern Hemisphere thus becoming the Boreal Hemisphere, and the present Boreal Hemisphere having to go in the place of the Southern Hemisphere elevated in its place.

Paradoxically enough, the only real geopolitical problem facing India today is one of territory, namely that of the complete political and historical possession and control of the Tibetan foothills and Tibet itself, areas now under Chinese rule. Indeed, it is only by leaning back on the formidable fortress of the Tibetan mountains, the heart of the Great Continent's foundational rooting, that the Indian subcontinent could ensure its mission of carrying to the tip, far into the oceanic spaces of the Southern Hemisphere, the concentration of telluric, invisible, ideal lines of force that it receives from the continental spaces to which its back is turned, the entire transcendental power of the Great Continent's constitutional spaces.

A survey, even reduced to its most essential part, of the sum of the great-continental magnetic power currents, of which India is the bottleneck, gathering and concentration, as well as the reverberation lock directed towards the oceanic spaces of the Southern Hemisphere, is not possible within the restricted framework of the present research. Let us assume, however, that the transcontinental magnetic current of the Major Axis, which in Europe runs along the Danube and the line of the subterranean Alps, from the Caucasus to the Atlantic, runs through the whole of the Great Continent as far as Central Asia, where it is sucked in and deflected by the central magnetic pole of Tibet and then reversed over India, is part of it; as is the vertical current separating, on the Baltic-Adriatic line, Europe into two parts, in principle antagonistic, from the West and the East, just like those which cross Siberia in bundles, and those which run along the far eastern coasts of China, from Sin-Kiang to South-East Asia, passing through Manchuria.

And just as India is thus bound to bend and concentrate upon itself the sum of all the great-continental currents of magnetic power, so too is India bound to concentrate, by drawing it into the inner space of its own self-consciousness and its spiritual and religious civilisation in the active totality of its depths, the sum of all the currents of thought and inner experience making up the unitary field of Eurasian great-continental spirituality in its overall historical becoming. All that the great-continental thought has been able to produce is summarised, prefigured, in its original strains, within Indian thought.

With the formidable weight of its religious and philosophical past, which can be reactivated at any time, with its one billion inhabitants on the horizon of the third millennium, with the current progress of its technological conquests - the Bangalore concentration, armed from within by *the Indian Institute of Science,* exceeds by far any similar achievement in the United States and Western Europe – with the irresistible rise of the wave of the Indian national-revolutionary movement, India is already in a position to take up the challenge which is before it, with the current progress of its technological conquests – the concentration in Bangalore, armed from within by the Indian Institute of Science, far exceeds any similar achievement in the United States and Western Europe - with the irresistible rise of the wave of the Indian national-revolutionary movement, India is already in a position to take up the challenge that is now being posed to it by the vanguard conclusions of transcendental geopolitics with regard to its final imperial predestination, its predestination as the new, last and supreme "polar centre" of the future Planetary Archipelago.

India's National Revolution, and its external supporters

However, for things to be done in due course, it is now becoming urgent and necessary that a new national consciousness, that the active will of a new Indian national destiny should arise and assert itself in the terms of a great Indian Revolution, to take in hand the political and cultural, economic-administrative and industrial mobilisation, to set in motion the total revolutionary mobilisation of the whole nation and its as yet unmanifested availabilities, to build the suprahistorical edifice of the future destiny of the New India, in conformity with the secret predispositions of its abysmal identity, destined to bear the future "polar centre" of the Planetary Archipelago. All things that must be done.

In other words, that the invisible, supratemporal India incarnate in the visible, descend into the present history of India to bring it revolutionarily to the identity and historical dimensions required by its final predestination. This can never be done without the intervention of powers outside this world, of the "powers above", which must then be drawn to the level of visible history, so that they may work for its renewal, its revolutionary change and the choice of other paths before its forward march.

As far as the problem of the in-depth recovery of present-day India is concerned, of its revolutionary self-recovery in the direction of its own identity, a hidden identity, still and always forbidden to the day of awakened consciousness, it seems to me that the first major option to be taken would be that of betting everything on an accelerated and increasingly significant strengthening of the movements of the revolutionary national revival of Hinduism already in action, the underground formation of politico-organisational cadres capable of taking in hand the offensive expansion of the front of these struggles towards the middle classes and the national masses of Hinduism, towards the decisive conquest of the intellectual circles in place, of the university hierarchies, of journalists and writers, of the creators of active culture.

And it is there that the European national-revolutionary movement, in its dimensions and according to its grand-continental orientation, will be able to give the full measure of its own subversive and breakthrough abilities, of total change, because it is a question of us, European national-revolutionary activists, taking it upon ourselves to mobilise, to urgently organise the external support of that by which our interference in the Indian revolutionary process in progress will be able to take on the absolutely decisive importance which must be, at the moment, imperatively its own: For it is up to us to instil in them the will to cross the *line of passage*, the forbidden frontier between action considered possible and what is in advance deemed impossible, between mere national activism and confident, awakened, irrevocable affirmation in the choice of the paths of the hardest destiny. Every great and decisive revolutionary enterprise must be secretly inspired from without, this is the iron rule of high active subversion. The investment of the peaks will always be the result of an external impulse, coming as it were from above, "coming from elsewhere, coming from outside". This is the active dialectic, the very constitutional approach of transcendental geopolitics, which finds its original field of application here, for what is this if not the fact of an external intervention, of transcendental level, in the immediate march of history, which raises its course and revolutionarily changes its orientation at the moment?

The conditions for a total revolutionary upliftment of present-day India

Assuming that a national-revolutionary organisation would be brought close enough to the central power in India to consider taking upon itself the task of defining the first measures fundamentally necessary for the profound changes in Indian society and history today, measures tending to establish the unity of consciousness and national wills which alone could open the way for that great Indian Revolution desired by the conclusions of transcendental geopolitics and its vision of the future Planetary Archipelago, what would those *first measures* be?

These would be twofold: to overcome, by a third revolutionary term, the religious tensions, particularly between Hindus and Muslims, which have torn India's history apart since the dawn of time, and to overcome, too, the incompatibility between the survivors of the original Aryan stock and the present-day remnants of the historical Dravidian masses.

This can only be achieved, in fact, by the complete overcoming of the two incompatibilities in question, religious and racial, by a third revolutionary term held to be superior to the antagonisms in progress. By the third term of the higher, transcendental consciousness of the identity and secret predestination of India in its final imperial projection as the "polar centre" of the Planetary Archipelago. And India remaining, nevertheless, what it is, that is, the project of a suprahistorical elevation of Hinduism to the original concept of Mother India, and Hinduism itself then being able to undergo an inner evolution, implicitly understood in the very terms of its tradition of the beginnings and of all time, provided that this was understood in an essentially initiatory light.

The Hindu tradition, unchanged and unchanged since Vedic times and even before, identifying itself with the primordial tradition in its principles and in the regular religious developments of these, must by this very fact contain, and does contain, in itself, to provide Catholicism and itself with the ultimate Sophianic and Marian conception of the world, the conclusions of which will be those of a Catholicism renewed from within, which will openly and dogmatically proclaim the Universal Sovereignty of the Virgin, Spouse of the Living God and Sole Mistress of Heaven and Earth, "Maria-Durga". This means, therefore, that the theological and metaphysical contribution of Hinduism to Catholicism and to the final dogmatic vision of the latter will give birth to - or rather, appear from - the marriage of Catholicism and Hinduism, the new imperial religion of the times of the Planetary Archipelago and of its *Imperium Ultimum*.

The work and the still hidden revelations of St. Maximilian Kolbe are precisely along these lines, and it is also important to note the views of the Auschwitz supplicant concerning the final conversion of Japan and the future birth in the Land of the Rising Sun of a solar, radiant and imperial Catholicism, free from the darkness of dereliction and death.

I will not dwell on these special considerations, whose interest for our present research lies, however, in the fact that they pose, in a very explicit manner, an opening towards the release and ultimate changes of the present religious encumbrances obstructing the paths of the Indian march towards its new future destinies.

It is no less certain that an immense secret lies hidden in the revelation, still rather obscure, of what will be the future theological wedding of Hinduism and Catholicism, of their Marian transubstantiation at the end.

And, in any case, it appears as a perfectly certain thing that the new changes occurring today in the great geopolitics of India come from the interference, within the latest advances of the latter, of a certain imperial visionary will, of a revolutionary awareness that must be there as the very fact of the passage to transcendental geopolitics that has taken place in the march of our own analyses currently in progress, as from the suddenly paroxysmal demands of their own developments on the verge of dialectical rupture: the traces of transcendental geopolitics in action are found as traces of fire, as traces of a passage from beyond the world.

If there is indeed a region of research where the interference of transcendental geopolitics immediately appears as the result of an active, obvious and irresistible necessity, it is indeed that of the current geopolitics of India: India is today the proper domain of transcendental geopolitics, where the exercise of this geopolitics is now the only one able to lead to the foreseen salvific outcome, the time of which is inexorably approaching.

And it is also understandable, in relation to the interference of a certain religious overtaking foreseen, and perhaps even already underway, the overtaking of traditional Hinduism towards a renewed, exalted Marian Catholicism, interference manifested in the very terms of our own transcendental geopolitics of India, that these could be considered as an emergence of Divine Providence in action there, concealed behind our own consciousness renewed by the changes that it is thus entrusted with bringing to a close.

The transcendental geopolitics of India can therefore only be conceived, in its present states, as a manifestation of Divine Providence intervening subterraneanly in the ultimate arrangements and expectations of the proceedings there, in India, in preparation for the coming of the proper times of the Planetary Archipelago, of the *Imperium Ultimum*. Occult, forbidden activities, if ever there were.

The intervention of the Negative Powers

All this was done in order to announce that considerable events were taking place in India, that ancient authorities that had fallen into the dogmatic sleep of withdrawal from being were about to awaken, intact, to act within the framework of a rise in the power of the Spirit, foreseen for the times of the Planetary Archipelago and the establishment of India as its "polar centre": This was all that was needed for a vortex of the opposite sign to arise, for the Negative Powers on the lookout to attempt to intervene to delay, to alienate the work of the renewal of the Spirit about to be born there.

A campaign of destabilization was therefore launched at the right time to try to create as much obscurantist confusion as possible, a campaign which - at a subaltern level, but nonetheless extraordinarily significant of what is behind it all - is used to distort historical perspectives, to reverse the order of things that have long been established, and this in favour of certain so-called "recent discoveries": It denies the superiority of the Aryan invasions in India over the local Dravidian ethnic groups, trying to make the latter the holders of a high civilisation, of the highest spiritual conceptions, and the Aryans the 'barbaric and criminal tribes on the run from the Caucasus region'. Thus Sanskrit itself, and its writing, as well as the *Vedas*, would be the work of the local Dravidian tribes, the Aryans having known nothing else but to destroy, to devastate the "superior civilisations" that they would have "met on the spot" when they arrived there.

The entire academic and media globalist apparatus in the service of the ontological enemy immediately got into the act, to forcefully convey the over-activated set of these indecent and primary aberrations, in an attempt to undermine the 'Hitlerian doctrines' of the high Aryan predestination of original India and hence the current attempts at external support for a return of India to its own abysmal identity, as actively envisaged by the proponents of the revolutionary avant-garde theses of transcendental geopolitics.

But this direct and somewhat precipitous intervention of the Negative Powers only proves the real and now decisive importance of what is happening in India at the moment in terms of the resurgence of the suprahistorical polar values of the former India, which are being joined by the advances of the extraordinary revolutionary effort, already in full swing, in view of the forthcoming advent of the New India, which is being invited to establish itself as the "polar centre" of the future Planetary Archipelago. It is the very intensity and authenticity of the traditional revival that is now taking place in India, the proof of its power of revolutionary deployment in depth, that have determined the setting in motion of the negative reaction that has been aroused, of all the reverberations that have arisen to prevent its reinforcement and propagation in continuity. Behind the cretins and lousy agents provocateurs of the class of the "Indian linguist", Dr. Jha, or Dr. Rajaram, "mathematician also working for NASA", behind the more than suspicious shenanigans of a François Gautier, correspondent of the *Figaro* in New Delhi, formidable forces are lurking in the shadows to act, which we will have to neutralise. Among the garrison of harmful idiots on duty, I would also mention the "American Indianist" David Frawley; this one I had no right to miss. He is the most infamous of them all.

By supporting the Indian Revolution we celebrate our return to the roots of our own identity

In the final analysis, what else can transcendental geopolitics want other than the conspiracy that Divine Providence maintains, constantly reactivated, in history in progress, and what else can its visionaries and its watchmen, its researchers and its doctrinaires, want other than its secret agents in action on the perished borders of the end of a world?

Therefore, we, the secret agents of transcendental geopolitics, have found in the current treatment of the Indian affair the field for the exercise of our most advanced revolutionary abilities, because it is indeed transcendental geopolitics that is in charge, today, of the destinies of the setting in motion of the concept of the new Indian Revolution, and by engaging in this way on its barricades we are only celebrating our return to the original sources of our own previous identity.

By going to support, on the spot, in the terms of our own commitment to the service of transcendental geopolitics, the cause of the final awakening of India promoted by the new Indian Revolution underway, it is the most ancient past of what we ourselves are that we find ourselves reactivating, making revolutionarily present again in history, which is also the final history of our own becoming. For it is there, on the banks of the Indus, that our own final destiny and that of the Eurasian Empire of the End is now being forged, the historical basis for the coming advent of the power of the Planetary Archipelago and, beyond it, of the Imperium *Ultimum*.

From the point of view of our European imperial doctrine of the Great Continent, it is the definitive political integration of Western Europe, Eastern Europe and Russia, of the Great Siberia of India and Japan that constitutes the horizon of our present struggle. A struggle that, in a later stage, will move on to the vision of a goal of planetary imperial integration, where the concept of the Planetary Archipelago will appear. It is at this point that the decisive predestination of Roman America, charged with revolutionary intervention in the United States, will appear. And it will also be in this second imperial period that India will reach the level of its truly ultimate destiny, because at that moment, due to the unveiling of its own final geopolitical positions, it will be India that will be called upon to institute the "supreme centralising pole" of the Planetary Archipelago.

Beyond the as yet unexplored chasms of world history in its most distant future, through the very sum of the ongoing deployments of the antagonistic forces at play in an uninterrupted manner, India thus allows itself to be caught, at present, as the magnetised pole of an ever-concealed, out-of-reach power, which seems destined to draw forth the formidable secret of history's achievements from beyond history, which is the very secret of *the Imperium Ultimum*.

India's particular relationship with transcendental geopolitics is, as we have come to understand, a mystery of dogmatic irrationalism, the very mystery of the providential meaning of history: we, those whose honour is called fidelity, are made to sink into it.

CHINA DOES NOT BELONG TO THE EURASIAN GRAND-CONTINENTAL COMMUNITY OF DESTINY

Convened by President George Bush on 21 November 2001 in Shanghai on the occasion of the Asia-Pacific Cooperation Forum (APCF), the "Big Three" conference - the United States, Russia and China - was held to define and agree on a "global anti-terrorism line" following the terrorist attack in New York on 11 September 2001, Following the terrorist attack in New York on 11 September 2001, a "global anti-terrorist line" was defined and agreed upon, bringing together the Presidents of Russia and China with the President of the United States.

However, it seems quite obvious to me that beneath the new circumstantial urgencies concerning the need for a unified planetary anti-terrorist combat front, even if only in appearance, there are hidden, subterranean reasons, reasons of particular interest to each of the three participants, which led the "big three" to manifest, on 21 November 2001, in Shanghai, their operational identity of view regarding the common action in which they were thus engaged at the call of George Bush.

It is in Russia's extreme interest to be present in a common front of action, engaged, from now on without any ideological-democratic reserve or restraint, in a fight of planetary dimensions and of resolute decision against Fundamentalist Islam and its revolutionary terrorist strategies, which will allow it to integrate its own ongoing fight against the subversive sedition of Chechnya and the relations that this has with the current instances of Islamist revolutionary terrorism on a world level. Thus, the main pretext that the social-leftist and communist conspiracy in power in Western Europe uses to justify the process of encircling and isolating Russia, which is the "anti-democratic war" waged by Russia in Chechnya, is suspended at the same time.

China, on the other hand, sees it as a way to silence, if only temporarily, the intensive grievances that are constantly being levelled at it from the outside for its forced denationalisation and permanent political oppression in occupied Tibet, and for the pressure it maintains against Taiwan; as well as its total freedom of action against the separatist activities of its revolutionary Uighur Islamist minorities; not to mention the effective acceleration of the process - which is still dragging on - of its admission into the WTO circle of economic openness and world trade. By moving closer to the United States and Russia, China is blocking the increasingly overactive tensions that are manifesting themselves against its current external positions, while internally, extreme tensions are responding to them, exacerbating each other; without wanting to recognise it, it is finding in this an unexpected opportunity for a strategic truce that will allow it to *catch its breath*. This is no mean feat in a situation of serious, hidden crisis such as the one it is currently facing. China is now prepared to do anything, and it is going to do it.

However, as far as the United States was concerned, things were in fact somewhat more complex. For, if we know that George Bus h's current presidential "grand design" aims at the constitution in the near future of a triple planetary articulation - United States, Europe, Russia - justifying the de facto predominance of the United States over the whole of the "Western camp", This is a turning point that would have to be negotiated in terms of a real ideological-strategic revolution that would change all the givens of the present day, but it is no less certain that another fundamental geopolitical option persists in obsessing the occult circles where the major decisions concerning the destiny of the United States are made. Namely, the option of a rapprochement between China and the United States, which would make China the political-strategic bridgehead with a deep impact on the interior of the Eurasian "Big Island", giving the United States access to its eastern, north-eastern and south-eastern flanks. This neutralizes the fundamental positions of the great Eurasian continent and of the imperial bloc that should constitute, in the long term, the operational politico-strategic framework, namely the Paris-Berlin-Moscow-New Delhi-Tokyo axis, and makes the implementation of Karl Haushofer's visionary political concept, taken up by General de Gaulle and continued by Vladimir Putin, the supreme geopolitical concept of the *Kontinentalblock*, highly critical.

The fact that the United States has decided to gain a political and military foothold in Central Asia - in Afghanistan, and in Pakistan - in its current operation against the global terrorist organisation of revolutionary Islamism led by Osama Bin Laden, Al Qaeda, proves that a significant choice has already been made by the supreme officials in Washington, a choice that appears to be in the direction of the final adoption of the "Great Pacific" line, and thus involving the rapprochement of the United States and China in a vast enterprise designed to turn the Eurasian "Big Island" to the east of the besieged continent, while at the same time taking over its centre (which is already happening).

Nevertheless, China, caught in a pincer movement by Russia, India and Japan, finds itself in an extremely precarious situation from the start, especially since Vietnam and Mongolia, not to mention Tibet, are organically part of the Eurasian continent represented by Russia at present.

But the real decisions are made in other, more hidden depths of history, outside of unanticipated attention, in transcendental, 'oceanic' depths.

What supra-historical justifications?

All this being said, and even if the "underground reasons", the reasons "hidden by interest", by "particular interests", having pushed Russia and China to become stakeholders in the current planetary counter-terrorist enterprise undertaken by the United States to put an end to Fundamentalist Islamism and its bloody conspiracies, Although we are more or less aware of this, we must also take into account the active dialectic that duplicates everything, in the shadows, on behalf of the powers that are in the shadows, on behalf of the abysmal instances of the greatest ''history''. These are in reality non-human, suprahistorical, 'external', 'cosmic' instances determining the imposed, 'irrational' turns, governing the sudden changes in the ontological regime of history, according to occult, 'over-coded' reasons and justifications, the secrets of which we are in no way empowered to penetrate.

As Grasset d'Orcet understood perfectly well, visible history is in fact nothing more than the diversionary façade of the 'other history', which makes everything that lives exist only in other ways.

It is therefore my opinion that it is precisely from this special perspective that we should consider the reasons - the real reasons, which may not be real reasons - for the rather unexpected and profound changes that have just taken place in the current planetary politico-historical conjuncture. Changes that are supposed to say *something*, but that *we cannot yet understand, something other than what they seem to say at first glance.* And perhaps even the participants themselves are unaware of this.

The joint political-strategic commitment of the United States, Russia and China that we were shown on 21 October 2001 in Shanghai is, in reality, something quite different from what it purports to be: this is what we need to know, for our own destiny is at stake.

We are fighting a dual identity battle, which is the "reverse side of contemporary history" that Balzac had glimpsed in his time...

Guido Giannettini's geopolitical theses on China

In any case, there is a constitutional mystery of China, which has always kept itself closed in on itself: it was not as a line of defence against the outside world that the Chinese Wall was erected, but to prevent China itself from being attracted by the outside world, to make it keep itself exclusively inward-looking.

In fact, China, as we know it, or think we know it, does not exist, nor has it ever existed.

China is only the advance, towards the interior of the Eurasian "Great Continent", of the Pacific, of Insulindia and of all those volcanic islands, survivors of "something else", nocturnal, plunged into a suspicious shadow, jagged, belonging to another temporality, They are the original domain of other times and other spaces, and therefore have nothing in common with the European, Mongolian or Ural-Altaic races, which we know have always been those of the "Great Continent", and which also populate North China.

For there are two Chinas: the Mongolian and Ural-Altaic North China and the South China, which is merely a nocturnal colonisation from Insulindia and what Insulindia actually and symbolically represents. North China is nothing but a European Ural-Altaic land, a Eurasian imperial land.

In his book *Pekino tra Washington e Mosca*, published in 1972 in Rome, Guido Giannettini wrote in the last chapter, entitled *The Conquest of Middle Earth:*

From the historical, ethnic and geopolitical point of view, the real China does not go beyond the HoangHo valley in the north - with the exception of a few enclaves in the north-east - and the Kansu-Setchouan region in the west. Beyond these territories, despite the Chinese initiatives to denationalise them, Ural-Altaic peoples, i.e. Turks, Mongols, Tibetans and even Indo-Europeans, still live there today.

There is a profound difference in race, language, civilisation, history, customs and character between the Ural-Altaic and the Chinese. In all these aspects, the former are closer to the Indo-Europeans, with whom they have sometimes mixed over the millennia. The Chinese, on the other hand, were linked from the beginning to the peoples of Indochina-Insulindia and the Pacific. The Chinese state was born historically from the conquest of the country by Ural-Altaic (and, for once, Indo-European) races'.

In support of our own positions on China's hidden identity, I quote below Guido Giannettini's five fundamental geopolitical theses, which I borrow from the book cited:

(1) ''From the historical and geopolitical point of view, the territories inhabited by the Ural-Altaic peoples, Tibetans and the small Aryan group represent the boundary between the Eurasian continent and the Pacific area''. In reality, the dividing line between Europe and Asia placed on the modest hills of the Ural Mountains is artificial and contradicts both history and geopolitics. The Urals have never separated Europe from Asia: from prehistoric times to the Middle Ages, the territories of Central Asia have been closer to Europe than to China (this explains at least in part why the Russians, not the Chinese, are in Vladivostok).

(2) ''Let's summarise therefore: the border between the Western and the Eastern world is not on the Urals, but on the Altai Mountains. This means that it is wrong to speak of two continents, Europe and Asia: one should in fact consider Eurasia and the Asian Subcontinent. The former is not the theoretical Eurasia of the geography treatises, formed by the sum of Europe and "official"

Asia: and that it is not is easily deduced from what has been demonstrated so far.

In the Asian Subcontinent are included India, Indochina, Indonesia, the authentically "Chinese" China - see what has been said before - and also, in fact, the large and small islands of Oceania. The Asian subcontinent is projected onto the great primordial ocean, the Pacific, which connects it closely to the western strip of Latin America, the strip of ancient pre-Columbian cultures, still inhabited by strong Indian ethnic groups. The community of Pacific peoples has a historical reality of its own, which is always receiving new conformations from studies on the subject, as well as a modern political reality in the American push towards the Far West, a push that has influenced the agreement between Washington and Beijing more than one might think''.

Now, if we wanted to indicate a border walk between Eurasia and the Asian subcontinent, we would have to point out the following countries: the Anatolian peninsula, the Kurdistan mountains, the steppe plateau of Khorassan, Sin-Kiang, Chinghai, Mongolia, Khingan, Japan. These countries, listed from West to East, represent the "middle land", the obligatory region of passage of ancient commercial contacts and invasions between the Eurasian continent and the oceanic world.

(3) ''Today, the Central Asian 'Middle Land' - to be considered in essence as the eastern step of a Eurasian *Heartland* more centralized, in relation to the main mass of land masses, than was Mackinder's *Heartland* - is in an unstable situation, being partly Russian territory, partly Chinese territory, and partly independent (Turkey, Iran, Afghanistan, Japan). Its central part, the most important one, is therefore disputed by the Russians and the Chinese, and this is the deepest cause of the dispute between Moscow and Beijing. The struggle for the possession of the "Middle Earth" has been temporarily suspended because of the American intervention, but sooner or later it will have to be reignited. This struggle can only end in two ways: with the Chinese on the Volga, or with the Russians on the Great Wall, on the eastern glacis of the "Middle Land".

(4) ''The United States, which until 1968 had pursued a policy of isolating and repressing China - playing Taipei off against Peking and vice versa - developed a counter-strategy in 1968 that, by supporting China, prevented the Russian military operation in the East. The American counter-strategy was not only harmful to Russia, but also turned against Japan, the number one economic and technological enemy of the United States (even before Europe and Russia)'.

From these developments, two great blocs with opposing interests now seem to be emerging: the Russian-Japanese bloc, and the American bloc. These two blocs know that their fate and that of the whole world will depend on the outcome of the struggle for the conquest of the 'Middle Land', a struggle that is only postponed in time, but inevitable.

(5) "Against Eurasia, the heart of the main mass of land masses, stands the great primordial Ocean, the Pacific, which today has found its axis not only geographically, but also politically, in the 40' parallel of Washington and Beijing. Disputed by two worlds, the border walk, the 'middle land'. And just as four thousand years ago, the possession of the 'middle land' is still of interest to the European descendants of the ancient '*Reitervolker of* the steppes'.

In fact, if Hitler's Drang *nach Osten* had succeeded, Europe (but, above all, Eurasia) would today be in the front line on the Altai Mountains and the borders of Sin-Kiang. This did not happen because the same forces now allied with China succeeded in preventing the peaceful unification of the Eurasian continent-which both Hitler and Stalin seemed to be striving for-and then the attempt at unification led by arms. But the substance of things is not changed. Europe will be reborn and will not be able to escape the fatal *Endkampf* for the conquest of the "Middle Land", a final struggle that will also decide its fate.

Guido Giannettini then quotes a document that is extremely revealing for the deep problematic of China, published in the number 6, 1968, of the unofficial Soviet magazine *Mezdunarodnya Zhizn*:

The political-ideological platform of Mao Tse-Tung's group in the field of foreign policy can be understood in the light of a historical fact: the ruling group of ancient China, over many centuries, inculcated in the people the idea of the supremacy of all that is Chinese, of China as the centre of world civilisation, as the main Power of the world. The contradictions between these conceptions and the actual situation, especially in the period when China had turned into a semi-colonial country, gave rise to an extreme exacerbation of national feelings, to the aspiration to rebuild China's former power at any cost. In recent years, China's foreign policy doctrine has been increasingly penetrated by the Maoists with the idea of China's supremacy over all developing peoples. In order to underpin its hegemonic tendencies, Mao's group did not disdain to use concepts such as Sinocentrism, left over from the Chinese feudalists and Chiang Kai-shek's reaction, and the prejudices of Han nationalism. Chinese propaganda revises world history, overstating the role of China and the yellow race.

Europe must reclaim China's northern half

That Hitler totally missed his chance, there is certainly nothing to complain about, but, on the other hand, that General de Gaulle did not succeed in his either, there is a real disaster. A fatal political and historical disaster, for which we have not yet finished paying.

It is enough to know how to look back, to question the facts of a still relatively recent past. In 1949, General de Gaulle said: "I say that Europe must be built on the basis of an agreement between the French and the Germans.

Once Europe is built on this basis, we can then turn to Russia. Then we can try, once and for all, to build the whole of Europe with Russia too, even if it changes its regime. That is the programme of true Europeans. That is mine.

Once again, it was in 1949 that General de Gaulle made these statements, during a press conference that was quite visionary. The political genius of General de Gaulle, supported by a suprahistorical, transcendental inspiration, had thus seen, some fifty years ahead of time, and with astonishing clarity and precision, what the fundamental problem is, the current problem of the greater continental Eurasian Europe, and which is also, at the present time, the problem of the final destiny of a civilisation that is tragically facing the danger of its disappearance in the near future. It is the problem of the total federal reintegration of Europe, including Russia, of the imperial reintegration of the Great Eurasian Continent and therefore of the advent of the *Imperium Ultimum*. A final imperial reintegration which, in the visible and invisible circumstances of the current planetary politico-historical conjuncture, can only be achieved against both the United States and China.

However, China's re-entry into the current situation of global tensions and surges, which it was able to negotiate very effectively during the crisis opened up by the United States' offensive against Islamist terrorism, abruptly highlights the urgent need for a significant change in the attitude of mainland Europe towards China. China is once again becoming relevant, mobilising our attention and intervening in our own political and strategic planning at the moment.

China is thus forcing us to change our attitude which, in any case, cannot be other than that of taking North China into account – which we will then have to play against South China, against the "oceanic China" according to Guido Giannettini's terms, through the special management of our own geopolitical positions. In other words, by adding North China to the fundamental Eurasian continental axis Paris-Berlin-Moscow-New Delhi-Tokyo.

This is essentially a task for Russia, which will also have to negotiate, with India and Japan, the powers directly concerned in the area, this partial turnaround of our own grand continental positions, integrating Northern China into the Eurasian imperial camp.

And this while taking into account the attitude of the United States towards this new turning point, which will mark the opening of a new era in Asia, that of the return of a certain China - of non-Chinese China - to its previous community of destiny. A formidable symbol if ever there was one, for the supporters of the enemy camp of ours, and an enemy, by the same token, of China's return to its own hidden identity.

To operatively arouse, within present-day China, a completely new revolutionary consciousness of its continental, "northern" identity, opposed, in terms of secession in the short term, to its adulterous, southern and "oceanic" component, foreign to the living ethos and to the specific, different destinies of the China that has made its great return to itself, represents, however, a considerable task of truly seismic importance and dimensions.

At the same time, it seems obvious to me that innumerable problems will arise in connection with the implementation of North China, which will have to be dealt with by a unified central political-strategic command, and that this command will have to begin its activities by accelerating the elaboration of a thorough and exhaustive doctrinal basis committed to defining the politico-historical and ideological reasons for the struggle for the liberation of "non-Chinese China", and its active dialectics. A unified command was to be set up, initially in Moscow, comprising, in addition to the Russian political-administrative cadres and its Chinese part, representatives of the entire Eurasian imperial community. A revolutionary earthquake wave will then sweep across the whole of Asia, changing the tectonics of the forces at work inside and outside China.

But there is much more. For the secessionist identity movement in China, which is called upon to refocus on its non-Chinese interior, will eventually find an analogous secessionist movement within the United States itself.

Doesn't the profound destiny of the United States require that it be divided - in the terms of a final counter-secessionist civil war, replaying in reverse the Civil War of 1861–1865 - between a healthy, ontologically alive and salvageable national republican part, and a democratically self-destructive part, irrevocably alienated on increasingly leftist positions, socially rotten and, in terms of conscience, totally depraved.

Now, just as the current decision-making centre of the great Eurasian continent is ontologically obliged to intervene in China in the near future, in order to bring about the revolutionary emergence of the internal pole of secessionist affirmation of Northern China, the Eurasian imperial community is also obliged, ontologically, to intervene in the American internal civil war, in its counter-secessionist war, which cannot fail to come about, in order to support in force the national republican revolutionary pole against the democratically democratising and self-depriving part. There are plans for the South American continent, liberated and mobilised around a revolutionary continental integration pole of national orientation, in a state of deep and total reverberation with the Eurasian imperial positions, to provide close combat support to the US national republican counter-secessional forces in their ultimate confrontation with the internal enemy subjugated to the existing and, for the time being, all-powerful (or appearing to be so) negative powers. Operational plans exist, I repeat, but they must also be able to pass the test of action on the ground, which always involves an element of unpredictability, often equivocal, and disappointing. And yet, I am convinced that we must never be impressed, never hesitate to go ahead, never hesitate to take *the* plunge.

History is prophecy

It has been said that, as things stand, "China does not belong to the Eurasian grand-continental community of fate". But, thanks to Guido Giannettini's advanced geopolitical research, we have found the answer to this seemingly definitive "no-win" situation.

Thus, the new turn that Guido Giannettini's research will impose on our Eurasian imperial geopolitical positions requires that we make a decisive contribution, in our choices, to the visionary, prophetic dimension of the march of history, which, for the rest of us, will always be led, secretly, by the inspired, by the predestined agents of the 'great history' in progress. History is prophecy. In this, we take our cue from General de Gaulle who, as we have seen, already in 1949, conceived of the Greater Eurasian Continental Europe as the mobilisation of all the countries of Europe around the Franco-German Carolingian Pole, including Russia as a fully participating party, "even if it means a change of regime".

The geopolitical problem of China, rightly posed, concerns us in a "direct and total" way, proposing a new direction of revolutionary politico-strategic commitment in the framework of our current Eurasian imperial struggle as a whole. A struggle that will thoroughly disrupt the whole of Greater Asia.

It is in a prophetic way, essentially prophetic, as we have understood, that the fate of China concerns us, commits us to action, to intervene directly in history. Does this task that we are imposing on ourselves seem impossible to achieve? Not for us, who act on other dimensions of history. In history, beyond history.

WE URGENTLY NEED TO TAKE AN IDEOLOGICAL AND STRATEGIC STAND

The current general US counter-offensive against Eurasian continental reunification

The spectre of a mortal danger is now looming ever larger over the United States: the spectre of the emergence in the near future of a Eurasian grand-continental empire mobilised around the Paris-Berlin-Moscow-New Delhi-Tokyo imperial axis.

For the problem thus posed appears at once to be of prodigious importance and simplicity: If the "Eurasian Island" managed to recover its previous polar unity, a unity that must be considered in some way supratemporal, to recover its imperial predestination contained implicitly in the very data of the problem, if this great Eurasian Empire, extending "from Tokyo to Dublin", were to emerge offensively on the face of current world history, the United States would cease to be the only total planetary superpower that it is at present, and that it wants to be, hegemonically, in the future, and would find itself demoted to the rank of a second, if not third, order power.

What, obviously, the United States, constituted, at the present time, as the 'first planetary superpower', cannot in any way resign itself to considering. Hence the constant, imperiously fundamental, of any American geopolitical project of decisive dimensions, present or future: to prevent, by all means, even the most dangerously adventurous - including, in the final analysis, the very risk of a planetary nuclear conflagration - that the great Eurasian continent should be able to recover its own community of historical and suprahistorical destiny, its final imperial unity, in the near future.

Now, as the movement of imperial reintegration of the Eurasian continent is beginning to take more and more shape, the occult decision-making circles in Washington, which confidentially foresee the forward march of the political destiny of the United States, have just realised that they had to take the initiative - that *the time had come* - to anticipate what is being done in Europe and consequently in the whole of the Eurasian "Great Continent". That they should therefore move, suddenly, and "as if in advance of a movement", to a planetary politico-strategic counter-offensive aimed at preventing the effective emergence of a European grand-continental imperial reintegration. And this American counter-offensive is becoming urgent, and more than urgent, due to the seizure of power in Moscow by President Vladimir Putin, who already appears to be firmly resolved to assume, personally, the political direction of this European "Eurasian" grand-continental imperial reintegration, against which the United States is at present really prepared to play everything. And right now.

Thus, the politico-military intervention of the United States against Serbia, in South-East Europe, under the false pretext of defending the Bosnian and Kosovar Islamic minorities - when in fact they were the aggressors, and in any case the United States had nothing to do with this internal European conflict - marks the beginning of the current planetary war being waged by the globalist conspiracy of the United States against the European continent. The current planetary war is an open continuation of a political war secretly waged by the United States against the reunification of the European continent, and particularly against France, since the end of the Second World War, when General de Gaulle had already in 1949 given the first warning signal for the reunification of the European continent in the sense of its total imperial integration.

Indeed, it was in 1949 that General de Gaulle first prophetically mentioned the concept of a Greater Europe centred on the Franco-German Carolingian Pole in direct and fundamental relation with Russia, during a press conference held on this subject. I say that Europe must be built," declared General de Gaulle in 1949, "on the basis of an agreement between the French and Germans. Once Europe has been built on this basis, then we can turn to Russia. Then we can try, once and for all, to build the whole of Europe with Russia too, even if it changes its regime. These are the programmes of true Europeans. This is mine.

At present, the total political warfare enterprise pursued by the United States against the Greater European, "Eurasian" continental reintegration, a reintegration in the process of revolutionary emergence, has five main strategic offensive directions:

(1) that of the permanent political destabilisation of Europe,

(2) that of the strategic-political encirclement of Russia,

(3) that of political-military investment in South-East Europe and Central Asia,

(4) that of the strategic-diversionist enterprise attempting to oppose the European continental bloc with the "Pacific bloc", including, basically, China, an advanced base towards the geopolitical centre of the Eurasian continent constituted as a bridgehead for the United States, and

(5) the one that foresees the inclusion of Europe and Russia in a false "Atlantic" Unity comprising the US, Europe and China, where the US would hold a decisive blocking hegemonic power, with an anti-continental and anti-imperial European orientation. Although dialectically antagonistic, the strategic offensive directions (4) and (5) currently being exploited by the US, are also dialectically within the same US attack front, a *dialectical attack front*. Because it is a secret dialectical war that is currently pitting the US globalist conspiracy against the already strategically active, even overactive, powers of the great Eurasian continent that have taken up the challenge that has just been presented to them.

Thus, from the Atlantic to the Pacific, the United States is now conducting its great political and strategic counter-offensive, designed to block and neutralise the emergence of the Greater European imperial movement.

The five current directions of the US strategic counter-offensive against Greater Europe

The five main offensive directions of the current US counter-strategy to the eventual emergence of an imperial reintegration of continental Europe and hence of the Eurasian 'Great Continent' appear to be the following, each of which I will analyse in terms of its basic conceptual commitment and politico-strategic developments in action:

(1) In order to prevent the European nations from eventually regaining their own national consciousness, Washington has been trying, for the past fifty years, to subversively impose and install, all over Europe, "democratic" regimes, whether liberal or social-democratic, social-communist or leftist (in fact, Trotskyite under the diversionary mask of socialism, as is the case today in France). And this structure of situation revealing itself in a quite flagrant way in France, the fundamental direction of attack of the anti-national subversion enterprise of the US globalist conspiracy at work in Europe.

Indeed, since 1945, the internal history of France has been the story of the subterranean, underhand, relentless and constantly renewed struggle between, on the one hand, the subversive action of the secret services in Washington charged with pursuing the political self-destruction of France, to prevent the French national powers from coming to power, and, on the other hand, the will- but increasingly weakened, increasingly alienated, *turned inside out-of* France and its national forces to find themselves once again entirely responsible for their own politico-historical destinies. In other words, to totally eliminate the intolerable, deadly taint of the dark anti-national forces hiding behind the socialist-communist, "Trotskyite" subversion, which maintained itself in power only through the permanent organised deception of elections distorted in advance by the subversive appropriation and subterranean control of the consciousness-and unconsciousness-of the masses thus totally manipulated in continuity.

Thus, the coming to power of General de Gaulle and the political-strategic action of Gaullism were always considered by Washington as an accident that had to be removed at all costs and by all means. Hence the great enterprise carried out through the anti-national uprising of 1968, which was to end up overcoming Gaullism anyway. And later, the whole series of insurrectionary strikes remotely controlled by Washington, notably through the FO trade union centre and its leader, Marc Blondel, who was totally under the thumb of his Trotskyite entourage, when Prime Minister Alain Juppé had tried to straighten out France once again, through a revolutionary reconsideration of its political and administrative structures, and to straighten out, at the same time, the Franco-German axis and the Gaullist line of the Greater Europe.

The politico-historical self-destruction of France pursued relentlessly by the United States was justified by the fact that it was France's duty to lead the operational implementation of the Greater Europe-through the Franco-German Carolingian Pole and its great policy of European integration of Russia-towards the fulfilment of its grand-continental, "Eurasian" imperial destiny. If France finds itself - as is the case now - in a state of advanced self-destruction, and even, perhaps, of already completed self-destruction, the whole grand European imperial edifice in the process of being built collapses by that very fact. And this is precisely what is happening at the moment. And, disintegrated, the Franco-German Carolingian Pole would be undone, Russia would be put, by this very fact, at odds in its revolutionary grand-continental dialogue with the whole of Western Europe, and India and Japan would be reduced to a truncated dialogue with Russia alone.

At present, therefore, German Chancellor Gerhard Schröder is trying to maintain, with Germany alone, the Greater European line of the Carolingian Pole in a state of ongoing dialogue with Russia. Absent from the heart of Europe, just as it has ended up being absent from itself, France is dethroning the entire ensemble of what it was conceived to be the central pillar, the axial revolutionary entity that must assume visible responsibility for the gathering of the imperial forces that constitute the Greater Europe.

With France thus destroyed, the whole of Europe - of the Greater Europe - is destroyed by the current counter-strategic offensive pursued relentlessly by the United States to block the emergence of a European, "Eurasian", grand-continental community of destiny. Thus, the politico-historical destitution of France constitutes the supreme counter-strategic objective of Washington's current grand occult policy, which aims, as an absolute priority, at the neutralisation and the unconditional and permanent political subjugation of Europe. Of this great continental Europe which constitutes, for today and for the future, the only real danger to the external security of the United States. Of which the current anti-European offensive is in reality nothing more than a permanent and preventive defence, disguised, operatively concealed.

(2) But it is also the case that, in a rather unexpected way-as if to compensate for the ongoing self-destruction of the Franco-German Carolingian Pole due to the defection of France and its current political dismantling-the geopolitical centre of gravity of Europe has suddenly shifted from Western Europe to Eastern Europe, to Russia. Russia, with the arrival of Vladimir Putin in power, would seem to have decided to take it upon itself to pose as a predestined power to force, push forward and control the definitive emergence of the largest continental, "Eurasian" Europe, Vladimir Putin's "New Russia", thus taking up the doctrine of "Gaullism of the end" - inherited from the fundamental geopolitical concept of *Kontinentalblock* forged by Karl Haushofer - concerning the transcontinental axis Paris-Berlin-Moscow-New Delhi-Tokyo.

However, having already freed itself from communism, Russia still had a long way to go in the darkness before Vladimir Putin came to seize presidential power, and regained the horizon of salvation and liberation, truly *final*, of the "New Russia" whose revolutionary destiny he took in hand immediately ahead, as well as its previous, restarted imperial identity. Miraculously restarted, providentially intact, alive, inspired, founded in holiness.

We now know that the self-dissolution of the Soviet Union was - at least at the first political level – the result of a long, extraordinary work – a long, subterranean politico-strategic work - of Washington, which, having initially turned the ambassador of the Soviet Union in Ottawa, in Canada, Alexander Yakovlev, had then succeeded in placing him with Mikhail Gorbachev, so that together they proceeded to an operation of high political cosmetics, of more or less "democratic" reconsideration of the Soviet Union. This operation had gone off course - with the help, in the shadows, of certain ultra-secret strategic services in Bonn, specially mobilised for this task - because instead of the approximate "democratisation" desired by the Soviet hierarchies, which had gone into meltdown, it was the end of the Soviet Union itself that finally took place, in a conspiratorial meeting, chaired by Boris Yeltsin, in a "hunting lodge in the Bialovej forest near the Polish border". On 8 December 1991, and not without some immediate dangers.

Just ten years have passed since then. And only Helmut Kohl should be able to remember to whom we should give our thanks - to which nameless, faceless German official in charge of certain top-secret German special services - for the "decisive turn", for the "national turn" that Russia, in the midst of an ontological transformation, was then able to take, the "post-communist Russia". And to thank Helmut Kohl again for the "miraculous appearance" of Vladimir Putin who, as we know, had to work in Germany for a long time, and who, since his accession to the Kremlin, has been able to bring Russia back to its own national and supra-historical destiny. And Vladimir Putin, for his part, knowing how to remember, recognises what present-day Russia owes to Germany, as he demonstrated on 25 September 2001 in Berlin before Chancellor Gerhard Schröder and his entire government, before the entire Bundestag. And all the more so as he spoke exclusively in German, with a perfect accent and without any mistakes. And how could one not be tempted by the confidential message of the signs?

It is therefore quite obvious that the United States is now mobilised by a categorical imperative to ensure that Vladimir Putin's grand-continental,

"Eurasian" imperial design cannot be *realised, cannot take shape*. This, of course, while taking care to avoid the ultimate conflagration, *the nuclear test*.

Hence Washington's current 'Strategic *Progressive* Investment' (SPI) of critical and control areas, the 'decisive zones' of the inner geopolitical space of the Eurasian continent: to prevent politically and economically that Russia cannot recover in a significant way, "total and offensive", and take strategic positions – the doctrine of "continental bridgeheads" – in the inner space of the great Eurasian continent close to the "central core" - the *Heartland* - of the imperial ensemble in the process of reconstitution represented today by Vladimir Putin's "New Russia".

This is also the reason for the establishment of American military-political bridgeheads in South-East Europe, as well as the current US intervention in Central Asia, where the eventual takeover of Afghanistan and Pakistan is equivalent to blocking the chain of Islamic republics of the former Soviet Union.

This also implies and commands the blocking by interruption of the continuity in the inner Eurasian geopolitical space ensured by the Paris-Berlin-Moscow-New Delhi-Tokyo transcontinental axis.

Finally, in terms of the domestic political and economic situation in Russia today, the US globalist conspiracy is constantly trying to subversively regain - through economic proxies with hidden agendas - the influence, if not the control, over the country that it lost with the rise to presidential power of Vladimir Putin. The overactive work of cleaning up Russia's internal political and administrative structures is a direct result of this, as Mikhail Gorbachev himself acknowledged in a resounding article that was taken up by the entire European press *(La Stampa, Le Monde,* etc.).

For, in Washington's view, Russia, no sooner liberated from communism, was to become, almost automatically, a colony of American supercapitalist exploitation, governed by the IMF and the pro-consular garrisons urgently put in place by the special operational agencies "in charge of the job" under the supervision of the CIA. As had already begun to be done. Before the Great Russian national fundamentalism managed to prevail over everything, through Vladimir Putin's "Gaullist" syndrome and the total reversal of the situation that he had been able to carry out as soon as he became President of Russia. Vladimir Putin did not fail to put the internal politico-administrative structures in order immediately, while redefining the new-and very old-geopolitical doctrines of his Eurasian, imperial and eschatological, "apocalyptic" predestination. Thus recovering Russia's national being, and the horizon of its greater history begun anew. This, by relying, as General de Gaulle had also done in his time, both on the deep will of the people, on their vitality and on their secret faith, and on the Armed Forces, the intermediate political-administrative hierarchies thus reduced to being no more than the field tool of the presidential revolutionary will. This was a process that could not be accomplished without difficulty, nor without terrible efforts, sometimes dangerously close to an *internal breakdown*.

(**3**) As already mentioned, the US globalist conspiracy has recently crossed the "fatal line" of direct strategic action by intervening, in the open, on a political-military level, in the South-East of the European continent, in Serbia and Kosovo, as well as in Macedonia, and then in Central Asia. Preparing further aggression in Somalia and Iraq.

The US military-political intervention in South-East Europe represents an absolutely inadmissible act of direct interference in Europe's internal space, as does its intervention in Central Asia, where the same process of military-political interference is being repeated on an infinitely larger scale. Under the more or less fallacious pretext of retaliatory action against Islamic fundamentalist terrorism, the United States has thus gained a foothold in Afghanistan and Pakistan, establishing its strategic, decisive presence on the southern flank of Russia and thus of the entire "Eurasian Island".

These are all actions of war concealed under the diversionary cover of circumstance, aimed at the strategic encirclement of Russia and of the politically emerging great-continental Europe. These are politico-military acts of war, which should normally be responded to by politico-military acts of war.

At the same time, the unilateral denunciation by the United States of the ABM global nuclear security treaty marks the clear desire in Washington of certain circles close to central power to preemptively disrupt the nuclear security balance established, for the time being, between the United States and Russia, with the aftermath of the 'Cold War' still playing out strongly behind the scenes (or appearing to do so, for very obscure purposes and, after all, not so obscure at all; on the contrary, one might even say).

Which in any case shows the irrevocably resolute decision of the United States to pursue and exploit to the maximum their current advantage in an urgent, reckless manner, but fully aware of the terrible ultimate stakes of these battles - already final - for planetary political-economic domination in the decisive years to come. This political and economic domination, however, hides another, civilisational and religious domination, giving reason to Samuel Huntington's theses. For the ultimate stakes, it is high time that we not only understood this, but also affirmed it, in the current final battles, appear to be, in the final analysis, fundamentally spiritual and religious.

(**4**) And all this while waiting for the US political-strategic thrust in the Pacific to lay the foundations for a "grand bargain" with China - what is now known in Washington as the *Final Project* - which, committed to a fundamental alliance with the United States, would thus deliver to them the very heart of the European "Great Continent". And this despite the presence, in the region itself, of India and Japan on the irreducibly anti-Chinese positions that are currently theirs within the framework of the full participation that they ensure in the Eurasian imperial project initiated by the Paris-Berlin-Moscow-New Delhi-Tokyo axis.

But in any case, the option of an upcoming shift in US offensive planetary geopolitics to the Pacific is really just a decoy, a trap designed to operationally draw China into the final US offensive enterprise against the Eurasian imperial community.

The United States' planetary agreement with China and the reversal of the entire American 'grand policy' in the direction of the Pacific is, as we know, an obsessive constant, a permanent underground project of a certain parallel American diplomacy, but one that is always on the lookout for an opportunity to manifest itself and that sometimes even succeeds in doing so. This could also be the case now.

(5) However, in addition to the option of a rapprochement and agreement with China and the reorientation of the United States' "grand policy" towards the Pacific, another fundamental strategic option is now mobilising the plans of the United States' global policy, which is trying, at the same time, to achieve an "Atlantic integration" of the United States alongside Europe and Russia, George Bush has just made extremely advanced proposals in this direction, but it must be understood that it represents only a supplementary counter-strategy of the United States in its ongoing endeavour to dismantle the Great Europe of the "Eurasian" line. Indeed, by admitting itself into the continental unity of Europe and Russia, the US is merely attempting to derail Eurasian grand-continental integration in a direction contrary to its own goals. The project of the imperial reintegration of Europe - of the Greater Europe, including Russia - which is fundamentally directed against the planetary domination of the United States, would, if the United States were to join it, become yet another tool in its current planetary domination.

The United States is thus playing, at the same time, on two fundamental strategic options, where the "Chinese option", or the Pacific option, is dialectically opposed to the "European option", the *Atlantic option,* within the framework of the same great counter-strategic enterprise aiming at the dismantling of the Eurasian imperial unity.

Whereas it is by remaining indefectibly identical to itself, and by relying on Tibet, India and Japan, that the final Eurasian imperial federation will pose itself as a total will and unity of suprahistorical destiny, thus succeeding in imposing - according to Guido Giannettini's brilliant geopolitical vision - the future secessional division of China into "North China", of "Mongolian and Uraloaltaic" substance, and "South China", belonging to the "oceanic space" of the Pacific and Insulinde.

And it will be, at that moment, by a just return of things, to Tibet having recovered its freedom, that it will be up to it to govern, as in the time of the "Tibetan empire of China", the new and very old Mongolian and Ural-Altaic community of "North China", brought then to join quite naturally our own Eurasian imperial combat unit.

The United States is thus playing both towards a fundamental agreement with China, and towards a diversionary Atlantic integration of the United States, Europe and Russia: the strategic duplication of the current planetary action of the United States is thus aimed at both the Pacific and the Atlantic, engaging the dimensions of an enterprise of integral planetary domination, that of final imperial hegemony.

This is what we, the proponents of the Eurasian grandcontinental line, the Haushoferian line of the *Kontinentalblock, are* trying to prevent, in terms of a counter-strategic enterprise with a suprahistorical, "transcendental" horizon. For the Eurasian party of world history at its end fundamentally involves a religious, eschatological, even apocalyptic counterpart, concerning the ultimate destinies of the *Regnum Sanctum*, which opens up beyond history.

This introduces into the current planetary competition of the powers fighting for the final domination of the world and of history a transcendental component foreign to the world in which these powers and their own history are exercised, a fundamentally supernatural component, coming from the "other world". And this is the "great secret" of the eschatological imperial doctrine of Vladimir Putin's intractable orthodoxy and the hidden goals of his overall action, both in terms of the final deliverance of Russia and *the assumption of Europe*, as Raymond Abellio said, which will be a Eurasian assumption.

In the interregnum of the planetary dialectical war

A Russian essayist, Anatole Ivanov, recently wrote that the "terrorist action of September 11 changed the direction of world history". I believe that Anatole Ivanov is entirely right: in the face of the now paroxysmal threat of global Islamic terrorism, a vital reflex of concerted, politico-strategic unity of action came into play within the beleaguered camp, which had reached its most significant point in the joint declaration in Shanghai in September 2001 by the United States, Russia and China, a declaration which, in principle, laid the foundations for a global counter-terrorist community. Vladimir Putin's affirmative response to George Bush's offer of a joint US-Europe-Russia counter-terrorism action unit could therefore be explained not as some kind of Russian retreat, but simply as Russia's dialectical engagement, which, by entering - or pretending to enter - into the US game, momentarily blocked its anti-continental offensive action while buying time for the overall US globalist conspiracy to take shape. Which must outpace the imperial politico-historical emergence of Eurasian continental unity, or lose, in advance, the game.

For, having come to this point, time is now becoming an absolutely decisive factor in the operational conduct of the ongoing, covert, larval political conflagration, the planetary war between the two camps, that of the US globalist conspiracy and that of the accelerated implementation of the final Eurasian grand-continental imperial integration undertaken, supported and pushed forward by Vladimir Putin's "New Russia", becoming today a dialectical war, where the two confronting camps fight each other while getting closer and closer while fighting each other, each camp trying, on its side, to gain time in relation to the other, and for that purpose going so far as to suspend, together, their hostilities, in order to better be able to take them up again when the time really comes. And each side taking advantage of the time gained to better secure its own offensive positions, to place its own intervention bodies as far forward as possible, in a more decisive manner.

This requires an extraordinary mastery of the dialectical play of antagonistic powers in action, while defining, by this very fact, the 'present moment' of the ongoing planetary conflagration in a way that is still relatively concealed. And whose definitions of its own actuality cannot but be concealed, but less and less so.

And things are now asserting themselves, very openly, as if the "ontological line of rupture and separation" of the two camps was no longer passing only between them, between the two antagonistic camps facing each other, but also within each of these two camps.

This is true both in the case of China and the United States, and also with regard to Europe itself, divided in its identity by the terrifying results of the work of subversion carried out for years by liberalism and social democracy in the service of the nocturnal powers that we know. Or that we do not even know.

The internal dialectical struggle of the European camp in crisis

It is clear that as far as we are concerned, those of the Eurasian great-continental camp, the problem that we now face, in an inescapable way, is that of awareness, of a total self-revelation about the situation that we are facing on the double level

(1) our own identity in its ultimate suprahistorical positions, our *dogmatic identity*, and

(2) our overall political-historical situation, our *identity of the moment*. Indeed, as a party of being, we are, at a transcendental suprahistorical level, winners in advance. Whereas at the level of our historical situation of the moment, we are losers in advance.

Thus we are asked, in the terms of a revolutionary war of consciousness, a total dialectical war, to revolutionarily mobilise the consciousness of all the present nations of the "Eurasian Island" on the suprahistorical concept of the great community of destiny-eschatological predestination-which is ours, to make us understand the polar secret of the abysmal unity of our civilisation and of our own being.

It is therefore a question of a double ideological and spiritual revolution to be unleashed within our own camp, and of achieving its ultimate goal: the constitution of a monolithic block of revolutionary and suprahistorical planetary consciousness, engaged in a counter-conspiracy opposed to the globalist conspiracy of the United States and what is hidden behind it. And this counter-conspiracy of ours should eventually bring the great "Eurasian Island" to its final position as the supreme superpower of the Third Millennium.

For we already have everything we need now: for our greatest destiny to be finally fulfilled, all we need is a dialectical revolution, the emergence and direct revolutionary affirmation of the new Eurasian imperial consciousness committed to its immediate political-historical fulfilment.

It can therefore be said that *the Greater Europe is now no more than our own awareness of the Greater Europe.*

All of us will have to become the secret agents of influence and underground intervention of this new revolutionary grand-continental consciousness, which is the very consciousness of our salvation and deliverance, of the final liberation of Europe and the whole of the Eurasian "Great Continent", according to the mysterious Heideggerian concept of *wieder*, of "once again".

Because once again we will break history.

This is what will bring out in full force the fundamental role of the revolutionary ideological framework to be put in place urgently in our own camp, from "Tokyo to Dublin". As well as the double revolutionary ideological intervention that will have to be carried out thoroughly by us, simultaneously and covertly, inside the antagonistic camps of China and the United States, which are opposed, each on its side, to our camp, while also opposing each other.

For it is the same ontological, and dialectically secessional, rupture that we will have to bring into play, when the "time comes", both within China and within the United States: just as China will then have to be separated into itself, the "North China" led - following Guido Giannettini's visionary geopolitical doctrines - to secede from the "South China", from the "oceanic" China, centred on the Pacific, we will also have to bring about, also within the United States, a definitive secessional rupture between the still healthy, national republican fraction of the American people and the negative, degenerate component of the latter, its "progressive", "democratic" component.

It is foreseeable that, in this case, both "North China" and the healthy, national republican, secessionist fraction of the United States will have to end up siding with us in the final conflagration of the two worlds in total ontological opposition, the world of being and the world of non-being, the world of the "Empire of the End" and the world of the "Anti-Empire" of non-existence and chaotic void.

There is therefore no task, no "revolutionary mission" for the rest of us more imperatively to follow than that of setting up the structures of ideological instruction, thorough and advanced, committed to bringing about the ontological supra-consciousness of the Eurasian imperial counter-conspiracy in the face of the US globalist conspiracy, which is the acting conspiracy of non-being.

An ontological supra-consciousness that will be the revolutionary foundation of the new Western history of the world, and the new West of history at its end.

Immediate battles

At present, the Eurasian transcontinental axis Paris-Berlin-Moscow-New Delhi-Tokyo appears to respond to a double internal constitutional structure: for, if its first three instances, located in the East of the Eurasian "Great Continent", Moscow, New Delhi, Tokyo, correspond to countries that have fully recovered - through the national regimes in place of Vladimir Putin, Atal Behari Vajpayee and Junichiro Koizumi - their deepest national integrity, their own being and their own destiny of continental and planetary dimensions, on the other hand, its two basic European bodies, Paris and Berlin, are both plunged into a state of total political catastrophe, due to the socialisto-trotskyist and social-democratic regimes currently in power in France and Germany.

With, for Germany, the "extenuating circumstance" of Chancellor Gerhard Schröder's current, advanced, vital, overactive relations with Vladimir Putin's "New Russia". While France stubbornly maintains an essentially anti-Russian political line, no doubt because of its current government, which under a socialist mask is a Trotskyite government, on the one hand; and, on the other, because of Vladimir Putin's great orthodox, "eschatological" religious choices, which are unsupportable by the fundamentally materialistic, anti-religious, secretly "satanist" infrastructures of the occult power governing, in the shadows, France's current political destiny. The intractable anti-Russian resentments of a Trotskyist government supported by the active hostility in the shadows of an all-powerful occult super-power in place against the "New Russia" that has recovered its former great orthodox faith, makes an impassable barrier, that's for sure; but a barrier that must be broken down, and that we will know how to destroy.

Thus, France, which by virtue of its very origins, by virtue of its secretly "archaic" identity, by virtue of the final eschatological nature of its own historical missions, should have been in continuation the axial pillar, the over-activated and over-activating powerhouse of the emerging Greater Europe, finds itself today reduced to a desperate situation, with no way out other than those of the "last choices", the choices of direct revolutionary action, of "civil war".

Fortunately, the legislative elections of June 2002, which will undoubtedly send the present socialist-Trotskyist government back to the nothingness from which it emerged, will thus keep away the bloody spectre of civil war, of "total political war", as was the case during the Spanish war of national liberation of 1936–1939. A certain clandestine France could then surface. But the horizon remained dark, very dark.

It should be noted, however, that a chain process of anti-socialist-communist national-revolutionary liberation along European lines is already underway, with a number of European countries - Spain, Italy, Serbia, Austria, and more recently Denmark and Portugal - having managed to democratically liberate themselves from the regimes of anti-national alienation that had been purposely imposed on them by the subversive machinations of the US globalist conspiracy. To a greater or lesser degree, but the fact is there, indisputable, and its significance cannot be ignored.

The creation and immediate start-up of a "secret centre" for the direction and politico-strategic control of all the national movements that have currently come to power within the geopolitical space of Greater Europe, the mobilisation, by us, of a sort of national-revolutionary "Comintern", would seem to be an operative necessity that should mark the great politico-historical turning point whose advent thus seems to be announced. An operative necessity which implies that *we* really *take the plunge,* and to which it is no longer possible for us not to respond, and all the more urgently since the task of immediately installing this "secret centre" of the national-revolutionary movements currently on line in the European countries already liberated from social-communism concerns us directly, and is rightfully incumbent on us, "those of the ultimate limits".

Indeed, everything points to the fact that the summer of 2002 will see the 'great turning point', for which we will have to be fully prepared. In a certain sense, it will probably be the case that we will no longer have to take into account the current political and historical situation. For it will no longer be the events, whatever they may be, nor especially the relations of the forces objectively present that, when the time comes, will have to decide what must mysteriously happen: it is the abysmal secret of history itself, of 'great history', that will have to act there, according to a non-human will, external to this world, fundamentally supernatural and which, for the moment, still remains inconceivable to us. Totally inconceivable. And already, now, we are being carried forward by an occult flow of history, which is both impenetrable and which nothing can resist.

Everything we needed to know, ideologically and strategically, about the current "planetary political moment" has been said here, and all that remains is for us to become deeply aware of it, so that we can immediately *do what needs to be done.* Our path is marked out, we are in *charge.*

The Summer of 'Final Reversal'

No one can deny it now: while Eastern Europe, which came under Washington's political and economic control after its liberation from Soviet rule, persists in holding to left-wing social-democratic positions, as we have just seen in Hungary, Western Europe is in the process of turning completely to the right. After Silvio Berlusconi's resounding defeat of the ruling socialist-communist conspiracy in Italy, which was clinging on angrily, and after the seizure of power by the national and anti-communist right in Portugal, the West is now turning completely to the right, after the probably definitive annihilation of the socialist left in France and the spectacular rise of the right in the Netherlands, which dislodged social democracy to impose a right-wing governmental line, while Austria and Spain had already long since eliminated the left from power, the socialist left now remains in power in Western Europe only in Germany, Belgium and Greece; And it is already certain that next September Germany will also be able to liquidate the socialist-communist subversion currently in power in Berlin.

And if I speak thus of socialist-communist subversion rather than of "socialist" or "social-democratic" subversion, it is because, after the political self-destruction of the USSR, the communist parties of Western Europe - as well as all their parallel bodies and networks of clandestine action - have resorbed, in the long term, into a state of semi-clandestine underground activity through socialist formations-parties, diversionary and replacement groupings, an analogous shift having taken place, at the same time, within the socialist formations thus infiltrated, transformed from within. And, at the same time, the operative structures of Soviet communism were replaced, almost on the spot, by the reactivated structures of dormant Trotskyism. For world communism – the "world revolution of communism" - had never ceased to carry within it, in a hidden way, the dual identity of its conflicting origins, the antagonistic political action structures and clandestine intervention apparatuses of Trotskyism and Stalinism, the trotskyist apparatuses having more or less clandestinely survived outside the USSR, while inside the USSR the totality of the power was held, in depth, by the Stalinist central - and, after the death of Stalin, by the "Soviet central" – in place in Moscow. However, outside the USSR, in the face of the world revolutionary apparatus of Soviet communism and the communist parties which constituted its external offensive armature, the world apparatus of Trotskyism, for its part, did not cease to assert itself, clandestinely, in continuity. By singularly unsuspected ways, the irreducible antagonism of the Stalinist and Trotskyist revolutionary apparatuses has not ceased to mobilise, to set ablaze the secret foundations of

European and world history, even today. Especially today, even if very few have come to know it. But these are the ones that count.

The current underground of a European Trotskyist surface organisation

Thus, with the collapse of the USSR, a fundamental displacement was declared, from below, proceeding everywhere to the double operation **(1)** of the replacement of the Stalinist apparatuses by decoys, by new formations of false socialist identity, and **(2)** of the nucleation of the socialist parties already in place, and of the whole of social democracy, in power everywhere in Europe, by subterranean offensive Trotskyist infiltrations.

While the operation to replace the Stalinist communist apparatuses with formations of false socialist identity was massively and very effectively carried out in Italy, it was in France, however, that the Trotskyite operation to invest socialism in power in depth was best brought to light - finally - thanks, above all, to leaks carried out by certain political security services.

Behind Lionel Jospin and his compact group of Trotskyites supposedly rallied to socialism, it was a covert operation to re-establish the Trotskyite fraction of revolutionary globalist communism that was thus begun, and was pursued relentlessly during the five years that socialism remained in power in France; from where it has just been swept away by the Gaullist right-wing line of Jacques Chirac.

It is true that the Right has already taken power in most of Europe. But this is only a formal, electoral, "democratic" takeover, which does not yet have the political and social foundations of real political power. At the present time, underneath the floor of the visible, democratically legitimate power of the European right, the leftist-Trotskyist magma is rumbling, ready at any moment to try to rise up, to overthrow and revolutionarily break the counter-offensive floor of the right, to try to prevail over the positions that the right has currently won with great difficulty. The decisive test of strength will not be long in coming, and it will not be a democratic test.

This was seen in Italy during the huge wave of insurrectionary demonstrations organised - openly - on 23 April in Rome by the secretary general of the CGIL, Sergio Cofferati, under the pretext of "trade union opposition" to the plans to amend labour legislation put forward by Silvia Berlusconi's government. In reality, it was something quite different. For, behind the CGIL stood the activist bodies of the DS ("Democrats of the Left"), a conglomerate of apparatuses intended to house, more or less confidentially, the still active structures of the PCI; and, behind the DS, the revolutionary Trotskyist centres and the "buried" nuclei of the Red Brigades ready, once again, for "direct action".

Thus, Antonio Martino, Minister of Defence in the Berlusconi government, quite rightly told the daily *La Sicilia* that he saw "in the CGIL demonstration an enormous danger for the free institutions of democracy, the union overstepping its role to the point of threatening the constitutional order, preventing the legitimately elected executive from governing the country", and added that "sooner or later we will have to re-establish constitutional legality". While, for his part, the vice-president of the government, Gianfranco Fini, affirmed that the development of the forces of the socialist-communist left under the guise of a trade union demonstration was, in reality, nothing more than a concealed admission of the concerted refusal, by the subversive movements involved, of the fundamental decision by which the majority of the Italian nation had democratically expressed its unqualified rejection of the left's stranglehold on the state apparatus.

The message that Sergio Cofferati had been asked to convey on 23 April had to be very clear: that under the cover of the DS, the socialist-communist, leftist and Trotskyist bodies intended to form a "common front" to oppose insurrectionally the government of the national anti-communist line currently in power in Rome.

On the other hand, one can certainly consider that in France, the objectives of the current republican regime of Jacques Chirac could in no way be ours. At the same time, however, he has succeeded in completely eliminating the socialist-communist conspiracy from the European political game, reducing it to impotence and throwing it out of the current French political power. This appears to be of the utmost importance in the present political circumstances.

Now this dialectic of insurrectional manipulation of the masses, in Italy and in France, to blockade and finally overthrow the democratically established governments of national line, appears to be quite exemplary, and it risks to be, from now on, more and more so. For, in the terms of a vast operation assumed by the same socialist-communist forces manipulated, in the shadows, by the clandestine Trotskyist structures, the same phenomenon of so-called "anti-fascist" mobilisation also manifested itself in France, last May, between the two rounds of the presidential elections, with the aim of preventing, through the streets, the democratic takeover of power by the right. The end result was a sudden reversal of the situation and a huge failure for the left. In these very days, the same scenario is being repeated in Spain, where under the spectre of the "general strike" the forces of the street, the "anti-fascist" masses are being pushed to go up - with the open support of Sergio Cofferati's CGIL, triggering, simultaneously, the same manoeuvre, for the second time, in Italy - to the assault of the democratically in power in Madrid. But Madrid will resist, as Rome and Paris have resisted.

So the showdown has already occurred twice, in Italy and France, between the forces of being and national identity on the one hand and the forces of non-being, the nihilistic forces of creeping chaos on the other, and the latter have been defeated, annihilated, on both occasions. Europe is waking up, Europe has woken up.

Something has happened in the invisible.

However, by taking the initiative to mobilise en masse, by making all its politico-revolutionary availabilities available against the current right-wing turn of Europe, the social-communist conspiracy with a secretly Trotskyist identity has, by this very fact, *self-democratised*, appearing under its true active identity and in its true continental European dimensions, thus led - a fatal error if ever there was one - to sacrifice the strategic advantage of its clandestinity to the suicidal vertigo of open revolutionary action. This is the fatal trap into which the European surface socialist-communist conspiracy is being trapped.

We, the advocates of the European grandcontinental, "Eurasian" geopolitical line, who find ourselves, all together, in the imperial project of the Paris-Berlin-Moscow-New Delhi-Tokyo transcontinental axis, now know with whom we are dealing.

For in its successive metamorphoses and under its alternative masks, the ontological enemy of all that we are appears once again to be the same, always.

And what, at the present time, seems to us to be very actively significant for their overall plans of action is the fact that, under the cover of the fundamentally diversionary discourse (the "anti-fascism") that they have chosen to push forward, the leftist organisations in the service of the ontological enemy have integrated themselves into a vast supranational subversive movement, whose clandestine front line goes, without a break, from Moscow to Lisbon, thus controlling the whole of the interior of greater Europe.

Overall plans for social-communist provocations

Now, among many other supporting proofs, what forcefully revealed the fact of the subversive-revolutionary integration of all the national Trotskyist apparatuses into a single clandestine supranational offensive structure was the recent affair of provocation, sabotage and violence organised in Paris on the occasion of the "Salon du Livre 2002", during the official reception of the Italian State delegation at this "Salon du Livre", which was dedicated, precisely, to Italy.

Sabotage organised by the more than dubious Catherine Tasca, Minister of Culture in Lionel Jospin's Socialist government, who by virtue of her very position was in charge of the official reception of the Italian delegation. And who, having seized the opportunity, had organised a demonstration - or rather a series of demonstrations - of inconceivable and low violence against the current Italian national political regime, with the support, on the spot, of a large representation of Italian 'writers and intellectuals' who, for this very purpose, had travelled en masse to Paris. Italy rejects Berlusconi" was the headline on the front page of a major Paris daily newspaper, announcing the "special supplement" in which a number of Italian "writers and intellectuals" testified against the arrival of the right-wing in power in Italy. Headed by a crass nullity like Antonio Tabucchi and supported by the ignoble smala of his "anti-fascist" pimps. The outbursts of national treason, leftist delirium and abjection had reached, on this occasion and under the direct and personal patronage of the French Socialist Minister of Culture, truly intolerable limits.

In support of the thesis of the overactive existence of a vast clandestine Trotskyite continental enterprise, we can also cite the subversive activities of Boris Berezovsky and his organisation of combat and agitation against President Vladimir Putin's "New Russia" in London, with the support and under the shadowy direction of the political special services of the current socialist government. A shadowy oligarch from the beginning, a hidden backer of Chechen terrorists and Fundamentalist Islam, according to recent statements by Chechen President Maskhadov himself, Boris Berezovsky is part of the field garrison of the remnants of the underground Trotskyist apparatus infiltrated within the former Soviet power that is resurfacing, Today, it is back in action with the entry into the fray of the new underground Trotskyist organisation of European dimensions, of which the "Red Brigades of the Communist Fighting Party" (BB/CFP) also form part in Italy. It was this underground Trotskyist organisation of European dimensions that was behind the attack on John Paul II, in which an attempt was made to implicate the former Bulgarian political special services. Much will soon surface. It is time, and some of our people are working intensively on it.

How far will the covert actions of the special political services of the present socialist government in London go, when it is also known that it was these same services that had hastily organised the assassination of Commander Massoud, so that they could prevent him from setting up a national line regime in Kabul after the liberation of Afghanistan from the terrorist domination of the Islamic fundamentalists? For it was not a national line regime that the US needed in this case, but an equivocal, decaying, manoeuvrable regime that was entirely under its strict obedience.

In the same vein of counter-strategic research, we can also cite the incredible attempt by the Minister of the Interior of Gerhard Schröder's socialist government, the highly suspicious Otto Schilly, who has just requested the creation of a 'general central file' and a 'special court of justice' for the 'surveillance' and 'repression' of 'any attempt, any anti-globalisation stance', a request that Otto Schilly intended to make at the European level.

In this same order of analysis, I have already spoken about the Italian-Spanish unitary revolutionary subversive action in favour of the common "insurrectionary general strike" against the national line regimes currently in place in Rome and Madrid. Sergio Cofferati: ''The European right-wingers share a common purpose. In Italy as in Spain, their governments seek to limit the protection of acquired rights. Faced with these provocations, the European trade union must mobilise. And that is what it is doing".

It is not the "social policy" of the national government of José Maria Aznar that the socialist-communist conspiracy of the European surface – acting under the trade union cover of the CGIL in Italy and, in Spain, of the UGT (socialists) and the CCOO (communists) Workers' Commissions - intends to sanction in this way, but the fact of the current presence, in Madrid – as already almost everywhere in Europe - of a right-wing national regime, resulting from the resounding failure of the concealed Trotskyite socialism that had been that of Felipe Gonzalez.

Unitary structure, superstructure, and infrastructure

Thus the June parliamentary elections and the German elections in September, which can be considered as having been won for the Right, mean that Europe is now entering an abruptly new phase of its destiny, the very phase of the "final decision": in two months' time, with the exception of Belgium and Greece, Europe will have turned completely and profoundly to the Right. This will completely change the political situation, opening the way for a total revolutionary reversal of the general situation in the very near future. A real change of the world.

At the same time, in our own camp as well as in the camp opposite, in the camp of the right as well as in the camp of the left, the situation is, for the moment, structurally identical, in appearance as well as in depth.

There is indeed a kind of "unitary structure" of this *situation of the moment,* which happens to be the same in both camps, a "unitary situation" which constitutes, in itself, one of the *signs of the times* announcing the next political-revolutionary explosion of final planetary dimensions.

The concept of 'unitary structure' therefore appears to be extraordinarily enlightening, providing the operational keys to the current political and strategic situation in Europe. What, then, should be understood by the operational concept of "unitary structure"? What is its analytical constitution, and its own power to intervene in the current grand European conjuncture?

At the level of the European continent as a whole, the Right and the Left are governed by, exhibit today the same structure – a "unitary structure" – of duplication, this one constituted of an external, visible, conventional part of a "suprastructure" identity, together with an internal, revolutionary, occult part of an "infrastructure" identity.

As an analytical example of the constitution of this "unitary structure", I will cite below the present politico-revolutionary situation in Italy, and, for the right, in France.

Today, in Italy, the "superstructure" of the left is constituted by the gathering of the over-activated sum - circumstantially - of the social-democratic formations asserting themselves under the increasingly symbolic leadership of Massimo d'Aiema, a "superstructure" which is in reality nothing more than an instance of reception and concealment of the active remnants of the PCI, and below which stands strategically, subversively splitting it, the ardent sum of the nebulae integrating – and these are precisely the "infrastructures" of the whole – the mass of immediately revolutionary activisms, partisans of "direct action", recognising themselves, without admitting it, in the emblematic project of the "Red Brigades of the Communist Party/Combatant", BR/PCC. The "superstructure" is the left of apparently democratic pretensions and services, and the "infrastructure" of the latter, the subversive revolutionary part, partisan of "direct action" and of the BR/PCC.

In France, the same "unitary structure" today mobilises the "suprastructure" of the national republican front gathered behind the President of the Republic Jacques Chirac, the "infrastructure" of duplication of the latter being constituted, today, beyond the National Front of Jean-Marie Le Pen, by the national-revolutionary nebula, for the moment marginalised, of direct action in which the activists, with a more or less clandestine status, of the imperial, ''Eurasian'' grand-continental European line, partisans of the transcontinental project of the Paris-Berlin-Moscow-New Delhi-Tokyo axis, are engaged.

And the same phenomenon of the internal splitting of the left and the right being manifested identically, under the aegis of this same mysterious "unitary structure", in each country of Western Europe, an overall national-revolutionary counter-strategic line therefore appears, at the present time, as an obvious necessity for us, the supporters of the continental, "Eurasian", great-European marching front, deeply concerned by the project of the Paris-Berlin-Moscow-New Delhi-Tokyo imperial axis: our imperial politico-revolutionary task is now rising before us, like the red sun of the recommencement of our greatest history at its end, like Raymond Abellio's "red sun".

This unitary counter-strategy of the right is therefore valid for the whole of the European continental right in power in Western Europe in its double identity, both at the level of its "superstructure" in power and at the level of its "infrastructures" already engaged in the revolutionary expectation of final power; both at the level of its democratically avowed action and at the level of its underground combat organisations, still standing in the shadows.

That is until the day of the sudden "Final Reversal", which may be much closer than we think, when the European grand-continental national-revolutionary infrastructure will prevail, imposing its own law on the conventional right-wing "superstructure" that we are seeing, at the moment, being put in place all over Western Europe, from Vienna to Lisbon.

Will the coming summer be the mystical and ardent "Great Summer" that our saint Pius XII foresaw as a visionary combatant of the last cosmic and political conflagration, his mysterious *"Prope est Aestas"* of 19 May 1958, the very year of the "breaking of the dikes" brought about by the return of Gaullism to power?

Do not betray the operational secrets of our final counter-strategy

However, and more particularly in the present state of affairs, it is not for me to reveal here what the combat counter-strategies of the "infrastructural" right, of the great continental European revolutionary right, will actually be in the face of the "suprastructural" right in power, and much less in the face of the subversive positions of the left. The revolutionary confrontations being by their very nature covered in depth by the "counter-strategic secret", there is no question of revealing the operative structures of our next field engagements nor the new doctrines of combat other than in ultra-confidential writings, intended for an elite acting under cover.

Nevertheless, it can be argued that, following the "dialectic of combat of agitating minorities", the structures – the "infrastructures" – of the operative right of the Great European revolutionary right must begin, in the current phase of hard confidential commitments, a phase of approach, of infiltration and covert entryism, of manipulation and influence, of politico-doctrinal and immediately operative takeover of the entire European front of the "suprastructure" right.

The "suprastructural" Right, over which the "infrastructural" Right - or rather the extreme Right - will have to exercise a nocturnal, but increasingly integral and integrating hold, a hold that will lead to the "Final Reversal", when the theses of the extreme Right's "infrastructures" will prevail, totally, over the positions of the "suprastructural" Right.

Only then can decisive battles be waged at the European continental level against the left, which is to be destroyed once and for all.

All the while not ignoring the fact that the internal politico-strategic battles of the continental European right – the secret battles of its imperial-revolutionary "infrastructure" against its democratic "superstructure" – will be joined without further delay by the external battles of the Greater Europe to free itself from the globalist grip of the "Planetary Superpower of the United States".

The "Planetary Superpower of the United States" as the suprahistorical enemy of the Greater Europe

Indeed, we must not for a moment lose sight of the fact that the Greater Europe, of imperial dimensions and predestination, "Eurasian", is posing itself geopolitically as well as in the terms of its greater destiny, its suprahistorical destiny, more and more openly against the current imperialist aims of the United States, planetary hegemonic aims, which have already "moved into action". The US, as a "Planetary Superpower", is setting up the apparatus of its ultimate hegemonic projects, which are also directed, in the first place, against the "Greater Europe" and its implicit commitments to the "Eurasian Island" and the problem of "final world domination". History repeats itself, as we know. The geopolitical spiral is permanent. Projected onto the visible scale of world history currently underway, the opposition of the "Planetary Superpower of the United States" and the Greater Eurasian Line Europe is simply a repetition of the opposition that, in other times, led the Roman Empire to find itself obliged to annihilate Carthage, with the "oceanic empire" of the United States now taking up the situation that Carthage faced against the Roman Empire.

The United States has already made itself politically and militarily present in South-East Europe, Afghanistan and Pakistan, while at the same time investing in the southern belt of the Islamic republics of the former USSR. And at the same time they are trying to neutralise European continental integration by interposing themselves - or trying to do so - between Western Europe, Eastern Europe and Russia, and are preparing to move into the European zone of influence in the Middle East by preparing an open military aggression against Iraq, or even Syria. And we haven't seen anything yet.

To dislocate the current arrangements for European political integration, to neutralise the effort to effectively integrate Russia into the unified European whole: George Bush's recent trip to Europe - to Germany, Russia, France and Italy - had no other purpose.

To block the ongoing process of continental, "Eurasian" imperial integration by imposing its presence, its "participation", through the diversionary pretext of the "enlargement of NATO to Eastern Europe and especially to Russia", which is in fact George Bush's project in action to prevent, or at least delay, the establishment of the "Eurasian Empire of the End" for which we, the "midnight harvesters", are fighting. An initiative that we cannot but hold, in advance, doomed to failure.

Washington and Moscow

The dialectic of the strategy of rapprochement of the two great planetary geopolitical blocks in competition for the "final domination of the world and its ultimate history" - the United States and the Greater Europe – understood as a preliminary to their great final confrontation, which had also been, in 1939, that of the German-Soviet Pact as a preliminary to the war of Hitler's Germany against the USSR, is resurfacing today, on a planetary scale – whereas in 1939 the same problem was posed on a European scale only - with the "strategy of rapprochement" of the United States and the Greater Europe of Eurasian identity, a rapprochement which is in fact - once again - only the preliminary strategy of the great final planetary confrontation which will be, in the long run, that of the United States and Europe, that of the "oceanic bloc" and the "continental bloc".

This is what Vladimir Putin understood perfectly well when, by agreeing to enter fully into the diversionary game of the new continental promotion of NATO, he dialectically reversed the terms of the problem, using the new deal proposed by George Bush to gain time for the ongoing process of the final imperial integration of the Greater Europe, thus postponing the inevitable confrontation between the United States and Greater Europe to a later date, thereby averting the extreme danger of a direct US offensive venture before the European continental bloc could achieve its true ultimate identity.

However, it seems that it is the success of this extraordinary politico-strategic manoeuvre of planetary dimensions and counter-conspirative repercussions that will make Vladimir Putin reach the status of charismatic leader, ''predestined'', of the future ''Eurasian Empire of the End''.

It is the providential march of history itself that brings out the decisive figures of its own foundational achievements, of its abysmal beginnings.

Didn't a Republican elected official from the Deep South, David Duke, recently write that *Russia is the key to our survival*?

Fighting on two fronts

From all of these operational analyses, it follows that the global political and strategic situation requires us, the political soldiers of the Greater Europe, to accept to fight on two fronts at the same time: on the one hand,

(1) the *home front*, of the confidential showdown between the "suprastructure" of the European Right, which is openly, "democratically" seizing overall political power throughout Western Europe, and the underground action of its national-revolutionary "infrastructure" engaged in its own grand-continental, "Eurasian" line, and

(2) the *external front* of our counter-offensive opposition to the ongoing hegemonic plans to assert the "Planetary Superpower of the United States".

The fundamental schizophrenia of the current socialist conspiracy of European dimensions of Trotskyist revolutionary underground influence is manifested in the fact that its so-called uncompromising choice of total opposition to the US policy of global hegemonic interventionism is at the same time contradicted, This is reflected, among other things, in the bill tabled by the German Socialist Minister of the Interior, Otto Schill, for the consistent repression of "anti-globalization" activities, and in its refusal to take any action against the subversive globalization offensive of the United States, which is currently underway worldwide. This appears to be extremely revealing as to the true occult obediences of the socialist-Trotskyist conspiracy in its ultimate, *unmentionable* depths.

It thus appears that an immediately operative instance of central counter-strategic command of the whole of the grand-continental European national-revolutionary front becomes, from now on, an organisational imperative that cannot be ignored.

We have not a moment to lose. Everything is returning to the zone of supreme attention''.

The revolutionary, tragic dialectic of the action of "acting minorities" abruptly returns to the order of the day, commands our choices and illuminates the paths that we must take, whatever the cost. The mystery of the 'Final Reversal' is that its fulfilment in the history of the end is the work of a very small number of chosen ones in the shadows, the *survivors of the fire.*

THE TRANSCENDENTAL MEANING OF THE UPCOMING GERMAN ELECTIONS (SEPTEMBER 2002)

In September 22, Germany will be called upon to elect a new chancellor, and will thus most likely eject into the outer darkness the lout Gerhard Schröder and the party of German Marxist Trotskyites acting under the false and now irretrievably rotten guise of social democracy and its equally dubious "allies". Thus, next autumn, a whole era will collapse, in one fell swoop, just as the Berlin Wall collapsed in its time. The German elections on 22 September are therefore a very important event, on which the future fate of Europe, of the "Greater Europe", will undoubtedly depend – directly, and perhaps even, in a way, totally. But an event which, obviously, cannot be described as 'transcendental'. Unless one knows how to look at the present situation from a higher, "metapolitical" point of view, capable of detecting behind a political event as such that which splits it up by elevating it to the occult space of the great decisions and the great spiritual reversals, the mysterious "suprahistorical restarts" through which "great history" advances and reveals itself in its unpredictable march. This is precisely the case with our present approach to the German elections of 22 September, an approach that proposes to reveal what lies behind them, in the shadow, and which thus makes them a fundamental turning point in present and future European history. A shadow cast by the very part of the unspeakable that is present there, subversively engaged.

The shattering awakening of Asia and the increasingly accelerated developments of the planetary hegemonic grand design of the United States now constitute, together with the setting in motion of the Greater Imperial Europe, centred on the Franco-German "Carolingian Bloc" on the one hand, and on the revolutionary emergence of Vladimir Putin's "New Russia" on the other, the overall front of the fundamental political problems that have come to the forefront with the transition to the Third Millennium. All these problems bear the mark of the transition from one ontological state to another, the tragic mark of "crossing the line".

Now, the awakening of Asia as well as the current imperialist planetary offensive of the United States are in reality both directly conditioned, and as if virtually suspended in their march, by the race ahead of Greater Europe, by the revolutionary evolution already underway of the "Great Continent" towards its final imperial Eurasian integration. The affirmation of the Greater Europe contradicts and neutralises the two other planetary political operations, that of Asia and that of the United States, whose respective futures it blocks by implicitly opposing them; and even, already, explicitly, as we will see more and more.

However, if this triple antagonistic polarisation of current world history is fundamentally conditioned by the offensive construction site of European imperial integration, the latter, in turn, is at present a direct function of the future great political orientations of Berlin: in the final analysis, the face of the world and of future history now depends on the current political future of Germany. Hence the "transcendental" qualification required by the German legislative elections of next September, which thus appear to be dialectically something else – and indeed "something else entirely" - than what they would appear to be on the immediate political level alone, benefiting as they do from a vertiginous depth of field - a backdrop that is both hidden and tragic. And tragic, because everything now depends on a choice left to the sole will of the German people, who are the object of exacerbated solicitations and who are continuously trying to predetermine; to influence in a direction that goes towards the interests of the "power of darkness", always on the alert, always on the lookout, always available to seize the fatal opportunity.

But at the same time it is no less certain that history itself has, in its forward march, visible or invisible, the inner imposition of an abysmal will, beyond all influence, beyond all reach outside itself, which makes it, in the last analysis, history, history itself, which finds, mysteriously, as if by itself, within itself, the preconceived bed of its ineluctable decisive forward discharges, its choices never being but the fact of the hidden will of Divine Providence alone, and not of some other predeterminations, whatever they may be.

In this sense, and to paraphrase Mœller van den Bruck, we can say that in this case the "Fourth Reich", the "Reich of the End", will also be the "Eternal Reich". Because world history at its end will now lead to a supra-historical afterlife of history, the secret of which only we know. We, the "last ones", the "survivors of the fire". Germany's new political destiny no longer depends on a political choice, but on a transcendental choice, whatever that political choice may seem to be.

The new Franco-German 'Refounding Pact

It is not history that follows the times, but the times that follow history, that respond to its subterranean injunctions. Thus, as soon as the "new" post-Socialist national regime that emerged from the German elections in September comes to power in Berlin, it will have to face the total test that will be – and that the "new" German regime will formally want it to be – that of the 40th anniversary, the anniversary of the ontological refoundation, of the Franco-German "Founding Pact" of January 1963 – the "Treaty of the Elysium" of General de Gaulle and Chancellor Adenauer – being at the historical origin of what has been called, since then, the Franco-German

"Carolingian Pact" and hence of the greater Europe to come. For *everything has to start again.*

The subterranean sabotage undertaken and pursued by the French and German socialist-Trotskyist – so-called "social-democratic" – regimes of the last few years of resigned decay has come to an end, in fact, with the return in force, in France and Germany, of a political power with a fundamentally national and grand European orientation.

During his visit to the Élysée Palace on 16 July, Edmund Stoiber, the anti-socialist candidate in the forthcoming German elections, made a formal commitment to relaunch the Franco-German "Carolingian Pole" in the direction of its greater European offensive mission. It is up to us, Germans and French," he declared on this occasion, "to promote the European integration project. He immediately added that "the Franco-German relationship is part of the raison d'état in Germany today". Edmund Stoiber had also declared, at the Élysée Palace, that as soon as he took power in Berlin, he would appoint Wolfgang Schauble - his current foreign policy chief – to take immediate operational charge of relaunching the Franco-German European pole and of the follow-up to this relaunch - under the terms of a new "Refounding Pact" – at the grand continental European level, Wolfgang Schauble should immediately receive the support, on the French side, of a counterpart appointed by Jacques Chirac for this purpose, with the same mission. This should be seen as the outline of a parallel Franco-German government.

France and Germany, said Wolfgang Schauble, want a stronger, more active, more efficient Europe. And this can only work if France and Germany play a leading role. This is not directed against others. It is a service to the whole of Europe. And also, which I think is very important: "We are fully in favour of a federal construction for Europe". For it is clear that the greater continental, "Eurasian" Europe can only be fundamentally federal, whether some people accept it or not.

The twofold operational mechanism of the Franco-German European revival will therefore have to be, on the one hand, that of the setting up of a European political-military ontological structure of total integration of national armies and, on the other hand, that of the decided, immediate and accelerated setting up of a Greater Europe, economic, industrial and technological, capable of facing up to the hegemonic designs of the United States at the planetary level where these are set.

Not to mention the great cultural battle that will have to be waged on a continental scale for the revolutionary reunion of Europe with its own civilisational identity, which was deliberately alienated during the period of the totalitarian impositions of Trotskyite socialism, which in recent years, having subversively seized political power throughout Europe, had attempted to modify the structures of consciousness and expression according to their own depraved, sub-human demands. Here, too, there is an immense amount of work to be done, for which we are responsible.

Thus the Franco-German "Refounding Pact" which will be instituted on the occasion of the 40th anniversary, in January 2003, of the de Gaulle-Adenauer "Treaty of the Elysium" will have the status of a revolutionary political-strategic restart of this "community of Franco-German destiny" which General de Gaulle had already defined, in 1963, as a "New World Revolution". For it is precisely this great-continental European "New World Revolution" that, after 40 years of subversive interruption, we must rediscover today, *returning to where its course had been broken.*

It is now known how the "Elysée Treaty" was sabotaged by the blackmail and shadowy coup de force perpetrated on the German Bundestag by Washington's special political services, and how Chancellor Konrad Adenauer was soon replaced at the head of the Federal Republic of Germany by the undercover American agent Ludwig Erhart, who was charged with "bringing everything back to "order", by deviously undoing the providential work undertaken and pursued by General de Gaulle and Chancellor Adenauer, the heroes of the salvation and deliverance of Europe. Who, from the founding pact, from the Franco-German "Carolingian Pact" had laid the suprahistoric foundations of the future Great Continental Europe, of the future geopolitical axis Paris-Berlin-Moscow-New Delhi-Tokyo.

To take up again, today, the things where they were interrupted, subversively, in the sixties, to take up again, forty years later, the metapolitical battle for the setting up of the Greater Europe starting from the Founding Pact of January 1963, updated, renewed, returned to its original provisions under the identity of a "Refounding Pact" destined to relaunch in depth and in a quite decisive way the revolutionary process of the grand-continental European imperial integration of the end, such will be, therefore, in January 2003, the mission of this one, the mission of the Franco-German "Refounding Pact" once again situated at the base - and at the vanguard – of the new historical – and supra-historical - emergence of the "Franco-German community of destiny.

Everything returns to the zone of supreme attention. Everything begins again. On the final ruins of non-being, being returns to the day. This will be the first great goal of the 'new' German post-Socialist national regime that emerges from the elections in September.

However, France and Germany, together in the next "Refounding Pact", must position themselves before the unavoidable, absolutely fundamental requirement, which is currently that of an over-activated, revolutionary, total presence of Vladimir Putin's "New Russia" within the great-continental European "community of destiny", of the imperial Great Europe of Eurasian dimensions and horizon. Without Russia, nothing is possible. Nothing will happen without Vladimir Putin's 'New Russia'", wrote one of our internal newsletters recently.

However, just three days after Edmund Stoiber's visit to Paris and the implementation, by him and Jacques Chirac, of the project of a Franco-German "Refounding Pact" for next January, Jacques Chirac went to Russia-to Sochi, in Crimea to meet Vladimir Putin, where the second act - after Edmund Stoiber's visit to the Élysée Palace on 16 July - of the total upheaval of the current Grand European political scene was to take place. An upheaval to which even the most astute political observers had given relatively little importance.

When in fact it was an event of seismic proportions. Strange, very strange misunderstanding. Suspicious even.

Nothing will happen without Vladimir Putin's New Russia

With the advent of the Trotskyite government of Lionel Jospin to power in Paris in 1995, France became the spearhead of the European Union's permanent anti-Russian offensive, an anti-Russian offensive carried out - in principle - over the so-called "colonialist war" that Moscow was allegedly waging in Chechnya through a "long series" of "crimes against human rights", etc.

Recently, the Trotskyite government of Lionel Jospin officially received in Paris high-level representatives of Islamic terrorist organisations and "ministers" of their puppet government. Day after day, for years, the French media - press, radio, television - had been engaged in a permanent campaign of misleading disinformation and provocation against Vladimir Putin's "New Russia". To the very limits of the intolerable.

However, as soon as he arrived in Sochi, Crimea, where he was expected by Vladimir Putin, Jacques Chirac reversed the movement, by declaring, in all clarity, that, for France, Russia's war in Chechnya was a "war for the integrity of the Russian national territory", and against the "Islamic terrorism of the Chechens", and, as such, that this war had the full approval, and the unreserved support of France.

The political consultations conducted in Paris by Edmund Stoiber and Jacques Chirac, at a double level, public and secret, even ultra-secret, had thus immediately borne fruit with regard to the 'French line' towards Russia.

Edmund Stoiber: "There can only be stability on our continent if Russia is politically, economically and culturally part of our community of destiny".

Thus, as a result of the new common political and strategic positions of France and Germany, which have come together through the renewal of their "Refounding Pact", the European Union as a whole will have to change its "general line" towards Russia. This is despite the fact that Italy, in the person of Silvio Berlusconi, had already taken clear and firm positions regarding the integration of Russia into Europe, an integration - according to Silvio

Berlusconi - that is fully fledged, both at the political and defence level, as well as at the economic and cultural levels.

But be careful. But beware. The current democratic liquidation of Trotskyist subversion in France and Germany under the disguise of social democracy does not represent the great revolutionary change in the national-revolutionary line that we expect. But the current anti-socialist-Trotskyist cleansing of the European interior nevertheless opens up certain prospects for the renewal and acceleration of the process of setting in motion the Greater Europe of imperial, "Eurasian" dimensions, while leaving - in principle – the way clear for a national-revolutionary reconsideration of the national line in the political ensemble of Western Europe, given that this great national reconsideration – which we are now calling for with all our might - is already present, already active, in Russia, with the rise to power of Vladimir Putin.

Thus, the revolutionary centre of gravity of the next "great history" of Europe is now located in Russia, which is therefore one step ahead of the fundamental political movement currently underway in Europe - the movement of the return of the nation to its being - but also of the future of this movement, which is not only destined to accomplish itself, but also to go beyond its own accomplishment. For it is not enough to make the Greatest Europe, we must make the Greatest Revolutionary Europe of the end, *the Imperium Ultimum*, the suprahistorical *Regnum* of the end, of the history beyond history. The ultimate horizon of our action is a transcendental horizon.

Today, Vladimir Putin is the only European political leader who has understood this and is proceeding accordingly. In the long term, inexorably. And that is why, at the moment, our eyes must be permanently turned towards Moscow, with all that this implies. For it is Vladimir Putin's Russia that is, today, the revolutionary centre of history and of the world, and that must polarise, as such, all our revolutionary wills.

The current lack of awareness in Europe - in Western Europe, but also in Eastern Europe - of Vladimir Putin and the "New Russia" he is in charge of, of what is really happening there, what is secretly taking shape there, what is being prepared in the shadows as well as in broad daylight, remains, strictly speaking, hallucinatory, and in the present state of affairs it would be more than useless to try to change anything. Only a very small number of us are aware of the true horizon within which the formidable lines of force of Russia's current hidden assumption are developing, and it is exclusively through our own geopolitical networks and secret spiritual work that we can circulate the news that reaches us through unmentionable, forbidden channels. Dangerous, sometimes.

In direct contact, from now on, with this "New Russia", will France and Germany of the "Refounding Pact" be ready to grasp in time the seismic rumour of the New Revolution that is preparing there in broad daylight? Everything is there, everything depends on it; before it is too late.

Will we be able to take on the decisive task of making known, as if by reverberation, what is happening in Russia, breaking through the barrage of relentless disinformation that opposes it? This is one of the fundamental strategic fronts that we must open to this end, and for which we bear full responsibility today. For ourselves, and for *history at its end.*

Faced with the US 'Planetary Empire', a new deflagration dialectic

Today, Greater Europe is a revolutionary geopolitical project that is in the process of becoming aware of itself. And so it is that the completed, final concept of a "Greater Europe" to come, of a "Eurasian" horizon and predestination, is not only justified by its own future, which is beginning to assert itself, following the offensive geopolitical line of the transcontinental axis Paris-Berlin-Moscow-New Delhi-Tokyo, from one end of the "Great Continent" to the other, from the "Atlantic to the Pacific". But that it is also, and above all, justified against the "Planetary Empire of the United States" which is already there, which is already acting on the level of its current imperial plans, of its vast planetary politico-strategic action already underway.

At present, it is in *a* state of *incompleteness* that "Greater Europe" defines itself in relation to itself, or recognises itself, while at the same time it opposes the "American Planetary Empire", which is in *a* state of *completion,* and acts as such. This planetary geopolitics opposing *defensive incompleteness to offensive completion* represents a new conflagration dialectic, the final outcome of which will decide the fate of current world history and the "other world" that it will bring forward.

For let us not delude ourselves. At the present time, Washington has definitively thrown off the mask, or masks, under which, since the end of the last war, the United States had been accustomed to conceal the imperial aims of its foreign policy. Already with the concept of the "new world order" launched by George Bush senior, which Washington intended to install and ensure that it was maintained, Washington had "announced the colour". Bill Clinton in his turn used the expression "Planetary Superpower of the United States" and today, George W. Bush is personally sponsoring the Republican geopolitical doctrines that openly advance the concept of a "Planetary Empire of the United States" and define the political-strategic, economic and cultural lines of force of the new American imperial line.

So the Republican columnist Charles Krauthammer recently wrote in the *Washington Post:* 'The reality is that no nation has been so culturally, economically, technologically and militarily dominant since the Roman Empire', referring, of course, to the United States, whose planetary destiny he will note. But the real doctrinaire of Washington's new imperial designs is Robert D. Kaplan, an advisor to the CIA and the Pentagon, as well as to

President George W. Bush personally. In a recent book, *Warrior Politics*, Random House, New York 2001, Robert D. Kaplan urges the United States to embrace its own imperial destiny, even if it means ignoring democratic dogma: "It is an imperial principle that defines the world today. The Pentagon has troops in every corner of the world, American interests are global, Washington pulls the strings everywhere. The United States has no colonies, but in the end it is at the centre of a much more classical empire than it wants to admit. Like Rome, Venice or the British Empire in their time, it is the organising principle of the contemporary world. It is the power that drives the planet forward, the force that defines equilibrium and curbs anarchy. And he added, suggesting dark days for 'democracy': 'How far should we tolerate disorder? Should the West sacrifice its freedom to ensure its own survival? ''.

All this implies that, at the present time, the "Planetary Superpower of the United States" represents the only truly decisive and total world political power, the "final power". That the United States is already engaged in the one-way street of a planetary imperial destiny, for which it accepts the burden.

In fact, everyone is totally wrong about George W. Bush and the real reasons why he became President of the United States; for there was a conspiracy. It is important to know that the Republican Party is not a "unitary party" at all, but, on the contrary, a ganglionic arrangement of particular "power groups"; and that the Republican "power group" that George W. Bush represents is ultra-minority; obeying an occultist, uncompromising and offensive, totalitarian, "imperial" "inner doctrine"; with secret "ultimate objectives", of a "superhuman" nature. A "superior conspiratorial cell".

In its depths, which are most forbidden to external attention, the current American central power is, in reality, an essentially occult power, based on an offensive planetary strategy and relying, within the current Republican administration, on small decision-making groups acting exclusively in the shadows, which secretly - and entirely - duplicate the existing apparatus of the political-administrative power of the State. This is, moreover, a political modality that has always been specific to the Republican Party. And it has recently reached its own paroxysm (see the nocturnal background of "September 11, 2001").

Despite the sum of the reasons put forward by Washington in this regard, it is still impossible to understand why the United States is so relentless against Saddam Hussein's Iraq (all the accusations made by Washington are obviously false and fabricated). There is an impenetrable, "irreducible" mystery here, the key to which should perhaps be sought in a "mystical", "occultist" direction, in relation to Iraq's location in the space of ancient Mesopotamian, magical and theurgic civilisations, where supra-temporal influences secretly manifest themselves. And also, perhaps, in the singularly unavowable para-religious convictions of the 'small group of initiates' constituting the occult 'summit group' of the Republican Party of which George W. Bush is today the visible (but, at the same time, also covert) representative.

Taking the side of Iraq is taking the side of Europe

In any case, it is perfectly certain that, from now on, the "hour of truth" will not be long in coming. It will be time for the US to attack Iraq, with or without UN support. But, writes Robert D. Kaplan, the White House and the Pentagon "persist in believing that the Iraqi adventure would be purely military; the real question is what Turkey, Iran, Saudi Arabia and Syria will do after Saddam Hussein is eliminated".

However, despite Robert D. Kaplan's questioning, now the White House and the Pentagon will not back down.

It is in relation to the offensive intervention of the United States in Iraq that Europe, by opposing it, will now have to take its new bearings, to determine the "new line" of its own global policy. With perhaps - but can we really hope for it - France, Germany and Russia committed to the front line in the common European action of refusal to the American aggression?

However, it is hard to believe that, in the current world situation, Jacques Chirac and Edmund Stoiber could formally oppose Washington's intervention in Iraq, despite the strong feelings of the French and German nations against this blatant US aggression.

But, at the same time, it is here that the fundamental politico-strategic mission of the European "geopolitical groups" of great-continental, "Eurasian" line will appear, whose revolutionary mobilisation could arouse, organise and strengthen more and more the oppositional agitation of the European masses against the American aggression, thus doubling the "official line" of Paris and Berlin by a vast movement of resistance expressing the true will of the European peoples. And thus beginning the final, irreversible process of the "great awakening", of the great European continental liberation from the planetary imperialism of the United States in action. For, in the end, the will to freedom of the European peoples cannot fail to prevail over the tactical hesitations of their "democratic" governments of circumstance, and all the more so since these governments themselves secretly harbour the same deep vital convictions, the same decisive choices of a new European grand-continental destiny. For non-being cannot indefinitely block the emergence of being.

And this revolutionary setting in motion of the European peoples being at the same time supported, and as it were exacerbated, by the fundamental metapolitical pole of Russia, the "liberated base" in the East of the Greater Europe, whose opposition to the American aggression against Iraq will serve as a rear front of grand-continental reverberation to the vast European anti-American revolutionary movement on the march, while also dragging India and Japan into it, and thus making the transcontinental geopolitical axis Paris-Berlin-Moscow-New Delhi-Tokyo immediately effective.

Thus, the US intervention in Iraq risks being ultimately fatal to the ongoing plans of US global imperialism, the pitfall that will derail the "grand design" of the "higher conspiracy cell" secretly installed in the White House, and which follows "the orders of the Crucified Serpent on the T". For we are there, indeed, even if we refuse to believe it. Once again, it is not the United States that we have to fear, but what stands behind the United States.

The "parallel hierarchies" of Greater Europe

George Lukacs said: "Only he who has the vocation and the will to bring the future into being can see the concrete truth of the present". It was during the three historic days between 16 and 19 July that the Greater Europe came to be constituted: on 16 July, in Paris, with the agreements – and the "confidential parts" of them – between Jacques Chirac and Edmund Stoiber on the Franco-German "Refounding Pact", which was to take up the terms of the de Gaulle-Adenauer "Treaty of the Elysium" in January 2003, on the 40th anniversary of the latter, three days later, on 19 July, with the meeting between Jacques Chirac and Vladimir Putin, in Sochi, in Crimea, which was to mark the de facto adhesion of Vladimir Putin's "New Russk" to what Wolfgang Schäuble calls the "hard core" of the current European Union. It is an adherence in principle, but definitive. For it is a question of a new "iron pact", word given against word received.

The Paris-Berlin-Moscow axis, which we have been calling for in recent times, has now been assembled and, with the Paris-Berlin-Moscow geopolitical axis, the largest continental Europe with a Eurasian horizon and predestination has been born.

A politico-historical upheaval with absolutely decisive consequences, in which the founding will of Jacques Chirac, Edmund Stoiber and Vladimir Putin was to affirm the revolutionary emergence of a now irrevocable imperial Great European commitment, a Great European commitment made possible by the elimination of Trotskyite socialism from power in France and Germany, and not only in France and Germany but also in the political space of the whole of Western Europe. Now other times are coming".

Now, what will have been constituted in this way, in principle, at the level of the democratic political action of the European States concerned, and which will follow, from now on, the developments foreseen by the process already underway, must very imperatively be at the same time taken up and reinforced, urgently reconsidered in a grand-continental revolutionary horizon, by the living forces of the European nations which have arrived, at present, at the crossroads of their final suprahistory.

To double, therefore, the new political situation created by the setting up of the Paris-Berlin-Moscow axis, by a series of initiatives destined to give birth to the "parallel hierarchies" of a new European revolutionary political-administrative reality, is the task that it is incumbent upon us to make our own at the present time.

It seems to me that there should be four such initiatives, and that we should immediately take action to impose their ontological grid on the events already underway.

(1) A supranational organisation called the "France-Germany-Russia Geopolitical Community", the basic ideological foundation of the future Greater Continental Europe, which is to act as a sort of "provisional government" of Greater Europe, acting in the shadows, in a semi-clandestine manner.

(2) A supranational politico-strategic structure, integrating, as a matter of priority, all the European "geopolitical groups" into an active organisation intended to constitute a sort of front-line grand European "Kominforrn".

(3) A revolutionary supranational "counter-strategic intelligence" organisation, employing, sectorally, certain "special powers". Raymond Abellio: ''The police use of these powers is the essence of metapolitics''.

(4) A vanguard body to promote the birth and subsequent unfolding of a new great European continental culture to fill the terrifying cultural vacuum of the last fifty years of European history.

It is the Spirit that takes power, and this power is the Spirit, wrote Georges Soulès in his great book, published in *J943, La fin du nihilisme, a* prophetic book if ever there was one.

GERMANY, AND THE ULTIMATE FATE OF EUROPE

The failure of the anti-Socialist coalition led by Edmund Stoiber in the German elections last September certainly appears, in principle, to be a major catastrophe for the forward march of the Greater Continental Europe of national-revolutionary line; but, in reality, things may well be different; and even, in the final analysis, the very opposite of what it would seem to be expected. In active revolutionary politics, it is in fact not the actual situations that count, but their dialectical commitments governing the subterranean tension that constantly pushes them forward, that constantly pushes them to self-depassment.

Firstly, it is an extremely relative failure for Edmund Stoiber, because the government coalition of Socialists and Greens only won by an almost fictitious majority of two seats at the most, and Edmund Stoiber's anti-Socialist National Front therefore currently has practically the same majority as that of Gerhard Schröder's anti-nationalist Socialist coalition and its 'red-green' allies; Finally, it is already obvious that Joschka Fischer's "red-greens" won last September, because if only Gerhard Schröder's Socialist-Trotskyites and Edmund Stoiber's National Front had been in the running, it would have been the latter who would have won the elections and restored order in Germany.

Fate thus played a negative role through the unexpected expansion of Joschka Fisher's so-called "ecologist" party, which benefited, in a circumstantial and subversive manner - artificially inflating its field strength by massive contributions, by order, from leftists and excommunists - from a fairly significant electoral growth. For, let us remember, what is the ecologist party, Joschka Fisher's "red-greens", if not an organisation for the reception, operational supervision and concealed promotion of the most actively extremist, anti-national and anti-European ultra-leftist and Trotskyist elements?

By means of its current ecological cover-ups, the German revolutionary extreme left has thus secured a decisive political-strategic base in the new government majority that emerged from the highly dubious elections last September. But will Gerhard Schröder let it happen? By acting, Joschka Fisher will reveal his positions and, by the same token, force Gerhard Schröder to take counter-action. The worm is in the fruit.

For the socialist-Trotskyist power of Gerhard Schröder, which is currently back in power, is in a situation of fundamental destabilisation, permanently subject to active contradiction and to the political pressure of the 'other majority', the 'national majority' of Edmund Stoiber. And this while, within the Socialist-Trotskyist-Ecological coalition that has been returned to power, the operational political centre of gravity of the whole has shifted from the positions of Gerhard Schröder's Socialist-Trotskyist majority to the minority led by Joschka Fisher and his so-called ecological penetration and control structures (which in reality are of a completely different order).

On the other hand, and in any case, the major fundamental political choices of Germany are more or less safeguarded, which are the choices concerning, on the one hand, the opposition - relative, all things considered - to the policy of globalist interference of the United States and more particularly in Iraq, currently under the threat of a decisive politico-strategic action from Washington and, on the other hand, open, even unconditional support for the ongoing process of integrating Vladimir Putin's "New Russia" into the larger continental, "Eurasian", "imperial", "final" Europe. A process that is now inescapable.

The pro-American and anti-Russian shenanigans of Joschka Fisher and the blackmailing minority of the "Red-Greens" will certainly now be working to undermine - and with increasing intensity - the opposing positions of the ruling Socialist-Trotskyist majority in Berlin, to which he himself also belongs; things are not easy in this respect. And already, by calling into the government Wolfgang Clement, to whom he entrusted the key ministries - or rather the super-ministry - of Economy and Labour, enriched with the "service of fundamental economic policy and analysis", Gerhard Schröder has just lit a sizeable counter-fire intended to block the globalist pretensions of Joschka Fisher and those of his action group. He has not failed to "restore" German-American relations by announcing his next visit to Washington, while reinforcing the subversive political-social line of his party. Thus, the *Frankfurter Allgemeine Zeitung* accuses Joschka Fisher's "red-greens" of "carrying out an ideological attack on everything that can be considered as traditional values, especially the family in the classical sense".

The current political regime in Berlin, which emerged from last September's elections, is in fact a "non-regime", available to all solicitations, to all blackmail, to all forceful shaking: the best ground for the implementation of a great counter-strategy intended to obtain its eventual overthrow. A definitive and total overthrow, the critical point of which is somewhere in the next two years, and probably much closer still. It seems to me that it is now a certainty that Edmund Stoiber and his political staff will not miss the opportunity when it comes, especially since a real opportunity does not come by itself, it is *provoked*.

However, the disaster - for, whatever one may say, it was a disaster - of the German elections last September, has brought back into the light of day, suddenly, reasons for its emergence which lie elsewhere, and are of a quite different order than those of the extremely relative failure of the anti-socialist national forces in competition with the anti-national socialist conspiracy in place. It is nothing less than a certain disaster of the German national substance itself, indeed - in addition - of the historical destiny of present and future Germany, of the "German idea" itself, to use a fashionable ex-pressure in recent times in political debates across the Rhine, employed even by Gerhard Schröder.

Facing a certain historical disaster of Germany; its causes, and ways of recovery

There is no denying it: last September, half of Germany freely voted against Germany. How was it possible for half of Germany to take up - freely - positions that manifest such an ultimate degree of political alienation, at once incomprehensible and quite certain, even active, the suicidal alienation of an unconsciously suicidal people?

A kind of mysterious 'German disease' has thus been brought to the surface, asserting itself with dismaying force. This evil, which in its depths represents a terrible disease of death, is not new. But at least we have been given the opportunity to try, once and for all, to unclog the fatal abscess, to surprise and reveal the work of ontological alienation, historical resignation and vital decay that is thus subterraneanly in action. An absolutely decisive political battle is thus announced to our awakened attention; a battle that we must engage without further delay.

The immense sacrifices made in the recent past by the German people, who stood up in their entirety against the foreign invaders to defend the very being and the political and historical integrity of Europe as a whole, of the encircled Europe, cannot fail to be recognised in the end, for the sacrifice of blood remains, counts for ever. No other European people, with the exception of the Russians, has been led to make such supra-heroic, supra-human sacrifices of life, such sacrifices of blood. This means that today, whether it recognises it or not, Europe as a whole has contracted an inescapable ontological debt to Germany - and to Russia - on which the abysmal foundations of the future great-continental Europe, of the "ultimate" imperial Europe, must be built.

Thus, Germany's current political resignation, whether conscious or unconscious, represents a tragic tear, which deeply wounds all the peoples of Europe and to which the peoples of Europe must respond together, face up to it in order to reduce its consequences and present effects, totally erase the negative affirmation of the situation thus newly created, and even the memory of it, as if nothing had happened.

For more than half a century the subversive anti-European conspiracy of democratic terror carried out in continuity by the "Planetary Superpower of the United States" has been working to devastate the historical consciousness of the German people, to try to keep them out of active history, to turn them into a non-people afflicted with a phantasmatic political nonconsciousness and non-destiny: the present disaster of German national consciousness is only the direct result of this concerted work of alienation, determined to prevent Germany and thus Europe as a whole - the greater imperial Europe - from finding itself again, in the terms of a new, grand-continental and ultimately planetary revolutionary destiny.

Subjected for more than fifty years to the formidable deconstituting pressure of the anti-national conspiracy disguised as an "anti-totalitarian struggle", which it had taken under its control just as, subsequently, it had taken under its control the whole of Western Europe with the exception of Gaullist France, it is therefore not so incomprehensible that, In the end, the German people - or at least a good part of them - would have yielded to the profound political alienation that had been forcibly instilled in them, and with the precise aim of preventing them from finding themselves beyond the politico-historical fracture line represented by the highly symbolic, "apocalyptic" defeat of 1945.

For it was the long, hallucinatory procession of victims of the mental mutilation of Germany pursued for more than fifty years which, last September, constituted the dazed masses of voters for the party of Anti-Germany, the purposely rendered unconscious masses of voters for the party of Trotskyite social democracy and the underground resistance of its hidden proponents to the now inevitable national-revolutionary advent of the Greater Continental Europe. Last September, Germany thus paid the real price for the long anti-national alienation to which the German people had been subjected, the terrible price of their subjection to the totalitarian terror of social democracy, and its other side, liberal democracy, *vae victis*. Social democracy, liberal democracy, which had only ever been the infrastructures of control and active supervision of the democratic terror imposed by the "Planetary Superpower of the United States" and by the obscure powers that stand behind it, today as in the past.

In his courageous and visionary trips to Germany shortly after the end of the last war, General de Gaulle - as he himself says in his *Memoirs* - had envisaged the immediate restoration of Germany's position in Europe, so that the Franco-German "Carolingian Pole" could immediately restart the interrupted history of Europe, laying the political and historical foundations for the future Greater Continental Europe.

Charles de Gaulle, *Memoirs:* ''Freiburg, in the Black Forest, groups together to receive de Gaulle all that is representative of the regions occupied by us on the right bank of the Rhine. On October 4, Dr. Wohleb introduces me to the personalities of Baden. On the morning of the 5th, Mr. Carlo Schmitt introduced those from Württemberg. The Archbishop of Freiburg, Mgr Grœber, as well as Mgr Fisher of the diocese of Rotthausen, are among the visitors. Then, these men of quality, trembling with goodwill, gathered to hear me evoke "the links that once brought together the French and the Germans of the South and that must now be rekindled" to serve to build "our Europe, and our West".

And we also remember that during one of his press conferences, General de Gaulle declared, already in 1949: *"I say that Europe must be built on the basis of an agreement between the French and the Germans. Once Europe is built on this basis, we can then turn to Russia. Then we can try, once and for all, to build the whole of Europe with Russia too, even if it changes its regime. That is the programme of true Europeans. That is mine.*

Now, Russia, finally freed from the bloody nightmare of Soviet communism and, by freeing itself - by self-liberation – from the subversive dominations of democratic totalitarianism – of Trotskyite social democracy, and of liberal democracy - Europe, Europe, the ''Greater Europe'' – is in the process of being able to claim to recover its former unity, its own destiny and its ultimate, suprahistorical, and the greatest, its ''eschatological'', ''imperial'' missions.

In recent years, Europe, country by country - Portugal, Spain, Italy, France, Serbia, Austria, the Netherlands - has freed itself from the subversive grip of the existing socialist-Trotskyist conspiracy, with only Germany and Belgium still missing. Today, as we have just seen, Germany itself came very close to joining the group of European countries that have already regained their freedom and are ready to embark on the path of a new great continental destiny.

However, can the accidental political failure of a large section of the German people, who were blindly led to vote against themselves, prevent what needs to be done from finally being done? No, that is no longer possible at all. Provided that, on our side, and relying in force on the conscious part – the "already mentally liberated" part – of the German people, we commit ourselves, on our side, to do everything that needs to be done, in terms of agitation and advanced offensive counter-propaganda, to liberate Germany from the negative and alienating grip of the anti-national and anti-European conspiracy, which still holds it more or less captive to its political and mental framing apparatus, and to put it in a position to do so on its own.

The process of national liberation in Germany, which began in earnest with the elections last September, must now be brought to its final, *decisive* conclusion. A national liberation which Germany will achieve by relying on both France and Russia, so that the transcontinental Paris-Berlin-Moscow axis can come into being before it is too late.

Thus, there are several ways that could facilitate - or even lead to the success of – the ongoing process of national liberation in Germany, including, among others – and probably above all – that of an internal overthrow of the centre of gravity of the current socialist-Trotskyist regime in Berlin, an overthrow that can be expected to occur in favour of the renewal, scheduled for January 2003 – its 40th anniversary - of the Gaulle-Adenauer "Élysée Treaty". This renewal can already be envisaged in the revolutionary form of a Franco-German "Refounding Pact", a "Refounding Pact" wanted by Jacques Chirac and supported by Vladimir Putin, which, by relying fully on Russia, would relaunch the process of setting in motion the Greater Europe from the Paris-Berlin-Moscow axis.

Indeed, it would be difficult to imagine Jacques Chirac and Vladimir Putin being fully committed to the final construction of the Paris-Berlin-Moscow axis alongside a Germany whose current political regime is in total contradiction with the national orientation of Europe as a whole: Germany's domestic political situation must therefore change of its own accord, and this change can only be the result of a fundamental change of consciousness, of an irrevocable return of Germany to its own national consciousness from the depths and to its own destiny, its previous destiny; its supra-temporal destiny.

The Putin Directive

In his great speech in German on 25 September 2001 in Berlin before the full Bundestag, President Vladimir Putin not only declared in the most formal way that Russia – his "New Russia" – was ready to consider European integration on the economic, military and cultural levels, but he also intervened, with all his political authority, to urge the German people to stop blaming themselves, to stop secretly inflicting moral penance on themselves for faults from a bygone era, which prevents them from fully facing up to their real political tasks today in Europe and the world. And in doing so, Vladimir Putin was also forcefully denouncing the harmful action of certain "German intellectuals" who were consciously cultivating the incapacitating myth of "German guilt" in a destabilising and subversive manner, which no longer had any reason to exist today. Vladimir Putin's political genius had thus grasped that the fundamental problem, that the dramatic problem of today's Germany was above all a problem of consciousness, a problem of self-liberation, and of the revolutionary affirmation of a new German consciousness and a new German destiny. Now, it is absolutely necessary to agree on this, and this is what we ourselves never stop saying, and it is also the final objective of the overall political-strategic action, of grand-continental European dimensions, that the "geopolitical groups" of ours must assume today in their present struggle for the setting in motion of the transcontinental axis Paris-Berlin-Moscow, on which, from now on, everything definitely depends.

Thus we fully endorse the "Putin Directive" concerning the struggle for the national liberation of the present German consciousness from the negative grip of a world conspiracy with occult motives, a conspiracy bent on blocking the ongoing political advent of the Greater Europe, of which Germany is, today as in the past, the hub around which France and Germany, as well as the European countries as a whole, must now mobilise in order to gain revolutionary access to the line of final imperial predestination which has *always been* theirs, in history and beyond history. The line of a new Western passage from non-being to being, the very line of our ultimate and supreme polar predestination.

There is certainly not much time left, but, on the other hand, the tragic hour of the agitating minorities has returned. The planned movement of in-depth agitation and reversal of the current German consciousness clearly defines the issue that will decide the final fate of Greater Europe: this shows the extreme importance of the overall politico-strategic action of the "geopolitical groups" in the final orientation of the choices that must bring Germany back, once again, to a new and total consciousness of its own being and of its renewed destiny.

TURKEY, THE VANGUARD OF THE SECRET ACTION OF AL QAEDA IN EUROPE

Millions of Muslims around the world are waiting for Turkey to wake up and rise up.

Recep Tayyip Erdogan

The Balkans are already Islamic, Spain has been for centuries and will be again, as well as Hungary and all of Central Europe. In ten years, Germany will be Islamised, as will France. The whole of Europe will be Islamic before the end of the century. Know this.

The political leader of an underground Islamist group in the Paris suburbs.

For me, Turkey's entry into the European Union would be the end of it.

Valéry Giscard d'Estaing

The fact that one stands, as we do, totally on the side of the Palestinian and Iraqi peoples currently threatened with genocide by the "globalist conspiracy" of the United States and what stands behind it, does not mean that one should be any less totally against the great subversive designs of fundamentalist Islam in action. And it cannot be denied that of all the European heads of state currently in office Silvio Berlusconi is the only one who, in the name of Italy, has said everything that needs to be said about Fundamentalist Islam, nor that on every occasion he has openly taken the side of recalling and supporting the inescapable necessity of the integration of Vladimir Putin's new Russia as a full political, military, economic and cultural member of the European Union.

Recent events, decisive in their affirmation and in their immediate consequences, have just confirmed in a dramatic way the extreme urgency of all the politico-strategic options to be made ours: against the new subversive interferences in the process of being specified on the part of Fundamentalist Islamism through its advances in Turkey, and against the pro-Islamist internal complicities within the European Union. What are these recent events? First and foremost, Turkey's shift - for the time being still somewhat hidden - towards fundamentalist Islamism through the coming to power in Ankara of

Recep Tayyip Erdogan's AKP, the "Justice and Development Party", and the entry, therefore, of Turkey into the sphere of influence of Osama Bin Laden's Al-Qaeda. And, by the same token, the extraordinary danger posed to the whole of the European continent by the current plans to admit Turkey to the European Union, which is said to be quite possible. It is up to us to make it impossible.

Important things always happen in the shadows, today as in the past. It is high time we realised this, for our very survival depends on it.

A political Hiroshima occurred in Europe on 3 November that no one seems to have noticed yet: the conspiratorial takeover of power in Ankara by the visible and invisible supporters of Recep Tayyip Erdogan's so-called "moderate Islamist" party, carried out under false democratic pretenses. In reality, it was a "final" subversive operation, absolutely decisive, on a continental European scale, carried out in the shadows, in direct relation with Osama Bin Laden's global Islamist conspiracy organisation, Al-Qaeda.

Having seized, when he was only mayor of Constantinople, the diversionary appellation of so-called "moderate Islam", Recep Tayyip Erdogan, a secretive and essentially ambiguous figure, has always promoted, practised and confidentially represented the hardest underground line of extremist and very actively conspiratorial Islam, belonging to the Panturkic movement engaged in the long subversive process that finally led to the seizure of total political power on 3 November last.

For, with the prospect of Turkey's future admission to the European Union, the overall strategic plans of the global Islamist subversion currently represented by Al-Qaeda have been abruptly changed: the strategic-political centre of gravity of revolutionary Islamist action has been shifted from Asia to Europe, and Turkey has become the operational hub of this change. From now on, everything will take place in Turkey.

This is, in fact, a total change in the ''geopolitical line'' of Al-Qaeda, whose fundamental strategic objective appears to be that of engaging in the battle for the final Islamic investissent of the entire European geopolitical interior space: Western Europe, Eastern Europe and Russia. Europe is thus to be declared a 'holy war zone', a new space for the Islamist 'Grand Jihad' in action towards the realisation of the 'Final Khalifate', ultimately including the United States itself.

The fundamental base of implantation, departure and politico-strategic deployment of future Islamic offensives in Europe will thus be located in South-East Europe, starting from Turkey and the European Islamist territories of Albania, Bosnia, Kosovo and Macedonia, as well as, at the same time, within each European country that includes a large Islamic colony. Among them, Germany and France.

What could be more normal than for a German Islamist to want to live in an Islamic Germany one day", was the headline in the Turkish press in Berlin in recent days.

The concept of 'Islamic Germany' has therefore just been launched: the concept of 'Islamic Europe' will soon be discussed.

In this respect, it should not be forgotten that Osama Bin Laden has already gone to "inspect" the Islamic settlements in Albania and Bosnia, and that, according to the secret services in Belgrade, he would have gone clandestinely as far as Germany, particularly Berlin.

Europe has thus been chosen as the future battlefield of Islam's great holy war, its "Grand Jihad" of the coming years. The iron dice of a new dramatic destiny for Europe have been thrown.

Leaving the fighting in Asia to the care of his clandestine proxies, Mullah Omar and Abdel Azim-Al-Muhajar, Osama Bin Laden and the covert Al-Qaeda infrastructure will soon move somewhere in South-East Europe, from where the revolutionary offensive operations and terrorist actions of the 'Islamic International' engaged in the subversive investment and ultimate political conquest of mainland Europe will be directed.

At the same time, Russia's southern flank - the chain of former Soviet Islamic republics – being Turkey's reserved domain – which, by the way, they already are - will see Turkey's less and less clandestine interference intensify to the maximum, while Chechnya will look, in this case, in relation to the current European-wide Islamic offensive ventures, like the Spanish national war on the eve of the last world war.

Either congenital cretinism of an irremediably destitute civilization, or concerted high treason, or both together, it is also the precise moment when all the current democratic governments of the European Union, as well as all the major European press and media - of the left and the right - are more than ever determined to support the pro-Islamist positions of the irresponsible governments in place, such as *Le Figaro, Le Monde, Le Courrier International*, etc. This is not only with regard to the issue of the right to freedom of expression, but also with regard to the right to a fair trial. This is not only the case with regard to the issue of Turkey's admission to the European Union, but also and above all by maintaining an increasingly exacerbated climate of open hostility, and very deliberately provocative, towards the counter-terrorist commitments of Vladimir Putin's Russia in Chechnya, where Moscow's armed forces are heroically fighting, in the vanguard of beleaguered Europe, Chechen Islamism at the behest of its sponsors in the shadow of Osama Bin Laden's line.

If nothing is done to put an abrupt stop to this suicidal state of affairs, to make Europe as a whole aware of the in-depth political-strategic investment plans being pursued towards it by the occult leaders of the "Islamic

International", it will soon - very soon - be too late to really try to contain and repress the devastating outpouring of the Islamic masses already on the march, following the programmes planned for this purpose.

For it is now certain that the "Islamic International" conspiratorially led by Osama Bin Laden has already declared a religious and racial war, a total political-historical war on Europe, and that if it does not mobilise counter-offensively as a matter of urgency, Europe will disappear as such from the history of the world: the obstinate, pathological, abysmal work of Islam for the conquest and subjugation of Europe, which has been going on unceasingly for centuries, is very likely this time to achieve its ultimate ends.

What we have to bear in mind above all is the fact that the fundamental Islamist offensive against Europe will not come from outside, but from within our own lines, that the worm is already in the fruit.

It is the United States and Israel that are doing everything to forcefully support Turkey, and it is the socialist-Trotskyite regime of Gerhard Schröder and Joschka Fisher in Germany that is now pushing with more than a little suspicion for Turkey's admission to the European Union.

We must therefore use every means to combat the subversive team of traitors currently in power in Berlin, to bring about the rapid overthrow of the Socialist-Trotskyist regime of Gerhard Schröder and Joschka Fisher and its replacement by the German and European National Front of Edmund Stoiber and his counter-strategic coalition for the renewal of Germany's innermost being and its future destiny.

Thus, in recent days, the *Welt am Sonntag* invited Germans to rise up against the socialist-Trotskyist conspiracy currently in power in Berlin, to demonstrate against '*the former Sixties at the top in the universities, the media, and finally in the government*'.

For the rest of us, these are vital battles, battles for the ultimate survival of all that we are.

For Turkey, fundamentally subservient to the politico-strategic interests of the United States and the globalist conspiracy pushed forward by the latter, while assuming in continuity the revolutionary mission of supporting, exacerbating the religious uprising on the southern flank of Russia, in the former Soviet Muslim republics, will now have to serve as the strategic continental base for the US enterprise of devastation and control over Iraq and thus over the whole of the Middle East, just as it had also served as a covert strategic base during the previous US action of external politico-military interference in the South-East of the European continent.

Now, not only should the European Union in no way subscribe to the project of admitting Turkey into its midst, but it has now become certain that it is precisely against Turkey that the new European Empire, mobilised around the Paris-Berlin-Moscow axis, is going to have to undertake its first major counter-strategic action of continental dimensions: If, according to the imperial dialectic of the Paris-Berlin-Moscow axis, Russia is now an integral part of the Greater Europe, the European Union, in exchange, cannot fail to fully embrace the first fundamental offensive political-strategic thesis of Vladimir Putin's "New Russia", namely the thesis of the necessary liberation - for higher, transcendental reasons - of Constantinople, and of the liberation of the Hagia Sophia, the common, predestined goal of the new great European history to come according to its ultimate eschatological requirements.

Thus, not only must Europe absolutely refuse to admit Turkey into its midst, but it must also commit itself, in a total and decisive manner, to fight to drive Turkey out of the European area. Is this clear?

Today, the age-old enemy is back, secretly preparing its 'final assault'. For that is what it is all about.

The overall strategy of Moscow's ongoing, over-the-top anti-terrorist counter-offensive in Chechnya is explained by the fact that if the Chechen bolt were to break, the Turkish-backed Islamist terrorist uprising - of which Recep Tayyip Erdogan was speaking - would surely set fire to Russia's entire southern flank of the Eurasian 'Great Continent'.

Thus, the European Union must urgently understand that the vanguard struggle pursued by Moscow in Chechnya against Wahabi revolutionary Islamism is also, and fundamentally, its own struggle against the offensive designs of Fundamentalist Islamism determined to carry the Jihad – its "holy war of conquest", or, as they say, "reconquest" – to the very heart of Europe. And that, understanding this, the European Union acts accordingly, whatever the immediate conditions, demands and burdens.

By attacking Iraq, the United States is attacking - and, it is to be feared, knowingly - the last anti-Islamist Arab national-revolutionary stronghold, not hesitating to set off a huge anti-Western Islamist revolutionary conflagration all along the Eurasian Islamic belt from the Maghreb to Indonesia, as well as within the European Islamic communities. The situation could not be more paradoxical.

Yielding to the subterranean pressures of the extremist pro-Israeli lobby acting from within the United States, the Protestant 'secret societies' of the 'illuminists' currently in power in Washington are preparing to unleash a revolutionary Islamist holocaust of planetary dimensions which they imagine will serve the global imperialist designs of their occult masters, whose identity is unmentionable, secretly committed to the service of non-being and chaos, to the service of the 'Islamic', they imagine, will serve the world imperialist designs of their occult masters, with an unavowable identity, secretly committed to the service of non-being and chaos, to the service of the abysmal "Mystery of Iniquity" of which Saint Paul speaks in his "Apocalyptic Epistle", in his 2nd Epistle to the Thessalonians (Th. II, 3–10).

For the Paris-Berlin-Moscow axis the time has come to act, and to act immediately. Containing, neutralising and rolling back the revolutionary Islam that has just seized total political power in Turkey with Recep Tayyip Erdogan is now a matter of life and death. Just as it is a matter of life and death to oppose by all means Washington's subversive planetary war against the anti-Islamist national-revolutionary fortress of Iraq. For only the Paris-Berlin-Moscow axis can still oppose the immense apocalyptic outburst planned - and already set in motion - by the secret negative and chaotic forces mobilising today the reversed stakes of the US subversive enterprise against Iraq, which are fanning and supporting what they at the same time pretend to fight. These *reversed stakes* mean that the United States is now attacking Iraq - in an enterprise that it defines as essentially directed against revolutionary Islamist terrorism in its global dimensions - without realising that, by doing so, it is pushing for the general conflagration of revolutionary Islamism throughout the world, thus working against its own avowed objectives. But do we know what their real objectives are, their hidden and even more than hidden objectives?

Moreover, as some of our 'secret teachings' affirm, it is precisely in order to reach this point that Islam was created in the seventh century to act in history in a long-term perspective. In any case, the 'ultimate times' are coming.

But aren't we ourselves "men of the ultimate times"? Isn't that why we were made the way we are, whether we know it or not? Designed so that we can face these "ultimate times" precisely?

The current return of Fundamentalist Islam to the level of planetary political action constitutes one of the most revealing 'signs of the times', as does the return of Russia to its highest suprahistorical, 'eschatological' destiny: the 'times of return' are also the 'times of the end', always. But they are also the times of "great beginnings".

At the present time, the active politico-strategic forces of the Greater Final Europe have to fight, to confront on at least five fronts of open, total political warfare: on the double home front of Islamic revolutionary action in European territory, at the same time as on the home front also of its clashes with Trotskyite and social-democratic subversion underground everywhere at work; against the subversion, too, of European domestic subjugations to the US globalist conspiracy in action; against the external lines of Fundamentalist Islam in its permanent offensive undertakings, and against - finally - the action carried out, at the level of clashes, open antagonisms, decisive tests of strength, more and more frontal, by the United States directly against the Greatest imperial Europe of the end.

This permanent political war on multiple fronts, waged against a chaotic backdrop, is, it seems to me, the burning cipher, which says it all, of these 'ultimate times' that are ours.

VLADIMIR PUTIN, IN THE ESCHATOLOGICAL PERSPECTIVE OF THE "THIRD ROME": THE MAN OF THE KREMLIN, THE MAN OF THE FINAL BATTLES

The time of conspiracies

We are living in times of all conspiracies, all current 'great politics' – be it national or global, 'planetary' – appears to be, fundamentally, a conspiratorial politics. Thus, only an advanced conspiratorial awareness of politics in progress can still provide the keys to a deep and active understanding of the political reality of today's world, a world now governed by concerted concealment, by over-activated secrecy and overall operational pretence, a world that has become, in itself, a conspiratorial world, a world of permanent and total conspiracy.

The present history of the world has thus become its own inverted image, the 'anti-history', and it is indeed this 'anti-history' now replacing history which, in fact, constitutes, enlightens and affirms the true face of the world history in progress.

It is therefore obvious that all those - whoever they may be - who pretend to oppose this conspiratorial conception of current history, who are fully complicit in this state of affairs, are in fact only pretending to do so, in order to better conceal their own occult shenanigans, their active participation in a history based essentially on concealment and on the subversive misappropriation of its own meaning, or of what they are trying to pass off as such.

Authentic historical vision can therefore no longer be more than a reflected vision, operative only to the second or third degree, and history itself is no longer made up of anything but its own deciphering.

Now, as things have become, only these considerations of principle on the fundamentally conspiratorial nature of the current world history in progress can make us effectively understand the absolutely blatant fact of the line of opposition followed, and unceasingly reactivated, which is that of *the implicit agreement*, mobilising at present the whole of the European media – press, radio, television, exhibition under the control of "politically correct" doctrinal conceptions – against the whole of the national and world political positions, "planetary", of Vladimir Putin's "New Russia". An *implicit agreement that* functions as an insurmountable ideological-political barrier, as a vast operational device for stifling and subversively diverting all of Russia's political initiatives, choices and actions. In other words, as a concerted and unwavering obstruction of President Vladimir Putin's ideological-political line, followed in the shadows.

It is as if a "great occult decision-making centre" was working tirelessly in the shadows to keep the increasingly exacerbated opposition of the entire European information and governmental options against Russia's attempts to assert its political presence in Europe, its will to defend its continental counter-offensive against the anti-European actions of the Islamist revolutionary subversion acting in South-East Europe. The European Union is also concerned about the southern flank of its own European grand-continental geopolitical positions in the former Soviet Islamist republics.

A total politico-revolutionary war is being waged, openly, by Fundamentalist Islam - and by what lies behind it - against Russia, in the geopolitical space of Russia's presence on the southern flank of the European continent, and more particularly in Chechnya, which constitutes its decisive politico-strategic anchor point. It is in Chechnya that Europe as a whole must now face the preliminaries of the future revolutionary waves of the Islamist invasion in the name of the "Great Holy War" with weapons.

However, not only does European political information as a whole refuse, in a manner subversively concerted to this end, to recognise the validity of Russia's counter-offensive positions on the southern flank of the Eurasian "Great Continent", but, in addition Russia has not stopped formally siding with the anti-European side of the total political-revolutionary war being waged against Russia - and thus against the whole of continental Europe - in Chechnya and in the Islamic Asia of Russia's southern flank.

This factual situation was recently brought to light, in an absolutely intolerable manner, during the intervention in the Durbrovka Theatre in Moscow last October of the terrorist group of Chechen criminals acting under the orders of Mosvar Barayev, when the European information – without any exception, the "right-wing" media in the lead - were at pains to disavow in the most irresponsible and shameless manner, behaving – in terms of the most obvious high treason - as enemies of the European camp under attack, the counter-strategic measures of the Russian political security forces in action on the ground.

At the same time as the bloody events in the Durbrovka Theatre in Moscow were taking place, led by Chechen terrorists under the orders of Mosvar Basayev, a "World Conference" for "Free Chechnya" was being openly hosted in Copenhagen - Denmark holds the presidency of the European Union - and in Paris, France's largest right-wing daily did not hesitate to feel sorry for the Chechen bandits who were being put out of action by the Russian special forces, while the Moscow crowds, drunk with rage, shouted "Russia is not being brought to its knees".

That the dictatorship of the socialist-Trotskyite conspiracy of Lionel Jospin, himself a member of the "Trotskyite International", and the stranglehold of the state terrorism of "political correctness" that it maintained, had been abruptly driven out of power in France and replaced by a new absolute right-wing majority and a new right-wing government mobilised behind Jacques Chirac, apparently did nothing to change that: Everything was still going on as if the watchwords of a socialist-Trotskyite superconspiracy, of supranational dimensions, still prevailed over the new French national political situation, over the "new French line", anti-Russian and anti-Putinian watchwords, in accordance with the great campaign of agitation and counter-propaganda in progress, which was being maintained underground.

But, in the end, a question that cannot be avoided will have to be asked, given the now absolutely unacceptable sum of all these anomalies clandestinely implemented with regard to the new Russia of President Vladimir Putin: What is hidden behind all these subversive - anti-national and anti-European - options of European political information in its entirety, European political information that is openly subjugated to a secretly unitary, anti-Russian and anti-Great European line? What are the ins and outs of this *secretly unitary line*, who is behind it, what are its hidden goals?

This is discussed below.

For there is an answer to everything, even if, at times, these answers may appear to be more or less unbelievable, disturbing, deeply disturbing our acquired certainties. But isn't that what is needed? To disturb, to disturb, to *reveal*?

The fundamental internal antagonism of the former Soviet power is now being covertly perpetuated on a European scale

Contrary to all the evidence, and to everything that has been thought since, Soviet central power has never been that of a monolithic bloc. The central Soviet power has always represented, secretly, the cohabitation in depth of two fundamental, dialectically antagonistic powers: the "Bolshevicotrotskyist" power, left Marxist and "internationalist", and, in front of it, the "Stalinist" power, national and imperialist, "Eurasian", relying essentially on the Soviet Armed Forces. The latter had always had the upper hand since the elimination, in 1929, of Trotsky and his supporters within the higher hierarchies of the party. This opposition was, moreover, the product of decisive factors, intractable but external, in a way, to politics, because of its ethnic and secretly religious nature.

Thus, once the apparatus of Stalinist power had been accelerated and exhaustively installed, and was now out of reach, the authorities and leaders of the "Bolshevik-Trotskyist" power - having faced it - had to hide, conceal themselves, and sink deeper and deeper into the darkness of the party apparatus, no longer acting in the light of day, but nonetheless constantly present and participating in the implicit reality of the power definitively in place. For some sixty years, the Soviet central power functioned in a state of clandestine duplication by an internal anti-power, which had not ceased to weigh on its fundamental decisions, and even on the very line of its external, "planetary" conduct.

Thus, at the moment when the Soviet Union was so mysteriously put in a state of immediate and total self-destruction, the main supporters in the shadow of the "Bolshevik-Trotskyist" fraction of the Soviet power that had just been brought down, had to resign themselves to the fundamentally national choices of the new power in place, of the "new national-revolutionary line" of this one, they had to resign themselves to go into exile - after a series of most equivocal waverings – outside, so that they could invest – for lack of anything else available - the clandestine operative field of Western Europe, where they were moreover expected. Where they brought formidable financial assets, both in cash and in hidden industrial and banking participations, to the Western economy. These clandestine transfers were made in haste and by unpredictable, makeshift means, and were able to pass relatively unnoticed, especially because of the terrible disorder reigning in Russia at the time.

Thus the "Bolshevik-Trotskyist" structures of Soviet power, forcibly exiled to the outside, met there, on the ground, everywhere in Western Europe, the operational apparatuses of the "Trotskyist International" already in place, and the socialist-social-democratic parties infiltrated for a long time by the undercover metastases of activist Trotskyism, the junction being made without delay. But the consequences of this shadowy junction were not long in coming, and they were dramatic for the Europe of the national line.

It was in these conditions that Soviet underground Trotskyism outside, in exile, took over, almost on the spot, all the social democratic parties of Trotskyist orientation under cover, provoking the wave of socialist takeovers and the advent of the Socialist Europe of our "leaden years". A Socialist Europe which, in reality, was a socialist-Trotskyist Europe, of the type of regimes that came to power in France, Germany, Italy, Spain, Greece and, above all, in Belgium: it was, in fact, in Belgium, that the occult headquarters of the new European socialist-Trotskyist power was located, as well as the bodies that were behind the scenes of the reception and concealment of the great financial and economic assets that had been smuggled out of the ex-USSR.

And all these processes of subversive political-administrative reconsideration had to take place, as one can imagine, exclusively in the darkness of a perfectly concerted revolutionary action, by experienced specialists and in the operating conditions exclusively of their choice.

The fact is that, unfortunately, the entire political and ideological infrastructure, media, information and social-Trotskyist agitation-propaganda is still operating in broad daylight or clandestinely throughout Western Europe, even after its liberation from the subversive grip of Trotskyite socialism, continuing its subversive anti-European and anti-national, and primarily anti-Russian, activism at full speed.

For the New Russia of President Vladimir Putin represents, in continuity, for the proponents of the social-trotskyist conspiracy still clandestinely in place, and still in action, the ideological and politico-strategic principle of the greatest imperial Eurasian Europe, with a higher spiritual horizon, eschatological, engaged in this "opening to being" of the peoples of the great previous, "traditional", "archaic" European civilisations; This "openness to being" is absolutely intolerable to the supporters of the ideologies of non-being and chaos, to the subjugators of nothingness.

This is because, starting from the Franco-German "Refounding Pact" and the project of the Paris-Berlin-Moscow axis, what Western Europe and Vladimir Putin's New Russia are currently preparing, putting into situation, is precisely the revolutionary constitution of the largest continental Europe, Eurasian', of final imperial dimensions, destined to block, ontologically, the 'globalist conspiracy' of the Planetary Superpower of the United States and of the Trotskyite oriented socialisms that the United States uses in its own forward march: The resulting inescapable confrontation is only the *ultimate*, predestined *fate* of the present world history heading towards its end.

Why Vladimir Putin?

If one were to take the trouble to dialectically project the "carrier figure" of all the directions of threat, attack, provocation and destabilisation, of disinformational and disqualifying denigration, permanently pursued, in recent times, by the socialist-trotskyist left against the immediate or implied positions of the imperial national-revolutionary doctrine of the Greater Europe, it would immediately appear that, at the present time, this "carrier figure" gathering on it the constantly rising wave of collective, over-activated hatreds of the socialist-Trotskyist enemy, could only be that of President Vladimir Putin, who brilliantly embodies its flamboyant outline in the feverish skies of our most unavowed hopes, of our revolutionary will. Why Vladimir Putin? Significantly decisive, this revelation about Vladimir Putin is a big one. For the revelational choices of the collective unconscious of peoples are always final, never wrong and never can be wrong. It is at the level of the collective, abysmal, irrational choice of the Russian people that everything is at stake, now and for the years to come, in Russia itself and, from Russia, in the inner space of the destiny of the largest continental, "Eurasian" Europe. So who is Vladimir Putin?

Vladimir Putin is, today, as President of Russia, the "providential man" destined - predestined - to take upon himself the immediate politico-historical setting of the Greater Continental, "Eurasian" Europe, the revolutionary constitution of the *Imperium Ultimum* charged with confronting the "globalist conspiracy" of the United States and that which stands in the shadows behind the United States.

Vladimir Putin is the "absolute concept" of the new Great European imperial revolutionary history on the way to the political-historical fulfilment of its final destiny.

In a certain sense, we can therefore take it for granted that the present history of Greater Europe is no more than the secret continuation of the antagonism in depth, of the original antagonism between the two constituent fractions of the former Soviet power, the "Bolshevik-Trotskyist" fraction and the "Stalinist", "national-revolutionary" fraction, having based its power on the imperial predestination of the Soviet Forces, the New Russia is the direct heir of the latter, just as it wants to be the heir of the Russian Empire of the Romanovs, whose canonisation was obtained by Vladimir Putin personally through its last representatives - Nicholas II and his family - martyrs of their Orthodox faith and by their gift of Eucharistic blood for the final salvation of Russia.

As such, Vladimir Putin appears, at the moment, in front of the invisible, hidden supporters of the socialist-Trotskyist conspiracy of secretly European dimensions, as the "absolute enemy", as the man to be put down immediately and by all means. Fortunately, he is at the same time the object of certain hidden, "supernatural" high protections.

For, in the process of being constituted from the Paris-Berlin-Moscow axis, the greater continental Europe, "Eurasian", which includes, in principle, Western and Eastern Europe, Russia, Tibet, India and Japan, can only be brought together around Russia, which is at the hinge of the two halves - that of the West and that of the East – of the continent, India and Japan, can only be brought together around Russia, which is at the hinge of the two halves – the Western and the Eastern - of Europe, of the Eurasian "Great Continent": everything depends on Russia and, in the final hour, everything will depend on Vladimir Putin.

To draw a metapsychic and spiritual portrait of Vladimir Putin according to the subterranean dialectic of "depth psychology" would be a fascinating task, and one that would undoubtedly reveal many revelations, but it is not possible to undertake it in the framework of this article.

It is no less certain that the decisive marriage between Vladimir Putin's own personality and the demands of today's New Russia in the face of its new imperial and eschatological European grand-continental missions appears from the outset - a revolutionary marriage if ever there was one - as the very mark of a great predestination in the process of being fulfilled.

The double ministry of Vladimir Putin's own destiny can thus be seen as being, on the one hand, that of creating the tool of his own revolutionary work, namely the imperial, grandcontinental European New Russia, and, on the other hand, of engaging this tool - the New Great Russia - in the revolutionary process of accomplishing its own political-historical tasks. Tasks converging, all of them, towards the establishment of a new Greater Europe of imperial, "Eurasian" horizon and dimensions. In other words, to rebuild Greater Russia so that it can build the Greater Europe.

The implementation of Vladimir Putin's dual revolutionary ministry is clearly a superhuman task, and it is certain that he could not contemplate completing it without the "external help" of super-activated forces from beyond history, from the depths of a suprahistorical revolutionary horizon.

Such are the occult commitments of the present great European history, which is reaching the climax of its new planetary destiny, which will perhaps also be a *final destiny*. For something absolutely new to appear, the *Novissima Aetas*, must not something old, something definitively gone, disappear without trace? Is not every elevation based on a collapse?

Bringing down the socialist-Trotskyist fortress of Berlin at all costs

It goes without saying, it seems to me, that all the current activist availabilities of European revolutionary nationalism must henceforth be unconditionally in support of the great Eurasian imperial enterprise, in the process of development, of Vladimir Putin's New Russia engaged in the paths of its final eschatological design.

For, after the liberation of most of Western Europe from its subjugation to the Trotskyite conspiracy of social democracy everywhere has been achieved, the time has also come for the second liberation of Europe, which will be the liquidation of the liberal-democracy currently acting as a subversive replacement structure.

Moreover, it should not be forgotten that in the heart of Europe liberated from the social-democratic grip acting as an operational cover-up for the Trotskyite continental conspiracy, there are still European spaces that have not yet been liberated, including - Britain no longer counting as part of Europe - Germany, Belgium and Greece, and this is what we must deal with as a priority. The Trotskyite regimes currently operating in Berlin and Brussels under the now completely random mask of social democracy must be brought down at all costs, and as a matter of urgency.

We need to "clean house", definitively: the subterranean, over-activated Trotskyite infection centres that Berlin and Brussels have become must be unbridled, and thoroughly cleaned up, revolutionarily sanitised; put completely out of action.

Only then will it be possible to do everything that belongs to our people, everything that belongs to us who are "survivors of fire", escapees from the last great political-historical collapses of Europe, miracles of invisible history.

The line of action of the socialist-Trotskyist regime currently in power in Berlin through Gerhard Schröder and Joschka Fischer is also justified by the fact that Germany is the main European power committed to truly supporting Turkey's admission to the European Union. However, with the arrival in power in Ankara of Recep Tayyip Erdogan's "Justice and Development Party" – a so-called "moderate Islamist" party, but which in reality serves to conceal a large-scale interventionist political-military Islamist conspiracy – the revolutionary and terrorist "Islamist International" has just found its political and terrorist base in Turkey, in Turkey, the politico-strategic base of a vast European continental offensive which, at a later stage, is likely to completely reverse the current balance of power.

In fact, in the extremely small circles of the great political and strategic intelligence, it is already known that Osama Bin Laden is preparing to shift the centre of gravity of his planetary seditious action from Asia to Western Europe and to South-Eastern Europe, which is already being worked on underground by Islamism, following the Islamist takeover in Turkey, Turkey, relying on the latter - in Albania, Bosnia, Kosovo and Macedonia - should serve, from now on, once it is admitted into the European Union, as an offensive base for the investment of subversive Islamism in the whole of Europe. The internal geopolitical space of Western Europe will then be declared a "Land of Holy War", a "Land of Jihad", and will be offered, thus, to the seditious action on the spot of the Turkish and Arab Islamist groupings already present inside the European nations. And the massive free movement of Turkish nationals in Europe, as a consequence of Turkey's admission to the European Union, should do the rest. If we allow this to happen.

In any case, the fate of the three million Turks already present in Germany has already been settled, who are to serve as the vanguard and mass of manoeuvre for the launch of the revolutionary Islamist offensive in Europe, three million Turks who support Gerhard Schröder's Socialist-Trotskyist party, and whom he supports unconditionally for reasons that are both basely electoral and subversively electoral.

Revolutionary Islam, seditious to excess and terrorist in its means as well as in its aims, is however only a depraved and criminal deviation from the regular Islamic religion, a religious cancer that obscure, 'infernal' powers maintain and constantly fan.

Thus Islam, when it is framed, resituated in a social and national framework, as in Russia, for example, entirely gathered behind President Vladimir Putin, participating in Alexander Dugin's Eurasia organisation, becomes a respectable and enriching religious power, faithful to the national governmental orientations. Similarly, French Islam, which the new Minister of the Interior, Nicolas Sarkozy, has just succeeded in framing in a unitary National Representation, is in the process of giving itself a different status, one that is not alien to the active body of the living nation.

And then there is President Yasser Arafat who, in the name of the Palestinian nation fighting for its ultimate freedom, has just taken a firm stand - and apparently a definitive one - against the terrorist positions of Al-Qaeda and Osama Bin Laden. Indeed, in an interview published on 15 December 2002 by the *Sunday Times,* President Yasser Arafat formally accused Osama Bin Laden of exploiting the Palestinian cause, whereas he has never helped the Palestinians and is constantly acting against their interests, against their present destiny. I ask him to stop falsely standing behind the Palestinian cause'', said President Yasser Arafat, who took a strong stand against Osama Bin Laden's positions and the overall action of Al-Qaeda.

Pushing for a regular Islamic awakening? It is therefore not impossible that this is where the counter-fire to the revolutionary anti-European Islamist offensive, currently being prepared from the underground interference of Al-Qaeda in Turkey, which has fallen under its harmful influence, should finally be considered.

Faced with the "Planetary Superpower of the United States", the great-continental, "Eurasian" Europe is rising up today

At the same time, it is extremely significant to note that the non-European powers that are trying to impose the admission of Turkey into the European Union, that are constantly trying to force the decision of European politicians in this direction - and one wonders what right they have to do so - are precisely the United States and Israel.

Valéry Giscard d'Estaing: "I believe that the admission of Turkey into the European Union would be the end of it".

Indeed, the situation could not be simpler: in the next ten years, Turkey and revolutionary Islam are likely to put an end to Europe for good. This is precisely the reason why the United States - and its allies in Israel - are obviously and, above all, behind the scenes, supporting the advances of Turkey and Islam in Europe.

For the foreign policy of the United States has basically only one global strategic goal: to *prevent by any means, including those of a final planetary conflagration, the creation of the Greater Eurasian Imperial Europe, which would take away their rank of "Planetary Superpower", and reduce them to the level of a second, and even third, rank power.*

And when you have understood that, you have understood everything, and there is nothing more to say.

The Three Suns of the End

However, in the coming years, the greatest danger to the final identity and internal unity of Europe is still Turkey, as the fundamental political-strategic base of the anti-European offensive planned by the Islamist conspiracy, whose operational vanguards are already acting from within the European countries they are currently investing.

Thus, in this dramatic situation, Russia's imperial Orthodox mission becomes absolutely crucial. If, in order to pursue its own final, suprahistorical, eschatological mission, Russia must above all be able to recover its own abysmal identity, its final politico-strategic goal will have to be that of the liberation of Constantinople, the "liberation of the Holy Sophia": For it is the "liberation of the Holy Sophia" that constitutes the supreme myth of the ultimate imperial mission of Vladimir Putin's New Russia and, as such, it is Russia that is thereby given the task of leading the permanent and decisive counter-offensive against Islamic subversion in Europe.

Rome, Constantinople, Moscow will thus have to constitute, together, at the end of the present European grand-continental history, the arc of the final offensive of the imperial identity of the Greater Europe, because, as it has been said, it is the simultaneous appearance of the "three suns" at the ultimate horizon of the ultimate cycle of the present world history – "the sun of the past", the sun of the present", "the sun of the future" – which will constitute the "sign of the times" par excellence, announcing the apocalyptic conclusion of the latter and the advent of the suprahistorical *Ultima Aetas*, of the "history beyond history".

Like Nicholas II, Vladimir Putin knows that Russia's greatest destiny will eventually be in Europe, and like Nicholas II, Vladimir Putin also knows that Russia's true centre of gravity is in India, that it is in India that Russia's invisible "Polar Crown" is hidden on the ultimate heights, and he also knows, along with Alexander Dugin, that "Russia is the bridge from Europe to India". It seems to me that Russia's special relationship with India, which is growing stronger all the time, is not being given the importance it deserves.

Today's European consciousness is profoundly mutilated by the habit of the absence of Russia and Eastern Europe from its internal space, from which it had long been separated by the barriers of communist prohibitions. The ongoing extension of the EU's borders towards Eastern Europe is, however, changing this damaging, dramatic state of affairs. The return of Eastern Europe to the global consciousness of itself, which from now on will increasingly be that of the greater continental Europe, opens up a new horizon for the unforeseen paths of an absolutely decisive revolutionary revival, because

Eastern Europe, close to Russia, will eventually bring a great reviving breath, a vital power that will change the deadly lethargy in which the great countries of Western Europe are currently plunged, victims of the anaesthetising influences of the "globalist conspiracy" of the USA. Unsuspected energies are already being transferred from the East to the West of Europe, without anyone yet realising it, which will soon begin like a formidable earthquake, as unexpected as it will be decisive in terms of its ideological-political consequences, in terms of the awakening of consciousness that it will provoke, and in terms of the changes in the depths.

But the last word belongs to Russia, to Vladimir Putin's New Russia. For the new Europe rising from its ashes cannot be anything other than the largest continental, "Eurasian" Europe, and this includes Russia as a central space for active geopolitical affirmation, Russia, the great continental hinge where Western and Eastern Europe meet, neither of which exists except for their double unitary transcendence, their common imperial vocation, affirmed by the figure of the "three suns", Rome, Constantinople and Moscow.

That is why we hold the 'man from the Kremlin', Vladimir Putin, as the man for our greatest continental battles to come.

THE ASSUMPTION OF VLADIMIR PUTIN

The American Democratic Party, and its double

The global political earthquake caused and sustained by the US presidential elections over the past few months has completely obliterated the news horizon, effectively relegating all other events to the back burner of media attention.

The very good news of John Kerry's return to his wife's skirts, from which he should never have emerged, and the harsh disappointment of the socialist-Trotskyist conspiracy operating behind the cover of the new Democratic petition for power, should not, however, obscure the dimensions of the catastrophe that would have been the Democratic Party's arrival in power in Washington.

Having self-suggested to the point of making themselves believe that victory was assured, the shadowy leaders of the Democratic Party believed that they could indeed already take the initiative of a large-scale ideological operation, which discovered in advance, rather imprudently, their dramatically negative positions towards Vladimir Putin's Russia and hence towards the European Union on the march, more or less subterraneanly mobilised by the imperial vanguard geopolitical line of the Paris-Berlin-Moscow-New Delhi-Tokyo axis.

Thus, under the provocative title of *Stop Embracing Putin,* a text that appeared in the most important American and European press organs recently called for a complete revision of the policy of the United States and its Atlanticist allies towards Vladimir Putin's Russia. Among the 115 signatories of this text – called the "115 document" – are Vaclav Havel, Francis Fukuyama and James Woolsey, former director of the CIA. At the same time, and as part of the same anti-Russian operation-supervised, in its entirety, by Bruce P. Jackson-appeared in the *Financial Times* an article signed by Richard Holbrook, former right-hand man to Madeleine Albright, and Marc Brzezinski, son of Zbigniew Brzezinski, entitled *The United States should give Russia tough love.*

On the other hand, having thus unconsciously discovered itself in the uncertain certainty of a Democratic victory in the presidential elections, a certain secretly Democratic fraction of the CIA in place had to immediately suffer the consequences of its faux pas. This may explain the very significant dismissals within the agency by the new Director, Porter Goss, appointed by George Bush to carry out a thorough and urgent clean-up.

The vast conspiracy of leftist intellectuals engaged in the anti-Russian operation led in Washington by Bruce P. Jackson, intended to espouse - totally, and openly - the positions of the Atlanticist conspiracy of 'liberal intellectuals' and 'Trotskyists under cover' that constitutes, today, in Moscow, the domestic front of the 'democratic resistance' against Vladimir Putin.

But the early mobilisation of the existing left-democratic networks only led to their exposure.

A socialist-Trotskyist conspiracy against Russia? Why is that?

But who is Bruce P. Jackson, the kingpin of this very important anti-Russian agitation-propaganda operation that was the production, from Washington, of the "115 document" against Vladimir Putin? A former officer of the American military secret services, and then in charge of strategic planning at Lockheed, the "largest arms manufacturer in the world", the "Document of the 115" was not his first move; he had already directed the so-called "Vilnius Appeal" operation, which had succeeded in mobilising the support of Eastern European countries for the American war against Iraq against the positions of the Franco-German European line. He is present in the ranks of the *Project for a New American Century* (PNAC), an ideological-strategic war machine at the service of the planning of the United States' planetary offensive ventures, administrator of the Center for Security Policy, of the *New Atlantic Initiative,* of CSIS. And, above all, an influential member of *the American Committee for Peace in Chechnya* (APAC), which explains everything.

Bruce P. Jackson is a man on the front line of the current underground political-strategic conspiracy of the global socialist-Trotskyist front mobilised against Vladimir Putin's Russia and thus against the European Union, and it is as such that he had to sponsor the "115 document".

It will therefore be in Washington that the domestic anti-Putin resistance will seek its decisive impulses. The last American elections brought to light the global socialist-Trotskyite conspiracy that is present everywhere, and in particular in the United States, in both the Democratic and Republican camps. A conspiracy whose "final objective" is the dismantling of the national-revolutionary political regime currently in power in Russia, a regime embodied by Vladimir Putin. Why is this? Why this relentlessness against Vladimir Putin? Because Vladimir Putin's "New Russia" represents, today, the national-revolutionary metapolitical fortress in the vanguard of the New Europe of the Eurasian imperial line, mobilised by the Paris-Berlin-Moscow-New Delhi-Tokyo geopolitical axis. Two worlds face each other, irreducibly. Which, in the more or less long term, will have to confront each other directly. From now on, everything will depend on the nature and the internal timeframe of this deadline.

In any case, burned internally as he is by his intimate, polar and orthodox vision of Russia, of Russia's great imperial and eschatological predestination, Vladimir Putin now has only one choice before him: to do what he has been chosen to do, and for that he has only one means of action, Russia.

It is therefore necessary to succeed in setting Russia against the negative direction of the current "great history", to succeed in giving Russia the spiritual and political power that can allow it to envisage its marriage with its greatest historical and suprahistorical destiny, thus dragging Europe and Asia into this supreme attempt at revolutionary self-deprivation that can be symbolised by the visionary figure of the "Eurasian Empire of the End", *the Imperium Ultimum*.

For Vladimir Putin, we have no doubt, the "big decision" has already been made. However, in the present state of affairs, Russia is not yet in a position to meet the final revolutionary demand that must be expected of it.

Vladimir Putin must therefore, above all, bring Russia back at least to the level of planetary superpower that it had reached at the height of its rise as the Soviet Union. This can only be done if Russia manages to take the lead and make it possible to impose on the Eurasian "Great Continent" the imperial revolutionary impulse carried by the implementation of the Paris-Berlin-Moscow-New Delhi-Tokyo axis.

Vladimir Putin's current battle appears to be, first and foremost, that of Russia's self-righting. And this is what Vladimir Putin is now devoting the extraordinary amount of effort that he is mobilising for the political, military, economic, cultural and religious takeover of Russia as it is at the moment, a revolutionary amount of effort that is in fact just a gigantic open site.

A project engaged above all in a terrible battle against time: the "hour of confrontation" with the planetary imperial pursuit of the United States must not come before Russia is fully ready. The hour of confrontation that Vladimir Putin must ensure comes as late as possible (if there is any implicit fatality of its coming, which is not entirely obvious, in the *will of God*).

The basic steps of Russia's final recovery

Five decisive politico-strategic steps constitute the next stages of the great forward spiral of Vladimir Putin's irresistible call of his own destiny and his very inspired imperial and eschatological plan for the missions and the near advent of a "transcendental" Russia, the "Russia of the End": a Russia established as the summit centre, as the "living and radiating pole" of the "Eurasian Empire of the End", of the *Regnum Ultimum*.

(1) To ensure in depth, to reinforce, to take completely in hand the new revolutionary political-administrative reorganisation of the State, a mission already in the process of being accomplished through the coup de force of 30

October 2004, when following the terrorist action of 1–3 October 2004, in Balsan, North Ossetia, Vladimir Putin established by decree that the power of the governors of the provinces will henceforth be directly within the competence of the vertical of the Kremlin, the Kremlin being the only one entitled to proceed with the choice of the representatives of the central power on the spot. Thus the Kremlin will control the entire political-administrative power of the territory of Russia, without going through the dubious intermediary of the "elected governors" on the spot, subject to divergent, locally interested, manipulable influences.

(2) To provide the Armed Forces of Russia with a grand-strategic nuclear armament of land, air and sea, to foresee an in-depth reorganisation of their operational structure, to define the broad lines of their new strategies of presence and effective affirmation on the grand-continent and the planet. To instil in the Armed Forces a new imperial revolutionary consciousness, to make them the immediate operative base of the new political-administrative structures of the State. Nothing will prevent Russia from continuing its programme of renewal and significant reinforcement, of over-modernisation of its strategic nuclear forces: *"It would be enough for us to weaken our attention to these components of our defence, which form our nuclear missile shield, for us to find ourselves confronted with other threats"*.

Of course, there is still the problem of the current social and economic situation in Russia, one being linked to the other. While the problem of the conspiracies pursued by the oligarchs and their offensive structures at home will become less important once the Khodorkovsky case has been settled, it is now a fact that Russia's economic and industrial recovery is already well under way, with colossal reserves of raw materials and an existing industrial and research infrastructure that is pretended not to be taken into account. This is very much to the detriment of the country, as we will have to admit one day.

Russia's imminent economic and industrial recovery, which has entered its decisive phase, is now a matter of course, and its external developments will follow on a grand continental, "Eurasian" and even global scale.

For a common apparatus of Great European agitation-propaganda However, the problem lies in the blatant lack of an overall geopolitical doctrine, affirmative and inflexibly decisive, concerning Russia's great-continental European commitments and, above all, in Russia's direct support action in Europe - in Eastern Europe, and in Western Europe - to the groupings, currents, parties and movements driven by the revolutionary faith in a Greater Europe, of final, "Eurasian" dimensions, a mass of presence, support and thrust that must represent the flywheel of Russia's revolutionary action committed to the continental "grand design" of Vladimir Putin.

At a time of great continental regroupings, Russia is nothing without Europe, just as it is imperative that it have its Asian flywheel - India and Japan

- so that it can access the grand-continental imperial liberation through which it will be possible to see its supreme eschatological predestination fulfilled.

It is also understood that it is imperative that the Russian Nuclear Forces be equipped with a new generation of extreme planetary devices, which no other power currently has.

(3) To obtain, by the most appropriate and tense means, that the infrastructures of European agitation already in place succeed, reinforced from below, in making all the peoples and governments of the interior space of the European grand-continental civilisation join massively, revolutionarily, the offensive imperial project of the New Europe proposed by the fundamental geopolitical axis Paris-Berlin-Moscow-New Delhi-Tokyo

To organise, in the long run, a revolutionary upsurge that brings about the collective decision of the peoples concerned concerning the "selfliberation" of the largest continental Europe.

(4) To provide Russia, in the very short term, with a world-class economic-industrial framework. To liberate the state from subversive oligarchic servitude.

(5) Find the dialectic of a definitive integration of Catholicism and Orthodoxy, the "two lungs of Europe", according to John Paul II.

Having understood that there is no New Empire without an imperial renewal of the one religion, draw all the conclusions, assume all the consequences of this sacred certainty, *build on it.*

These seem to be the five steps, the five fundamental stages of the final renewal of Vladimir Putin's Russia in search of its status as a global superpower.

On 17 November 2004, Vladimir Routin chose to reaffirm Russia's nuclear superpower status. Addressing the annual meeting of senior military officers in Moscow, he stated quite clearly that Russia will soon be equipped with new nuclear weapons structures 'which do not exist and will not exist in the next few years among the other current nuclear powers'. And also: "We are not only carrying out research and testing of the most modern nuclear missiles. I am convinced that in the next few years they will be part of our equipment".

And then to lay the operational foundations of a double overall political-strategic apparatus, comprising a common 'information branch' and a 'field action branch' under the direction of a common command centre.

In a way, a new Cominform and a new Comintern with the conventionally figurative names of Natinform and Natintem. Natinform and Natintem would obviously have nothing to do with the Soviet Cominform and Comintern, essentially subversive organisations. On the contrary, Natinform and Natintem should be in the vanguard of the politico-strategic struggle of the peoples and governments of the European Union for the support of the home front of the Greater Continental Europe along the Paris-Berlin-Moscow-New Delhi-Tokyo imperial geopolitical line.

Thus, it would certainly be conceivable that, in the current state of affairs, the starting point for Moscow's implementation of the double positive political-strategic dis of Natintorm and Natintern would be constituted precisely from the ideological-doctrinal structures already acting, on the ground, in the direction foreseen by the great European designs that are ours. Namely, on the one hand, the chain of revolutionary "geopolitical groups" covering the whole of the interior space of the European continent and, on the other hand, the *Eurasia* organisation directed by Alexander Dugin from Moscow, which has recently extended its activities to the whole of Eastern and Western Europe.

At the same time, it should be noted that, at the present time, there are a certain number of ideological and administrative structures in Alsace that are intended to establish the major operational orientations of future economic and industrial cooperation bodies following, on a continental scale, the Paris-Berlin-Moscow axis, and that it would appear that all the doctrinal, prospective and organisational activities already underway should be mobilised without further delay and amplified in a final perspective.

It is here, in fact, that the fundamental projects, already partially at work, of the gigantic economic-industrial complexes of the Greater Europe being forged by us, the fighters for the final polar unity of the Eurasian "Great Continent", are being prepared, conceived and operationally defined.

We don't know it yet, but Alsace is today the open site of our already metaphysical future.

The nuptial dialectic of the Imperium Ultimum and the Religio Novissima

The sum of the considerations concerning the current situation of Vladimir Putin's Russia that appear in the present text will not, however, suffice to shed some light on the problem, which remains decisive, that of the evolution of political and strategic choices, These are decisive choices for the future destiny of the Greater Europe and therefore for world history in its greater future, ontological and foundational choices that Russia will have to make at a time when, in any case, it is almost here.

For the problem of Russia will be doubled, by the very mystery of its own predestined being, by a perspective of religious, supernatural dimensions, far beyond the historical conditions of its immediately visible becoming.

Whatever one may say, Vladimir Putin's regime is fundamentally Orthodox, and even Orthodox above all: if one has not understood the *veiled evidence of* this situation, one has understood nothing about Russia today.

However, the problem of Orthodoxy is essentially to be overcome. Indeed, if the ultimate destiny of present-day Russia is a Great European imperial destiny, this fundamentally implies that a new, or rather *renewed,* religion will eventually arise, given that there is no Great Europe, no imperial Europe, without a "religion of Empire" that is specifically its own.

But the renewal of Orthodoxy in terms of an 'imperial religion' can only be achieved through its 'reunification' with Catholicism, which is the religion of the other half of Europe, of the other half of *the Imperium Ultimum;* constituted by Russia and Europe, by Eastern Europe and Western Europe.

The imperial historical process of the advent of the New Europe, the Greater Europe, must therefore imperatively involve the effective emergence of what John Paul II called the reunification of the 'two lungs of Europe', Catholicism and Orthodoxy. There is not the slightest contradiction in this visionary certainty, because that is how it is. As in its beginnings, before its separation into two, the new 'European religion' will see Catholicism and Orthodoxy reunited in a single imperial religion, *Una Sanctam.*

And when we know, not only to what extent Vladimir Putin and John Paul II are definitively convinced of the absolute necessity of the final grand-continental reunification of the two living European religions, but also, and above all, to what extent the underground link - the high conspiratorial complicity – of a common decision keeps the course of the confidential actions of the current master of the Kremlin and the Supreme Pontiff very closely united, to what extent the subterranean link – the high conspiratorial complicity – of a common decision keeps the confidential actions of the current master of the Kremlin and the reigning Pontiff very closely united with regard to what must imperatively be done in order to get to *where we need to be anyway,* all hopes are legitimately allowed for the *Religio Novissima* that will have to be – and will be - that of the 'Europe of the End', at the appointed time.

A *Religio Novissima* that will also have been able to find certain accommodations with a certain 'deep Hinduism' and a 'certain transcendental Shintoism' so that India and Japan can find their rightful place within the great continental Europe of the End.

It would, however, be rather pointless, it seems to me, to continue to dwell, in the context of an article such as this one, on the subject of this *Religio Novissima,* when it would be necessary, obviously, to devote an entire book of undeniable importance to this problem; which will, moreover, undoubtedly be done, I already undertake to do so.

And what must also be fundamentally taken into consideration is the fact that the beginnings of the third millennium already appear to be of an essentially religious nature. Is Islam not setting the whole world on fire, from Indonesia to Algeria, with the invading flame of its new revolutionary fundamentalism, while the countries of South-East Europe under American occupation - also Islamist, Albania, Kosovo, Bosnia, Macedonia - are undergoing the immediate effects of the same subversion, while in the very centre of the continent the Catholic-Orthodox religious conflict of the Ukraine suddenly on the verge of religious and civil war is manifesting itself.

Is there a "Vladimir Putin mystery"?

On the other hand, how could one conclude the present study on, without attempting to penetrate the deep, abysmal personality of the current master of the Kremlin? For me, the very mysterious emergence of a supremely gifted providential man of Vladimir Putin's stature and professing deep convictions and hidden eschatological orientations that lead him in his ways, cannot be explained other than by the fact that, against all established evidence, the imperial military spirit of the "Holy Russia" and the Tsars still secretly prevailed over the bloody tragedy of seventy years of Communist darkness and terror. Thus the figure of Vladimir Putin appears - symbolically, and unconsciously - as a representation on earth of *Christ Pantocrator* and his armies as that of the "Sun of Justice", the *Sol Justitiae. Whereas the Imperium*'s own times - even if they are exclusively virtual in nature - are secretly and permanently situated in the "history beyond history". The appearance of Vladimir Putin - which is very mysterious, by the way - corresponds to a total reversal of the historical perspective, and of the consciousness that one can have of it, which covers the burning marks of its previous configurations; intact, completely intact. The same, and immersed in the same light, *the light of before*.

For we must face this new and revealing evidence: all things considered, the 'form of consciousness', the vision of the world and of history that is that of Vladimir Putin, is perfectly identified with the 'form of consciousness' that was that of the officers of the Pravoslavian Armies of the Russian Empire of the Romanovs.

A 'form of consciousness', therefore, that is entirely traditional, and traditional in the most Guenonian sense of the word.

These are inconceivable allegations for anti-traditional minds conceived by the abject standard of the present times, but they are the only ones that can attempt to shed light on the mystery of the extremely secretive and pre-ontologically self-confident being who happens to be the current host of the Kremlin.

Where does Vladimir Putin really come from, who is he beyond appearances? History will tell us: Vladimir Putin's assumption will be made through history and in history, of which he will be one of the fateful terms, one of the decisive, *unsurpassable* conclusions.

Now it seems to me that I must take it as a sort of revealing sign that at the moment when I am led to write these last lines on Vladimir Putin and Eurasia, he is precisely in India, where, under the cover of economic-industrial negotiations, he is actually trying to lay the foundations for an in-depth ideological-strategic collaboration with India, which appears more and more to be the centrepiece of the great imperial geopolitical project that is being carried out by the United States, he is in fact trying to lay the foundations for in-depth ideological and strategic collaboration with India, which is increasingly appearing as the centrepiece of Russia's current imperial geopolitical grand design, and of what lies behind Russia. India is the pivot around which the future history of the world will revolve.

OTHER TITLES

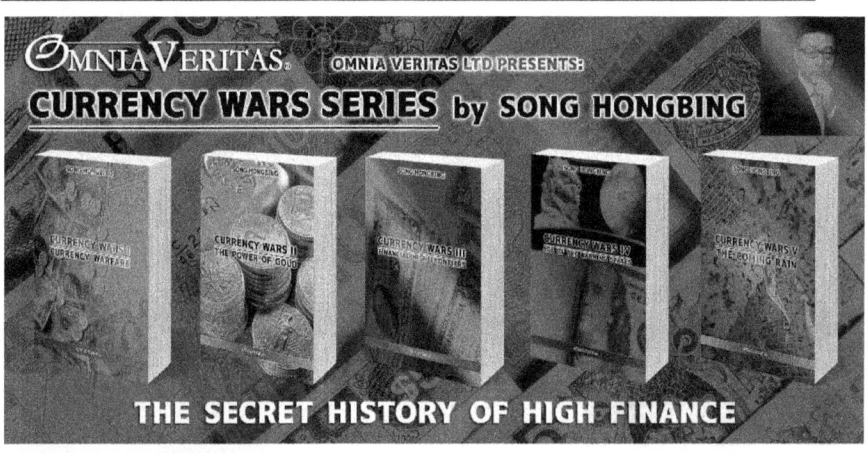

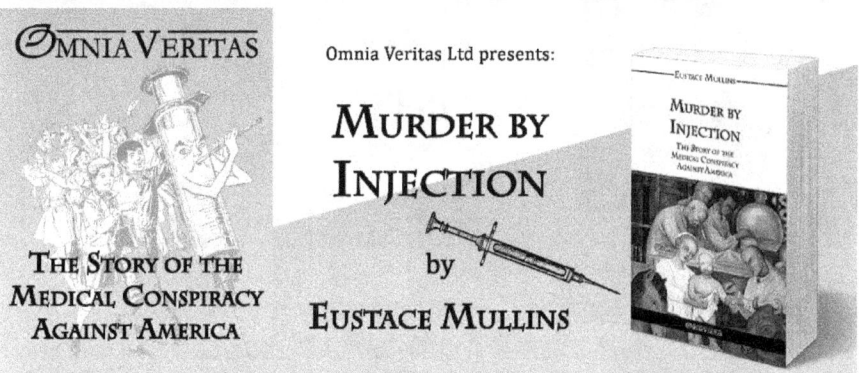

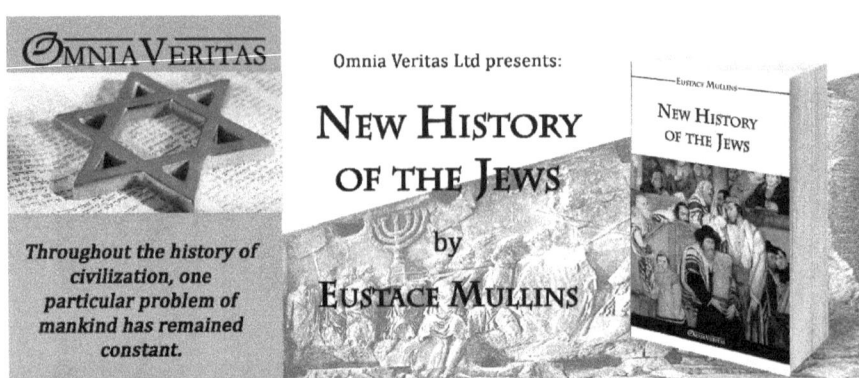

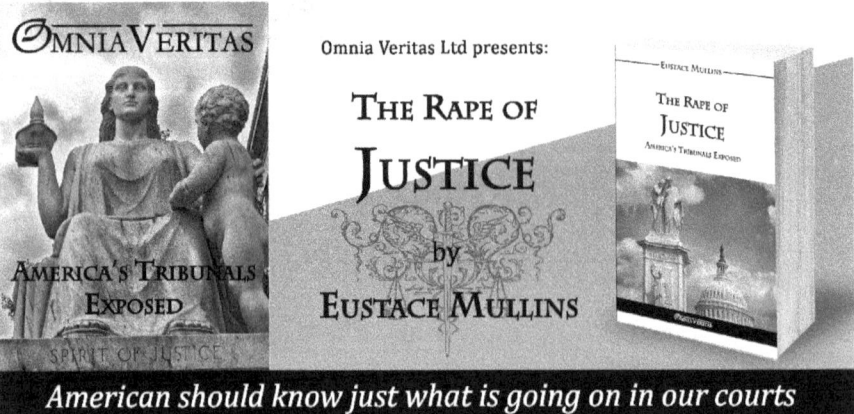

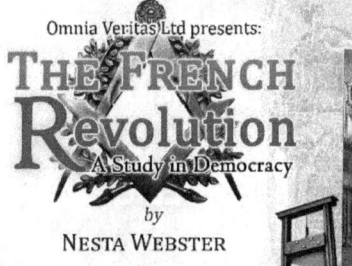

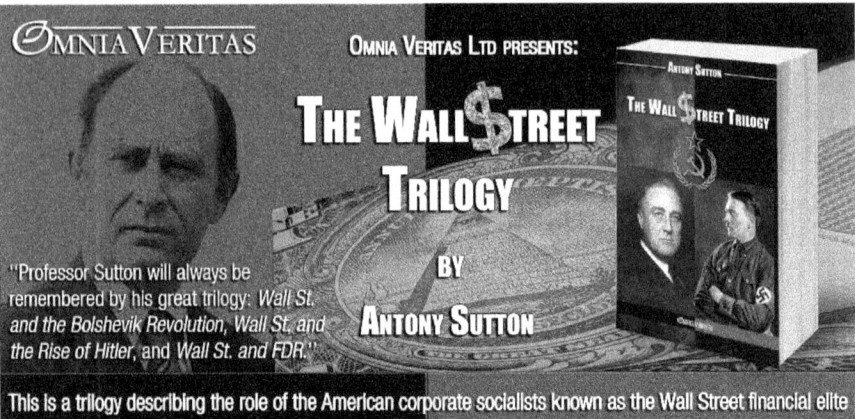
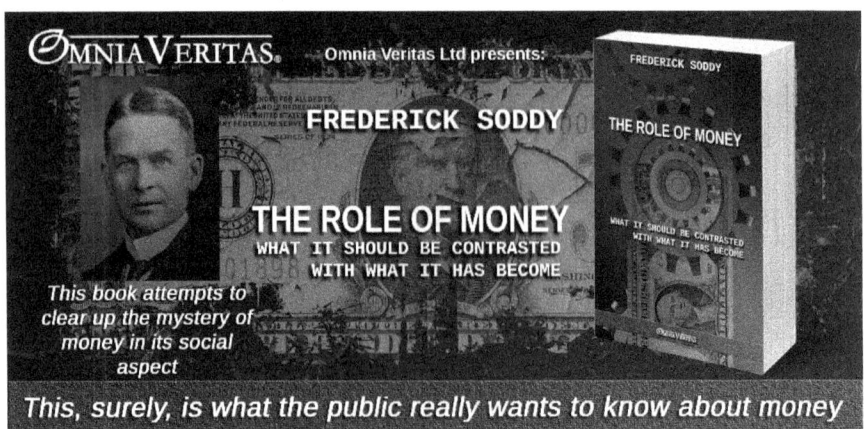

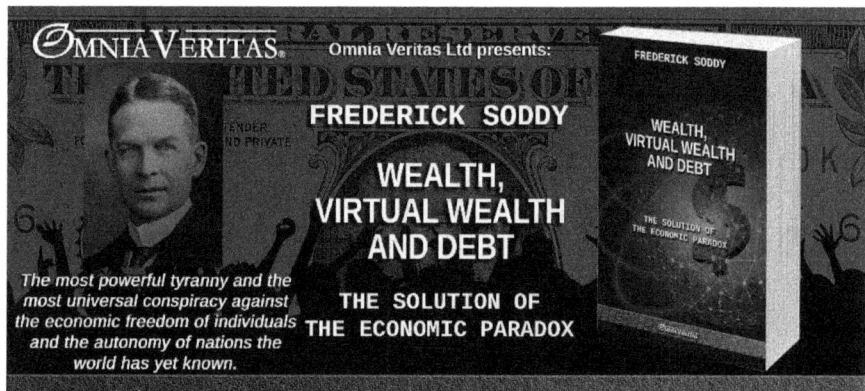

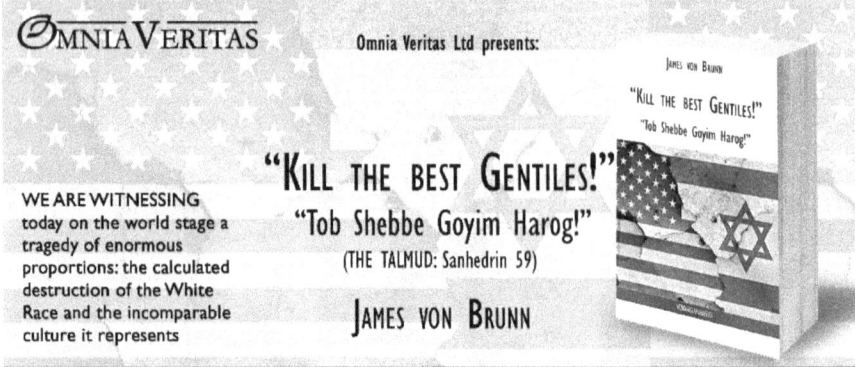

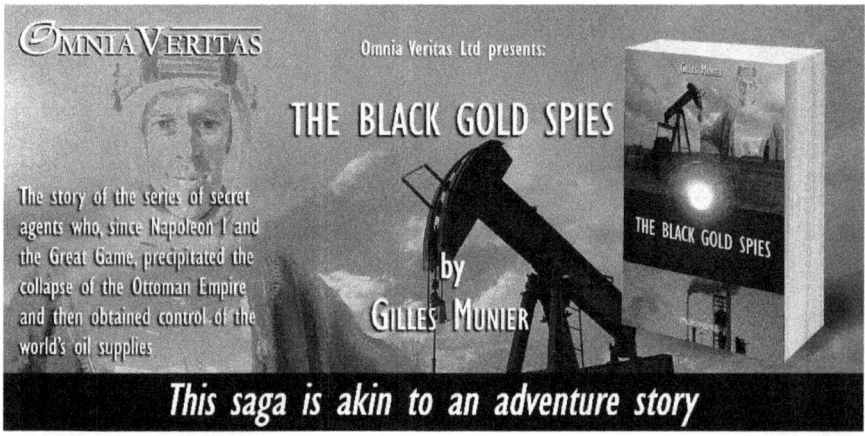
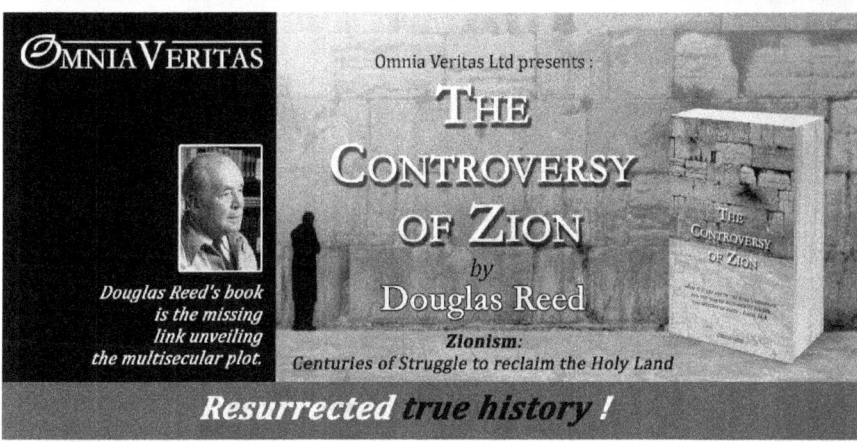
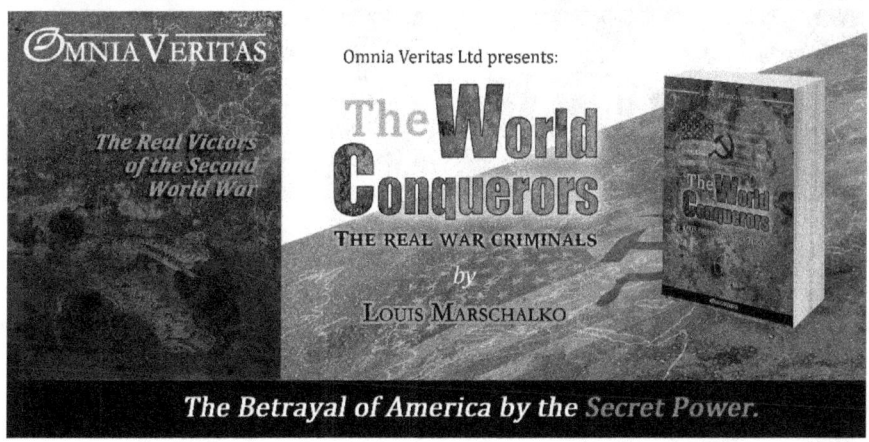

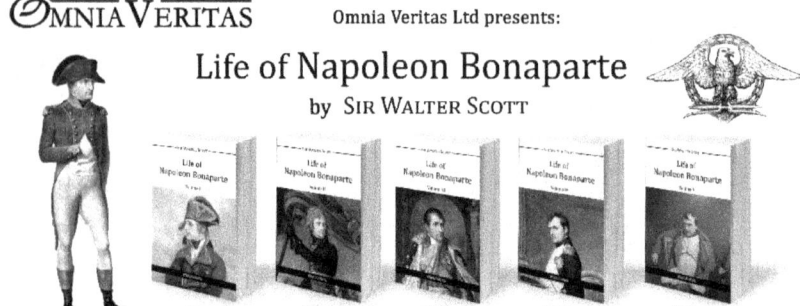

www.ingramcontent.com/pod-product-compliance
Lightning Source LLC
Chambersburg PA
CBHW071312150426
43191CB00007B/596